Feminism and Documentary

VISIBLE EVIDENCE

Edited by Michael Renov, Faye Ginsburg, and Jane Gaines

Public confidence in the "real" is everywhere in decline. This series offers a forum for the in-depth consideration of the representation of the real, with books that engage issues that bear upon questions of cultural and historical representation, and that forward the work of challenging prevailing notions of the "documentary tradition" and of nonfiction culture more generally.

Volume 5 :: Diane Waldman and Janet Walker, editors
Feminism and Documentary

Volume 4 :: Michelle Citron
Home Movies and Other Necessary Fictions

Volume 3 :: Andrea Liss
Trespassing through Shadows:
Memory, Photography, and the Holocaust

Volume 2 :: Toby Miller
Technologies of Truth:
Cultural Citizenship and the Popular Media

Volume 1 :: Chris Holmlund and Cynthia Fuchs, editors
Between the Sheets, In the Streets:
Queer, Lesbian, Gay Documentary

VISIBLE EVIDENCE, VOLUME 5

Feminism and Documentary

Diane Waldman and Janet Walker, Editors

University of Minnesota Press

Minneapolis

London

Every effort was made to obtain permission to reproduce the illustrations in this book. If any proper acknowledgment has not been made, we encourage copyright holders to notify us.

A different version of chapter 1 appeared in *Media International Australia* (1996). An earlier version of chapter 2 appeared in "The Flaherty: Four Decades in the Cause of Independent Cinema," *Wide Angle* 17, nos. 1–4 (winter 1996): 197–216; reprinted with permission. Chapter 3 was originally published as "New Subjectivities: Documentary and Self-Representation in the Post-Verité Age," *Documentary Box* 7 (July 1995): 1–8 (Tokyo); reprinted with permission of the Yamagata International Documentary Film Festival and *Documentary Box*.

Published by the University of Minnesota Press
111 Third Avenue South, Suite 290
Minneapolis, MN 55401-2520
http://www.upress.umn.edu

Library of Congress Cataloging-in-Publication Data

Feminism and documentary / Diane Waldman and Janet Walker, editors.
    p.   cm. — (Visible evidence ; v. 5)
  "Selected filmography/videography" : p.
  Includes bibliographical references and index.
  ISBN 0-8166-3006-2 (acid-free paper). — ISBN 0-8166-3007-0 (pbk. : acid free paper)
  1. Feminism and motion pictures. 2. Documentary films—History and criticism. I. Waldman, Diane. II. Walker, Janet, 1955– . III. Series.
PN1995.9.W6F447 1999
070.1'8—dc21   98-45119

Printed in the United States of America on acid-free paper

The University of Minnesota is an equal-opportunity educator and employer.

11 10 09 08 07 06 05 04 03 02 01 00 99   10 9 8 7 6 5 4 3 2 1

Contents

Acknowledgments   vii

Introduction   JANET WALKER and DIANE WALDMAN   1

PART I
HISTORICIZING DOCUMENTARY   37

1 ▶ Sentimental Contracts: Dreams and Documents of
American Labor   PAULA RABINOWITZ   43

2 ▶ Flaherty's Midwives   PATRICIA R. ZIMMERMANN   64

3 ▶ New Subjectivities: Documentary and Self-Representation
in the Post-Verité Age   MICHAEL RENOV   84

4 ▶ Bad Girls Come and Go, But a Lying Girl Can Never
Be Fenced In   ALEXANDRA JUHASZ   95

PART II
FILMMAKER/SUBJECT: SELF/OTHER   117

5 ▶ (Pass through) The Mirror Moment and *Don't Look Back*:
Music and Gender in a Rockumentary   SUSAN KNOBLOCH   121

6 ▶ Identities Unmasked / Empowerment Unleashed:
The Documentary Style of Michelle Parkerson
GLORIA J. GIBSON   137

7 ▶ Cross-Cultural Filmmaking, Japanese Style
ANN KANEKO   158

PART III
GOING BACK (WITH A CAMERA):
GENDER, NATION, AND DOCUMENTARY RETURNS   183

8 ▶ Return, Transference, and the Constructedness of Experience
in German / Turkish Documentary Film
SILVIA KRATZER-JUILFS   187

9 ▶ Melancholic Memories and Manic Politics:
Feminism, Documentary, and the Armenian Diaspora
ANAHID KASSABIAN and DAVID KAZANJIAN   202

10 ▶ Fetishes and Fossils: Notes on Documentary and Materiality
LAURA U. MARKS   224

11 ▶ On Silence and Other Disruptions   DEBORAH LEFKOWITZ   244

PART IV
INNOVATIVE (AUTO)BIOGRAPHIES   267

12 ▶ Fleeing from Documentary: Autobiographical Film / Video and
the "Ethics of Responsibility"   MICHELLE CITRON   271

13 ▶ From Rupture to Rapture through Experimental Bio-Pics:
Leslie Thornton's *There Was an Unseen Cloud Moving*
CHRIS HOLMLUND   287

14 ▶ Women's Fragmented Consciousness in Feminist Experimental
Autobiographical Video   JULIA LESAGE   309

Selected Filmography / Videography   339

Selected Bibliography   347

Contributors   353

Index   357

Acknowledgments

Both feminism and documentary stress collaboration and collectivity, and thus it's only fitting that the editors of a book on this subject have many people to acknowledge. First, we'd like to thank our contributors for writing or adapting essays specifically with the goals of this project in mind and for putting up with our less-than-laissez-faire approach to editing. Friendships formed or deepened through the process of sharing ideas are particularly sweet. We also thank Bill Nichols for his constructive comments and suggestions first in response to the proposal and then the manuscript, and Charles Wolfe for his comments on our introductory essay. We also thank our series editors, Michael Renov, Jane Gaines, and Faye Ginsburg, for their support of the project. Thanks are also due to the people at the University of Minnesota Press, especially Micah Kleit for his interest and constant encouragement, and Jennifer Moore, who negotiated the details with such skill. Louisa Castner is a dream of a copy editor: her eye for inconsistencies, her command of style, and her professionalism are much appreciated.

Both the University of Denver and the University of California, Santa Barbara provided financial support through two faculty research grants and a summer stipend, respectively. The University of Denver also provided support for the many phone calls, faxes, and overnight mailings without which collaboration across the miles would have been impossible. Special thanks are also due to Kat Paez, whose eagle eye and facility with languages made her a particularly good research assistant for this project; Peggy Marlow, who can wend her way through any bureaucratic maze; and Jeff Rutenbeck and Jennifer Moore-Evans, who helped to avert some potential computer disasters.

Finally, we would like to thank our colleagues in documentary studies for many stimulating conversations and presentations at Society for

Cinema Studies and Visible Evidence conferences, for the brilliant literature of documentary studies, and for the strong commitment so many of you have to addressing the real world issues, problems, and sometimes joys that documentaries depict.

An anonymous undergraduate student wrote to Janet in a teaching evaluation that she or he now had a good grasp of the fictional and rhetorical strategies of documentary but still wondered about its relationship to reality. Janet offers her part of this book in response to that perceptive student and to the other wonderful undergraduate and graduate students in documentary courses at the University of Southern California, University of California (Los Angeles and Santa Barbara), and California State (Los Angeles), who inspired her thinking and shared her passion for nonfiction film. Janet would also like to thank her own first teachers and fellow students of documentary Howard Suber, Steve Mamber, Frank Tomasulo, Maria LaPlace, and Greg Lukow; her former colleagues at Wayne State, especially Robert Burgoyne, Jackie Byars, and Cynthia Erb for many intense conversations on questions of film, history, and politics; and her departmental colleagues Edward Branigan, Anna Brusutti, Donna Cunningham, Dana Driskel, Anna Everett, Constance Penley, and Charles Wolfe, all of whom think, teach, and/or write documentary (among many other things) with tremendous talent and insight. Janet especially thanks Charles Wolfe for entrusting her with 125B, for talking documentary whenever, and for setting a standard of scholarship, pedagogy, and humanism to which she still aspires. Janet also thanks her family, especially her mother, sister, and daughter, Ariel, for their unconditional encouragement; and Steve, intelligent and constant participant-observer of it all, love and thanks as always. Finally, Janet thanks Diane, once again, ideal collaborator and friend extraordinaire.

Diane would like to thank the students, colleagues, friends, and family who sustained her during the writing and editing of the volume. Special mention is due to students in documentary history, theory and production, and women and film classes, coteachers Tony Gault, Phil Stephens, Sieglinde Lug, and Laurie Schulze; departmental colleagues; and the Loose Canon. Thanks to the former members of the Madison Women's Media Collective, especially Fina Bathrick and Maureen Turim, for getting her started on the issues she would return to in this volume and for their steadfast friendship; to David Tafler for accompanying her to the Wiseman series at the Madison Art Center so many years ago; and to Chris Holmlund and Patty Zimmermann for pushing her intellectually and physically on hikes all over the western United States. She'd also like to thank her mother and sister for their unflagging support, Rachel for her patience with her mother's big "chapter book," and Neil, for sharing her love of documentary and for his unselfish willingness to empathize with her struggles and delight in her triumphs. And finally, to Janet, for a great working relationship and a wonderful friendship.

JANET WALKER
DIANE WALDMAN

Introduction

▶

Orientations

The importance of the *and* in the title of this volume cannot be overstated.[1]
Women's studies and documentary studies have been separated by disciplinary as well as prejudicial boundaries, and it is the aim of this volume to
poke holes in those boundaries so that ideas from the two areas may flow,
or possibly crash, together.

Those of us who are aware of the feminist literature of women's studies can become frustrated when we see ideas that have circulated in that literature get ignored, discounted, or reinvented in another field as if for the
first time. Adrienne Rich was right to quote Susan B. Anthony's words
upon the death of her friend and colleague Elizabeth Cady Stanton in
1902: "How shall we ever make the world intelligent on our movement?"[2]
The entreaty resonated when Rich quoted it in 1979 and it resonates now.[3]

Because women speak and write (and we use the term *write* in the
larger sense of "writing" as tangible expression in any medium) from the
margins of patriarchy, we who are conscious of this phenomenon have
wrestled strenuously with the problem of using language against itself—the
joint impossibility and necessity of speaking and writing. Because women's
history is a counterhistory, we have been particularly attuned to the necessarily partial and subjective nature of history writing. Because the interests
and needs of various groups of women are always going to be different, we
have grappled with the problem of securing the common goal of human
rights for women while dealing with constituent interests that may be at
odds. And because the commitment to social change underlies all of this,
we have come up against the need to acknowledge simultaneously the

discursive nature of representation and also the material realm that writing, including filmmaking, contends with.

Documentary studies could benefit greatly, we submit, from the attention women's studies has already paid to these conundrums. For a developing documentary literature concerned with the relation to the real that does after all inhere in documentary representation (Bill Nichols's "difference that makes a difference"),[4] feminist attempts to voice revolutionary agendas while deconstructing language are illuminating. Or, consider the potential use of feminist work on autobiography, identity, and memory for a documentary theory charged to explain the operations of documentary film as historiography. As Paula Rabinowitz asserts in the introduction to her book *They Must Be Represented: The Politics of Documentary*, "gender is a central category within documentary rhetoric, though one often ignored, suppressed, or resisted, because it is not always clear who occupies what position when."[5]

But at the same time that we read feminist studies literature, we write from a disciplinary position within documentary studies. (Another case of women's double duty—it's tough, but it has its uses.) And from this perspective, too, it seems that the relationship between feminism and documentary must be reciprocal. Being documentary scholars faced with a wide range of fascinating films that don't shrink from difficult, multidimensional, and topical issues has kept before us the limitations of any feminist view focused solely on gender and sexual differences without sufficient regard for the way these differences are always caught up in other determinations of subjectivity that affect the reality of women's lives.

It's not that feminist studies has been totally blind to issues of race and class. Sometimes the white, middle-class part of the women's movement forgot its uniqueness, forgot, in fact, its own minority status. But we would be loath to recapitulate that narrowness by writing as if that wing of the movement exhausted the voices of the movement overall. There have long been white, middle-class feminists, both lesbian and heterosexual, who were cognizant of race and class.[6] And there have long been women of color, some of whom are also working class and/or lesbian, who have been publishing from a radical women's perspective.[7] The challenge, as we see it, is to further this evident but often overlooked interest in the connective and conflictual tissues of sexual, racial, and class differences as applied to documentary studies; that is a main goal of this volume.

Happily, documentary studies is a place where such connective theorizing can flourish. Films such as *Harlan County, USA; Intervals of Silence; Seeing Is Believing; An Armenian Journey;* and *Don't Look Back* (discussed in this volume) push us to recognize how gender issues link up with other categories of what Michael Renov has termed the "historical 'real'"—the real people and events that are the subjects of documentary films and videos.[8] Gender is never figured in isolation but always in relation: to class in *Harlan County,* to ethnicity/nationality in *An Armenian Journey,* to religion/nationality in *Intervals of Silence,* to race/nationality in *Seeing Is Believing,* and to sexuality/performance/verité in *Don't Look Back.*

Feminist studies will also be enhanced, we believe, by a fuller incorporation of the theoretical work on representation being done in film studies as a whole and documentary studies as a result. As we will discuss below, non–film studies feminist articles on documentary films and videos have tended to be issue oriented, vulnerable to the charge that they fail to take into account the specificity of film and video media.[9] But in feminist film theory, where authors *have* engaged with issues of representation, there has been a tendency to avoid documentary forms or to focus solely on feminist documentaries as if feminist thinking were inapplicable to documentary films in general.

Each of the articles we gathered and/or commissioned is both solidly feminist and grounded in the theoretical work on representation being done in film and documentary studies. Our choice to offer this volume engendering documentary is expressive of our desire to consider jointly two multiple terms, two complicated disciplines that have evolved, in too large part, as parallel universes. The essays in this collection illuminate feminism and documentary as one unbounded and mostly uncharted universe.

▶ ───

Mutual Myopia

The early-to-mid-1970s witnessed an explosion of writing both in the area of documentary studies and in the area of feminist film criticism in the United States.[10] Fueled by the revival of documentary filmmaking in the post–World War II period and by the recognition of the specifically cultural manifestations of women's oppression, respectively, documentary studies championed nonfiction film as an alternative representational practice while feminist film studies criticized the depiction of women in dominant commercial cinema and sought to develop feminist alternatives. Given the documentary form's long-standing association with progressive social movements, the opposition of both documentarians and feminists to the dominant commercial cinema and the interest of both in developing and supporting alternatives to it, one might assume that these areas of study would have much in common. But, for the most part, the two have had little to say to each other, and here we attempt to explore some of the reasons why.

The relationship of '70s documentary studies to feminist concerns was primarily one of omission. Early '70s work on documentary neglected both the representation of women in the classics of the documentary tradition and the contributions of women to the documentary form. For example, although Erik Barnouw's chapter on Robert Flaherty in his 1974 *Documentary: A History of the Non-Fiction Film* begins with a breathtakingly beautiful still of Nyla and her child from *Nanook of the North*, she receives nary a mention in the written text. In Lewis Jacobs's 1971 anthology *The Documentary Tradition*, there are intriguing allusions to about a dozen and a half films by women such as Nancy Naumburg, Helen Grayson, Ruby Grierson, Nicole Védrès, Madeleine Carroll, Helen Levitt, Agnes Varda, Shirley Clarke, Nelly Kaplan, and Nell Cox, yet only work by Esfir Shub and Leni Riefenstahl receives more than a passing reference. Richard Barsam's 1973 *Nonfiction Film* and Barnouw's *Documentary* do even less to recognize women as makers of or writers on documentary.

In part, the absence of women in the historical surveys may be attributed to the fact that relatively few women up to that point had directed documentary films compared with their male counterparts. But as Patricia Zimmermann argues in her essay in this volume, conventional documentary history's overemphasis on the film text and its director as opposed to the institutional structures that sustain and nurture documentary erases the contributions women have made to documentary film culture: as cinematographers, editors, sound persons, fund-raisers, organizers of festivals, and writers and lecturers.[11]

Characterized primarily, then, by their *lack* of analysis of the representation of women in the films they discuss and their *neglect* of the contributions of women to the documentary form, the masculinist perspectives of the early '70s work on documentary occasionally stand out in sharp relief. Someone reading Jacobs's anthology in 1971 might be intrigued by the inclusive-sounding title of Robert Gardner's chapter, "A Chronicle of the Human Experience," only to find that it refers to his justification for the selective focus—on the Dani's involvement with violence—of his 1963 *Dead Birds*:

> It meant, among other things, that most of my time was spent observing and filming in the men's world. It was almost impossible to concern myself with women except when their lives touched on their husbands' or children's. Actually Dani women maintain a rather formidable and exclusive female company. Had I chosen agriculture as the dominant topic for a film, there would have been considerable difficulty entering that domain, since women do most of

the productive work. In deciding to focus on the topic of violence I was well aware that much of Dani existence would elude me. On the other hand, I was convinced that the topic I had chosen was of such central importance to the whole nature and significance of the Dani world that by treating it exhaustively I had my best chance to illuminate the culture as a whole.[12]

Laudable for his consideration of gender (and the difference that the gender of the filmmaker makes) in a genre of writing from which it was customarily absent, Gardner still attempts to convince himself and his readers that what he openly acknowledges as a selective and partial masculine focus "was of central importance to the whole nature and significance of the Dani world" and could "illuminate the culture as a whole."[13]

Another reader might be shocked—even (or maybe especially?) in 1973—to come across certain aspects of Barsam's analysis of Frederick Wiseman's *High School*. Barsam begins by discussing the way the film demonstrates "the rigid mechanical nature of authority in this self-contained society." So far, so good, but then he adds, "To make his account complete, Wiseman continually intercuts with reminders of aspects of the school that are somewhat more admirable: generally mature and intelligent lectures on sex, for instance."[14] This assessment of what has to be from a feminist perspective one of the smarmiest sequences in the history of cinema—in which a male gynecologist jokingly lectures to an all-male assembly about female anatomy and sexuality—clearly illustrates that the critique of representation fostered by the women's movement in this period was not yet "penetrating" traditional documentary studies.[15]

At the same time that documentary studies was ignoring feminist perspectives, however, the women's movement had discovered the documentary form. Relatively cheap, accessible, and lightweight 16mm film and later video equipment enabled many females to enter media production for the first time and/or to turn their filmmaking skills to issues of particular concern to women.[16] By the late 1970s, documentary studies could not help but notice the abundant number of these works: in the second edition of his book, for example, Jacobs refers to "the arrival of scores of women filmmakers" as "the single most conspicuous development in the seventies."[17] This was, therefore, the manner in which documentary studies took notice of feminist perspectives: by including chapters or essays devoted to a discussion of explicitly feminist work.[18] Yet with very few exceptions,[19] the discussion of nonexplicitly feminist work remained unaffected by feminist thinking. And the questions that were by now animating feminist discussion of other genres of filmmaking—the representation of women; gendered address through formal structures and specifically cinematic techniques of camerawork, editing, and sound; the response of the cinematic spectator to that address—were absent. For this reason alone, over and above the specific arguments they make, the essays in this volume by Susan Knobloch, Paula Rabinowitz, and Anahid Kassabian and David Kazanjian are crucial, for in their discussions of a classic of direct cinema—films about labor struggles and films about the Armenian diaspora, respectively—they bring feminist approaches and concerns to bear on works usually exempt from them. It is only recently that documentary theorists and historians have begun to engage seriously with feminist film theory and to write women back into documentary history.[20]

To explain this prior state of affairs, it is necessary to turn now to a discussion of feminist film studies and its relative lack of attention to the documentary form and the discourse that describes it. First, as asserted above, the most urgent project of feminist film work has always been twofold: a critique of the dominant cinema (defined as Hollywood fiction film) and support for the development of an alternative feminist cinema. This is true whether the first part of the project is described as understanding Hollywood film as "the country's principal vehicle for ideological oppression,"[21] defining "the place that women are fixed in,"[22] or using psychoanalytic theory to "advance our understanding of the status quo, of the patriarchal order in which we are caught."[23] Analysis of the classics of the documentary tradition, representative of an already marginalized cinema, seemed a less pressing (and perhaps less fascinating) topic to address.[24]

As indicated above, activists from the second wave of the women's movement were initially attracted to the documentary form for a multitude of reasons, and early feminist film writing enthusiastically embraced these films as well.[25] Looking back at this early reception of feminist documentaries is enlightening, for it reveals not only what was exciting about these films to these early writers but also the grounds for the later feminist critique of them. For example, in her review of Kate Millett's *Three Lives* in the first issue of *Women & Film,* Susan Rice argued:

> *Three Lives* is a Women's Liberation Cinema Production, and it is the only feature film I know of that not only takes women as its subject-matter, but was produced, directed, shot, recorded, lit, and edited by women. What makes this more than a stunt is the intimacy that this female crew seems to have elicited from its subjects. The element I find most compelling about the film is that it captures the tone and quality of relationships and significant conversation between women. If the film were to fail on every other level, this would stand as a note-worthy achievement.[26]

Similarly, in the second issue of the same journal Dora Kaplan reported on the excitement generated by some of the nonfiction films and the "Making Documentaries" panel at the First International Festival of Women's Films in New York. In her discussion of how events of the '60s facilitated the up-surge in feminist documentaries, Kaplan commented on the invention of lightweight equipment associated with cinema verité, described as "the documentary which allowed reality to happen on the screen."[27] "Capturing" aspects of women's lives, "allowing reality to happen"—these are precisely the assumptions about these early documentaries that would cause other feminist writers to reject them in favor of a modernist, feminist counter cinema.[28]

Claire Johnston's important 1973 essay "Women's Cinema as Counter-Cinema" took issue with a number of positions represented by *Women & Film,*[29] but most crucial for our analysis of feminist writing on the documentary is her discussion of strategies for an oppositional women's cinema. Drawing on developments in contemporary film theory that in turn drew on a (somewhat selective) reading of Bertolt Brecht's and Walter Benjamin's critiques of realism,[30] Johnston argued against what she saw as the prevailing aesthetic of women's documentaries:

> Much of the emerging women's cinema has taken its aesthetics from television and cinéma vérité techniques (eg *Three Lives, Women Talking*). . . . These films largely depict images of women talking to camera about their experiences, with little or no intervention by the film-maker. (214)

Crucial to Johnston's argument was a view of cinema as *mediation*, not a neutral record of reality:

> Clearly, if we accept that cinema involves the production of signs, the idea of non-intervention is pure mystification. . . .Women's cinema cannot afford such idealism; the "truth" of our oppression cannot be "captured" on celluloid with the "innocence" of the camera: it has to be constructed/manufactured. New meanings have to be created by disrupting the fabric of the male bourgeois cinema within the text of the film. (214)

Another aspect of Johnston's argument (and an assumption of the theoretical tradition informing it) was the notion of the effects these different strategies had on the cinematic spectator:

> The danger of developing a cinema of non-intervention is that it promotes a passive subjectivity at the expense of analysis. Any revolutionary strategy must challenge the depiction of reality; it is not enough to discuss the oppression of women within the text of the film; the language of the cinema/the depiction of reality must also be interrogated, so that a break between ideology and text is effected. (215)

We will leave aside for the moment the question of whether these early documentaries were actually noninterventionist or whether textual strategies alone can determine reception. Here we simply want to make the point that this wedding of the critique of realism with the goals of feminism was a crucial development that had enormous consequences for the direction of feminist film theory and the marginalization of documentary within it.

That this position was influential in feminist film circles is revealed by a *Women & Film* editorial the following year. Explaining the addition of three new sections—"The Ideological Massage/Reviews of Commercial Cinema," "Third World Perspectives," and "Independent Women's Cinema"—the editors wrote of the third section:

> Each of the forms—political documentary, fictional narrative, biographical portraits, experimental—requires a specific mode of analysis. We hope to address ourselves most exhaustively to those feminist films which attempt to deconstruct the aesthetic/political codes of patriarchal culture.[31]

The position against direct cinema or cinema verité[32] documentary as an effective strategy for doing so was solidified the following year when the journal published Eileen McGarry's "Documentary, Realism and Women's Cinema." Taking off from Johnston's brief comments on the inadequacy of the aesthetic of cinema verité for a feminist countercinema and drawing on the antirealist critiques of Johnston, Paul Willemen, and others,[33] McGarry launched a full-scale attack on current theorizing about documentary, particularly Stephen Mamber's *Cinema Verite in America: Studies in Uncontrolled Documentary.* As such, her essay is notable for being one of the few feminist works of that period to actually confront and engage with the tradition of documentary studies. And in her discussion of the mediations that occur both at the levels of documentary production (intervention in the profilmic event and through the processes of filming, sound recording, and editing) and reception, she anticipated much later documentary theorizing.[34]

McGarry's essay, however, was not a polemic against documentary per se, only the specific practice of American cinema verité or direct cinema. In fact, she argued that many political filmmakers, including feminists, aware of the "transparent ideologies of the aesthetic of realism," tended to eschew styles of documentary relying on such an aesthetic. Instead, they were returning to "what are now considered to be older, less *realistic* and more propagandistic styles of non-fiction film," styles favoring techniques such as intellectual montage, expressionistic sequences, music, voice-over, and dramatization.[35] Indeed, the last part of her essay was devoted to an analysis of several women's films (New York Newsreel's *Makeout* and *She's Beautiful When She's Angry* and San Francisco Newsreel's *Herstory* and *The Woman's Film*) that she found exemplary in their use of antirealist techniques to expose and examine aspects of women's oppression.[36]

Moreover, McGarry made it clear that hers was not just a formalist argument: she also contrasted the above films "with revolutionary content" to *Fifty-One Per Cent,* a film that uses many of the same formal devices (voice-over narration, dramatization, and so forth) but in ways that reinforce rather than challenge dominant ideology. Here, then, McGarry avoided some of the pitfalls of the antirealist position noted later by critics such as B. Ruby Rich, Judith Mayne, and Alexandra Juhasz, who saw the problems inherent in valorizing form "above and independent of other criteria."[37]

Thus, feminist film theory, after McGarry, might have gone in the direction of work on strategies for the feminist documentary that avoided the noninterventionist, positivist stance of the direct cinema movement. However, the publication of Laura Mulvey's groundbreaking "Visual Pleasure in the Narrative Cinema" in that same year (1975) focused feminist attention on the narrative fiction film and encouraged feminist film theorists to look to the avant-garde rather than the documentary tradition for strategies for an oppositional feminist cinema. Bringing together such sources as Juliet Mitchell's *Psychoanalysis and Feminism* and much of the work on the so-called cinematic apparatus,[38] Mulvey's essay is primarily an argument for the use of psychoanalysis to understand the fascination of mainstream fiction film. As is well known, much of the essay is devoted to delineating the narrative and cinematic structures that underlie that fascination and work to avoid "unpleasure" for the masculine subject. These are structures of identification, voyeurism, and fetishism that seem less applicable to the documentary or nonfiction film. (But see Susan Knobloch's essay in this volume, applying feminist psychoanalytic models developed by Mulvey and Kaja Silverman[39] to Pennebaker's *Don't Look Back*).

But Mulvey's essay was also a polemic, especially in its introduction and conclusion, for an alliance between a feminist project and the strategies of the experimental avant-garde. Thus in her introductory section, "Destruction of Pleasure as a Radical Weapon," Mulvey argued:

> The alternative cinema provides a space for the birth of a cinema which is radical in both a political and an aesthetic sense and challenges the basic assumptions of the mainstream film. This is not to reject the latter moralistically, but to highlight the ways in which its formal preoccupations reflect the psychical obsessions of the society which produced it and, further, to stress that the alternative cinema must start specifically by reacting against these obsessions and assumptions.[40]

And in her famous conclusion, after summarizing the "complex interaction of looks" specific to mainstream fiction film, she asserted:

The first blow against the monolithic accumulation of traditional film conventions (already undertaken by radical film-makers) is to free the look of the camera into its materiality in time and space and the look of the audience into dialectics and passionate detachment. There is no doubt that this destroys the satisfaction, pleasure and privilege of the "invisible guest," and highlights the way film has depended on voyeuristic active/passive mechanisms. Women, whose image has continually been stolen and used for this end, cannot view the decline of the traditional film form with anything much more than sentimental regret. (26)

And in her "Film, Feminism and the Avant-Garde" Mulvey made this alliance even more explicit, recapitulating the arguments against early feminist documentaries,[41] drawing on the linking of the "crisis that produced the language of modernism with 'the feminine'" in the work of Julia Kristeva, and connecting the goals of feminists working in the cinema with those of the modernist avant-garde, especially the political avant-garde of Sergei Eisenstein and Dziga Vertov, Bertolt Brecht, and Jean-Luc Godard.

Among the things Mulvey championed in this tendency within the avant-garde was the way in which it had "broken down rigid demarcations between fact and fiction and laid a foundation for experimentation with narrative."[42] And indeed, this advocacy of works that mixed modes or "blurred boundaries"[43] between documentary and fiction was (and still is) one important way feminist film theory and practice would go. (See, for example, Paula Rabinowitz's discussion of the work of Yvonne Rainer, Jill Godmilow, and Trinh Minh-ha in *They Must Be Represented* and the essays in this volume by Michelle Citron, Chris Holmlund, Alexandra Juhasz, Silvia Kratzer-Juilfs, and Julia Lesage.) But at this point we invoke Mulvey's essay in our explanation of the ways in which the critique of realism and the alliance of feminism and the avant-garde rendered documentary, in Constance Penley's words, "a neglected area in feminist thinking about film."[44]

We think this neglect of the documentary in feminist film theory and criticism was (is) unfortunate in several respects. First, and most obviously, it allowed documentary theory and practice to continue largely without the benefit of feminist insights. But second, since documentary film and video-makers (and feminists writing about documentary film and video) frequently represent subjects and struggles that indicate the messy imbrication of gender, race, class, nation, and sexuality, neglect of the documentary may have allowed feminist film theory to move away from its initial engagement with such questions to focus more exclusively on sexual difference. Third, as Alexandra Juhasz has persuasively argued, the hegemony of the antirealist position in feminist film theory has meant the actual loss of many of the '70s so-called feminist realist documentaries, given "the economic relationship between film scholarship and alternative film distribution: only twenty years later, they are very difficult, if not impossible to find."[45] And finally, we would argue, especially since feminist filmmakers and activists have continued to use the documentary form, the overbroad critique of realism obstructed discussion of specific issues, how to represent them, and how to think them through in ways that could advance feminist political practice.[46]

But around the same time that "Film, Feminism and the Avant-Garde," was written, some feminist critics began mounting a critique of the antirealist position and its implications for feminist filmmaking. We think these responses might prove instructive for documentary studies as a whole—indeed, we see this as one of several areas where feminism could enrich documentary studies and vice versa—and it is to these responses we now turn.

▶ ──

Defense of Documentary—The Realist Debates

Documentary studies seems to have reached a point of reckoning around the issue of documentary's relationship to the material world. Once the '70s critique of realism began to affect documentary as well as feminist film studies, writing on documentary began to challenge the truth claims of documentaries themselves and to stress the form's necessarily constructed or mediated nature and its dependence on narrative patterning.[47] However, recent approaches to documentary (notably Bill Nichols's *Representing Reality*) have begun to acknowledge the "authenticating trace" that does connect the documentary film to its real referent. After all, there is a crucial though not categorical difference between the documentary and the fiction modes. It becomes apparent, therefore, that there remains a need to distinguish among, and not collapse, what Hart Cohen terms the various "modalities of the visible."[48]

It seems to us that this "point of reckoning" can be illuminated by a reconsideration of issues initially brought up in the responses by feminist scholars to the critique of realism and early feminist documentaries in the late '70s and early '80s. In other words, feminist writing has already figured, we argue, and it can be made to illuminate further what has recently come to be a defining dilemma of documentary studies. While often accused of falling into the realist illusion that documentary films present real women, feminist documentary practices and studies have in fact looked for ways to avoid that illusionist pitfall while at the same time acknowledging the political stakes in representing the images and voices of women who are not professional actors and whose documentary representation seeks to build consensus with actual women for the audiences of these films. Feminism's political grounding has mitigated any facile reduction of documentary to its fictive properties by retaining the paradox of the "reality fiction"[49] as a *paradox,* and moreover, as a paradox in which there is much at stake.

Feminist criticisms of the antirealist position and the defense of documentary took several different tacks. One such tack defended the use of realist strategies under certain conditions, or at least pointed to the limitations of an overly broad critique that does not allow for distinctions between the use of those strategies for different political ends.[50] To cite a contemporary example, Julia Lesage's tape *In Plain English,* featuring University of Oregon students of color describing what life is like on the predominantly white campus, confers on these students what must be for them the rare privilege of being "talking heads." To read this film as if it were a conventional network news documentary is to miss the significant nuance of who is doing the talking.

Several writers noted that realism is often the first recourse of oppressed groups wishing to counter vicious stereotypes or lies. Sometimes it is politically important and effective to show what is usually hidden from view, as Kimberly Safford argued in her defense of the filmmakers' use of documentary realism to counter beliefs about the easy reversibility of sterilization in Ana Maria Garcia's *La Operación.*[51] In Jane Gaines's words, "Leftist media workers cannot afford to undertake an abstract analysis or make an educational statement *about* representation if it is politically imperative that they make a representational reference to a 'brutal actuality' in order to counteract its ideological version."[52] Many also pointed to the problems of a stance that discourages identification or ignores the affective side of spectorial response.[53] E. Ann Kaplan put it eloquently: "What I have in mind here is the danger of a theory that ignores the need for emotional identification with people suffering oppression."[54]

It is important to emphasize that feminist critics of antirealism have not simply embraced the realist aesthetic. Both writers and filmmakers have pursued experimental or innovative means through which to use, and at the same time critique, traditional documentary forms to challenge, as Julia Lesage writes in this volume, "the prevalent assumption that documentation of one's own past or of social process requires a realist aesthetic."[55] But at the same time, many feminist critics rejected a formalism that assumes that textual strategies alone can determine reception, and they recognized the necessity of working with audiences to create a public for more difficult or complicated works.[56]

All of these arguments, we would maintain, are productive for thinking through documentary's relation to the real and to its audiences because they refuse to disallow the opinions expressed in and by the films simply because the means of expression are not immediately acknowledged as such. The feminist critique of antirealism is a way of conserving the baby of vocalized struggle while draining out the bathwater of pseudotransparency.

▶ ──

Filmmaker/Subject: Self/Other

> *As a filmmaker, you're always exploiting. It's part of modern life.*
>
> :: Marcel Ophuls, quoted in Calvin Pryluck, "Ultimately We Are All Outsiders"

> *Being a woman of working-class origins myself, that also makes me want to make films by, for, and about working-class women.*
>
> :: Julia Reichert, quoted in Alan Rosenthal, *The Documentary Conscience*

Another strain of the argument in defense of feminist realist documentaries has emphasized that, while they seem the same as the American direct cinema and cinema verité documentaries, these feminist works are actually rather different, especially in the relationship of the filmmaker(s) to the subjects represented. Whereas American direct cinema and cinema verité traditions downplay the role of the filmmaker in the production process (the filmmaker-as-fly-on-the-wall theory), feminist filmmakers have thought long and hard about the politics of people filming people.[57] But since writings about direct cinema and cinema verité have dominated documentary studies in the past few decades, a historian must be particularly attuned to the filmmaker-subject relationship to find literature dealing with it.

One area of nonfeminist documentary studies where this relationship is dealt with is image ethics literature. There, direct cinema, cinema verité, and expository modes are all addressed in terms of how they figure filmmakers and subjects. In 1976 Calvin Pryluck published an article called "Ultimately We Are All Outsiders: The Ethics of Documentary Filming," in which he drew attention to a power imbalance between documentary filmmakers and documentary subjects that, while not exactly inherent to documentary filmmaking, was and is certainly endemic.[58] Reminding documentary practitioners and other readers that "we can take our gear and go home" while "they have to continue their lives where they are," Pryluck called on documentarians to acknowledge and practically observe the moral and ethical dilemmas and responsibilities of the act of filming. Filmmakers, he urged, should exercise "extreme caution . . . in dealing with potential infringements on the rights of subjects" (258, 260).

Pryluck's call was not sounded in total isolation,[59] but Brian Winston later criticized documentary studies for its neglect of these ethics issues. The field, Winston argued, developed so as to become overinvolved in "issues of transparency and narratology" and "mediation and reconstruction," and underinvolved with "the people whose cooperation is crucial to documentarists."[60] The volume *Image Ethics,* in which Winston's position paper appeared, was designed to fill this oversight by using case-specific "theoretically informed analyses" to "[call] attention to an important but neglected domain of moral accountability" in documentary filmmaking—that of filmmakers to subjects.[61] In our view, this image ethics discourse is indeed an important one, and the eponymous volume a varied and valuable contribution. We do need to pose the question of who is ultimately served, to borrow Winston's examples, by Griersonian social documentaries such as *Housing Problems, Industrial Britain,* or *Enough to Eat.* We must also ask whether there are cases when a filmmaker should stop filming and act to save a life or come to the aid of a subject, or, more commonly, whether the act of filming subjects does not tend to set them up for ridicule.[62] In general, we need to develop such discussions of filmmakers and subjects and, in particular, the recognition that filmmakers are really also coparticipants, along with subjects, in the power dynamic of the operation of direct cinema filming.

But it is also crucial to note the perspective from which the image ethics discourse proceeds. With some few exceptions (notably Thomas Waugh's essay in *Image Ethics*),[63] discussions of documentary ethics tend to be framed in terms of the "we" of Pryluck's "we can take our gear and go home" and the "they" of "they have to continue their lives where they are." These discussions tend to concentrate on documentary encounters in which filmmakers are privileged by conventional valuations of class and race (the middle-class filmmaker shooting footage of the poor, the Western reporter in troubled Africa, and so on). In "The Tradition of the Victim in Griersonian Documentary," Brian Winston makes the point that socially conscious films and filmmakers tend to "concentrate on the lower classes as victims."[64] Our point here is that the image ethics discourse echoes this pattern—at a theoretical level. True, the point of the ethics discourse is to find ways to level out or ameliorate the inegalitarian power relations it correctly identifies, but by concentrating on what the filmmaker can do to protect the rights of the subject ("the image maker's obligations to his/her subject"), this discourse actually reiterates the very power imbalance it seeks to redress.

Furthermore, because the image ethics discourse concentrates on presumably clear-cut we/they situations to evaluate, it tends to neglect from the start another large area of documentary practice where the boundaries between we's and they's are not so clear. That is, image ethics discourses tend to neglect documentaries initiated jointly by subjects and filmmakers who come, very often, from the same milieu and who wish to articulate in documentary form their shared position in the world. The image ethics discourse remains, therefore, within parameters we think are too narrow because (1) it originates from the perspective of the empowered self, and (2) it ignores a whole group of documentaries that are made and function in a very different way.

Both of these pitfalls have been astutely addressed, we believe, by feminist writing in response to an area of study we deem congruent to image ethics. The area is that of new ethnography, and the books *Writing Culture*, edited by James Clifford and George Marcus, and *Anthropology as Cultural Critique*, by George Marcus and Michael Fischer, may be regarded as foundational.[65] Like writing on image ethics, writing in the area of new ethnography begins from the assumption that the ethnographer-subject or self-other duo (the anthropological counterpart to the filmmaker-subject duo) imbeds a power imbalance that is, in this case, undergirded by the whole history of colonial imperialism and the maintenance of a First World–Third or Fourth World split. New ethnography seeks, therefore, to theorize ways to rehabilitate this power imbalance. In the spirit of the image ethics self-critique, new ethnography calls for the writing of "other" stories, the listening to "other" voices, and the development of a "reciprocal context" for research that would take participant observation even further in the interest of ethnographic justice.

But fair-minded and sophisticated as it might seem, new ethnographic literature has been subject to the feminist critique we alluded to on the grounds that such literature remains inegalitarian because its representative new ethnographers speak from the position of the dominant Western self.[66] Women feminists, on the other hand, speak from different positions in the First, Second, Third, or Fourth Worlds, and, at the same time, they (we) speak, as females, from the position of a "gender other."[67] As Frances Mascia-Lees, Patricia Sharpe, and Colleen Ballerino Cohen discuss in "The Postmodernist Turn in Anthropology: Cautions from a Feminist Perspective," feminist-informed new ethnography would emphasize the solidarity between and the joint interests of feminist ethnographers and ethnographic subjects, as well as trying to redress any existing power differentials between ethnographers and subjects. As in the case of the image ethics discourse, therefore, the discourse of new ethnography is laudatory in the invitation to participate that it extends, in principle, to the diverse constituencies formerly excluded from the ethnographic project. But both discourses would benefit, we submit, from a fuller consideration of the case of the speaking "other" — the other not merely seen as subjected to the operations of the self but the other *as* self.

New ethnographers are also distanced from the side of the other because their very discourse crystallizes the categories of self and other, categories that feminist literature, in contradistinction, tends to take as artificial. In the words of Lila Abu-Lughod:

> If anthropology continues to be practiced as the study by an unproblematic and unmarked Western self of found "others" out there, feminist theory, an academic practice that also traffics in selves and others, has in its relatively short history come to realize the danger of treating selves and others as givens.[68]

Faye Ginsburg, an anthropologist who has written extensively on gender and culture, comes to a similar conclusion about the danger of "treating selves and others as givens" in her exploration of whether indigenous groups (ethnographic others) should submit to ethnographic representation by First World selves or whether they should take up the means of representation them*selves*. The "Faustian contract," as Ginsburg poses it, is that, in taking up First World technology, indigenous groups risk altering beyond recognition the cultures they intend to represent.[69] But Ginsburg suggests that only an immutable or "essentialized" notion of indigenous cultures would necessarily prohibit cultural change including the incorporation of outside technologies such as film and video. If, on the other hand and following cultural studies models, cultural identity "is a projection that is never complete, always in process, and always constituted within, not outside, representation," then indigenous groups might well use media as an evocation of their own identities-in-process (60).[70] The self-other dyad, like its filmmaker-subject counterpart, is an overly rigid construction that fails its second term.

The third prong of the feminist critique of new ethnography is that, although new ethnographies acknowledge that "culture is contested" and that "cultural analysis is always enmeshed in global movements of difference and power,"[71] they do not actually deal with the real ramifications of such conflicts of interest. As Abu-Lughod asserts about anthropology in general,

> despite a long history of self-conscious opposition to racism, a fast-growing, self-critical literature on anthropology's links to colonialists . . , and experi-

mentation with techniques of ethnography to relieve a discomfort with the power of anthropologist over anthropological subject, the fundamental issues of domination keep being skirted."[72]

For example, Clifford discusses a four-volume edition of documents collected by and credited to James Walker, who worked as a "physician and ethnographer on the Pine Ridge Sioux Reservation between 1896 and 1914."[73] He characterizes the work as "a collaborative work of documentation, edited in a manner that gives equal rhetorical weight to diverse renditions of tradition. Walker's own descriptions and glosses are fragments among fragments" (15). And yet, although Clifford calls for a time when collaborators could receive authorial credit for such a work, he never suggests that the viewpoints contained within diverge in any substantial ways. Either they don't, leading one to suspect a central authorial voice after all, or they do, leading one to suspect that it is Clifford who neglects such differences.

Feminist theory, on the other hand, has by necessity grappled with just these issues of identities and power sharing, and grappled with them in a way we find valuable for documentary theory and practice. White, middle-class, heterosexual feminism has been forced by the response of lesbians and women of color and by some white, middle-class, heterosexual feminists themselves to acknowledge its boundaries and limitations and to redefine its terms inclusively, but in recognition that the goal of strategic unanimity brings with it the reality of divergent interests. The goal is "a politics of solidarity, coalition, or affinity built on [a genuine and firsthand] recognition of difference."[74]

The feminist correctives to new ethnography, then, highlight the importance of works by racial, cultural, and gender others, encourage skepticism of writing that takes the self and other categories as discrete and coherent, and are realistic about genuine power differentials. These points, we believe, could be much more fully incorporated into documentary studies to the great benefit of the field.

Documentaries initiated by people who take up a camera to film their own lives or by people and filmmakers coming together to tell common stories must be appreciated as at least potentially radical, and these documentaries must be instated in the archives of documentary history. Many documentary films and videos spring from deep convictions held jointly by filmmakers and subjects and by subjects *as* filmmakers. For example, Jill Godmilow's *Antonia: Portrait of a Woman,* about the orchestra conductor Antonia Brico who is interviewed by Judy Collins, tells in different ways the artistic aspirations of all three women. The same is true of Michelle

Citron's film *Parthenogenesis,* about Citron's sister, the sister's violin teacher, and Citron herself.

Moreover, shared-goal filmmaking has served an important role in getting the word out about the experiences of people in communities with histories of oppression and where access to national platforms has been blocked. Jacqueline Bobo's introduction to her collection on black women and film is suffused with language trumpeting the solidarity of filmmakers and subjects in their struggles for recognition of their social goals. "Congruence between the personal histories of filmmaker and subject is a predominant feature of Black women's biographical documentaries," she affirms.[75] And regarding Michelle Parkerson's *Gotta Make This Journey: Sweet Honey in the Rock* and Joanne Grant's *Fundi: The Story of Ella Baker,* Bobo attests that "the films are compelling examples of art transforming people's consciousness, facilely intertwining cultural expression with cogent political analysis" (5).

Such film and video work is part of the tradition of the "committed documentary," clearly defined as such by Thomas Waugh in his anthology *"Show Us Life": Toward a History and Aesthetics of the Committed Documentary.* As Waugh wrote in his introduction to the 1984 book, committed documentaries

> attempt to act, to intervene—whether as gut-level calls to immediate, localized action, or as more cerebral essays in long-term, global analysis . . . [—they] were made under an important additional assumption; if films are to be instrumental in the process of change, they must be made not only *about* people directly implicated in change, but *with* and *for* those people as well. (xiii)

Expressed by Julianne Burton, the goals of the committed documentary are to "us[e] the film medium to expose and combat the culture of invisibility and inaudibility."[76] These documentaries are about "coming out" or "declaring oneself" (Waugh),[77] about "*testimonio* acted as a counterdiscourse" designed to "inform the world at large about the conditions of [the speaker's] people and of the urgent need for social change" (Chon Noriega).[78] This is a documentary practice and supporting literature concerned with the empowerment of disenfranchised constituencies. It is a film and video practice and literature, in the words of Thomas Waugh, of "Minority Self-Imaging" in "Oppositional Film Practice."[79]

Here we want to affirm the common interests of feminist and other committed documentary makers and scholars (without glossing over any specific points of difference), and the need to attune ourselves to the battles and discourses of other "others." Parochial feminism isn't good enough. Thus, Laura Marks rejects Kristeva's psychoanalytically informed analysis of the maternal because in her view it "muffl[es] vast cultural differences" that *must* be brought to the fore. And Chris Holmlund praises Leslie Thornton's experimental biography of Isabelle Eberhardt because, unlike some avant-garde works, this one is not "blind to the ways feminists participate in Orientalist fantasies" (see chap. 13).

Given that the mainstream of documentary studies has focused primarily on documentary situations where the makers' and the subjects' lives and goals for the film are different, we call for more attention to shared-goal documentary practices such as those that have characterized feminist documentary practice in its many incarnations. But we would also emphasize that filmmakers and subjects in a documentary film are always cast in relation to one another, whether or not that relation is acknowledged and whether or not that relation is one of shared aims. Most of the essays in this volume deal explicitly with the filmmaker-subject relationship, and they foreground that relationship as a site of negotiated power.

▶ ──────────────────────────────────

Historical Nonfictions: Feminism and Documentary as Counterhistory

The struggle of filmmakers and subjects to tell their stories is particularly acute when these stories hark back to the past—that is, when they are histories. It is triply acute when these stories contest common explanations of causality and change—that is, when they are counterhistories. This is often the case with feminist historical documentaries, which we think provide a good case study of how feminist insights can aid historical thinking about documentary and thinking about the historical documentary.

In a 1981 article in the British film journal *Screen,* Noel King criticized *Union Maids* (Reichert, Klein, Mogulescu, 1976) and *Harlan County, USA* (Kopple, 1976) on the grounds that they are overly realist instead of being innovative and self-reflective, and on the grounds that they are "humanist-historicist." According to King, these films mystify rather than reveal the textual mechanisms through which their historical discourses are articulated. Beginning from what he saw as Christian Metz's and Dan Georgakas's misplaced unconditional acceptance of the films based on the "good intentions" of their makers, King called for a rigorous interrogation of the humanist-historicist meaning "that it is the work of their textual systems to secure."[80] The problem for King is that the films emphasize "individual responsibility" and therefore fail to contend with "the social and linguistic formation of subjects." They prioritize a moral or ethical discourse over one of politics, and they employ "a series of mini-narratives, biography, autobiography and popular narrative history," to construct a teleological history that advances "from a past to a present, from a point of origin or genesis along a casual [*sic*] chain until we reach the present" (11–12).

King's concerns seem to be echoed more than a decade later in Charles Wolfe's essay on a 1988 episode of the PBS series *The American Experience*, titled *Let Us Now Praise Famous Men — Revisited*. The gist of Wolfe's intricate argument is that this documentary, an updated filmed rendering of the well-known 1941 photo book of Alabama tenant farmers by James Agee and Walker Evans, is ultimately unsatisfactory because it substitutes a pattern of historical closure for the open-endedness of the source book. The photo book, Wolfe adduces, is formally innovative, aware of power imbalances in the social field itself and in the relationships between authors and subjects, and sensitive to the indelible links between history and memory and between the psychological and the social determinants of subjectivity. The documentary film, on the other hand, resorts to conventional strategies that "close down the challenging dimension of Agee's experimental method."[81] These strategies, like those that King attributes to *Union Maids* and *Harlan County*, involve the "foreground[ing] of narrative continuities over and against Agee's self-consciously opaque structure," the suppression of the "auto-inquiry" that "drives" Agee's project, the adoption of a "prescribed [and tragic] historical plot," and the appropriation of subjects' stories for the melodramatic plot (206–7).

But there is a crucial difference between the King article and the one by Wolfe. Whereas King criticized *Union Maids* for naively attributing agency to its subjects, Wolfe criticizes *Let Us Now Praise Famous Men — Revisited* for usurping the irreducible subjectivity of the people staring back at the camera from Evans's photos. Whereas the photographs of sharecroppers in the Agee-Evans photo book were presented in a section free of commentary, the interviews in the documentary film were staged to address an unseen interviewer. The result, argues Wolfe, "allows for the inscription of these figures into an anonymously narrated story" (207). Similarly, in a discussion of *Vietnam: A Television History*, Michael Frisch demonstrates how the thirteen-episode documentary largely made up of witness testimony nevertheless reserves for "outside experts" the roles of interpretation and historiography.[82]

It seems to us that the difference in reading has to do with how King, on one hand, and Wolfe and Frisch, on the other, understand the relations of power that underlie the formal attributes of documentary films in general and historical documentaries in particular. In objecting to critics who hold "political films" to different standards from those to which entertainment narratives are held, King is arguing for a kind of "color/gender/class blindness" in which all films should be read according to one set of critical standards. We take issue with such prescriptions. As we have discussed, the same formal attributes (the use of "talking heads" interviews, photographs, or voice-over narration) may serve very different functions in different films.

With regard to feminist historiography in particular, King's evaluation of *Union Maids* and *Harlan County* ignores the very specificity of the socio-political context of historical subjectivity that he purports to hold dear.[83] Recognition of past struggles of working-class women like and including those depicted in *Union Maids* is precisely what ignites the realization that individual volition and equal opportunity may be illusory or at least conditional. King ignores, in short, the status of *Union Maids* and *Harlan County* as feminist *counterhistories* that point up the political contingencies of agency. Wolfe and Frisch, on the other hand, regret the unrealized potential of the documentaries they analyze to mount counterhistories based on the testimony of the working poor, which in both cases include, very prominently, women.

An article by Sonya Michel written at the same time as King's article and about a similar group of documentaries did a better job of holding the necessary critique of realist representation together with a commitment to the political context and efficacy of the historical documentary. "Feminism, Film, and Public History" is, therefore, an example of the way in which a feminist perspective brought to the historical documentary can work through—or abide—the ambiguities and outright conflicts inherent in mounting a politics by way of a historiographic form. Like King, Michel called for the use of self-reflexive techniques that "foster not certainty but a critical consciousness."[84] But very likely because of a felt affinity for these working-class heroines, she also recognized that privileging the voices of subjects resonates differently in the history of representation when those subjects are women whose voices have been suppressed from mainstream histories. It is not that women's experiential information should be taken as universal truth, she points out, but, rather, that the information provided by these newly heard voices is precisely "fragmentary" and "idiosyncratic"—not the stuff of traditional, seamless, narrativized historiography.

While King called for an equal-opportunity aesthetic, Michel called for one that recognizes both the difficulty and the necessity for the disenfranchised to find a way to speak their interest and relation to the past while at the same time acknowledging the historiographic mechanisms of the medium through which they speak in the present. As Judith Newton puts it, "changing 'history' . . . depends on having that first kind of power, on speaking from somewhere other than the margins, although speaking from the margins has its uses too."[85]

As the quotation from Newton implies, Michel's insights are consistent with those of other feminist authors on women and history writing. Since the 1970s, women's history has been theorized as sociocultural history out of the mainstream, as a history written through gaps and silences as well as tangible text.[86] In this volume, Alexandra Juhasz and Patricia Zimmermann take up the historiographic project as regards women and documentary, with Juhasz focusing on two shows of feminist videos separated by a decade and forgotten in between, and Zimmermann on the annual Flaherty documentary film festival and the role of women in its inception and history. Both authors engage in historiographic meditations on the need to retrieve their evidence from the margins of history and to surmount a kind of periodic amnesia for women's works.

▶

Innovative (Auto)biography

Feminist literature on autobiography is another place where problems of agency, and specifically of historiographical agency, have been dealt with extensively.[87] This literature, while not monolithic, aims in general "to reconsider the imbrications of subjectivity, textuality, and community" as regards the self in history.[88] Here the "I" is conceived not as a monadic essence but, rather, as a "site and source of written subjectivity, investing that individual body with the shifting ethics of a political, racial, and sexual consciousness."[89] But although "I's" may be shifting, subjective, and fragmentary, it is also true that "all 'I's are not equal."[90] Thus, autobiography must be a practice in which identity is "assumed" for strategic political reasons.[91]

And if the self is complicated, the past in relation to the self must be all the more so. Not surprisingly, feminist theory–informed literature on (auto)biography points out the "gaping inadequacy of the lives of great men and public chronicled events to constitute a stable personal or Historical truth" and calls for more attention to the lives of everyday women.[92] But this literature is not blind to the inevitable indirection through which we struggle to gain our purchase on people and events of the past. A picture is painted of the past as a landscape "altered by the often aleatory processes of choice and the uncertainties of recollection."[93] Formulations of pastness, therefore, offer a similar paradox as formulations of agency, and of documentary, for that matter: while the past is not directly knowable, it may still present what Linda Williams aptly terms a "receding horizon of truth."[94] As Raylene Ramsay writes, the past although no longer unproblematically an immediate apprehension of the real, is, at the least, a material remembered from the experiences of the past, re-worked self-consciously and analytically in the present experience of the writing, mediated by the body and offering occasional glimpses of an obscure or unconscious origin.[95]

Another characteristic of feminist theories of autobiography is the emphasis on the lasting significance of the past not only for the present but for the future. The "autobiographical manifesto" outlined by Sidonie Smith emphasizes the "generative and prospective thrust of autobiography," its attempt "to actively position the subject in a potentially liberated future distanced from the constraining and oppressive identifications inherent in the everyday practices of the *ancien regime*."[96] The past, we could say, like subjectivity is in a way "assumed" for strategic reasons in the present with an eye toward the future. In this volume, many of the essays (including some not located in the book's section on autobiography) address the vicissitudes of (auto)biographical representation in documentary film and video. All are concerned with the vagaries of subjectivity and with the simultaneous impossibility and necessity to trawl the past in the interest of a humane and equitable present.

These insights, gleaned from feminist studies, may sound familiar to readers of the philosophy of history. Indeed, writers in that field including, very prominently, Hayden White, Saul Friedländer, Dominick LaCapra, and Michael Frisch, have been thinking in parallel with feminist scholars about issues of identities and histories.[97] A question arises, though, about any inherent differences between the thinking that follows from Hayden White's more recent work and that which stems from feminist studies. We would suggest at least one significant difference in the attributed impetus for postmodernist historiography. White sees a new sociopolitical reality specific to the twentieth century, and he calls for a new form of historiography to address it.[98] Feminist thinking, on the other hand, conceives of reality as having always been traumatic and conceives of traditional realist historiography as having always been descriptively inadequate to anything but the thinnest crust of historical reality. In this volume, for example, Julia Lesage links the fragmented form of many feminist autobiographical videos to the traumatic personal histories of the videomakers.

This difference between mainstream and feminist historiographies is surely a matter of perspective with the perceived traumatic content of history being proportional to the subject's distance from the corridors of power. As Judith Newton states, "Writing women into 'history'" meant "that traditional definitions of 'history' would have to change."[99] But our aim here is not to resolve this inconsistency in favor of one discipline or the other but, rather, to suggest that the maximum benefits of each approach will be enjoyed by reciprocal reading and thinking. As long as documentary makers are driven to represent the past, and given our increasing realization of the stakes of that project, documentary studies must strive for the fullest possible purchase on the historiographic impulse. That, we contend, comes from feminism and historiography both.

▶──

Psychoanalysis

In arguing the importance of feminism and historiography for documentary studies, we are talking about two disciplines deeply influenced by psychoanalysis. What, then, does this imply about the role of psychoanalysis for documentary studies in general and for the study of the historical documentary in particular? Our view is that documentary studies will be all the richer for the incorporation of psychoanalytic thinking. But the terms of that connection will have to be redefined.

As discussed above, psychoanalytically informed approaches to film have been confined, almost exclusively, to fiction film.[100] Michael Renov and Bill Nichols have speculated that this is very likely to do with the perception that documentary is a realm of "conscious inquiry," in Renov's terms, or a "discourse of sobriety" that lacks "a royal road to the unconscious," in Nichols's terms.[101] Even William Guynn, who does consider documentary film in relation to Christian Metz's and Jean-Louis Baudry's psychoanalytic theories of spectatorship, reaches the conclusion that documentary film works against the "artificial psychosis" produced by the fiction film's cinematographic apparatus—in short, that it undermines the cinematographic effect.[102]

Renov and Nichols, however, insist on the applicability of psychoanalysis for the study of documentary film (though neither really models the project). Renov stresses that documentary films are "fictive" (if not fictional) and rely, therefore, on patterns of spectator inscription described by psychoanalytically informed close textual analysis of narrative cinema (7). Similarly, Nichols points out that documentary films "are part and parcel of the discursive formations, the language games, and rhetorical strategems by and through which pleasure and power, ideologies and utopias, subjects and subjectivities receive tangible representation" (10).

Our take on the matter is that psychoanalysis is instrumental to documentary study not only because documentaries draw extensively on fictive strategies, documentary films as "reality *fictions*," but because documentary films are "*reality* fictions."[103] Psychoanalysis, we believe, figures psychic structure as a fusion of fantasy constructs and real remembered experience.

Of course, there are feminists who would disagree. American feminists especially have dismissed Freud's work in large part for his abandonment of the seduction theory, for his retraction of his own earlier finding that hysterical reactions in adult women are the result of childhood sexual "seduction" (read: molestation). On the other hand, there are feminists, especially those influenced by British and/or continental theory, who celebrate Freud's work and its application to film for its insistence on the centrality of fantasy and unconscious processes to psychic construction. To confine one's thinking to real experience, they believe, is to reduce psychic life to nothing. And with psychic life reduced to nothing, psychosexual identity becomes once again a matter of anatomy as destiny. As we have argued elsewhere, our own impression is that Freud's work surmounts the either-or dilemma posed by these other interpretations and instead retains throughout, both in single essays and in his repeated return to the signficance of patients' life events, a productive tension between experience and fantasy.[104] The events of a life are important, but they are important precisely in the way that these events get carried forward as mental constructs. And the mental constructs of an incested daughter will be different, we think, from those of a daughter who desires but does not receive her father's sexual attentions. We believe that psychoanalysis is fruitful for documentary study because it can help theorize the relationship between real events and ongoing psychic representations.[105]

Moreover, psychoanalysis is important for the study of documentary films, we claim, not only because it approaches "reality fictions" but because, like a significant proportion of documentary films and videos, it levels its aim at the psychic intersection of past and present events. The theories and findings of psychoanalysis emerge from Freud's revelation that infantile sexuality is instrumental to adult psychic makeup, and from the insight that a person's past is both ultimately unknowable and yet crucial for psychic constructions in the present. The meeting of past and present is staged in psychoanalytic transference, in the analytic confrontation between analyst and analysand, where conflicts of the past reemerge so that they can be worked through in the process of reconstruction. There is an immediacy to the personal interaction that can be used strategically. But emergent past conflicts are always mediated by memory, free association, and other psychic processes. The total result is that the past, however misremembered or charged with psychic conflicts, is made operative in actions and resistances in the present. This resonates well, we believe, with the intrinsic features of the historical documentary: to retrieve a past that is both eminently tangible *and* ultimately ephemeral, and to laminate that past to an equally mediated present and an imagined future.

Because psychoanalysis understands histories as texts in which past events may be figured, albeit indirectly, it can be used to maintain some of the findings of oral histories without necessarily taking them at face value. In other words, psychoanalytic methodology can help clarify—or complicate—the pervasive use in documentary films of "talking heads" and the truth value attributed to them. For example, when Linda Williams argues in "Mirrors without Memories" that the present anti-Semitism of Polish peasants in *Shoah* is a link to their anti-Semitism in the past, she is using (without identifying it as such) an inherently transferential model.[106] Psychoanalytic methodology can also be brought in to illuminate documentary films, such as Rea Tajiri's *History and Memory,* that acknowledge the impossibility of direct access to the past.[107]

Several of the essays in this volume incorporate psychoanalytic ideas from this new perspective. Silvia Kratzer-Juilfs uses the concept of transference in a discussion of how historiographic and psychoanalytic pasts intertwine in documentries about Turkish women in exile in Germany. Anahid Kassabian and David Kazanjian use Freud's essay "Mourning and Melancholia" to show how the film *An Armenian Journey* represents the Armenian homeland as simultaneously lost and present in the "melancholic" figure of the woman who is the main subject of this documentary.

In this introduction, then, and in our selection of articles for the volume, we propose that psychoanalysis holds great promise for documentary's historiographic project.

▶

Contributions

With only three exceptions, the essays in this volume are appearing in print for the first time, and they were written or adapted expressly for this book. We have made the choice to concentrate on new work even though (as the length of our introduction testifies) there are many existing articles that fall within the purview of this study and merit republication. By offering all of these essays, we hope that this book will model, but not by any means exhaust, the possibilities for a return engagement between feminist and documentary thinking and practice. We are wowed by the erudition of the authors whose works are contained herein, but we aim, in drawing their essays together, toward the suggestive rather than the definitive and toward the risky rather than the commonplace—hence, Ann Kaneko's journal of her ideas and interactions with people in the course of shooting a film that she was still editing, Laura Marks's highly original piece about the non-visual and nonaudio aspects of film and video, Julia Lesage's speculations on why women seem to take pleasure in "stories of violence against ourselves," and more.

The book is organized into several distinct thematic sections, each of which we describe at the beginning of the section itself. But the pieces are at the same time united by certain fundamental impulses. All of the pieces evince a deep appreciation of the documentary form as a palimpsest for the marking of history and memory. And all throw their attention outward beyond the inordinately cloistered horizon of white, middle-class, U.S., male perspectives. Turkey, Germany, Armenia, India, Peru, Pakistan, Japan, and North Africa are some of the places discussed in essays in this volume; and being black, Jewish, lesbian, working-class, Asian, female, incest-surviving, or some combination thereof are some of the realities or heritages of the women and men who people the documentaries discussed herein. We offer these essays on feminism and documentary, then, in the substance and the spirit of historiographic and future practice. The points of contact between these two areas of study must be remembered and also reimagined if we are to become "intelligent on" feminism and documentary.

◆————————————————————————————————

NOTES

1. In conceptualizing *feminism* and *documentary* as terms that come together across an *and*, we acknowledge a debt to Constance Penley's edited volume *Feminism and Film Theory* (New York: Routledge, 1988), whose titular *and* marks the way the feminist articles in that collection "criticize or revamp many of the premises of recent film theory," while at the same time acknowledging its attention to sexual difference and its "anti-establishment iconoclasm" (3).

2. Adrienne Rich, *On Lies, Secrets, and Silence: Selected Prose 1966–1978* (New York: W. W. Norton, 1979), 9.

3. There is actually a genre of feminist writing that seeks to secure for feminist work the attention of male-dominated theory. See, for example, Judith Newton, "History as Usual? Feminism and the 'New Historicism,'" *Cultural Critique* 9 (1988): 87–121; Frances E. Mascia-Lees, Patricia Sharpe, and Colleen Ballerino Cohen, "The Postmodernist Turn in Anthropology: Cautions from a Feminist Perspective," *Signs: Journal of Women in Culture and Society* 15, no. 11 (Autumn 1989): 7–33; Paula Rabinowitz, "Labor and Desire: A Gendered History of Literary Radicalism," in her *Labor and Desire:*

Women's Revolutionary Fiction in Depression America (Chapel Hill: University of North Carolina Press, 1991); Judith Stacey and Barrie Thorne, "The Missing Feminist Revolution in Sociology," *Social Problems* 32, no. 4 (April 1985): 301–16; and Marilyn Strathern, "An Awkward Relationship: The Case of Feminism and Anthropology," *Signs* 12, no. 2 (1987): 276–92.

4. Bill Nichols, *Representing Reality: Issues and Concepts in Documentary* (Bloomington: Indiana University Press, 1991), 7.

5. Paula Rabinowitz, *They Must Be Represented: The Politics of Documentary* (London: Verso, 1994), 6.

6. At opposite ends of a timeline see, for example, Rich's "Disloyal to Civilization: Feminism, Racism, Gynephobia" (1978) in *On Lies, Secrets, and Silence* and Ruth Frankenberg, *White Women, Race Matters: The Social Construction of Whiteness* (Minneapolis: University of Minnesota Press, 1993). For an account of feminist articles on film that deal with issues of class and race, see notes 16 and 25 below, and Diane Carson, Linda Dittmar, and Janice R. Welsch, eds., *Multiple Voices in Feminist Film Criticism* (Minneapolis: University of Minnesota Press,

1994). Finally, for writing about lesbian sexuality and documentary film and video, see volume 1 in University of Minnesota Press's Visible Evidence series, Chris Holmlund and Cynthia Fuchs, eds., *Between the Sheets, in the Streets: Gay, Lesbian, Queer Documentary* (Minneapolis: University of Minnesota Press, 1997).

7. Toni Cade Bambara, ed., *The Black Woman: An Anthology* (New York: New American Library, 1970); Cherríe Moraga and Gloria Anzaldúa, eds., *The Bridge Called My Back: Writings by Radical Women of Color* (New York: Kitchen Table Women of Color Press, 1981); bell hooks, *Ain't I a Woman? Black Women and Feminism* (Boston: South End Press, 1981); hooks, *Feminist Theory: From Margin to Center* (Boston: South End Press, 1984); hooks, *Talking Back: Thinking Feminist, Thinking Black* (Boston: South End Press, 1989); Barbara Christian, "Trajectories of Self-Definition," in *Conjuring: Black Women, Fiction, and Literary Traditions*, ed. Marjorie Pryse and Hortense J. Spillers (Bloomington: Indiana University Press, 1985), 233–48; Christian, "But Who Do You Really Belong To—Black Studies or Women's Studies?" special issue, Across Cultures: The Spectrum of Women's Lives, *Women's Studies* 17, no. 1–2 (November 1989): 17; Michele Wallace, *Invisibility Blues: From Pop to Theory* (London: Verso, 1990).

8. Michael Renov, "Re-Thinking Documentary: Toward a Taxonomy of Mediation," *Wide Angle* 8, no. 3–4 (1986): 71–77.

9. See, for example, Ruth McCormick, "Union Maids," *Cineaste* 8, no. 1 (Summer 1977): 50–51; and Linda Gordon, "Union Maids: Working Class Heroines," *Jump Cut* 14 (1977): 34–35. Noel King takes both articles to task in "Recent 'Political' Documentary—Notes on *Union Maids* and *Harlan County, USA*," *Screen* 22, no. 2 (1981): 7–18. We discuss the King article below.

10. On the documentary side, see, for example, Lewis Jacobs, ed., *The Documentary Tradition: From Nanook to Woodstock* (New York: Hopkinson and Blake, 1971); Alan Rosenthal, *The New Documentary in Action: A Casebook in Film-Making* (Berkeley: University of California Press, 1971); Richard Meran Barsam, *Nonfiction Film: A Critical History* (New York: E. P. Dutton, 1973); Erik Barnouw, *Documentary: A History of the Non-Fiction Film* (New York: Oxford University Press, 1974); Stephen Mamber, *Cinema Verite in America: Studies in Uncontrolled Documentary* (Cambridge: MIT Press, 1974). For examples of early feminist film criticism, see the journal *Women & Film* (1972–1975); Marjorie Rosen, *Popcorn Venus: Women, Movies and the American Dream* (New York: Avon, 1973); Molly Haskell, *From Reverence to Rape: The Treatment of Women in the Movies* (New York: Holt, Rinehart, and Winston, 1974).

11. Rosenthal, to his credit, does mention "the failure [in much critical discussion of direct cinema films] to accord recognition to the part played by the editor" (86), and he includes interviews with Arla Saare and Charlotte Zwerin in *The New Documentary in Action*, and Mamber (*Cinema Verite in America*) includes brief references to women's work as editors and sound persons. Because it reprints contemporary source materials, Jacobs's anthology implicitly gives an indication of the rich contributions of women as writers about documentary film. Such fleeting references and/or inclusions might provide the basis for future feminist rewriting of documentary history.

12. Gardner, "A Chronicle of the Human Experience: *Dead Birds*," in Jacobs, *The Documentary Tradition*, 435.

13. The role of women in Dani society receives much more extensive elaboration in Gardner and Karl Heider's prose/photographic essay *Gardens of War: Life and Death in the New Guinea Stone Age* (New York: Random House, 1968). For other references to debates over the gender politics of Gardner's films see, for example, David MacDougall, "The Subjective Voice in Ethnographic Film" and Peter Loizos, "Robert Gardner's *Rivers of Sand*: Toward a Reappraisal," both in Leslie Devereaux and Roger Hillman, eds., *Fields of Vision: Essays in Film Studies, Visual Anthropology, and Photography* (Berkeley and Los Angeles: University of California Press, 1995), 217–55, 311–25, respectively.

14. Barsam, *Nonfiction Film*, 276.

15. That Barsam is likely discussing this sequence is evidenced by the phrase immediately succeeding the passage quoted above, "But these are lectures given by a local doctor." To his credit, Barsam eliminates this passage from the 1992 second edition of his book, perhaps a testimony to the process of "re-vision" that Adrienne Rich argues feminism can provoke ("When We Dead Awaken: Writing as Re-Vision," *On Lies, Secrets and Silence*, 35).

It should be clear that we are not implicating the film itself in this discussion of the analysis. In fact, it might be argued that one of the things *High School* demonstrates is the construction of masculinity, femininity, and patriarchal (hetero)sexuality in and through the institution of public secondary education.

16. For a discussion of these developments see, for example, Julia Lesage, "The Political Aesthetics of the Feminist Documentary Film," *Quarterly Review of Film Studies* 3, no. 4 (Fall 1978), reprinted in Patricia Erens,

ed., *Issues in Feminist Film Criticism* (Bloomington: Indiana University Press, 1990), 222–37; John Hess, "Notes on U.S. Radical Film, 1967–80," *Jump Cut* 21 (1979), reprinted in Peter Steven, ed., *Jump Cut: Hollywood, Politics and Counter Cinema* (Toronto: Between the Lines, 1985), 134–50; and Patricia Erens, "Women's Documentary Filmmaking: The Personal Is Political," *Women Artists' News* 1, no. 3 (Fall 1981), revised and updated in Alan Rosenthal, ed., *New Challenges for Documentary* (Berkeley and Los Angeles: University of California Press, 1988), 554–65.

17. Lewis Jacobs, ed., *The Documentary Tradition*, 2d ed. (New York: W. W. Norton, 1979), 516.

18. Jacobs also includes Ruth McCormick's "Women's Liberation Cinema," reprinted from *Cineaste* (Spring 1972); Barsam and Barnouw add chapters or sections of chapters on women's and gay liberation cinema and/or emphasize the role of women in other contemporary genres of documentary in the revised editions of their historical surveys.

19. For examples of work that brings feminist perspectives or concerns to nonexplicitly feminist documentaries, see Thomas Waugh, "Filming the Cultural Revolution," *Jump Cut* 12/13 (1976), reprinted in Rosenthal, *New Challenges for Documentary*, 148–64; Julianne Burton, "Film and Revolution in Cuba: The First 25 Years," *Jump Cut* 19 (1978); Waugh, "In Solidarity: Joris Ivens and the Birth of Cuban Cinema," *Jump Cut* 22 (1980); and Julia Lesage, "For Our Urgent Use: Films on Central America," *Jump Cut* 27 (1982). The latter three are reprinted in Steven, *Jump Cut*, 344–85. It is no coincidence that all these essays appeared first in this journal, which since its inception in 1974 has insisted on feminist approaches to films of all kinds.

Additionally, for examples of work from this same period in which feminism at least informed attempts to theorize the documentary, see Annette Kuhn, "The Camera I: Observations on Documentary," *Screen* 19, no. 2 (1978): 71–83; and Bill Nichols, *Ideology and the Image* (Bloomington: Indiana University Press, 1981).

20. See, for example, Nichols, *Representing Reality* and *Blurred Boundaries: Questions of Meaning in Contemporary Culture* (Bloomington: Indiana University Press, 1994); Rabinowitz, *They Must Be Represented*; Michael Renov, "New Subjectivities: Documentary and Self-Representation in the Post-Verité Age," this volume, and reprinted from *Documentary Box* 7 (July 1995): 1–8 (Tokyo); and Barry Keith Grant and Jeannette Sloniowski, eds., *Documenting the Documentary: Close Readings of Documen-*

tary Film and Video (Detroit: Wayne State University Press, 1998).

21. "Overview," *Women & Film* 1, no. 1 (1972): 3.

22. Pam Cook quoted in E. Ann Kaplan, "Interview with British Cine-Feminists," in *Women and the Cinema: A Critical Anthology*, ed. Karyn Kay and Gerald Peary (New York: E. P. Dutton, 1977), 401.

23. Laura Mulvey, "Visual Pleasure and the Narrative Cinema," *Screen* 16, no. 3 (Autumn 1975); reprinted in Laura Mulvey, *Visual and Other Pleasures* (Bloomington: Indiana University Press, 1989), 15.

24. This aspect of feminist attention to the texts of Hollywood must also be acknowledged and addressed.

25. By no means were they addressed exclusively or uncritically, as has sometimes been asserted. For example, although generally lavish in her praise of the San Francisco Newsreel Collective's *The Woman's Film*, Siew Hwa Beh (later one of the founders and coeditors of *Women & Film*) took the film to task for its exclusion of Asian women and for its underplaying of the process by which the women interviewed became politicized to the point of taking up collective action (Siew Hwa Beh, "The Woman's Film," *Film Quarterly* 25, no. 1 [Fall 1971]; reprinted in Bill Nichols, *Movies and Methods: An Anthology* [Berkeley: University of California Press, 1976], 201–4). Similarly, although largely supportive of the films she discusses (Kate Millet's *Three Lives*; Midge MacKenzie's *Women Talking, A Woman's Place*; Amalie Rothchild's *It Happens to Us*, the *Bail Bond Film*; New York Newsreel's *Janie's Janie, The 5th Street Women's Building Film*; and Julia Reichert and Jim Klein's *Growing Up Female—As Six Become One*), Ruth McCormick was critical of what she saw as the liberal-reformist politics of some of them—what she calls their "all women are sisters" line—and their inattention to the differences between women and the ways in which class, race, and sexual orientation interact with gender and shape the material circumstances of women's lives (Ruth McCormick, "Women's Liberation Cinema," in Jacobs, *The Documentary Tradition*, 2d ed., 523–35).

26. Susan Rice, "Three Lives," *Women & Film* 1, no. 1 (1972): 66. This passage is also cited by Laura Mulvey in "Film, Feminism and the Avant-Garde," reprinted in *Visual and Other Pleasures*, 117.

27. Dora Kaplan, "Part III: Selected Short Subjects," report on the First International Festival of Women's Films, *Women & Film* 1, no. 2 (1972): 37.

28. The term *counter-cinema*, as David Rodowick notes, was coined by Peter Wollen in a 1972 essay on Jean-Luc Godard's *Vent d'est* to describe "the emergence of a number of

independently produced films characterized by a militant hostility to commercial, narrative cinema as well as a commitment to radical politics and formal experimentation" (D. N. Rodowick, *The Crisis of Political Modernism* [Urbana: University of Illinois Press, 1988], 1). Wollen's essay originally appeared in *Afterimage* 4 (Autumn 1972).

29. Claire Johnston, "Women's Cinema as Counter-Cinema," *Notes on Women's Cinema*, ed. Claire Johnston (London: Society for Education in Film and Television, 1973); reprinted in Bill Nichols, *Movies and Methods*, 208–17. Johnston, for example, took issue with the journal's opposition to the auteur theory (212).

30. For example, the British journal *Screen* reprinted Benjamin's "A Short History of Photography" in 1972. For discussion of the selective ways in which contemporary film theory appropriated Benjamin and Brecht see, for example, Dana Polan, "Brecht and the Politics of Self-Reflexive Cinema," *Jump Cut* 17 (1978): 29–32; Sylvia Harvey, "Whose Brecht? Memories for the Eighties," *Screen* 23, no. 1 (May/June 1982): 45–59; Abigail Solomon-Godeau, "Reconstructing Documentary: Connie Hatch's Representational Resistance," *Camera Obscura* 13–14 (1985): 113–46; and Rodowick, *The Crisis of Political Modernism*.

31. "A Note from the Editors," *Women & Film* 1, no. 5–6 (1974): 5. By this point, Sandy Flitterman, Julia Lesage, Elisabeth Lyon, Janet Parker, Constance Penley, and Bill Nichols had joined coeditors Siew Hwa Beh and Saunie Salyer as associate editors. Flitterman, Lyon, and Penley would shortly leave the journal and start up *Camera Obscura* with Janet Bergstrom.

32. Perhaps this is the place to take up the ambiguity of the term *cinema verité* and the way it was (and continues to be) used to describe a variety of documentary practices. Although both direct cinema and cinema verité had their roots in the reaction against traditional expository documentary and in the technological developments (lightweight, portable equipment and synchronous sound) that made alternative modes possible, most writers in the documentary tradition currently follow Erik Barnouw's distinction between direct cinema as practiced in the United States by Robert Drew, Richard Leacock, Donn Pennebaker, Albert and David Maysles, Frederick Wiseman, and others and cinema verité as practiced in France by Jean Rouch and Edgar Morin. In an often-quoted passage Barnouw argues: "The direct cinema documentarist took his camera to a situation of tension and waited hopefully for a crisis; the Rouch version of *cinéma vérité* tried to precipitate one. The direct cinema artist

aspired to invisibility; the Rouch *cinéma vérité* artist was often an avowed participant. The direct cinema artist played the role of uninvolved bystander; the *cinéma vérité* artist espoused that of provocateur" (Barnouw, *Documentary*, 254–55). At the time the debates over realism were occurring this distinction was not yet widely in use; for example, Stephen Mamber, although aware of the distinction in practices uses the term *cinema verité* to describe the distinctive style of practitioners in the United States. It seems to us that the critique of realism as expounded in the early '70s is most applicable to direct cinema, with its discourse of nonintervention and its practice of indirect address, the long take, synchronous sound, and so on. But it is questionable whether or not these early feminist documentaries, with their emphasis on the interview and direct address, actually were noninterventionist and hence subject to this critique. For a contemporary discussion of the nontransparent aspects of the so-called feminist realist documentaries, see Alexandra Juhasz, "'They Said We Were Trying to Show Reality—All I Want to Show Is My Video': The Politics of the Realist Feminist Documentary," *Screen* 35: 2 (Summer 1994): esp. 187–88.

33. McGarry cites, for example, Willemen, "On Realisms in the Cinema," *Screen* 13 (1972); Brian Henderson, "Towards a Non-Bourgeois Camera Style," *Film Quarterly* 24 (Winter 1970); and Christopher Williams, "The Deep Focus Question: Some Comments on Patrick Ogle's Article," *Screen* 13 (1972).

34. See for example Michael Renov, "Re-Thinking Documentary."

35. McGarry, "Documentary, Realism, and Women's Cinema," *Women & Film* 2, no. 7 (1975): 50–59.

36. McGarry actually argues that *The Woman's Film* "comes closer to a *realist* aesthetic in technique than previous Newsreel films," but that "in the almost *heroic* coding and use of women who would perhaps not appear in a favorable light in more traditional film (black, Chicana, welfare mother, working-class, Jewish, middle-aged, 'unfashionable,' etc.) the film elevates *real* women beyond traditional *natural* and *filmic* sexual stereotypes" (57). This latter point was taken up by Julia Lesage in "The Political Aesthetics of the Feminist Documentary Film," when she argues that "among the connotative elements to which feminist documentaries draw our attention and give an added complexity are the visual cues that define womanliness in film. The women characters' gestures, clothes, age, weight, sexual preference, race, class, embeddedness in a specific social milieu elicit our reflection on both the specificity of the subjects' and our own lives,

and on the difference between these cinematic representations and those of dominant cinema" (233).

37. B. Ruby Rich, "In the Name of Feminist Film Criticism," *Jump Cut* 19 (1978); reprinted in Steven, *Jump Cut*, 209–30. See also Judith Mayne, "Visibility and Feminist Film Criticism," *Film Reader* 5 (1982), esp. 123–24; and Alexandra Juhasz, ". . . The Politics of the Realist Feminist Documentary," esp. 188–90.

38. Juliet Mitchell, *Psychoanalysis and Feminism: Freud, Reich, Laing and Women* (New York: Random House, 1974); Louis Althusser, "Ideology and Ideological State Apparatuses" and "Freud and Lacan," in *Lenin and Philosophy and Other Essays*, trans. Ben Brewster (New York: Monthly Review Press, 1971), 127–219; see also Jean-Louis Baudry, "Ideological Effects of the Basic Cinematographic Apparatus," *Film Quarterly* 28, no. 2 (1974–75): 39–47; Stephen Heath, "Film and System: Terms of Analysis, Part I," *Screen* 16, no. 1 (1975): 7–77, and "Film and System: Terms of Analysis, Part II," *Screen* 16, no. 2 (1975): 91–113; and Christian Metz, "The Imaginary Signifier," *Screen* 16, no. 2 (1975): 14–76.

39. Kaja Silverman, *The Acoustic Mirror* (Bloomington: Indiana University Press, 1988).

40. Mulvey, "Visual Pleasure and Narrative Cinema," 15–16.

41. Mulvey argues: "Although it is hard to overestimate the vigour and immediacy of some of these films, they are closely tied to the ideology of consciousness-raising and agitation around particular feminist issues. This is their strength; their weakness lies in limitations of the *cinéma vérité* tradition. While as documents they can have an immediate political use, their aesthetics are bound by a concept of film as a transparent medium, reproducing rather than questioning, a project which reduces the camera to a magical instrument. There lies behind this a further assumption, that the camera, by its very nature and the good intentions of the operator, can grasp essential truths and by registering typical shared experiences can create political unity through the process of identification. The politics are thus restricted to emotion and the cinema stays trapped in the old endless search for the other self on the screen" ("Film, Feminism and the Avant-Garde," 117–18).

42. Mulvey, "Film, Feminism and the Avant-Garde," 124.

43. Of course, this term is borrowed from Bill Nichols's title (see note 20).

44. The phrase comes from Penley's introduction to a section on "Documentary/Documentation" in *Camera Obscura* 13–14 (1985): 85. "Talking about Our Lives and Experiences: Some Thoughts about Feminism, Documen-

tary and 'Talking Heads,'" Barbara Halpern Martineau points out that at a conference on feminist film criticism held at Northwestern University in 1980, hers was the only paper out of about forty presented that dealt with documentary film criticism. In Waugh, "*Show Us Life*": *Toward a History and Aesthetics of the Committed Documentary* (Metuchen, N.J.: Scarecrow Press, 1984), 271.

45. Juhasz, ". . . The Politics of the Realist Feminist Documentary," 173. Juhasz describes, for example, the difficulty she encountered in attempting to rent *Self-Health*, a film discussed at length in Julia Lesage's widely anthologized essay "The Political Aesthetics of the Feminist Documentary Film."

46. Sonya Michel's "Feminism, Film, and Public History," *Radical History Review* 25 (1981), and B. Ruby Rich's "Anti-Porn: Soft Issue, Hard World," *Village Voice* (1983) (both reprinted in Erens, *Issues in Feminist Film Criticism*, 238–49, 268–87) are exemplary counterexamples in the ways in which they go beyond the critique of realism to discuss such issues as the mystification of the relationship among women, the labor movement, and the organized left in feminist labor documentaries and the ways in which the redemptive structure and voyeuristic cinematography and editing of *Not a Love Story* limit or undermine its antipornography stance.

47. See, for example, Kuhn, "The Camera and I," and Renov, "Re-Thinking Documentary."

48. Hart Cohen, "The Ax Fight: Mapping Anthropology on Film," *Ciné-Tracts* 2, no. 2 (Spring 1979): 61–73. Cohen is not speaking of the fictional mode per se, but his phrase captures effectively the idea that representations can employ various avenues to truth.

49. Thomas Benson and Carolyn Anderson, *Reality Fictions: The Films of Frederick Wiseman* (Carbondale: Southern Illinois University Press, 1989).

50. See, for example, Christine Gledhill, "Recent Developments in Feminist Film Criticism," *Quarterly Review of Film Studies* 3, no. 4 (1978); reprinted in Mary Ann Doane, Patricia Mellencamp, and Linda Williams, eds., *Re-Vision: Essays in Feminist Film Criticism* (Frederick, Md.: University Publications of America, 1984), 18–48; E. Ann Kaplan, "Theories and Strategies of the Feminist Documentary," *Millennium Film Journal* 12 (Fall–Winter 1982–83); reprinted and revised in Kaplan, "The Realist Debate in the Feminist Film: A Historical Overview of Theories and Strategies in Realism and the Avant-Garde Theory Film (1971–81)," in *Women and Film: Both Sides of the Camera* (New York: Methuen, 1983), 125–41; Annette Kuhn, "Real Women," in *Women's Pictures:*

Feminism and Cinema (London: Routledge and Kegan Paul, 1982), 131–55; Jane Gaines, "Women and Representation: Can We Enjoy Alternative Pleasure?" *Jump Cut* 29 (1984); reprinted in Erens, *Issues in Feminist Film Criticism*, 75–92; and Alexandra Juhasz, ". . . The Politics of the Realist Feminist Documentary."

51. Kimberly Safford, "*La Operación*: Forced Sterilization," *Jump Cut* 29 (February 1984): 37–38, cited by Gaines, "Women and Representation," 91.

52. Gaines, "Women and Representation," 83.

53. See also Jane Feuer's conclusion to her discussion of Citron's *Daughter Rite*: "In its emotive power, *Daughter Rite* might well teach a lesson to those avant-garde radical filmmakers set upon sacrificing identification and emotional involvement on the altar of mere cognition" ("'Daughter Rite': Living with Our Pain and Love," *Jump Cut* 23 [1980]: 30); and Juhasz, ". . . The Politics of the Realist Feminist Documentary."

54. Kaplan, *Women and Film*, 217, n. 21.

55. See for example, Lesage, "The Political Aesthetics of the Feminist Documentary Film"; Kuhn, *Women's Pictures*; Kaplan, *Women and Film*; Charlotte Brunsdon, "General Introduction" and "Introduction" to the documentary section in *Films for Women* (London: British Film Institute, 1986); Jane Feuer, "'Daughter Rite': Living with Our Pain and Love," and Sylvia Harvey, "An Introduction to 'The Song of the Shirt,'" *Undercut* 1 (1981); both reprinted in Brunsdon, *Films for Women*, 24–30, 44–48; Constance Penley, "Documentary/Documentation"; Constance Penley and Andrew Ross, "Interview with Trinh T. Minh-ha"; Abigail Solomon-Godeau, "Reconstructing Documentary: Connie Hatch's Representational Resistance"; "No Essential Femininity: A Conversation between Mary Kelly and Paul Smith"; Jane Weinstock, "A Post-Post-Partum Document"; all in *Camera Obscura* 13–14 (1985): 85–161; Paula Rabinowitz, "National Bodies: Gender, Sexuality, and Terror in Feminist Counter-Documentaries," in *They Must Be Represented*, 176–204; Valerie Smith, "Telling Family Secrets: Narrative and Ideology in *Suzanne, Suzanne* by Camille Billops and James V. Hatch," and Amy Lawrence, "Women's Voices in Third World Cinema," both in *Multiple Voices in Feminist Film Criticism*, ed. Diane Carson, Linda Dittmar, and Janice R. Welsch (Minneapolis: University of Minnesota Press, 1994), 380–90, 406–20.

56. See, for example, Leslie Sterne, "Feminism and Cinema-Exchanges," *Screen* 20, no. 3/4 (1979–80): 89–105; Sonya Michel, "Feminism, Film, and Public History"; Kuhn, *Women's Pictures*; Kaplan, *Women and Film*; and Brunsdon, *Films for Women*.

57. See, for example, Lesage, "The Political Aesthetics of the Feminist Documentary Film"; and Rich, "In the Name of Feminist Film Criticism." Rich (somewhat playfully) suggests changing the ways such films are classified from cinema verité ("where they reside in decidedly mixed company") to "validative:" "By employing the name 'validative' in place of *cinéma vérité*, we can combat the patriarchal annexation of the woman filmmaker as one of the boys, that is, a professional who is not of the culture being filmed" (222). See also the report on the "Making Documentaries" panel of the First International Festival of Women's Films mentioned above. See also Martineau, "Talking about Our Lives and Experiences."

58. Calvin Pryluck, "Ultimately We Are All Outsiders: The Ethics of Documentary Filming," in *New Challenges for Documentary*, ed. Alan Rosenthal (Berkeley and Los Angeles: University of California Press, 1988).

59. See, for example, James Linton's "The Moral Decision in Documentary," *Journal of the University Film Association* 28 (Spring 1976): 17–22; or Jay Ruby, "Image Ethics," in *The Documentary Today* (working papers) (Minneapolis: Film in the Cities, 1983). Both are cited in *New Challenges for Documentary*, ed. Alan Rosenthal (Berkeley and Los Angeles: University of California Press, 1988).

60. Brian Winston, "The Tradition of the Victim in Griersonian Documentary," in Rosenthal, ed., *New Challenges*, 269–70.

61. Larry Gross, John Stuart Katz, and Jay Ruby, eds., *Image Ethics: The Moral Rights of Subjects in Photographs, Film, and Television* (New York: Oxford University Press, 1988), vi.

62. In their introduction to *Image Ethics*, Gross, Katz, and Ruby mention the famous case of the WHMA-TV (Anniston, Alabama) cameraman and sound recordist who were sent out to cover the story of an unemployed roofer who called the station to report that he was about to set himself on fire (16). The sound recordist put down his equipment and went to the aid of the roofer, but not before the roofer was seriously burned. The story was reported on television with excerpts from the tape, creating a case study in documentary news ethics. The *Image Ethics* editors also quote Harold Evans's description of an incident in Bangladesh in which Biharis were bayoneted as a "photo opportunity" for still photographers and television news cameraman, some of whom departed the scene and some of whom stayed and won Pulitzer Prizes (17).

63. Thomas Waugh, "Lesbian and Gay Documentary: Minority Self-Imaging, Oppositional Film Practice, and the Question of Image," in Gross, Katz, and Ruby, eds., *Image Ethics*, 248–72.

64. Winston, "The Tradition of the Victim," 271.
65. James Clifford and George E. Marcus, eds., *Writing Culture: The Poetics and Politics of Ethnography* (Berkeley and Los Angeles: University of California Press, 1986); and George E. Marcus and Michael M. J. Fischer, eds., *Anthropology as Cultural Critique: An Experimental Moment in the Human Sciences* (Chicago: University of Chicago Press, 1986); see also Lucien Taylor, ed., *Visualizing Theory: Selected Essays from V.A.R. 1990–1994* (New York: Routledge, 1994); George E. Marcus, *Rereading Cultural Anthropology* (Durham, N.C.: Duke University Press, 1992); and Leslie Devereaux and Roger Hillman, eds., *Fields of Vision: Essays in Film Studies, Visual Anthropology, and Photography* (Berkeley and Los Angeles: University of California Press, 1995).
66. James Clifford and George Marcus have been taken to task for their volume's exclusion of feminist contributors and perspectives. See, for example, Deborah Gordon, "Writing Culture, Writing Feminism: The Poetics and Politics of Experimental Ethnography," *Inscriptions*, 3/4 (1988): 7–24, and Mascia-Lees et al., "The Postmodernist Turn in Anthropology." For a further critique of masculinist perspectives in new ethnography see Margery Wolf, *A Thrice-Told Tale: Feminism, Postmodernism, and Ethnographic Responsibility* (Stanford: Stanford University Press, 1992); and Lila Abu-Lughod, "Writing against Culture," in *Recapturing Anthropology: Working in the Present*, ed. Richard G. Fox (Santa Fe, N.M.: School of American Research Press, 1991), 137–62.
67. Mascia-Lees et al., "The Postmodernist Turn," 11.
68. Abu-Lughod, "Writing against Culture," 139.
69. Faye Ginsburg, "Mediating Culture: Indigenous Media, Ethnographic Film, and the Production of Identity," in Devereaux and Hillman, eds., *Fields of Vision*, 259–60.
70. Ginsburg is drawing here on the work of Stuart Hall, particularly his article "Cultural Identity and Diaspora," in *Identity, Community, Culture, Difference*, ed. J. Rutherford (London, 1990).
71. Clifford and Marcus, *Writing Culture*, 20, 22.
72. Abu-Lughod, "Writing against Culture," 143.
73. Clifford, *Writing Culture*, 15.
74. Abu-Lughod, "Writing against Culture," 161, n. 5. Here Abu-Lughod is paraphrasing Sandra Harding, *The Science Question in Feminism* (Ithaca, N.Y.: Cornell University Press, 1986). Abu-Lughod writes: "Within the women's movement, the objections of lesbians, African-American women, and other 'women of color' that their experiences as women were different from those of white, middle-class, heterosexual women problematized the identity of women as selves"

(140). See also Mascia-Lees et al., "The Postmodernist Turn in Anthropology": "The need for building recognition that what once appeared to be theoretically appropriate mandates for change may have very different results for different populations of women. For example, some scholars claim that anti-rape activism has served to reinforce racial stereotypes (the rapist as black male), that pro-choice legislation has provided a rationale for forced sterilization and abortions among the poor and women of color, and that feminist-backed no-fault-divorce legislation has contributed to the feminization of poverty" (23).
75. Jacqueline Bobo, "Black Women's Films: Genesis of a Tradition," in *Black Women Film and Video Artists* (New York: Routledge, 1998), 6.
76. Julianne Burton, "Democratizing Documentary: Modes of Address in Latin American Cinema, 1958–1972" in Waugh, *"Show Us Life,"* 376.
77. Thomas Waugh, "Lesbian and Gay Documentary," 265. In fairness to the editors of *Image Ethics*, we acknowledge that the article by Thomas Waugh is included in that volume. But we believe that the nature of Waugh's project is in fact quite different in the ways we have attempted to describe in the text.
78. Chon Noriega, "Talking Heads, Body Politic: The Plural Self of Chicano Experimental Video," in *Resolutions*, ed. Michael Renov and Erika Suderburg (Minneapolis: University of Minnesota Press, 1996), 223, 210.
79. Waugh, "Lesbian and Gay Documentary."
80. King, "Recent 'Political' Documentary," 9.
81. Charles Wolfe, "Just in Time: *Let Us Now Praise Famous Men* and the Recording of the Historical Subject," in *Fugitive Images: From Photography to Video*, ed. Patrice Petro (Bloomington: Indiana University Press, 1995), 199.
82. See also Frisch's discussion of how expert voices usurp the authority of regular people who are interviewed in "Oral History, Documentary, and the Mystification of Power: A Critique of *Vietnam: A Television History*," in *A Shared Authority: Essays on the Craft and Meaning of Oral and Public History* (Albany: State University of New York Press, 1990).
83. King also ignores the specificity of the representational mode: Brecht was discussing drama.
84. Sonya Michel, "Feminism, Film, and Public History" (1981), reprinted in Erens, *Issues in Feminist Film Criticism*.
85. Judith Newton, "History as Usual?" 92. Newton also cites Elizabeth Meese's recommendation that we try "to win that authority in an in-situation we ceaselessly attempt to undermine and unsettle" (92, note).

Elizabeth Meese, *Crossing the Double-Cross: The Practice of Feminist Criticism* (Chapel Hill: University of Northa Carolina Press, 1986), 148.

86. For some early examples see the following works identified by Judith Newton (105, note): Lillian Robinson, "Modernism and History" (with Lise Vogel, 1971), in her *Sex, Class, and Culture* (New York: Methuen, 1986); Kate Millett, *Sexual Politics* (New York: Doubleday, 1970); Elaine Showalter, "Literary Criticism," *Signs* 1, no. 2 (Winter 1975): 435–60. For more recent examples see Patricia Erens, "Women's Documentaries as Social History," *Film Library Quarterly* 14, nos. 1, 2 (1981): 4–9; Patrice Petro, "Historical *Ennui*, Feminist Boredom," in *The Persistence of History: Cinema, Television, and the Modern Event*, ed. Vivian Sobchack (New York: Routledge, 1996), 187–200; Mary Beth Haralovich, "Film History and Social History: Reproducing Social Relationships, *Wide Angle* 8, no. 2 (1986): 4–14; Linda Gordon, "What's New in Women's History?" in *Feminist Studies/ Critical Studies*, ed. Teresa de Lauretis (Bloomington: Indiana University Press, 1986), 20–30. See also two essays in *Listening to Silences*, ed. Elaine Hedges and Shelley Fisher Fishkin (New York: Oxford University Press, 1994) that deal to some extent with the historical component of writing through silence: King-Kok Cheung, "Attentive Silence in Joy Kogawa's *Obasan*," and Kate Adams, "Northamerican Silences: History, Identity, and Witness in the Poetry of Gloria Anzaldúa, Cherríe Moraga, and Leslie Marmon Silko" (113–29, 130–45).

87. For some among many examples see Annette Kuhn, *Family Secrets* (London: Verso, 1995); *Autobiography and Questions of Gender*, ed. Shirley Neuman (Portland, Ore.: Frank Cass, 1991); *The Private Self: Theory and Practics of Women's Autobiographical Writings*, ed. Shari Benstock (Chapel Hill: University of North Carolina Press, 1988); *Women's Autobiography: Essays in Criticism*, ed. Estelle C. Jelinek (Bloomington: Indiana University Press, 1989); *A Poetics of Women's Autobiography: Marginality and the Fictions of Self-Representation*, ed. Sidonie Smith (Bloomington: Indiana University Press, 1987); *Black Women Writing Autobiography: A Tradition within a Tradition*, ed. Joanne Braxton (Philadelphia: Temple University Press, 1989); *De/Colonizing the Subject: The Politics of Gender in Women's Autobiography*, ed. Sidonie Smith and Julia Watson (Minneapolis: University of Minnesota Press, 1993).

88. Jeanne Perreault, *Writing Selves: Contemporary Feminist Autobiography* (Minneapolis: University of Minnesota, 1995), 2.

89. Ibid.

90. Sidonie Smith, "The Autobiographical Manifesto: Identities, Temporalities, Politics," in Neuman, *Autobiography and Questions of Gender*, 186.

91. Ibid., 189.

92. Raylene L. Ramsay, *The French New Autobiographies: Sarraute, Duras, and Robbe-Grillet* (Gainesville: University Press of Florida, 1996), 51.

93. Ibid.

94. We will discuss Linda Williams's work on postmodern documentaries below.

95. Ramsay, *The French New Autobiographies*, 52–53.

96. Smith "The Autobiographical Manifesto," 194.

97. Hayden White, *Metahistory: The Historical Imagination in Nineteenth-Century Europe* (Baltimore: Johns Hopkins University Press, 1973), *The Content of the Form: Narrative Discourse and Historical Representation* (Baltimore: Johns Hopkins University Press, 1987), *Tropics of Discourse: Essays in Cultural Criticism* (Baltimore: Johns Hopkins University Press, 1978); Saul Friedländer, ed. *Probing the Limits of Representation: Nazism and the "Final Solution"* (Cambridge: Harvard University Press, 1992); Dominick LaCapra, *Rethinking Intellectual History: Texts, Contexts, Language* (Ithaca, N.Y.: Cornell University Press, 1983), *History and Criticism* (Ithaca, N.Y.: Cornell University Press, 1985); Michael Frisch, *A Shared Authority*.

98. Hayden White, "Historical Emplotment and the Problem of Truth," in *Probing the Limits of Representation*; and "The Modernist Event," in *The Persistence of History*.

99. Newton, "History as Usual?" 100.

100. An excellent exception is Dan Armstrong's "Wiseman's Realm of Transgression: *Titicut Follies*, the Symbolic Father and the Spectacle of Confinement," *Cinema Journal* 29, no. 1 (Fall 1989): 20–35.

101. Michael Renov, "Introduction: The Truth about Non-Fiction," in his *Theorizing Documentary* (New York: Routledge, 1993), 6; Bill Nichols, "The Domain of Documentary," in *Representing Reality*, 9.

102. William Guynn, "The Nonfiction Film and Its Spectator," *A Cinema of Nonfiction* (London and Toronto: Associated University Presses, 1990).

103. We borrow this term from Thomas Benson and Carolyn Anderson's book on Frederick Wiseman, *Reality Fictions* (Carbondale: Southern Illinois University Press, 1989).

104. We discuss our reading of Freud and his interpreters at greater length in Janet Walker and Diane Waldman, "John Huston's *Freud* and Textual Repression: A Psychoanalytic Feminist Reading," in *Close Viewings: An Anthology of New Film Criticism*, ed. Peter Lehman (Tallahassee: Florida State University Press, 1990), 282–99.

105. Janet Walker, "The Traumatic Paradox: Documentary Films, Historical Fictions, and Cataclysmic Past Events," *Signs* 22, no. 4 (Summer 1997): 803–25.

106. Linda Williams, "Mirrors without Memories—Truth, History, and the New Documentary," *Film Quarterly* 46, no. 3 (Spring 1993): 9–21.

107. See Maureen Turim's psychoanalytically and historiographically informed discussion of memory and history in the modernist cinema of the post–World War II era in *Flashbacks in Film: Memory and History* (New York: Routledge, 1989), 212–26. Although the book concentrates mainly on fiction film, this passage deals with the "modernist flashback" in several nonfiction films by Alain Resnais and his hybrid film *Hiroshima, Mon Amour.*

I Historicizing Documentary

Historicizing Documentary

The first section of this book, "Historicizing Documentary," owes its titular gerund to Michael Renov's edited volume *Theorizing Documentary* and
is compiled, like its namesake, of essays that understand the history (rather
than the theory, though the two are not mutually exclusive) of documentary and feminism as an uncompleted writing action about two terms that
frequently relate to each other in a periodic historiographic "interval."[1]
The essays in this section are counterhistories of feminism and documentary that aim, as counterhistories do, to correct misapprehensions, to reclaim "lost" percepts and pen scripts, and, mainly, to rethink how documentary and feminist practices have been (historio)graphed so far and
imagine how they might be in the future.

The essays in this part appear in loose chronological order based
on the subject matter of each essay. Paula Rabinowitz's "Sentimental
Contracts: Dreams and Documents of American Labor" contextualizes the
discussion of contemporary films with reference to texts of the 1930s and a
heritage of struggle. For Rabinowitz, moreover, the compelling, resurgent
history is one of bloody labor strife, reportage, and tears traced back to
eighteenth-century sentimentality. Class, gender, and filmmaking strategies
are here explicitly linked, as are filmmakers, subjects, and viewers: the
tears are not only those of the combatants in labor strikes, nor only those
of the writers behind the lines where there could be no neutral ground, but
those as well of audience members sitting at a screening of *American
Dream* more than half a century later. Rabinowitz's chapter considers
"gendered discourses of sentimentality" in labor documentaries with a
focus on *Roger and Me,* a "modern male workers' melodrama," and
American Dream, a "dark romance" for the postmodern era.

In "Flaherty's Midwives," Patricia Zimmermann's adaptation of an
article that appeared initially as the introduction to her *Wide Angle* special

issue on the Robert Flaherty Film Seminar, Zimmermann casts herself as a "scholarly midwife to documentary history."[2] Chock full of references reflecting Zimmermann's personal and scholarly connections and commitment to the seminar, her essay puts spaces of exhibition on the map as alternative public spheres for women and argues for the incorporation of feminist exhibition histories into documentary cartographies of conscience. Michael Renov's "New Subjectivities: Documentary and Self-Representation in the Post-Verité Age" appeared initially in 1994 in the Yamagata International Documentary Film Festival catalog. We have chosen to reprint it here because the article is one of very few documentary histories to acknowledge the crucial influence of feminist thinking on the changed face of documentary film from the 1970s to the present.[3] Whereas it is commonplace to link Richard Leacock, Jean Rouch, and Ross McElwee in a patrilineal geneology of the subjective documentary form,[4] Renov's essay sketches in the maternal line, identifying video artist Wendy Clarke (creator of the diaristic video project *The Love Tapes*) along with Rouch as precursors of a new generation of makers (including Marilou Mallet, Raul Ruiz, and Rea Tajiri) in the act of "historical self-inscription."

Alexandra Juhasz's "Bad Girls Come and Go, But a Lying Girl Can Never Be Fenced In" shares the corrective historical impulse of the other essays in this section. But in this case, the history being restored is not women's history lost to masculinist historiography but, rather, feminist history itself, forfeited by our postmodern "culture of oblivion."[5] Juhasz writes as a young feminist curious not only about what was, but also about why we have forgotten. Arguing for an expansive definition of documentary, Juhasz analyzes two shows of art videos, presented more than ten years apart. These videos, she demonstrates, incarnate the forms of transgressive expression, and they allow her to explore how "documentary and avant-garde form (and their hybridization) . . . allow feminists to mold a medium to the shape of their anger and desire."

Individually and as a group, then, the essays in this first section participate explicitly in the project that guides this whole collection: to engage in dialogue with the dominant strains of documentary history from the perspective of feminism.

◆――――――――――――――――――――――――――――

NOTES

1. In *Theorizing Documentary*, "Introduction: The Truth about Non-Fiction," Michael Renov identifies "a whole series of intervals" (the latter term taken from Trinh T. Minh-ha's essay "The Totalizing Quest of Meaning," in *Theorizing Documentary*, 90–107) on which his volume reflects. The intervals include those "between truth and beauty, truth and reality, science and art, fiction and nonfiction . . . history and the-

ory (11)." In the chapter he contributes to *Theorizing Documentary*, "Toward a Poetics of Documentary," Renov characterizes his project as one that is "necessarily open-ended and demands extension in several directions" (36).

2. Erik Barnouw and Patricia Zimmermann, guest editors, *The Flaherty: Four Decades in the Cause of Independent Cinema, Wide Angle* 17, no. 1–4 (1995).

3. We disagree between ourselves about the extent to which Bill Nichols in *Representing Reality* has acknowledged a debt to feminism in the development of documentary modes from the expository, to the observational, to the interactive, to the reflexive. But we agree that he has always been exceptionally well informed about feminist documentaries themselves and has discussed them extensively in his writing.

4. Ross McElwee himself acknowledges the influence of Richard Leacock, who participates in *Sherman's March*. See also James Lane, "First Person Filmmaking," Ph.D. diss., University of California, Los Angeles, 1991.

5. Juhasz is quoting Carolee Schneemann interviewed in *Angry Women*, ed. Andrea Juno and V. Vale (San Francisco: Re/Search Publications, 1991).

PAULA RABINOWITZ

[1]   *Sentimental Contracts: Dreams and*
        Documents of American Labor

"Do not ask me to write of the strike and the terror. I am on a battlefield. . . .
But I hunch over the typewriter and behind the smoke, the days whirl, confused as dreams," declared the young Tillie Olsen during the 1934 San
Francisco General Strike.[1] In this classic example of reportage the division
between observation and participation, between fact and fantasy, has broken down. "I am on a battlefield," not merely as a war correspondent but
as one of the combatants. In Florence Reece's ballad trumpeting the news
of the 1934 Kentucky coal strikes in bloody Harlan County, one must decide "Which Side Are You On?": "If you go to Harlan County / there is no
neutral there, you'll either be a union man / or a thug for J. H. Blair."[2] The
bloody labor strife of the 1930s had clearly defined battle lines, and everyone sympathetic to workers knew which side was right; yet the engaged
writer, knowing she was on a battlefield, was left "behind the smoke . . .
confused as dreams" by her double duty—to march and to type. Contemporary labor documentaries owe much to the literary genre of reportage,
especially as practiced in the 1930s by committed journalists and worker
correspondents. This form collapses distinctions between reader and participant by placing the observer/writer in the midst of the action as it happens, and because the two poles are clearly marked—you either are a union
man or a thug—sentiment lodges on the side of labor. Florence Reece and
the other balladeers could march *and* sing, but writers eventually left the
line to tell the story. By leaving the line, the writer momentarily escaped the
conflict, confusing her class allegiance; however, an either-or situation demands that both reporter and reader must choose sides within a dichoto-
mous class structure. In reportage, documenters serve not only to witness,
but to intervene.

During the 1930s, many writers forged these sentimental contracts as
they journeyed in search of "the trouble" befalling a nation suffering

through extreme economic crisis.[3] In many ways, reportage mediated the feminized stance of the novelist—whether male or female, the writer was viewed by the Left as effete, bourgeois—and that of the hard-boiled reporter, as tough masculine worker, because these writers did not simply report from the sidelines; they put their bodies on the line. In modern times, radical intellectuals often have romanticized the industrial worker as the authentic vessel of revolution. This may stem from Karl Marx's infatuation with the French socialist workers he met "smoking, eating, drinking, etc." together in the Paris cafés while living in exile there as a young man. He notes that "the brotherhood of man is no mere phrase with them, but a fact of life, and the nobility of man shines upon us from their work-hardened bodies." Joining these "communist *artisans*" to produce "theory, propaganda" leads Marx to realize that "they acquire a new need—the need for society." He, too, seeks "company, association, and conversation" among them.[4]

So moving into workers' homes to march with them became a standard activity of radical journalists following the strikes in coal, rubber, and steel during the 1930s. For instance, in 1934, a young Smith College graduate, Harriet Gilfillan Woodbridge, writing as Lauren Gilfillan, traveled to the coal fields of fictional Avelonia, Pennsylvania, to report on the strikes there. She entered the struggle only to be reminded that she was an outsider. *I Went to Pit College* described her position as radical journalist within a mining community, riven by rival unions, political enmity, class conflict, and racial, ethnic, and religious divisions, which at least coalesced around a mutual suspicion of outsiders, especially those sporting linen dresses. Her book, widely reviewed and often denounced as sentimental tripe, a melodramatic portrayal of middle-class feminine thrill-seeking, was also praised for her willingness to bare herself as a voyeur and explore these class confusions, as well as provide a vivid portrait of a community torn apart by labor strife.[5] Reportage, "in no way content simply to depict facts," risked sentimentality, according to Georg Lukács, because it "does indeed appeal to our feelings, both in its depiction of the facts and in the call to action."[6] Too much investment in one side of the battle, too much detail, a fetishistic "portrayal" of the victims of capitalism, however, got in the way of clear-sighted, "scientific" analyses of the prevailing economic and political crisis. Because its strength is that it opens the way for tears, reportage treads a fine political line, locating sentiment in the house of labor.

Sentimentality emerges in eighteenth-century Britain under curious and contradictory conditions. On the one hand, discussions about the proper use of tears were linked to a long history of antirational conservatism starting with the embarrassingly sentimentalized male philosophers, such as Edmund Burke, resisting the Enlightenment revolutions in France.

Claudia Johnson argues persuasively that "the welfare of the nation and the tearfulness of private citizens—actual as well as fictional—were understood in the 1790s to be urgently interconnected."[7] I would add that this is no less true of the 1990s. On the other hand, the rise of the bourgeois state required a break with the teary-eyed men who maintained a chivalric honor unnecessary under a new democratic regime. Men's tears are throwbacks to an era when the spectacle of men crying could be understood as part of the workings of an aristocratic order of "sentimentality [under which] the prestige of suffering belongs to men."[8] Within the culture of middle-class sensibilities, women were to be the repositories of feelings. The new forms of gendered subjectivity developing within bourgeois culture, argue feminist literary historians such as Nancy Armstrong, Cathy Davidson, and Jane Tompkins, require the "cultural work" of women's sentimentality to establish the modern subject, a being drenched in emotion and encased in privacy during the age of revolution and after. Sentiment became private because its public expression threatened social order. According to Raymond Williams, what Burke resisted was the incursion of the rational state into zones previously cordoned off as civil society. Emotions publicly displayed by citizens of a democracy led to the frightening spectacles of mobs and masses in the streets.[9] Bourgeois culture thus contained sentimentality within women's domain. Its leakage into "the methods of science" appropriate to journalism,[10] especially in the service of that most melodramatic staging, the strike, threatened to undo political authority. That would seem a good thing if one's goals, like those of the literary radicals of the 1930s, were to overthrow a failed capitalism.

However, in the rhetorics of both the Left and modernism, bourgeois culture as a whole had taken on the sentimentalized characteristics of feminized, aristocratic decadence—an image repeated in iconography of the International Workers of the World, socialist cartoons, Thorstein Veblen's *Theory of the Leisure Class*, communist pamphlets, modernist manifestos, and even in Teddy Roosevelt's speeches.[11] Only the heroic workers (or modernist poets, but that is another story) standing shoulder to shoulder in solidarity could break with sentimentality and usher in a new world. This picture of masculine triumph had its own sentimental logic, which also dates from the eighteenth century. According to Raymond Williams, "the first great tribune of the industrial proletariat," William Cobbett, declared collective action to be "a movement of the *peoples's* own," a concerted response to the "masters [who] combine against them," leaving them barely able to feed themselves and their families.[12] If a strike provides a stirring, emotionally saturated, political tableau, its visual economy owing much to melodrama where the forces of good and evil are decisively separate, that is because since the late eighteenth century, the working class has been cast in both heroic and victimized poses.[13]

In twentieth-century America, the most powerful icons of this dual image of the working class have been found within the traditions of the documentary photography inaugurated by Lewis Hine. Hine's 1932 photographic record *Men at Work: Photographic Studies of Modern Men and Machines* offers a vision of labor poles apart from his earlier images of children dwarfed by massive looms. This children's book carefully integrates the male body into the machinery of construction (many of the images are from Hine's on-location photographs of the Empire State Building rising from the streets of Manhattan as it was built). The scale of the masculine body establishes the size of the machine it works. Some of the "men of courage, skill, daring" are "heroes," says Hine, paraphrasing Karl Marx in his introduction, "the spirit of industry." They are heroes because "cities do not build themselves; machines do not make machines . . . real men make and direct them."[14] Hine shoots individuals intimately curled over and around their tools, but he also provides a vision of the collectivity of labor in shots showing how modern work requires cooperation among many men on the job.[15] This highly erotic, actually homoerotic, vision of men and machinery became a staple of documentary, culminating in Robert Flaherty's *Louisiana Story,* in which the arrival of the enormous oil derrick moves the young boy to explore the world of machinery as he had once covered the natural landscape. The boy, embraced (literally) by this all-male world, ultimately integrates nature and machine and his body in the penultimate shot as he curls himself around the "Christmas tree," the above-ground (or in this case, above-water) cap to a gas main tap, left standing in the bayou. Flaherty's film was hardly a left-wing celebration of machinery and labor; Standard Oil footed the bill for this "fantasy," as Flaherty referred to it.

Hine's 1932 photographs initiated a visual rhetoric of sentimentality that cloaked workers' bodies and gigantic machinery in a celebration of the collective labors required to build America. In this, his images were visual updates of Herman Melville's ecstatic whale-rendering scenes in *Moby Dick.* This new sentimentality contrasted with Hine's earlier portraits of America's working victims suffering under capitalism's brutality. The recourse to sentiment among labor's documenters is tied at once, I want to stress, to confusing gender codes that have historically dictated who can and cannot cry, and to conflicting class and national allegiances, which also involve delegating the proper expression of sentiment. Modern national allegiance requires tears; one need only watch any athletic segment or any commercial during NBC's broadcast of the 1996 Olympics to get a shorthand lesson in the centrality of tears to national identity. We watch as athletes cry in victory or sob in defeat; we cry with them at home, our living rooms linked mysteriously through the flowing tears. Like nations, class formations, precisely because they require imaginative communities linked through ideas and sentiments, resemble these emotion-laden fantasies in that they do not inhere on the bodies' surfaces in the ways that genders or races appear to. It is for this reason that class is a slippery analytic category, even among feminists otherwise sensitive to nuanced gender and racial differences. In the differing views of Burke and Cobbett, workers combined, either sinisterly as a mass or rationally as a class, in response to the workings of the capitalist state, a state formed in the interests of one class, the bourgeoisie, in part by cordoning off sentiment and putting it to its own use. This is also the reason, I want to argue here, that the rhetoric of sentimentality—so crucial to modern national and class formations—still circulates within labor documentaries, even those questioning the form of documentary itself.

In differing ways, *Roger and Me* (Michael Moore, 1989) and *American Dream* (Barbara Kopple, 1990), the two films under consideration here, tap this long-standing tradition of figuring class conflict through gendered discourses of sentimentality.[16] *Roger and Me,* ever ironic about documentary, General Motors, and government policies that favor corporate greed over human need, cannot escape its heritage. In the 1930s, Hugo Gellert, a cartoonist for the left-wing journal *New Masses,* illustrated a selection of writings from Marx's *Capital* with his drawings of solidly muscled workers.[17] The butt of in-jokes within the Left, these heroic figments of radical imagination were fantasies of excessive virility.[18] A strong working class could overcome both the crisis of capitalism and the malaise the Lost Generation was suffering after the First World War. A heavy load to bear—making the revolution and saving American masculinity at once—this construction of the manly worker occluded any other vision of the working-class woman than the one in Gellert's drawings who bulges with hefts of muscle nourishing her buffed-out baby boy at her muscled breast, the kind of "revolutionary girl" celebrated in proletarian poems. By contrast, the bourgeoisie was a feminized and decadent class: corpulent men stuffed into top hats and tails, like the man on the Monopoly game (first marketed in 1936), sucking the vitality from the labor of others, or desiccated spinsters whose dried-up lives were doomed to disappear once the new working-class family took possession of its rightful place.

It was a ludicrous picture, then, when at least a quarter of the workforce was female. In the 1980s, it should have been trotted out only as

Karl Marx, "Capital" in Lithographs, by Hugo Gellert (New York: Ray Long and Richard Smith, 1934).

parody, yet *Roger and Me* returns to these stock types with a straight face to cast its saga of deindustrialization. Almost all the scenes with women target the lavish lifestyles of the rich and infamous of Flint, Michigan, and feature chiffon-dressed women sounding like Marie Antoinette before the revolution. The one exception—the lonely rabbit breeder whose uncanny pragmatism (pets or meat) seems demented at best, vicious at worst— clearly survives outside the economy of contemporary American late capitalist relations. She is a holdover from another era and another place, perhaps the mountains of Kentucky from which many autoworkers migrated during and after the Second World War, like a character out of Harriet Arnow's 1954 novel *The Dollmaker,* devastated by city life and industrial work discipline.[19] Director Michael Moore is drawn to this odd woman; she reappears as the star of his short sequel *Pets or Meat: The Return to Flint,* which also aired on PBS stations.[20]

Sentimentality requires a hero, just as melodrama demands clearly defined sides. But Moore is a contemporary (anti)hero, a goofy guy who has shed his class origins just barely because his skills lie in intellectual labor—the production of words and images—not the backbreaking assembly work of his father's generation.[21] His film unveils "an aesthetics of failure" in contemporary documentary,[22] an absence that looms enormous in this story of contemporary labor: no strikes; no "men at work." What *Roger and Me* finds instead is lack: the lack of union militancy, the lack of work as thousands of autoworkers have been laid off, the lack of industry as plants close and move their operations overseas. Flint, Michigan, stands as an emblem of militant union organizing, the site of the 1936 sit-down strike, the most effective use of the strategy in American history, whose stirring images of men curled amid their tools and machinery asleep on the shop floor galvanized generations of organizers. Josephine Herbst had caught this scene, connecting it to the rise of "the worker-writer," when she closes her 1939 novel *Rope of Gold* with an autoworker penning his autobiography.[23] This quintessential modernist figure—a striking worker sprawled across the plant floor recording the details of the strike for the *Daily Worker*—has no place in a deindustrializing economy. The strike appears ineffective against plant closures. The story has shifted elsewhere to the corporate and financial boardrooms where the flows of capital, not productivity (which requires bodies), are key to profits.

Without the bodies of workers at their machines or the masses on the picket line, Moore's saga comes down to a lone quest for an elusive figure, CEO Roger Smith. Smith's continual absence is one more hole in the fabric of American industry; a boss can no longer be embodied either. The rotund, cigar-smoking capitalist who lorded over a semifeudal "industrial valley" has also been displaced.[24] For example, in the new world order of virtual strikebreaking, to combat striking unions at Detroit's two largest newspapers, *The Detroit News* and *The Detroit Free Press* no longer need hire thugs. They have set up home pages on the World Wide Web denouncing union tactics on the picket lines and praising those who cross the lines, including stories about the terrific food served to those who show up for work.[25] Moore fails to get close to the real boss, Roger Smith, so he goes for the cheap shot, the vacuous country club wives of Chevy's middle

Standing in front of the Buick City sign in Flint, Michigan, are Rhoda Britton, holding her pet rabbit; writer, producer, and director Michael Moore; and deputy sheriff Fred Ross. All are involved in Moore's documentary film *Roger and Me*, about the closing of General Motors plants in the town and the effect on the residents there. The film was released by Warner Bros.

managers who declare Flint a wonderful city and wonder why everyone is complaining.

If the CEO cannot be located, neither can the worker; he is neither on the picket line nor on the assembly line. Charlie Chaplin's working Tramp represented the modern antihero of labor—dwarfed by the machine, encompassed by the masses. The counterpart to the Tramp's incorporation into the machine of capital is Chaplin's wonderful overhead crane shot, which offers a visual joke on working-class unity as the Tramp, after picking up a red flag that has fallen off the back of a carriage, unknowingly leads a demonstration of protesting workers, only to find himself beaten and jailed by the police. Instead, Moore finds his postmodern Worker-Tramp in Ben Hamper, a contemporary worker-writer, now a novelist, the "rivethead" whose column had previously appeared in Moore's alternative newspaper, *The Flint Voice*. Hamper explains, while aimlessly shooting hoops, that he was laid off with a medical disability because he had cracked up on the shop floor. He feels like a fraud, though, compared to the women he met in the hospital—suicidal and depressed—whose mental illnesses were somehow more real, caused as they were by domestic, personal troubles. The public world of work is not supposed to cause mental breakdowns, but without the masses to provide a collective shelter for the worker, his psyche becomes as fragile as a housewife's.[26] Moore empathizes with his high school buddy; they share history, each with a middle-aged, working-class inelegance that has no place, despite their new roles as intellectuals, circulating language and images.[27]

Moore's film, picked up and distributed by Time-Warner, which also published Hamper's tale, sparked a major debate within corporate boardrooms and across business and industry pages.[28] His wry humor showed GM as callous, the Flint Chamber of Commerce and Mayor's Office in the pockets of GM, and a citizenry suffering from delusions and privation so extreme that "recovery" appears unlikely.[29] Moreover, his decision to tamper with history, revising chronology to suit his narrative, caused a minor stir.[30] Moore's recourse to staged melodrama—placing Ronald Reagan in Flint in the midst of the shutdown—gave ammunition to GM, who wanted to defuse the film's effects.[31] But Moore's manipulations came from a long tradition of documentary filmmaking. As he remarked, "With nonfiction, you have no idea when you go out to shoot what's going to happen, and you have to figure it all out once you're in the editing room."[32] Dziga Vertov's scissors cutting celluloid in *Man with a Movie Camera* had foregrounded the editing process as crucial to *Kino-Pravda*—a job requiring the hands of his female assistant editor, Yelizaveta Svilova. With absence its central feature (no jobs, no organization, no boss, as capital flows elsewhere and workers sit idle), Moore's postmodern portrait of labor still rests on the prehistory of modern male workers' melodramas, now embodied only by the two forces—Roger, endlessly beyond the camera, and M(oor)e, endlessly performing for it.[33]

American Dream follows Barbara Kopple's magisterial view of worker solidarity in *Harlan County, USA* (1976) with a darker vision of the contradictions and complexities of contemporary union organizing in the heartland. Despite the more amiable atmosphere of Lake Woebegone, Minnesota, Austin's Hormel plant and the efforts of meat packers at Local P-9 of the United Food and Commercial Workers (UFCW) to maintain union solidarity present such a wretched scene, it lends bloody Harlan County a nostalgic glow. Kopple's complex gesture in *American Dream* traces the present conditions for union militancy in a typically midwestern industry—hog processing—during this era of multinational corporate flight; its story of the multiple forces working at odds confounds the melodrama of union men versus scabs staged in *Harlan County, USA.* The 1984–85 strike against the Hormel plant dramatized how the arena has been complicated with a proliferating cast whose allegiances and identities are not so easily coded as good or bad. This corrective seems in part a response to critiques of her earlier film as overly humanistic; perhaps deindustrialization forces another cinematic document as much as another political dream.[34]

American Dream begins with shots of the hog kill room, which Kopple was able to film with a hidden camera by posing as a New York high school student doing a report on the meat industry. The job of turning pigs into bacon is dangerous and disgusting work. The work site and work process, which are not central to the film's story (focusing as it does on the intricacies of local and international organizing and bargaining, then the strike and its aftermath), establish the source of the action. In the brief encapsulated history the film provides, we hear Ronald Reagan's "off-the-cuff" remark about the economy: "I'm prepared to tell you it's a hell of a mess." Jesse Jackson then tells a packed crowd in 1986 that "what Selma was to the civil, Austin is to the movement for workers' rights." The scene shifts two years earlier and follows two men past a playground where children swing and climb and slide to the front door of a large house where the wife of a Hormel executive lectures the men to be grateful they now receive $8.75 an hour: "When we were your age," she begins, but the men cut her off: "Give us a fair shake, like you got." Although a town like Austin represses its class structure, visible evidence lies everywhere. In Austin, twenty-two thousand people live in "a little world by ourselves," Hormel counsel Charles Nyberg explains, echoing the boosterism found at the town's border: "Enjoy Austin, where the good life is here to stay." To some extent this civic hype rings true; as the Hormel promotional film Kopple insets outlines, the social contract the corporation struck with its workers decades ago guaranteed good wages, lifetime benefits, and profit sharing. But the ragged years of recession and corporate mergers and wholesale assault on unions fostered by Reagan's administration have taken their toll. "Let us live in our house," pleads one woman stuffing envelopes at the union hall, "our $32,000 house." The company that makes that quintessential American product, SPAM, staple of U.S. Army k-rations during World War II, now expresses "the mood of the industry," as CEO Richard Knowlton declares; despite record $29.5-million profits in 1984, Hormel workers receive a 23 percent wage cut.

Thus the stage is set for the nightmare to unfold; a dark romance Kopple scripts around the struggle of a "new family," as the striking P-9ers describe their changed relationships to each other and to their formerly paternalistic employer, to come to terms with the betrayal by the new "father," Jay Hormel, son of the corporation founder who instituted the "social consciousness" of the company. But the real battle in Kopple's eyes involves a conflict waged by outsiders, distant cousins arriving to contest the company's will: on the one hand, Ray Rodgers, New Yorker and vegetarian head of Corporate Campaign, whose successful national boycott of J. P. Stevens Company finally resulted in union recognition in many southern textile plants; and on the other, Lewie Andersen, hard-bitten vice president of UFCW, former hog butcher and tough negotiator, who has finally accepted the UFCW's strategy of across-the-board contracts to bring up the wage floor in nonunion meat-packing plants. These giants battle on a grand scale for the hearts and minds of the P-9ers; their personalities are so charismatic that they seem to be determining the action, sweeping the quieter, more restrained Minnesotans along with them. Yet the determination of the strikers and their families is the real story: they keep on with the strike even after P-9 has been decertified by the UFCW; they keep gaining support from unions around the country even after the AFL-CIO, America's central union organization, has warned against this; they keep showing up at the picket lines even after the National Guard has been called out and some local members defy the strike. Playing out against the bleak snow-covered landscape is the new "American dream" of community and family and their fracture, with brother turned against brother, another civil war the inevitable result.[35]

Kopple's fascination with grand melodramatic historical epics owes as much to D. W. Griffith as to the fragile voice of Hazel Dickens's ballads in

Harlan County, USA, but in Austin the heroes are less pure and villains less obvious, if more devious. Unlike the coal miners' strike in Kentucky, where "you either are a union man or a thug for J. H. Blair," the complexities of fighting on three fronts—against the corporation, against the state, and against the union's international—unhinge melodrama. Interestingly, however, this multiplying set of powerful forces allied against the tiny P-9 local does not automatically call up even greater sympathy for the strikers. Instead, the rhetoric of sentimentality was invoked by those who gave up and crossed the picket line in the face of community censure. Shedding tears is central to the labor documentary—Lawrence Jones's martyred body and his mother's wailing marked the turning point for the United Mine Workers in *Harlan County, USA*—but in *American Dream* it is the scabs who mourn themselves as outcasts. The question is: do we care about these crying men?

When I saw *American Dream* at its public debut in Minneapolis (following its premiere in Austin) at a fund-raiser for the Pittston, West Virginia, miners' strike, the stage was crowded with Kopple; Senator Paul Wellstone, author of the Replacement Worker Bill barring the hiring of permanent replacements for strikers; striking miners from West Virginia; as well as the remaining striking P-9ers still out of work yet offering donations to the strikers in West Virginia. I, along with the rest of the audience, was moved to tears by the spectacle of solidarity. The context in which I saw the film suggested that Kopple's interpretation of the dream came from a nuanced and textured vision of class in contemporary America as deeply contradictory and overdetermined. As a newcomer to Minnesota, only later did I learn that many local union activists and P-9 supporters condemned the film; they felt it to be a betrayal for failing to capture the culture that grew during the strike. Kopple's conclusions question P-9's tactics, even blame them for losing the strike; but evidence to the contrary remained on the cutting room floor. (Actually, unused footage for *American Dream* is housed in University of Wisconsin's archives.) Is the picture nuanced because the politics are unclear when the profound shift in the economy alters this historic battlefield and its melodramatic representation?

An inheritance from the CPUSA's 1930s Popular Front attempt to meld Communists (overwhelmingly urban and immigrant and Jewish) into the People, the sentimental invocation of "family," "movement," "community," "culture" can insidiously repress conflicts and differences within America's class and racial structure. In 1938, General Secretary of the CPUSA Earl Browder outlined *The People's Front* as a program whose "first consideration in promoting new forces is to find native Americans" to lead its organizations, because the Communist Party was "destined to carry on and complete the work begun by Tom Paine, George Washington, Thomas Jefferson and Abraham Lincoln."[36] To an extent, *Harlan County, USA* participated in this "archaic aesthetic," as Jesse Lemisch calls it,[37] and Kopple received a series of critiques for her "conventional" portrayal of social events from a position of "knowledge" available to the outsider.[38] The postmodern condition of labor in the 1980s demanded another story; Kopple responds by exaggerating the rhetoric of sentimentality until its claims collapse. Kopple manipulates the codes of sentimentality to the point that our tears seem to merge us with the scabs and against the strikers, but only apparently.

This direction comes in part because the situation in Austin, unlike that in Harlan County, is multiply fractured. Kopple may just be doing her job as a documentary filmmaker by presenting a comprehensive picture of strikers, scabs, and international representatives; or she may be paying a debt to the many locals and internationals that contributed funding for the film; or she may be attempting to enter the action, much as she did in Harlan County, at the picket line, by witnessing the sense of emptiness and hostility of those who break ranks. In Kentucky, her presence at the daily "sunrise revivals" became a factor in the escalating violence during the strike. At times it appeared that Kopple's crew egged on the scabs and company goons; at others, the camera clearly helped avert violence. In Austin, when she shows the scabbing P-9ers (the P-10ers, as they were derisively called) crying as they decide to cross their union's picket line, Kopple would seem to be siding with their unpopular decision. Yet the scene is filled with bathos, its emotional timbre highly suspect as the men cry on cue about how hard it is when you can't feed your family. Tears are supposed to elicit sympathy, but why?

Unlike me, most critics of the film, such as Peter Rachleff who wrote *Hard-Pressed in the Heartland* in part to counter her Academy Award–winning portrait of the Hormel strike, consider Kopple a sellout because she provides a forum for these men who from the first worked hand-in-hand with the UFCW leadership to undermine the strike and now run the trusteeship union that replaced P-9.[39] Rachleff refers to the local treasurer, John Williams, as Kopple's "star" because he gets so much screen time to anguish over his actions.[40] Maintaining the kind of nostalgia for working-class authenticity and community characteristic of America's Left since the Popular Front, Rachleff fails to register the squeamishly maudlin and trite picture being painted. Kopple is relying on left-wing conventions of picturing the scab as feminized (a scab, like a thug, is not a union *man*). The men's tears are powerful visual cues calling forth audience sympathies, so the picture is confusing. This seems to be precisely the point: in the era of deindustrialization, it is not so easy to distinguish the union man from the scab.

While the strikers are presented as full of conviction—perhaps a bit naive in their faith in Ray Rodgers—they are still proud and angry folks, even if their militancy includes media-savvy campaigns. The scabs snivel about their lost manhood and the betrayal they feel: they hate to cross a line; the union has driven them to it. Lewie Andersen may steal the screen with his hard-nosed cynicism about P-9, but the UFCW comes off as retrograde and suspect, especially after UFCW President William Wynn storms into a meeting shouting that he will make the P-9 local sign the contract: "All it takes is a few good men (oh, and some women, too)," he nods to "the little lady there with the camera." Perhaps because Kopple's style is so consistently illusionistic—she appears to offer a pure vision of the struggle in Harlan County and a balanced version of the strike in Austin—the excesses in *American Dream* don't read as critique, but I think they should—not necessarily of the P-10ers but of the aesthetics and politics lodged in the sentimental itself as much as in the paradox of union politics in postindustrial America.

Although correcting Kopple's film served as one impetus for both of the book-length accounts of the Hormel strike, neither does more than mention Kopple's presence in Austin.[41] Her authority is implicitly challenged by the reports of these partisan insiders who were active in the support systems—either Corporate Campaign (Hardy Green) or Twin Cities Support for P-9 (Rachleff); Kopple remained an outsider, falling for the charismatic Lewie Andersen and thus failing to see the transformative effects of the strike on the lives of the union members and their families as she had in *Harlan County*. This transformation from alienated labor to a "movement culture" requires the creation of the alternative "prefigurative" institutions through which working people can galvanize into a collective agent for social and economic change.[42] To understand this process, outsiders need to get inside the homes, churches, meeting halls of the strikers, but Kopple's up-close-and-personal moments more often come between her and the P-10ers or Andersen. Rachleff provides a prehistory of P-9 through analyses of its earlier incarnation in a consumer and producer union that had achieved wall-to-wall unionization in Austin in the 1930s, establishing the base for the militancy and solidarity of the 1984–85 strike, the first against Hormel in fifty-two years. The two books also explain the changes in the meat-packing industry as a whole since the 1970s and in the contracts at Hormel that led the company to slash wages 23 percent after promising to maintain them. What had been a locally owned, paternalistic company in a homogeneous town in southern Minnesota became a lean and mean corporation with national and international subsidiaries linked to other major corporations during the era of mergers and buyouts. Kopple fails to give this kind of background from the point of view of Austin; instead of letting the strikers speak as she had in Harlan, where old-timers recounted the bloody days of the 1930s strikes for her through memories, songs, and photographs, she leaves it to Andersen to fill in the background.

Rachleff accuses Kopple of turning the P-9ers into "victims" rather than seeing them as victimized by the collusion of business unionism, state and local police, and corporate conglomerates all working in tandem to destroy a renegade local that had taken on enormous symbolic significance in the antiunion climate of Reagan America. Yet the only ones to appear as victims, in the classic melodramatic sense, are the "P-10ers," who sob before the camera after deciding to cross their union's picket line: "A person takes a lot of pride in being a breadwinner," says Ron Bergstrom. Since the eighteenth century, sentimentality, argues Robert Markley, has served as a "theatrics of virtue" for the display of feminized emotions; within the sentimental, the "passive victim" is always female, and it is up to the sensitive male to sympathize with her.[43] This is a class politics of bourgeois affects, thus hardly the virile profile of labor militancy so crucial to left-wing romance; the P-10ers vamp as hero(in)es. These men with whom Kopple positions her camera when they do cross the line are barraged with insults from neighbors, friends, even brothers, such as R. G. Bergstrom, a firm supporter of the strike. He lives outside Austin on a 4¾-acre farm with his wife and three kids and explains that he goes to the picket line to watch his brother cross it as much as to perform strike duty. Ron Bergstrom has accepted the logic of Hormel and 1980s corporate concessions for workers: "If you want a job," he tells Kopple, "you're going to have to take it." He becomes one of the original seven local members to return to work after twenty weeks on strike. In a telling scene later on, these seven watch themselves crossing the picket line and being jeered on the television news that evening: "The minute we crossed that line," remarks one, appealing to the sentiments offered to orphans in the storm, "we left them, left that organization," and the "whole new family" P-9 had created.

Because the union itself, Hormel's policies, and the subsequent reconstructions of the events have turned on the familial makeup of the town, its workforce, and its organizations, the act of scabbing is more than a betrayal of a lifetime of working-class upbringing and consciousness; it is also a divorce, a disownment, a severance of all family ties. These men have placed themselves outside the gates of the city when they reenter the factory gates. Their overly melodramatic responses to their own acts fail to exculpate them: they may have been forced by circumstances to return to work, yet the circumstances are outdated, based on an ideal of the male breadwinner providing fully for his family. In working-class and middle-class American homes alike, the family wage has failed to provide adequately since the 1970s. These men are victims as much of a passé vision of masculinity as of an outmoded form of unionism apparently ineffective against vicious corporations, but they do all right for themselves. Lewie Andersen has predicted from the start that the P-9 strike will fail, and it appears—though not so clearly in the film as in the written accounts of the strike—that the UFCW has actually worked to ensure failure, in part by courting these few dissident critics of Corporate Campaign. In a reversal of fortune reminiscent of melodrama, these men assume leadership of the local after it is put into trusteeship.

If the P-10ers are pathetic, the P-9ers occasionally appear misguided. Lacking strategy, lacking a program, they are a bit too smitten with the New Age self-esteem, assertiveness-training mentality that Ray Rodgers trumpets with quotations from Bruce Springsteen. Yet when one of the women leaves the "war department," the office in the union hall for strike committee meetings, after a meeting with Lewie Andersen, she explains, "I want a union for the 1980s." The strikers are trying to explain to Andersen that something more than wages is at stake in this strike. In part, they have bought Ray Rodgers's theory that traditional organizing tactics are ineffective under current corporate structures with easy flows of capital allowing quick relocation. Unions must use intensive media campaigns to dishonor companies by targeting investors and stockholders. More important, however, is the alteration of the community's social fabric. P-9 President Jim Guyette and many others describe how the union hall became a "fun place to be," where people "did what they liked to do"—car repair, carpentry, cooking—in an informal bartering economy set up during the strike. Vying for the power inhering in its sentimental invocation, they claim that "a whole new family" was formed through their union activism. This is especially true of the women's support network, which both Hardy and Rachleff contend accounts for the widespread "movement culture" P-9 was able to create. That Austin is an extremely homogeneous and insular small town with a paternalistic company that stably employed generations contributed to the ease with which a "new family" could be formed within and through the union; but it also explains the sense of betrayal the Hormel workers felt at the concessions demanded of them by both the company and the UFCW and set the stage for rupturing Local P-9. But this (women's) story does not grab Kopple as it did in Harlan County; this time she is watching the men cry.

This feel of intimacy is a modern feature characterizing both oral history and documentary. Kopple had moved in with the miners' families in Harlan County; her attendance at meetings and on the picket lines and road blocks happened because of her connections with the strikers even though she came from the outside. The presence of her camera became central to some of the actions that happened. When Kopple is asked by the coal company thug for her press pass after she comes up to him with camera and tape recorder to ask his opinion of the strike, she turns the question on him, demanding to see his identification. They come to a testy truce, after each refuses to produce these documents of identity. The camera watches as he turns his pickup truck around and leaves, averting violence. When a miner's wife pulls a revolver from her bra, she directly addresses the camera, daring her viewers to judge how violence escalates. The media contribute to its eruption, heightening the rhetoric and action of the strikers, even as the camera and tape recorder may rein in the actual expression of violence. The camera's presence sometimes provokes confrontation and violence, as when the armed thugs single out the camera as if it were a body to be beaten. As in the infamous scene in *The Battle of Chile*, in which cameraman Leonardo Henricksen filmed his own murder at the hands of the Chilean army, this scene suggests that, despite a legacy of bloody confrontations, the filmmaker's presence also may be provoking violence. However, Lawrence Jones's death occurs offscreen, leaving us to wonder whether he might still be alive if the crew had ventured out that morning. Instead, Kopple films the emotion of the funeral, lingering on the anguished cries of Jones's mother, tracking her collapsing body as it is carried from the church. The raw feeling spilling out inappropriately for public consumption accentuates the keenly divided world of victims (strikers) and tyrants (mine owners and their goons).

Watching *Harlan County, USA* recently I was again moved to tears by the film despite my recognition of the discourses of sentimentality at work; the carved worn-down faces of the old-timers and the incredible youth and poverty of the others, the violence and fear, the haunting ballads pull at the heart strings just as any tearjerker out of Hollywood might. Yet the tough-talking women; the humorous encounter between the miner picketing the Wall Street offices of Brookside's parent corporation and the New York City cop comparing benefits, wages, and working conditions; the old miners (black and white) suffering from black lung joking that while they entered the mines each day they were different colors, when they left they were all "soul brothers"—all temper the pathos with humor, giving *Harlan County, USA* the feel of solidarity: the escalating crisis and its violence are offset by the heady sense of power gained through collective actions; the sheer brutality of the labor that miners perform pales compared to the degree to which companies will go to keep workers from improving their lives. In the United States in the mid-1970s people who worked full time in a major industry still lived without plumbing or heat, in rickety shacks. Despite her obvious differences as a young, single New York Jew with a camera, she entered the privacy of the miners' lives. Unlike Lauren Gilfillan's more ambivalent attempt in her 1934 book *I Went to Pit College*, Kopple's move had opened a hidden world of exploitation to public view and garnered tremendous support for the mineworkers. A strike still looked noble in 1976, especially when it was clear which side one was on.

American Dream, unlike *Harlan County*, slips the veil of sentimentality over the wrong faces. When Peter Rachleff refers to the P-10ers as the "stars" of Kopple's film, is it because they get too much screen time? Or is it because they get to explain their decision more fully than those who remain on the line? Or is it because in their explanation they resort to emotional outbursts of tears rather than the anger expressed by R. G. Bergstrom at his brother's betrayal and so appear conventionally sympathetic? Kopple's grim tone, set early in the film and accentuated by the bleak Minnesota winterscapes of Austin, the tacky interiors of meeting rooms and negotiating suites in hotels, the gruesome images from inside the Hormel plant, offers none of the elevating and alleviating humor, hope, warmth, or sarcasm that occasionally lightened *Harlan County, USA*. The miners' pine-board shacks nestled in the hollows of West Virginia participated in the picturesque elements aestheticizing poverty that James Agee deplored even as he lyricized the perfect symmetry of the tenants' housing he found in Hale County, Alabama, in *Let Us Now Praise Famous Men*.[44] Nothing of the sort exists in Austin, a tidy middle-American town of postwar tract housing. The spirit of possibility following the democratization of the United Mine Workers is also missing from *American Dream*. Clearly, the dream of solidarity is over, too, another casualty of Reaganomics. If Moore undermined the heroic male worker through satire, Kopple finished off his image as the one who will lead us from the brutality of capitalism through united movements of militant solidarity. That American dream of the Left, that the virile working class holds the keys to revolution, rests on modernist economic relations and their melodramatic stagings. Kopple undercuts the rhetoric of the labor documentary by thoroughly inscribing the sentimental, using men's tears against their modern origins to tell a postmodern tale still unfolding around us.

NOTES

1. Tillie (Olsen) Lerner, "The Strike," *Partisan Review* 1 (November 1936). Reprinted in Charlotte Nekola and Paula Rabinowitz, eds., *Writing Red: An Anthology of American Women Writers, 1930–1940* (New York: Feminist Press, 1987), 245.

2. Florence Reece, "Which Side Are You On?" in Nekola and Rabinowitz, *Writing Red*, 182.

3. Lallah Davidson, *South of Joplin* (New York: W. W. Norton, 1939); Ruth McKenney, *Industrial Valley* (1939, reprinted Ithaca, N.Y.: Cornell University Press, 1992); Martha Gellhorn, *The Trouble I've Seen* (New York: William Morrow, 1936); and the nonfiction selections in Nekola and Rabinowitz, *Writing Red*.

4. Karl Marx, *Economic and Philosophic Manuscripts of 1844*, trans. Martin Milligan, ed. Dirk J. Struik (New York: International Publishers, 1964), 155. The original German manuscripts were first published in 1932, but they offer a far more ambivalent image of the "work-wearied figures" than the English translation I quote.

5. Lauren Gilfillan, *I Went to Pit College* (New York: Literary Guild, 1934). For a detailed discussion of this book, see my *Labor and Desire: Women's Revolutionary Fiction in Depression America* (Chapel Hill: University of North Carolina Press, 1991), chap. 4.

6. Georg Lukács, "Reportage or Portrayal?" (1932) in *Essays on Realism*, ed. Rodney Livingstone, trans. David Fernbach (Cambridge: MIT Press, 1981), 49.

7. Claudia L. Johnson, *Equivocal Beings: Politics, Gender and Sentimentality in the 1790s: Wollstonecraft, Radcliffe, Burney, Austen* (Chicago: University of Chicago Press, 1995), 2.

8. Ibid., 17.

9. See Raymond Williams, *Culture and Society: 1780–1950* (New York: Columbia University Press, 1983), 3–12 (originally published in 1953). For a brief dissection of the literary/political history of the term *sentimental*, see Raymond Williams, *Keywords: A Vocabulary of Culture and Society*, rev. ed. (New York: Oxford University Press, 1983), 281–82.

10. Lukács, *Essays on Realism*, 50.

11. On the ways in which the rejection by modernism of sentimentality is tied to a denial of femininity, see Rey Chow, *Women and Chinese Modernity: The Politics of Reading between East and West* (Minneapolis: University of Minnesota Press, 1991); and Suzanne Clark, *Sentimental Modernism: Women Writers and the Revolution of the Word* (Bloomington: Indiana University Press, 1991). On the gendered iconography of the Left, see Rebecca Zurier, *Art for the Masses: A Radical Magazine and Its Graphics, 1911–1917* (Philadelphia: Temple University Press, 1988); Barbara Melosh, *Engendering Culture: Manhood and Womanhood in New Deal Theater and Art* (Washington, D.C.: Smithsonian Institute Press, 1991); and Rabinowitz, *Labor and Desire*.

12. Cobbett is quoted in Williams, *Culture and Society*, 3, 17.

13. For critical analyses of melodrama, especially as a debased form that allowed marginalized peoples, especially women and the working class, a popular platform for resistance within containment, see Martha Vicinus, "Helpless and Unfriended: Nineteenth-Century Domestic Melodrama," *New Literary History* 13 (Autumn 1981): 127; Jackie Byars, *All That Hollywood Allows: Re-Reading Gender in 1950s Melodrama* (Chapel Hill: University of North Carolina Press, 1991); Christine Gledhill, "The Melodramatic Field: An Investigation," in *Home Is Where the Heart Is: Studies in Melodrama and the Woman's Film* (London: BFI, 1987); Lynn Hunt, *The Family Romance of the French Revolution* (Berkeley and Los Angeles: University of California Press, 1992); Ien Ang, *Watching Dallas: Soap Opera and the Melodramatic Imagination* (London: Routledge, 1989); Michael Denning, *Mechanic Accents: Dime Novels and Working-Class Culture in America* (London: Verso, 1987). The standard theoretical work on the mechanics of melodrama is Peter Brooks, *The Melodramatic Imagination: Balzac, Henry James, Melodrama and the Mode of Excess* (New Haven, Conn.: Yale University Press, 1976).

14. Lewis W. Hine, *Men at Work: Photographic Studies of Modern Men and Machines* (New York: Dover Publications, 1977). Originally published in 1932.

15. Terry Smith's *Making the Modern: Industry, Art and Design in America* (Chicago: University of Chicago Press, 1993) comprehensively analyzes the way in which 1930s celebrations of the machine enabled the rise of a corporate state. This was hardly the image that Marx presented when he noted, "The machine accommodates itself to the *weakness* of the human being in order to make the *weak* human being into a machine" (*Economic and Philosophic Manuscripts*, 149). Left-wing filmmakers such as Leo Hurwitz, however, celebrated the "machine itself, as an instrument for the transformation of labor and material into what people need."

Michael and Jill Klein, "*Native Land*: An Interview with Leo Hurwitz," *Cineaste* 6 (1974): 7. The aesthetics of streamlining, as Raymond Loewy, one of its most creative designers, told *Life*, meant "that society could be industrialized without becoming ugly." Quoted in Jane N. Law, "Designing the Dream," in *Streamlining America*, ed. Fania Weingartner (Dearborn, Mich.: Henry Ford Museum and Greenfield Village, 1986), 21.

16. See Joan W. Scott's critique of Gareth Stedman Jones's reading of the Chartists' political claims in *The Language of Class* in *Gender and the Politics of History* (New York: Columbia University Press, 1988); and Elizabeth Faue, *Community of Suffering and Struggle: Women, Men and the Labor Movement in Minneapolis, 1915–1945* (Chapel Hill: University of North Carolina Press, 1987) on women's organizing during the 1930s Minneapolis Truckers' Strike.

17. Hugo Gellert, *Karl Marx, "Capital" in Lithographs* (New York: Ray Long and Richard Smith, 1934).

18. But there is some truth to it. In an interview Mary McCarthy describes the faces of the men in the Gdansk shipyard as familiar, like those of the workers in this country she watched picket the great industries during her youth in the 1930s, their supple muscles and slender figures assuming the heroic poses Hine pictured: "Those young workers [in Solidarity] . . . I've never seen such handsome men. . . . You know, we haven't had a worker in this country that looked like that in fifty years. Railway men used to be very good looking in this country, very handsome. And an occasional lineman" (in Carol Brightman, "Mary, Still Contrary," *Nation*, May 19, 1984, 611–20). The bodies of 1930s American workers photographed by Hine have Renaissance proportions in stark contrast to the physiques of contemporary workers pictured by Milton Rogovin in Rogovin and Michael Frisch, *Portraits in Steel* (Ithaca, N.Y.: Cornell University Press, 1993).

19. This story had been a staple of 1930s proletarian fiction. The many novels about the Gastonia, North Carolina, mill workers strike centered on the transition from folk culture to a culture of capitalist exploitation and the especially difficult time that women, as repositories of family lore and tradition, had adjusting to the changes.

20. While the Corporation for Public Broadcasting has been a primary funder for many documentaries, including those investigating class relations in America, its audience is decidedly middle class. In *Pets or Meat*, Moore may have been working out a certain ambivalence toward PBS, which funded his films but which does not "bring the working class of this country into its network . . . they don't ever seem to speak to people like us." Jay Bobbin, "Moore Moves 'Nation' to Fox," *Post-Star* (Glens Falls), July 20, 1995, D8.

21. Speaking of *TV Nation*, Moore comments that "it's very bizarre and rare that a group of people such as me and my friends would be able to come from Flint, Mich., and have a network TV show." Bobbin, "Moore Moves," D8.

22. Paul Arthur, "Jargons of Authenticity (Three American Moments)," in *Theorizing Documentary*, ed. Michael Renov (New York: Routledge, 1993), 128.

23. This is Douglas Wixson's term for those Midwestern proletariat authors, such as Jack Conroy, who came out of the working class; see *The Worker-Writer in the Midwest: Jack Conroy and the Tradition of Midwestern Literary Radicalism, 1898–1990* (Champaign: University of Illinois Press, 1993). In the late 1920s, Mike Gold's editorial in the *New Masses* often called for a new movement of worker-correspondents to "tell us your story . . . in the form of a letter. . . . Write as you talk. Write." Gold, "A Letter to Workers' Art Groups," *New Masses* 5 (September 1929): 16.

24. In her reportage novel about the United Rubberworkers Union strike in Akron, Ohio, *Industrial Valley*, McKenney remarks on the geography of the company town in which the heights are reserved for the ruling families, with managers situated midway between the vast working-class neighborhoods spread around the plants in the valley.

25. Walter R. Baranger, "On Line, Management Also on Picket Line," *New York Times* July 24, 1995, D6. Work stoppages are effective still. During the summer of 1998, however, workers striking at two GM parts plants in Flint have shut down almost all the company's North American operations, costing it billions of dollars in profits.

26. See Ben Hamper, *Rivethead: Tales from the Assembly Line* (New York: Warner Books, 1991), for a full accounting of Hamper's fascinating gendering of mental illnesses. Thanks to Carol Mason for bringing this to my attention. The effects of unemployment occasion some of the most devastating chronicles of work life in late twentieth-century America—stories of alcoholism, depression, suicide, abuse, and so forth. The alienation of labor Marx detailed in his 1844 manuscripts is even more exacerbated by the loss of self accompanying loss of work. See the interviews in *Portraits of Steel* conducted by oral historian Michael Frisch for moving accounts of the psychic wreckage caused by plant closures.

27. Jay Bobbin, columnist for the Tribune Media Services, quotes Moore's remarks on "one of a series of really wonderful ironies" that his television show, *TV Nation*, aired the summer

of 1994 on NBC. The show, which often scrutinized corporate America, was shown in 1995 on Fox, which is among many other tabloids owned by international media tycoon Rupert Murdoch, CEO of the News Corporation. *Post-Star*, (Glens Falls) July 20, 1995, D8.

28. "Warner Acquires "Roger" Docu for World Distribution," *Variety* 337 (November 1, 1989): 12.

29. See Chester Burger, "What Michael Didn't Say about Roger," *Public Relations Journal* 46 (April 1990); Susan Duffy, "The Real Villain in *Roger & Me*? Big Business," *Business Week* (January 8, 1990); David C. Smith, "Michael & Roger: GM Critic's Film Makes No Pretense at Fairness," *Ward's Auto World* 25 (November 1989): 5.

30. See Carl Plantinga, "Roger and History and Irony and Me," *Michigan Academician* 24 (Spring 1992): 511–20; and Carley Cohan and Gary Crowdus, "Reflections on *Roger & Me*, Michael Moore and His Critics," *Cineaste* 17:4 (1990): 25–30.

31. This controversy was played out in the pages of the *New York Times* among other widely read national media venues and took on new life after it was learned that the film was not nominated for an Academy Award: on January 19, 1990, D. P. Levin reported that "Maker of Documentary That Attacks G.M. Alienates His Allies" (C12); then on February 1, 1990, Richard Bernstein asked *"Roger & Me*: Documentary? Satire? Or Both?" (C20); on March 2, 1990, D. Bensman contributed an op-ed piece stating, *"Roger & Me*: Narrow, Simplistic, Wrong" (A33); on March 26, 1990, V. J. Dimidjian responded in a letter to the editor, *"Roger & Me"* (A16). In the midst of this *Newsweek* asked "Will GM Retaliate?" February 26, 1990, 4.

32. Quoted in Bobbin, "Moore Moves," D8.

33. In *The Family Romance of the French Revolution* historian Lynn Hunt argues that melodrama was a key factor in the decision to behead royalty because this popular theatrical form securely differentiated between the righteous and evil ones and applauded ridding the stage of evil power. Moore is hardly advocating Roger's death, but his ability to collapse the situation into a struggle between himself and his adversary— richer, more powerful, more deceitful— recalls this plot.

34. James Guimond, *American Photography and the American Dream* (Chapel Hill: University of North Carolina Press, 1991). The title of his first chapter, on American documentary still photography, is "Dreams and Documents." Obviously, I see the parallels and contradictions extending into moving pictures.

35. Of course, the title *American Dream* refers to the post-World War II promise made to the white working class of a home, a car, a sta-

ble job, and so forth, earned at the expense of militant unions and through the buildup of a militarized federal budget. But I also think that because of the way the film portrays family conflicts, it is not entirely wrong to sit Freud before this dream and put his analytic powers to work. Hence my recourse to Freud's dissection of the family romance.

36. Earl Browder, *The People's Front* (New York: International Publishers, 1938), 56, 235.

37. For a devastating (and right-on) critique of the vestiges of Popular Front culture lurking within contemporary left-wing expressions of solidarity with the working class, see Jesse Lemisch, "I Dreamed I Saw MTV Last Night," *The Nation*, October 18, 1986, cover, 374–76.

38. Anthony McCall and Andrew Tyndal, "Sixteen Working Statements," *Millennium Film Journal* 1 (Spring/Summer 1978): 36. See also Noel King, "Recent 'Political' Documentary: Notes on *Union Maids* and *Harlan County, USA*," *Screen* 22 (2) 1981: 7–18.

39. See his review of the film in *The Oral History Review* 20 (Spring/Fall 1992): 94–96.

40. See Peter Rachleff, *Hard-Pressed in the Heartland: The Hormel Strike and the Future of the Labor Movement* (Boston: South End Press, 1993) for a history of the UFCW in Austin, as well as a completely different picture of the effects of the P-9 strike for the U.S. labor movement. A labor historian at Macalester College in St. Paul, Rachleff was instrumental in establishing the Twin Cities' support for P-9. Rachleff alerted me to the footage stored in Wisconsin's archives (personal communication, April 21, 1996).

    Tim Leland, business agent for the building trades union in Minnesota, voiced a great deal of criticism of the P-9ers, echoing Andersen that the strike was hopelessly doomed and thus resulted in hundreds of Hormel workers in Austin and Ottumwa, Iowa, losing their jobs (interview, November 10, 1994).

41. Rachleff's book is one of the two; the other is Hardy Green, *On Strike at Hormel: The Struggle for a Democratic Labor Movement* (Philadelphia: Temple University Press, 1990).

42. See Wini Breines, *Community and Organization in the New Left, 1962–1968: The Great Refusal* (New York: Praeger; South Hadley, Mass.: J. F. Bergin, 1982) on the adoption of this model for organizing by 1960s movements.

43. Robert Markley, "Sentimentality as Performance: Shaftesbury, Sterne and the Theatrics of Virtue," in *The New Eighteenth Century*, ed. Felicity Nussbaum and Laura Brown (New York: Methuen, 1987), 211–12.

44. James Agee and Walker Evans, *Let Us Now Praise Famous Men* (Boston: Houghton-Mifflin, 1941).

PATRICIA R. ZIMMERMANN

[2] *Flaherty's Midwives*

▶

Midwifery as Feminist Film History

The name *Flaherty* is inextricably coiled into the very foundational mythologies of documentary film history: Robert Flaherty as the father of documentary, the "Flaherty way" of shooting through immersion into a culture, Flaherty's ability to render poetry out of the everyday lives of others, Flaherty as purveyor of the imperialist gaze.[1]

The annals of Flaherty—whether myth, man, mania, or movement—expose the excessively patriarchal residues infiltrating the cultural/psychic formation of documentary itself. At documentary's core dwells a patriarchal fantasy of origins, birthrights, territorialization, disciplinary procedures of beautiful aesthetics to control unruly natives and racialized narratives, materialized images as the ultimate experience. In these foundational mythologies of Flaherty (a conception of fathering a new film movement; a notion of individualism in vision, purpose, and identity; an allegiance between the imperialist state and the patriarchal father), fathering is privileged without much critique as to its epistemological implications for a feminist historiographic project.[2]

And in this context, the history of documentary translates into the history of control over space(s) by individuals, a fiction that maintains order when disorderly discourses and intractable practices threaten. Documentary comes forth from its originary moment in a singular form, emptied of conflict, collectivities, messes, birthed without blood, without pain, without battles, without people, without places. In this history, everything is a traceable bloodline.[3] There are no adoptions, no identities formed out of need beyond textual familialism, political dynasties, and formal strategies. It is a fantasy of singularity, of omnipotence, of aesthetic biologism. With few exceptions, nearly every historical study of documentary ignores the institutions that house film movements, that nurture work, that provide communities when nations, capitalism, and patriarchy destroy them.[4] And, in these psychic configurations of documentary, as Slavoj Žižek would argue, all that is feminine, feminist, interactive, collective, confrontational is repressed.[5]

Yet since his death in 1951 Robert Flaherty also has come to mean something beyond the man and his films, something larger and more complex: the Robert Flaherty Film Seminar, the oldest seminar in the world supporting independent film, started in 1954 by his widow, Frances Flaherty, to commemorate and celebrate the cause of independent cinema outside the studio system.[6] The seminar was (and still tries to be) a place where aesthetic and political ruptures as well as differences among people could be provoked within a safe, mobile territory to produce something called independent cinema, itself a shape-shifting construct that changes throughout different historical periods. I will assume the identity of scholarly midwife to documentary history, bringing forth an entity not always foregrounded as an agent of historical change in documentary: the institution for exhibition that creates an alternative public sphere where women's contributions may be acknowledged.[7]

Simply constructing new feminist mythologies about repressed or forgotten documentary goddesses to replace old, patriarchal, dead Flaherty would fail to engage and dismantle these foundational myths and images.[8] As historiography, that practice would merely create a competitive history rather than one that rethreads the very processes of historiography, a history of great women makers-of-conscience in opposition to the history of the great men of documentary exploitation. A truly feminist historiography must analyze the institutions that created spaces where cinema could be imagined both outside and as infiltrating the commodity exchange system of Hollywood and American nationalism.

By flushing out the Robert Flaherty Film Seminar from a feminist historical perspective as a safety zone for independent film—rife with debates, denunciations, excisions—I hope to shift documentary film history toward a larger terrain beyond films and toward an analysis of the institutions that give public life to most independent work and produce noncommercial media culture. These various institutions, ranging from the Robert Flaherty Film Seminar, to Cinema 16, to black theaters, to a multitude of alternative film festivals (women, gay and lesbian, black, Latino, diasporan, Asian), to various state arts councils and public and private foundations, provide remnants of oppositional public spheres, material places where people and films created meaning and inaugurated change. In his massive archaeological project, Scott MacDonald unearthed the infrastructure of Cinema 16, arguing that we need to understand the historical places where experimental film operated as a cultural intervention as well as a public exhibition practice.[9]

These reclamation projects are especially urgent now: nearly all public space worldwide for the arts and culture is being sold off to transnational corporations, privatized, deregulated, and defunded.[10] Even the Robert Flaherty Film Seminar, despite its famous nomenclature and prominent genealogy, faces extinction as the welfare state dismantles itself and embraces vicious market forces.

▶

Births and Afterbirths

Birthing, editing, and domestic labor—three jobs associated with women—had a crucial role in the very first Flaherty Seminar in 1955. I deploy the word *birthing* here deliberately: not as some masculinist, modernist reincarnation of originary moments, but as a feminist revisioning of film history's sites. Birthing commands moving history from the film as static object to the making of the film, from the thing to the process, from the private to the public, from the fetishized text to its circulations, disruptions, social changes. I use *birthing* not in its maternalized, idealized, biologized form of patriarchal production of children, but in its feminist form as convulsions, pains, disruptions, blood, struggle. Because it creates new subjects and new subjectivities, it demands the remaking of social relations and institutions.

At the Flaherty Seminars, women have acted as high priestesses providing space for community rituals of renewal for isolated independent filmmakers. They have served wine and films. They have battled for space for films and for words. They have argued across genders, races, and nations.

The 1955 Flaherty Seminar inscribed women in film in multiple, contradictory, serpentine ways outside the regulated norms of conventional film historiography: from representation, to postproduction, to the social, to the griots of submerged histories, to young warriors and amazons, to listening to the tales of the elders. The Flaherty Seminar delivered a vision of independent film as an international community, moving it beyond the nation-state. Discourses and practices were continually redefined and remade throughout the four complicated decades of the seminar in heated interventions about women and their place in film, in documentary, in the seminar, in the world.

Flaherty Seminar records refute the individualism of film annals, challenging historians to rethink how feminism morphs documentary history.[11] At the institutional birth of the Flaherty, women occupied not one position but many: producers of life, behind-the-scenes quilters of documentary fragments, chroniclers of a collective, diverse alternative film culture, impresarios of debates.

The trajectory of women at the Flaherty Film Seminar falls into two historical periods. The early period, from 1955 to about 1970, could be termed the protofeminist, great "mother" era. In this period, women worked for the Flaherty Foundation as trustees, organized the seminar, led discussions on editing and curating, and screened some documentary and experimental films. The Flaherty provided space for women in film at a time when few public film venues would admit them.[12] Although feminist film as a political movement does not fully emerge until about 1970, the fifteen years leading up to that moment show that one of the few places for women in film to be nourished and to thrive as intellectuals, artists, and discussion leaders was the Flaherty Seminar.

The second era, from around 1970 to the present, is clearly the period of feminist film grounded in criticism of patriarchal forms of representation and connected to the women's movement and other identity politics. In the first period only a few women showed works. Shirley Clarke's experimental work was screened in 1957, 1958, 1959, and 1960, her documentary work in 1964, and her video installations in 1970. Maya Deren made many films during this period, but they were not screened at the Flaherty until programmer D. Marie Grieco's 1984 tribute to her during the feminist era, which included most of her films as well as film fragments and unfinished Haitian work. After 1970, programs were packed with nearly every major feminist film of the following decades.

▶ ───

A New Language

The 1955 Flaherty Seminar begins with black women giving birth on screen in George Stoney's landmark film about Georgia midwives sponsored by the Georgia State Department of Public Health, *All My Babies*. Stoney was one of the founding policy advocates of public access television. Shot by a white crew in a deeply segregated South during the beginnings of the civil rights movement as a government-sponsored training film, *All My Babies* is remarkable for its beautiful lighting and sync-sound, which allowed a black woman to speak about delivering babies in exquisite lighting usually reserved for white movie stars. Unlike most narrative films, it has significant political, social, and health connections to its community, with the goal of upgrading the practice of midwifery.

As a film for a specialized audience featuring a live birth, *All My Babies* could only be screened in private settings like the Flaherty Seminar. Unlike almost any other documentary of the period, *All My Babies* is structured to follow the course of a pregnancy from prenatal care, to birth and postpartum. It serves as an imaginary map for the history and experience of the Flaherty Seminars.

All My Babies imagines the borders of race and gender differently, interrogations that jut in and out of nearly every seminar like forceps. But read within contemporary theorization, the film also produces a more politically complex image of gender and racial frontier crossings: white male filmmaker and black women subjects, midwives versus the medical system, a state-sponsored film shown surreptitiously in a more liberal North, a film that wins the Robert Flaherty Award for documentary but scripts and stages its narrative.

The inaugural Flaherty Seminar, attended mostly by whites, conferred screen time and space on black mothers and midwives. The Flaherty Film Seminar has also functioned as a kind of midwife for North American independent film across four decades. For at that first seminar, women had something that patriarchal 1950s American culture had robbed them of: language. In *All My Babies* an African American midwife spoke in synchronous sound about birthing details. Helen Van Dongen, Joris Ivens's longtime editor, conducted a lengthy session on the editing of Robert Flaherty's *Louisiana Story,* shot by a young Richard Leacock. Van Dongen symbolically spoke for Ivens, at that time barred from the United States because of his communist affiliations. Frances Flaherty, Flaherty's widow and collaborator, hosted an assorted group of film aficionados, filmmakers, and intellectuals at the family farm on Black Mountain, Vermont. She fashioned a liberated zone for film talk in the stultifying context of 1950s Cold War culture.

▶

Bob's Boot Camp or Frances's Zen Retreat

The legends clouding the Robert Flaherty Seminars betray a masculinist, homogenizing deification of Flaherty the man as spawning an institution in his own likeness, a sperm bank from which future generations of documentarians could clone the so-called Flaherty style of romanticized imagery of innocent primitives. These fables concoct Robert Flaherty as a stern founding patriarch who envisioned the seminars as a boot camp to produce good soldiers of straight, explorer-style documentary. Like most fairy tales, these apocryphal stories displace women as well as more heterogeneous, gnarly histories where race, internationalism, and gender entwine in extremely contentious, difficult ways.

Librarians, programmers, and administrators like D. Marie Grieco, Barbara Van Dyke, Cecile Starr, Erik Barnouw, and Sally Berger reaffirm Frances as the founding mother of the seminar. Frances Flaherty rerouted the competitive individualism of postwar filmmaking into a more collective, fiery vision of artistic practice that upsets consciousness through a very simple, almost trivial concept: storytelling and seeing.

Frances Hubbard Flaherty created the seminar in memory of her deceased husband, a tribute to his vision of embracing a multifarious world of film artists and film explorers outside the standardized Hollywood studio system committed to a new vision of the world. The seminars, then, originated not in Robert Flaherty's individual escapades, as most seminar participants even now presume, but in Frances, who recast the collective parts of his spirit into a group experience, fueling new artistic explorations and new film movements through dialectical combustions and face-to-face interactions.[13] Seeking to monumentalize her husband's contributions to documentary, Frances actually drew on the least individualist aspects of his life: his attachment to younger filmmakers with whom he argued about life. Robert Flaherty's most famous mentoring relationship was his "discovery" of Richard Leacock, a childhood friend of his daughter Monica.

In fact, Robert Flaherty never attended the seminar: he died from cerebral thrombosis in 1951. Only his films have reappeared each year like the returning ghost of the father, an enduring seminar tradition that is less deification than a historical space to anchor new debates, practices, and theorizing. This fantasy reenacts the old Freudian theme of killing the father to seize one's own identity and voice. The seminars dance, quite literally, on the grave of the father, a tribal gathering of the various sectors of independent media: makers, scholars, librarians, distributors, students, curators. In place of the idolatry of one great man arose a public space where contradictions and arguments were de rigueur.

As envisioned by Frances and the first trustees, the seminars continued this legacy of a salon for serious artists outside of the debilitating realms of commerce, capitalism, and the daily grind of film production.[14] Many of those who convene in the name of Flaherty tend to feel that contemporary media practice has moved beyond him. What would Flaherty, the aesthetic conservative and romantic, have thought about new communications technologies like satellites, CD-ROM, the World Wide Web, and even camcorder video?

The Early Years: The Seminar as Film School

In the 1950s, only two or three formal university-level film schools (New York University, Columbia University, and University of Southern California) existed. Paralyzed by anticommunism, the ideology of the nuclear family, the hermeticism of suburbia, and mind-numbing corporate bureaucratization, the larger culture was not an inviting place for free thinkers—especially if they were women—interested in visionary film that questioned social norms. Hollywood focused its resources on technological rather than artistic innovation, for example, the developments around 3-D, while television shows idealized families.

The earliest seminars were organized like a university-level course in film analysis and often included professors like David Reisman, author of *The Lonely Crowd*,[15] media historian Erik Barnouw, and noted curators like Iris Barry, first Director of the Film Library at the Museum of Modern Art, who gave informal talks. Frances Flaherty believed that artistic vision was not innate but could be coaxed into being by seeing differently, with new eyes, through a series of juxtapositions. Film programming was designed to ambush the spectator's expectations, forcing new insights. Inspired by the Zen philosophy of releasing both the past and the future to submit to the flow of the present, the early seminars gave commercial, academic, and artistic filmmakers a metatheoretical experience anchored in the practical realities of filmmaking. The retreat space she created, removed from the domesticated grind of life, unleashed an international vision of independent film outside of Hollywood and commercial television straitjackets.

Frances Flaherty's own ideas about the role of The Flaherty demonstrated a shaman-like sense of film curating: she frequently proclaimed that the creative process itself could be explored through juxtapositions. The programming resembled a curator's interpretation of Eisensteinian montage. Through close film viewing, the seminar could produce thinking filmmakers to intervene in the world, take risks, and see in new ways.

Eclectic Groupings and Legendary Debates

Two real achievements were propagated out of the convoluted, lived reality of the seminar: unusually eclectic groupings of films and legendary, incendiary debates. For example, the 1964 seminar reveals an amalgam of countries and genres that belies the idea that the Flaherty Seminar emphasizes

North American documentary exclusively: animation and cinema verité documentary from the National Film Board of Canada, films by Yasujiro Ozu (Japan), Satyajit Ray (India), Ygang Hang Hae (Korea), Jerzy Bossak (Poland), and Amilcar Tirado (Puerto Rico); along with work from Ricky Leacock, Albert and David Maysles, Joyce Chopra, Shirley Clarke, experimentalist Ed Emshwiller; and the U.S. Department of the Interior as well as CBS News.

Intense debates were generated from the actual film and the presence of the filmmaker, not abstract theorizing. Across four decades, seminar participants were forced to make conceptual leaps, vaulting over philosophical and practical ideas about film by thinking across genres, forms, and national cinemas that was more Dziga Vertov than Flaherty in conceptual design. Second, intense interactions between an assortment of programmers, different kinds of filmmakers, funders, scholars, curators, television executives, women, men, blacks, whites, international makers, seasoned pros, and young acolytes let what was boiling up on the margins of commercial film culture—experimental film, sponsored documentaries, cinema verité, international art film, feminist film, regional film collectives, video, queer cinema, identity politics, video installations, CD-ROM— overflow within the nurturing clan of the like-minded supporters of noncommercial film.

Commercial television, Hollywood studios, and public television would suppress friction and conflict, rechanneling it into consumerism, pacification, and politeness. In the Cold War culture of political isolation and anticommunism, the internationalism of the seminars refused linking cinema with nationalism. Flaherty Seminar elders who have regularly attended the seminar for nearly four decades insist that without conflict there can be no change.[16] Most Flaherty programmers still resist sanitizing conflicts. It is exactly this dialectic that opened a space for women in film at the Flaherty Seminars at a time when women had very few cinematic spaces.

▶

Maternity Ward and Trauma Unit for Cinema Verité

Robert Drew (as well as many documentary film historians) contend that U.S.- based direct cinema was born at the Flaherty, where Drew met Ricky Leacock, and Jean Rouch met Michel Brault. The Flaherty Seminar operated as an incubation center—and trauma unit—for cinema verité as all of the above, plus D. A. Pennebaker, Fred Wiseman, the Maysles brothers, and many others showed their pathbreaking works at the seminar during the 1960s. Their films subtly exposed large institutions like the music industry, the U.S. presidency, and high school by using lightweight cameras as passports to forbidden public territories to destroy illusions.

However, most historians have overlooked the important interventions into the race, gender, and power blindness of cinema verité by experimental filmmaker and early Flaherty organizer Shirley Clarke. Her films from the 1950s like *Bridges Go Round, A Moment in Love, Skyscraper,* and her films for the United Nations criticized the observational distance of cinema verité through foregrounding film form. Almost all Shirley Clarke's work was screened during the first ten years of the seminar. *The Cool World* and *Portrait of Jason* questioned the racialized divide between camera and subject that most cinema verité repressed. Blurring the lines between fact and fiction, between nonintervention and theatricality, Clarke's works prefigure current interest in performativity in documentary.

The birth of direct cinema was not so simply a consortium of founding fathers from the United States, Canada, and France operating like a tribe of lightweight camera worshippers smoking cigars in a hospital waiting room. Instead, Clarke's experimental and documentary work, as well as the work of international narrative directors like Aaejay Kardar (Pakistan), Satyajit Ray (India), Jean Renoir (France), Michelangelo Antonioni (Italy), Yasujiro Ozu (Japan), pushed race, gender, and formal interventions into the maternity ward. Their films disturbed the cozy male bonding between cameraman and subject. These films also countered the moving camera of direct cinema with more graphic, stylized compositions that suggested visuality as a construction. That Clarke's involvement in these debates as well as her early administration of the Flaherty Seminars have been excised from most documentary history illustrates how the messy afterbirth of film movements is repressed, exiled into absence, where nothing is disturbed.

Other expurgations emanate from the male mythology of cinema verité's beginnings. *Happy Mother's Day,* an early cinema verité documentary about the Fischer family quintuplets in Aberdeen, North Dakota, often attributed to Ricky Leacock, was actually a collaboration between him and Joyce Chopra, who became a major figure in feminist film in the 1970s and North American independent narrative film in the 1980s. The film exposed how capitalism and state agendas exploited motherhood for consumerist agendas. Recutting the film to mute its stinging critique of capitalist motherhood, ABC lured Beechnut Baby Foods as a sponsor.

The juxtaposition of the independently produced version and the network recut of *Happy Mother's Day* has been repeated several times as a programming strategy at the Flaherty Seminar to prod audiences into considering the institutional parameters of filmmaking. Resonating with *All My Babies,* this pairing exorcises the differences between corporate network neutralizations of argument and independent film's critical interrogations by foregrounding how editing strategies shift the relationship between maternity, the state, and capitalism.

▶

Birth (Not Origin) of the Feminist Film Movement: The 1970s

Feminist film was also incubated at the Flaherty Seminar. Most historians agree that feminist film developed within the multiple trajectories of the women's movement in the late 1960s and 1970s rather than from one alternative film institution like the Flaherty Seminar. However, the important contributions of feminist infrastructures have been virtually ignored: early women's film festivals, the use of films as political organizing tools for the women's movement, and the role of nonprofit institutions like the Flaherty, Women Make Movies, and New Day Films.

Feminist film scholars like B. Ruby Rich, Elizabeth Lyons, and Julia Lesage have noted the tensions between a more sociological, realist form of filmmaking exemplified in feminist appropriation of cinema verité techniques during the early 1970s and a more psychoanalytic and avant-garde approach that interrogates patriarchal representation through formal invention.

During the late 1960s and through the 1970s, Flaherty Seminar programming clearly sided with the more realist, cinema verité side of feminist documentary. Yet these early feminist projects often interrupted the seamless narratives of cinema verité with talking head, Murrow-style techniques, carving out more discursive space for women. The feminist documentary films of the 1970s shown at the Flaherty displace the state, Kennedy liberalism, the fathers, the big institutions, and traditional cinema verité. They recast documentaries with working mothers, children, feminist politics, and smaller institutions like family life or union locals: for example, Joan Churchill's *Sylvia, Fran and Joy* (1973), Liane Brandon's *Not So Young Now As Then* (1974), Martha Coolidge's *Old-Fashioned Woman* (1974), Barbara Kopple's *Harlan County, USA* (1977). Amalie Rothschild's *Nana, Mom, and Me* (1974) sparked a heated debate about the efficacy of the filmmaker's putting herself into her own film.

The monumentally significant shift from the great white male auteurs of cinema verité realism to the incendiary, analytical compilation films of radical political movements coalesced at the 1970 seminar. The 1970 seminar refutes the segregation of black, feminist, antiwar, Latino, national cinemas, and experimental film history, demonstrating the convulsive inter-actions between movement films and formal experimentation, between in-dependent films produced within our nation and those produced in other countries.[17]

For example, in 1970, films by Bruce Baillie, Standish Lawder, and Hollis Frampton were screened with feminist work like *Woo Who? May Wilson* by Amalie Rothschild and *I Am Somebody,* a film about a black women's strike, by black feminist and future International Film Seminar trustee Madeline Anderson. Bolivian Jorge Sanjine's *Blood of the Condor* was screened. Symbolically refuting the auteurism and institutional privi-lege of cinema verité on public television and in festivals, films from collec-tives and regional workshops were shown: Newsreel, the radical antiwar film collective, screened *Amerika* and *People's War,* and community film workshops from Appalachia, New York, California, and Puerto Rico showed selected shorts.

The Flaherty Seminar gestated parts of the feminist film infrastruc-ture as a direct result of debates and meetings between enemies and soul mates. New Day Films, one of the first feminist film distribution compa-nies in the United States, grew out of the 1971 seminar programmed by Willard Van Dyke, a forceful curator who put politically radical American independent cinema on the map by screening it at the Museum of Modern Art. Julia Reichert and Jim Klein screened *Growing up Female: As Six Become One* and met Amalie Rothschild, whose film *The Center* had also been shown. Heated controversies about the function of women's cinema erupted in the seminar discussion of *Growing up Female.* They galvanized all the women at the seminar to meet for breakfast the next morning to discuss the limited distribution and exhibition venues for women's films. Over eggs and bacon they developed the organizing committee for what was to become the First International Women's Film Festival in 1972. The next year, Reichert, Klein, and Rothschild met Liane Brandon, who screened two historically significant feminist films at later seminars, *Anything You Want to Be* and *Betty Tells Her Story.* Reichert, Klein, Rothschild, and Brandon discussed distribution of feminist work to women's political organizations, and New Day was born by cesarean section, lifted out of the belly of that Flaherty.[18]

The political sea changes of the antiwar, the women's, and civil rights movements called for films that critiqued institutions to mobilize audiences to action, an epistemology alien to the refined, almost mystical distance of cinema verité. It is no mere coincidence that the birth of New Day Films as an alternative distribution collective for community-based, feminist filmmaking happened during a period of heightened internationalism at the Flaherty Seminar.

Within a five-year span, the Flaherty Seminars unspooled major retrospectives from five of the most daring, analytical, and influential male compilation documentarians of the past quarter of a century: Dziga Vertov (U.S.S.R.), Dusan Makaveyev (Yugoslavia), Emile De Antonio (United States), Marcel Ophuls (France/United States), and Chris Marker (France). These filmmakers shifted the documentary episteme away from shooting to editing. Their more philosophical deconstruction of ideology through assemblage of film fragments annihilated the individualism inscribed in a single cameraman. Compilation films assaulted cinema verité for believing too much in the real as a unified construct.

Similarly, many film historians ignore the complex interactions and debates among the early women's, antiwar, and black movements, typified in the 1971 seminar juxtapositions between *The Woman's Film,* a Newsreel feminist film by Judy Smith, Louise Alarmo, and Ellen Sorrin, *The Murder of Fred Hampton* by Mike Gray, and *The Selling of the Pentagon* by Peter Davis.

During the 1970s, virtually every important American feminist filmmaker had been screened at the seminar: Julia Reichert, Amalie Rothschild, Liane Brandon, Claudia Weill, Joyce Chopra, Cinda Firestone, Jill Godmilow, Madeline Anderson, Barbara Kopple. Their historical importance for delivering a nonpatriarchal, critical image of women during a period of intense organized feminist political activity demands their revival as heroic texts.

▶

Gaps and Absences

The history of the Flaherty Seminars reveals other layers of repression. More formally combative, international films that functioned as theoretical workings out of feminist film theories of representation are often curiously absent. Significant works by Laura Mulvey, Chantal Ackerman, Sally Potter, Betty Gordon, and Yvonne Rainer are missing. International feminist filmmakers like Tracey Moffat, Marta Meszaros, Helke Sander, Marlene Gorris, Sara Maldoror, and Margarethe Von Trotta have been placed in neonatal quarantine by seminar programmers.

Over four decades of the Flaherty Seminar, only four women have been featured artists with major retrospectives. The first was Agnes Varda from France in 1976, a figure of great interest to North American, British, and French feminist film theorists. The second was Sachiko Hidari of

Japan, who had begun her career as a glamorous star but retooled herself into a documentarist. Her gripping feature film on a railroad strike offered a Japanese parallel to the work of Barbara Kopple. The third, in 1993, was Marta Rodriguez, a Columbian filmmaker and one of the few women associated with the New Latin American cinema movement. The fourth was Japanese video artist Mako Idemitsu at the 1994 seminar. From France, Columbia, and Japan, they show the transnational linkages between women and social movements that feminism demands.

▶ ───

Collaborators and Editors: The Repressed of Film History

As a working seminar to study the art, practice, ethics, and philosophy of film, the Flaherty Seminar has always featured film editors and film collaborators. Many of these editors and collaborators have been women, functioning in some of the few roles available when the doors of Hollywood were closed shut and a Mason-Dixon line existed for gender relations even in independent cinema.

Seminar programs underscore that these canonical films were not produced by lone male directors but were in fact collaborations, often with women. Despite years of dismantling the myth of authorship, much film history has difficulty theorizing collaborations. Some Flaherty elders contend, for example, that all of Flaherty's films except *Nanook* were actually collaborations between Robert and Frances.

Other collaborative efforts emerge. One of the first gatherings dedicated exclusively to Third World and black film was sponsored by the Flaherty Seminar in 1975. Featuring the films of Sembene, Greaves, Latham, as well as work from other countries of the black diaspora, it was organized by the multiracial team of Barbara Van Dyke, Madeline Anderson, and Pearl Bowser. The Appalshop program of 1973 was not only Bill Richardson, heralded as the founder of regional cinema, but Mimi Pickering as well. *Hiroshima Nagasaki August 1945*, often referred to as Erik Barnouw's film, was actually a joint international collaboration between Barnouw, Paul Ronder, Japanese cameraman Akira Iwasaki, and Barbara Van Dyke.

Many other collaborations surface: *Antonia: Portrait of a Woman* by Judy Collins and Jill Godmilow and *Union Maids* by Julia Reichert, Jim Klein, and Miles Mogulescu. *Harlan County, USA*, the Academy Award–winning documentary about a Kentucky coal miners' strike, was screened at the 1977 seminar with Barbara Kopple and Hart Perry, her cinematographer and collaborator.

Although programmers like D. Marie Grieco and Willard Van Dyke showcased emerging feminist documentaries, it was not until the mid-1980s that significant amounts of feminist work appeared. In 1983, at a seminar programmed by Bruce Jenkins and Melinda Ward, five events asked the audience to rethink authorship and authority by looking at feminist films.

Trinh T. Minh-ha screened *Reassemblage,* provoking debate about the assault on traditional aesthetics by a racialized, experimental feminism. Dee Dee Halleck brought work produced by the New York cable access collective Paper Tiger. *Seventeen,* a film that created an uproar for PBS over race, gender, and representation of teenagers, was screened by Joel DeMott and Jeff Kreines. Evoking the early seminar with Helen Van Dongen, two works-in-progress were screened with their editors: *Far From Poland,* with Jill Godmilow and Susan Delson, and *Seeing Red: Portraits of American Communists,* with Julia Reichert and Jim Klein.

By the 1980s, the rise of small-format video, increased distribution and exhibition outlets in federally funded media centers and university venues, and increased public funding helped to establish feminist media as a major force in independent film. Feminist work at the Flaherty during this later period was concentrated in documentary (Pamela Yates, Sarah Elder, Christine Choy, Leslie Thornton, Andrea Weiss and Greta Schiller, Jennie Livingston) and experimental work (Su Friedrich, Cauleen Smith, Lynne Sachs, Barbara Hammer, Sadie Benning, Cheryl Dunye). Male independent producers increasingly traded the marginal world of documentary for narrative filmmaking with greater commercial viability.

During the past decade of the Flaherty, about one-third to one-half of the films shown were directed by women, an amazing accomplishment for any arts organization. If the 1970s spotlighted documentary work by mostly white, middle-class women, the past ten years have witnessed an explosion of work from artists of color and lesbians. International feminist work mushroomed, signaling feminism as a transnational site: Anne Clair Poirier (Canada), Mira Nair (India), Jane Campion (New Zealand), Maureen Blackwood (England), Gloria Ribe (Mexico), Racquel Gerber (Brazil), Pratibha Parmar (England), Shani Mootoo (Canada), Yau Ching (Hong Kong/U.S.A.) Mary Jimenez (France), Ngozi Onwurah (England), Ana Maria Garcia (Puerto Rico), Mako Idemitsu (Japan). American and diaspora feminist filmmakers of color appeared for the first time in thirty years at the seminar: Ayoka Chenzira, Michelle Parkerson, Trinh T.

Minh-ha, Lise Yasui, Camille Billops, Lourdes Portillo, Jackie Shearer, Ela Troyano, Indu Krishnan.

Video increased at the Flaherty, delineating the 1980s as an era when oppositional work migrated from 16mm film to the cheaper, more accessible video format. Video resolved the debate between realist cinema and textual interventions by layering them into one project: Cecelia Condit, Max Almy, Kathy High, Vanalyne Green, Rea Tajiri, Mona Hatoum, Sadie Benning, Karen Ranucci, Helen De Michiel, Martha Wallner, Tami Gold, Sherry Milner, Aline Mare.

▶──

Curators and Programmers: The Forgotten Subjects

Several historical factors can explain the large amount of feminist work screened in the 1980s and 1990s compared to the 1970s. In contrast to the first three decades of the seminar, more women curators programmed the seminar. In the annals of conventional film history, curators and programmers are often overlooked. In the 1980s, many women who were trained in university film programs entered the infrastructures of independent film— exhibition, distribution, and nonprofit organizations. Many of these women explicitly identified with feminism as well as other identity politics movements: Linda Blackaby, Melinda Ward, Pearl Bowser, Coco Fusco, Marlina Gonzalez Tamrong, Margarita de la Vega Hurtado, Jackie Tschaka, Ruth Bradley, Lise Yasui, Julie Levinson, D. Marie Grieco. But the movement to screen feminist work was not just an old girls' club. Male curators like Erik Barnouw, Richard Herskowitz, Somi Roy, Chon Noriega, and Steve Gallagher were also interested in the new emerging social movements of the 1980s.

The infusion of New York State Council of the Arts (NYSCA) grants money precipitated shifts in programming as well. Under the imaginative and dynamic leadership of B. Ruby Rich, an established feminist film critic, the NYSCA film and video division pushed the Flaherty to broaden its range of invited filmmakers to include more women and people of color.

▶──

Hostesses: Stories from the Belly

The story of women at the Flaherty Seminar is also about recovering women's invisible labor in running the infrastructures that provide the physical spaces for independent film. These reclaimings, restorations, and recoveries, however, do not mean creating new unities but, rather, displacing false homogeneities.

Hostessing—my preferred term for volunteerism—poses a knotty feminist historiographic problem. How do we unravel, describe, and analyze women's often invisible labor that was the lifeblood of the Flaherty Film Seminar as well as other nonprofit independent film organizations? Volunteer work is often erased, with no archival record beyond the memories (and complaints) of the women who engineered mailings and meals. Unrecognized and undocumented, women's "domestic" work requires rethinking the patriarchal presumptions about what constitutes evidence as well as analyzing the movements and contradictions between public and private spaces.

Within film studies, however, scant attention has been devoted to even beginning to map the domestic aspect of various film practices; the glamorous labor of film production—war stories, if you will—has been privileged over the hard work of getting those same films exhibited and discussed. Oral histories, memories, stories, and even imaginings enlarge documents. Trinh T. Minh-ha would identify this history as a story from the belly rather than a narrative: a story passed down by women, revitalized through its public expression but private in origin, continually reborn in new ways with each retelling.[19]

Rather than thinking solely in the maternalized terms of birthing and hostessing, we need to recast these histories as stories from the belly by excavating how these infrastructures were administered, operated, and functioned. Women librarians, archivists, programmers, filmmakers, and arts administrators who served as board members and executive directors like Frances Flaherty, D. Marie Grieco, Esme Dick, Barbara Van Dyke, Elodie Osborne, Edith Zornow, Nadine Covert, Dorothy Olson, Cecile Starr, Shirley Clarke, Mary Lea Bandy, Madeline Anderson, Sally Berger, Ruth Bradley, Michelle Materre, Deirdre Boyle, Christine MacDonald, Pearl Bowser, Faye Ginsburg, Carroll Blue, and Jackie Tschaka need to be reconsidered as important historical agents. The invisible, domesticated labor of these women kept the Flaherty Film Seminar going through writing memos, fund-raising, hosting board meetings at their homes, registering participants, making food, greeting filmmakers. Because a seminar, where people gather and disperse, is so immaterial, the labor of these women has simply evaporated into the historical ozone, with the films and filmmakers assuming a privileged place in various annals.

▶

Collisions and Detours: Feminist Historiography

Feminist rummagings into the multiple, layered histories of independent media institutions demand that we get off the straight superhighway of conventional historiography that seeks a public destination and denies it its privatized origins. History is not only what is on the road but is also collisions, accidents, near misses, intersections, absences, and detours. Feminist film historiography, then, is also what *built* the road, and what maintains it.

The histories of women's film and feminist film—two different but connected registers—at the Flaherty are not linear narratives moving easily toward greater visibility and voice. If anything, these histories are marked more by exclusions than inclusions. In the Flaherty, feminist film discourses are submerged in deleted names, collaborations that erase women, debates for which there is no record, women's covert discussions fueled by cold beer outside under stars after screenings.

Histories of feminist film practices should also recognize the behind-the-scenes labor of every film, every seminar, every film festival, and every arts organization: how women did the physical labor of serving food, delivering drinks, projecting films, greeting filmmakers, writing name tags, organizing barbecues. Beyond political and aesthetic debates about cinema, these activities sustain a collective experience on a much more material level as triage to the precarious and endangered world of independent cinema. Women scholars, curators, and librarians whose names are not printed in programs or left in letters must be named. As volatile absences, they disrupt the smooth linear flow of masculinist film history with their forgotten words and actions.

▶

Coda: 1996

With the theme "Landscape and Place," the forty-second Robert Flaherty Film Seminar manifested what a feminist-forged seminar would look like: creating hybrid mixtures of different media forms; promoting a range of national, gender, sexual, and technological boundary crossings; rejecting an essentialist identity politics; and pluralizing the space of exhibition. For the very first time in more than four decades, three women, who were committed feminists, coprogrammed the seminar: Ruth Bradley, the Athens International Film Festival programmer and editor of the journal *Wide Angle*; Kathy High, an established New York video artist and curator; and Loretta Todd, a noted First Nations/Canadian writer, director, and curator. Their political and aesthetic differences yielded a seminar that did more than simply celebrate diversity: it plunged the audience into border crossing(s).

Together, Bradley, High, and Todd scheduled more women makers than any other preceding seminar, including Ngozi Onwurah (England/Nigeria), Merata Mita (New Zealand), Steina Vasulka (Iceland/The Netherlands), Marcelle Pecot (U.S.), Alanis Obomsawin (Canada), Elizabeth Barret (U.S.), Ellen Spiro (U.S.). Male filmmakers whose work is heavily inscribed by feminist ideas about public/private space, perception and interrogation of patriarchal representational forms included Leighton Peirce (U.S.), Herb E. Smith (U.S.), Marlon Fuentes (U.S./Philippines), Austin Allen (U.S.), Zachary Longbow (First Nations/Canadian), James Benning (U.S.), Alex Rivera (U.S.), and George Kuchar (U.S.).

A plethora of film and video utilized hybrid forms of documentary, fiction, and experimental film to dismantle nationalistic identities, such as *PapaPapa* (Alex Rivera), *Personal Belongings* (Steve Bognar), *Roam Sweet Home* (Ellen Spiro), *The Devil Never Sleeps* (Lourdes Portillo), *Weather Diaries* (George Kuchar), *Welcome II the Terrordome* (Ngozi Onwurah), *Bontoc Eulogy* (Marlon Fuentes), *Deseret* (James Benning), and *Richard Cardinal: Cry from a Diary of a Metis* (Alanis Obomsawin).

Alanis Obomsawin, perhaps the most influential aboriginal mediamaker in the world, was scheduled to show a miniretrospective. Loretta Todd explained that Alanis would be welcomed in a manner different from the "white western" norm of recounting the accomplishments of an artist. In a stunning scene where nations emerged as transnations, where ritualized communication forms blended with film exhibition, Merata Mita, a Maori mediamaker, chanted a traditional greeting song walking from the back of the theater down the aisle toward Alanis. In this moving and singing, western white norms of distance and othering were sung into extinction.

After the screening and discussion of Obomsawin's awesome and fierce epic on the Mohawk occupation of Oka, *Kanehsatake: 270 Years of Resistance* (where she had risked her life to smuggle cameras behind the Canadian army barricades to record the Mohawk's voices), the audience was escorted out the delivery door of the movie theater. The audience gasped in awe: hundreds of luminaria radiating with candles flanked a path leading into the woods. A translucent screen hung like an oversized fairy's wing in an open clearing at the end of the path. Slowed down, reversed, and upside down images of fire, water, lava flows, glaciers poured off the suspended screen. Water, lava, and ice-cracking sounds roared from speakers hidden deep in the woods. The candles, the sound, and the woods summoned spectators to a ritualized performative place that required active participation because there was no place to sit. People milled around the screen from every direction, expressing their joy and wonderment at watching exquisitely intimate images of incredibly violent natural acts of landscape alteration in Iceland within the forest of upstate New York. *Borealis* was the work of well-known video and installation artist Steina Vasulka, the grand diva of experimental work. Through its juxtaposition of real and mediated landscapes, *Borealis* also recast exhibition itself for feminist interventions, disrupting patriarchal orders through transnational, psychic, and aesthetic connections as well as abrupt cuts.

These two extraordinarily moving, breathtaking moments signified how collective experimental feminist exhibition practices can invent new architectures of spectatorship. They can create new institutional landscapes and imaginary places to rewire relationships between nations, genders, tribes, spaces.

▶

Beginnings

For feminist film/media histories to be vital and significant, younger emerging artists and scholars need to be constantly invoked. In clamping their psychic imaginaries and real bodies onto filmmakers, scholars, curators, and administrators whose work carved out public space for women at the Flaherty Seminar, emerging artists assert the generative powers of women's solidarities across differences of age, race, sexual orientation, and nation.

In the future, feminist film historiography will need to embrace new technologies like CD-ROM, the Internet, the World Wide Web, and virtual reality. We urgently need to not get stuck in the analog, but to ruthlessly combine the analog and the digital in our fight for feminist media spaces and places. We need to distribute our historical, theoretical, and creative work in engaging, pleasurable ways to new audiences. We need to discover how the next generation surfs the gendered, racialized global streams of the new world order to create new kinds of feminist imaginings. For it is in the anger and hopes of these still-forming mediamakers and writers that new ways of imagining media, the Flaherty Film Seminar, and a feminist future will be gestated and reborn.

◆

NOTES

1. This essay is a more extended version of my "Midwives, Hostesses and Feminist Film," in Erik Barnouw and Patricia R. Zimmermann, eds., "The Flaherty: Four Decades in the Cause of Independent Cinema," *Wide Angle* 17, nos. 1–4 (Winter 1996): 197–216. I thank Janet Walker and Diane Waldman for their helpful suggestions in expanding the original essay, and Ruth Bradley for her endless inspiration. I thank Zillah Eisenstein for her

astute reading of an early draft of this essay and Erik Barnouw for his insights and criticisms.

2. See Jack C. Ellis, *The Documentary Idea* (Englewood Cliffs, N.J.: Prentice Hall, 1989); Richard Barsam, *The Vision of Robert Flaherty* (Bloomington: Indiana University Press, 1988); Fatimah Tobing Rony, *The Third Eye: Race, Cinema and Ethnographic Spectacle* (Durham, N.C.: Duke University Press, 1996); Brian Winston, *Claiming the Real* (London: British Film Institute, 1995).

3. Most film history is organized around national cinemas or commercial institutions helmed by men. For salient examples, see David Bordwell, Janet Staiger, and Kristin Thompson, *The Classical Hollywood Cinema: Film Style and Mode of Production to 1960* (New York: Columbia University Press, 1985); and Thomas Schatz, *The Genius of the System* (New York: Pantheon Books, 1988); Richard Abel, *The Cine Goes to Town: French Cinema, 1896–1914* (Berkeley and Los Angeles: University of California Press, 1993). Rare exceptions are Geoffrey Nowell-Smith, ed., *The Oxford History of World Cinema* (Oxford: Oxford University Press, 1996); and Judith Mayne, *Directed by Dorothy Arzner* (Bloomington: Indiana University Press, 1994).

4. Several exemplary exceptions to these gaps in noncommercial institutional media history are Alexandra Juhasz, *AIDS TV: Identity, Community, and Alternative Video* (Durham, N.C.: Duke University Press, 1995); Bill Nichols, *Newsreel: Documentary Filmmaking and the American Left* (New York: Arno Press, 1980); Deirdre Boyle, *Subject to Change: Guerrilla Television Revisited* (Oxford: Oxford University Press, 1997).

5. See Slavoj Žižek, *The Sublime Object of Ideology* (London: Verso, 1989), 55–75.

6. For a more in-depth history of the Robert Flaherty Film Seminar, see Barnouw and Zimmermann, "The Flaherty." This large monograph includes scholarly essays, seminar transcripts, primary source materials on Flaherty as well as the seminar, first-person accounts from participants, and a complete listing of all works screened at the seminar for forty years.

7. Most scholarly historical work analyzing the institutions of cinema has concentrated, not surprisingly, on Hollywood and national cinema. Institutional histories of the independent sector have yet to appear in great numbers. Douglas Gomery has brilliantly argued for the importance of film exhibition for historical and political economy analysis, extending from the Hollywood studio system's vertically integrated theaters to black, alternative, and art cinemas to HBO and home video. Douglas Gomery, *Shared Pleasures: A History of Movie Presentation in the United States* (Madison: University of Wisconsin Press, 1992).

8. Hélène Cixous, "Castration or Decapitation," in *Out There: Marginalizations and Contemporary Cultures*, ed. Russell Ferguson, Martha Gever, Trinh T. Minh-ha, and Cornel West (Cambridge: MIT Press, 1990), 345–56.

9. Scott MacDonald, ed., "Cinema 16: Documents toward a History of the Film Society Part I and Part II," *Wide Angle* 19, nos. 1, 2.

10. See John Hess and Patricia R. Zimmermann, "Transnational Documentaries: A Manifesto," *Afterimage* (January/February 1997): 10–14.

11. Evidence is based on four decades of Flaherty Seminar programs, International Film Seminar publicity material, and interviews with participants.

12. See Lauren Rabinowitz, *Points of Resistance: Women, Power and Politics in the New York Avant-Garde Cinema, 1943–71* (Champaign-Urbana: University of Illinois Press, 1991); and Diane Carson, Linda Dittmar, and Janice R. Welsch, eds., *Multiple Voices in Feminist Film Criticism* (Minneapolis: University of Minnesota Press, 1994).

13. Information on Frances Flaherty's ideas was garnered from interviews with D. Marie Grieco, November 14, 1994; Cecile Starr, January 20, 1995; and Barbara Van Dyke, October 12, 1994.

14. I thank Jack Churchill, Erik Barnouw, George Stoney, Cecile Starr, and William Sloan for their numerous, generous conversations with me about the early seminars.

15. David Reisman, *The Lonely Crowd* (New Haven, Conn.: Yale University Press, 1961).

16. I thank Erik Barnouw and George Stoney for instructing me in this method at the 1994 seminar. Scott MacDonald has also made the case that violent conflict in spectators has always been the mission of the avant-garde.

17. For a historical discussion of these interactions between political and aesthetic movements in the 1970s, see essays in Peter Steven, ed., *Jump Cut: Hollywood, Politics, and Counter Cinema* (New York: Praeger, 1985). I also thank Bill Nichols and John Hess for discussions with me on this topic.

18. Based on interviews with Jim Klein, May 13, 1994; Amalie Rothschild, August 3, 1995; and Julia Reichert, August 12, 1995.

19. See Trinh T. Minh-ha, *Woman Native Other* (Bloomington: Indiana University Press, 1989).

MICHAEL RENOV

[**3**] *New Subjectivities: Documentary*
and Self-Representation in the
Post-Verité Age

▶

Cinema and the Secularization of the Divine

The documentary film has long been tied up with the question of science.
Since the protocinematic experiments in human and animal locomotion by
Eadweard Muybridge and others, the cinema has demonstrated a potential
for the observation and investigation of people and of social/historical phenomena. In the 1930s, noted avant-garde filmmaker Hans Richter described this potential with particular urgency:

> Technology, overcoming time and space, has brought all life on earth so close
> together that the most remote "facts," as much as those closest to hand, have
> become significant for each individual's life. Reason has given rise to a secu-
> larisation of the divine. Everything that happens on earth has become more
> interesting and more significant than it ever was before. Our age demands the
> documented fact. . . . The modern reproductive technology of the cinemato-
> graph was uniquely responsive to the need for factual sustenance. . . . The
> camera created a reservoir of human observation in the simplest possible
> way.[1]

As an instrument of "reproductive technology," the cinema was endowed
with the power to preserve and re-present the world in real time. "The
(apparent) incorruptibility of optics," wrote Richter, "guaranteed 'absolute
truth'" (43).

But as Richter's parenthetical qualification of cinema's veridical status
indicates ("the [*apparent*] incorruptibility of optics"), few have ever trusted
the cinema without reservation. If ever they did, it was the documentary
that most inspired that trust. For the young Joris Ivens, the small, spring-
driven Kinamo camera was a tool for investigating the natural world. Having learned "all its advantages and also its weaknesses from Professor

Goldberg, the inventor of this practical little instrument," Ivens set out in 1928 to make a film about a railroad bridge over the Maas River in Rotterdam:

> For me the bridge was a laboratory of movements, tones, shapes, contrasts, rhythms and the relations between all these. I knew thousands of variations were possible and here was my chance to work out basic elements in these variations. . . . What I wanted was to find some general rules, laws of continuity of movement. Music had its rules and its grammar of tones, melody, harmony and counterpoint. Painters knew what they could do with certain colors, values, contrasts. If anyone knew about the relation of motion on the screen he was keeping it to himself and I would have to find out about it for myself.[2]

Ivens was researching the unique characteristics of a *cinematic* rendering of the world, already aware that the laws of optics and of chemistry alone could guarantee nothing. If, as he was to discover in his making of *The Bridge*, there were real possibilities for a felicitous translation onto film of this engineering marvel, there remained much to be discovered about how this medium could best evoke the dynamism of the bridge's mechanical action without, for example, sacrificing a sense of the monumentality of its scale. The making of the film was a kind of laboratory experience.

Of course, Ivens's enthusiasm for a systematic understanding of cinema's representational potential was partially historical, a by-product of modernism. Note in this context the writings of Dziga Vertov, who in his "We: Variant of a Manifesto" (1922) produced blissful accounts of man's "desire for kinship with the machine" and of "our path [which] leads through the poetry of machines, from the bungling citizen to the perfect electric man."[3] Vertov, trained in medicine, described his cinematic labors as a "complex experiment" and film itself as "the sum of the facts recorded on film, or, if you like, not merely the sum, but the product, a 'higher mathematics' of facts" (84).

All of these desires evinced by the early practitioners of the cinema — factual sustenance, the discovery of the laws of cinematic motion, and the perfectibility of perception — are deeply implicated with the scientific project. It is the domain of nonfiction that has most explicitly articulated this scientistic yearning; it is here also that the debates around evidence, objectivity, and knowledge have been centered. I would argue, then, that nonfiction film and the scientific project are historically linked. The work of a number of scholars offers further corroboration of this point.[4] I would also argue that the perceived relations between the two (perceived, that is, by the community of practitioners, critics, and scholars) have shifted in important ways over the years. In the post–World War II period, the status of the documentary/science dyad has most frequently centered on the particularly vexed question of objectivity.

While the difficulties surrounding the distinctions between subjective and objective knowledge in the European intellectual tradition are ancient, Raymond Williams points to the developments in German classical philosophy from the late eighteenth century on as crucial to current understanding. Especially in the aesthetic realm, an explicit dualism was forming by the midnineteenth century. But important changes were under way. Where in previous centuries, the prevailing scholastic view of subjective was "as things are in themselves (from the sense of subject as substance)" while *objective* was "as things are presented to consciousness ('thrown before' the mind)," the emergence of positivism in the late nineteenth century effected a radical reorientation of meaning. Now *objective* was to be construed as "factual, fair-minded (neutral) and hence reliable, as distinct from the sense of *subjective* as based on impressions rather than facts, and hence as influenced by personal feelings and relatively unreliable."[5] Attentive as ever to the "historical layering" of meaning in intellectual concepts, Williams suggests that the coexistence of an increasingly dominant positivist ideology with the residual idealist tradition has created considerable misunderstanding:

> In judgments and reports we are positively required to be *objective*: looking only at the facts, setting aside personal preference or interest. In this context a sense of something shameful, or at least weak, attaches to *subjective*, although everyone will admit that there are *subjective factors,* which have usually to be put in their place. . . . What must be seen, in the end, as deeply controversial uses of what are nevertheless, at least in *subject* and *object,* inevitable words, are commonly presented with a certainty and at times a glibness that simply spread confusion. (312)

Given nonfiction's historical linkages to the scientific project, to observational methods and the protocols of journalistic reportage, it is not at all surprising that, within the community of documentary practitioners and critics, subjectivity has frequently been constructed as a kind of contamination, to be expected but minimized. Only recently has the subjective/objective hierarchy (with the latter as the favored term) begun to be displaced, even reversed.

▶————————————————————————————

The Observational Moment

In his elucidation of four documentary modes of exposition, Bill Nichols has described the observational mode as that approach to documentary filmmaking often called direct cinema, characterized by the prevalence of indirect address, the use of long takes and synchronous sound, tending toward spatiotemporal continuity rather than montage, evoking a feeling of the "present tense."[6] Throughout the 1960s and well into the 1970s, this mode was in its ascendancy in the United States and Canada, with a related but philosophically antagonistic approach (deemed by Nichols the interactive mode) developing in France at about the same time under the aegis of Jean Rouch. Brian Winston has argued that the American practitioners tended, like Richard Leacock (trained as a physicist) and Albert Maysles, to be under the influence of the natural sciences in their early pronouncements of an ethic of nonintervention, even artistic selflessness: for example, one critic's description, "It is life observed by the camera rather than, as is the case with most documentaries, life recreated for it," or Robert Drew's statement, "The film maker's personality is in no way directly involved in directing the action."[7] Winston suggests that Rouch, an anthropologist, and his occasional partner Edgar Morin, a sociologist, had "the advantage of a more sophisticated conception of the problems raised by participant observation" than their American counterparts.[8]

But even in the heyday of direct cinema, the specter of subjectivity could not be wholly expunged. According to Stephen Mamber's account, a disagreement arose between producer Robert Drew and D. A. Pennebaker during the shooting of *Jane* (1962) as to whether or not the sound of the camera should be filtered out during an extended sequence with Jane Fonda, sitting alone before her dressing room mirror: "Pennebaker felt that the noise should remain, making it clear that the audience was not seeing Jane alone in her dressing room, but Jane alone in her dressing room with a camera observing her."[9] By the time of the making of *An American Family* (a twelve-part documentary series about the William C. Loud family of Santa Barbara, California, shot in 1971, broadcast on the Public Broadcasting System in 1973), there could be little doubt that the filmmaker's personality was rather intimately involved in the creation of the final product.

In several scenes with Lance or Grant, the two most active "performers" among the five Loud siblings, a conspiratorial glance is exchanged with the camera as a kind of confirmation of its role as witness. In episode four, Pat Loud journeys to Eugene, Oregon, to help celebrate her mother's birthday. As Pat and her mother settle down with cocktail glasses in hand, the daughter offers a toast to her aging parent: "To lots of birthdays!" Apparently misunderstanding the intent of the wish (she reads it as a toast to all those celebrating their birthdays rather than as a wish for many more years of her own good health), Mrs. Russell replies, "Who else has a birthday?" From off-camera, Pat rather flatly intones, "Susan has a birthday." Mrs. Russell's gaze shifts from her daughter to some point offscreen and to her right: "Oh yeah, sure, I knew it was something else. I'm not the only one having a birthday." This rather puzzling exchange is clarified only with the realization that mother and daughter are sharing this scene with filmmakers Alan and Susan Raymond, the latter of whom is the Susan in question. Indeed, the Raymonds shared a life with the Loud family for seven months, this despite the fact that their off-camera presence and the effects of their personalities on the seven principal subjects are only rarely acknowledged. By the time of the Raymonds' *American Family Revisited* (broadcast in 1983, updated in 1990), only remnants of the invisible fourth wall remain. Each of the Louds in turn speaks to the occasionally imaged filmmakers about the impact of the series on their lives as well as the effects of the presence of the camera on their behavior. (Remarkably, the ever rational Bill Loud calibrates his response to Pat's on-camera announcement that she is filing for a divorce in episode nine in the following way: 80 percent or 90 percent spontaneous, only 10 percent for the camera.) The Raymonds choose to end the follow-up piece on the fate of this American family, which had unraveled years earlier for all the world to see, with a reference to themselves, announcing that indeed *they* were still married and that in 1988 Susan had given birth to a son, James. Covering nearly two decades, the updated *American Family* saga offers dramatic evidence of the shift away from a self-consciously observational approach to a more interactive, even reflexive modality. Again, as with the modernist yearnings of Vertov, Ivens, and Richter, this transformation is historically contingent.

▶──────────────────────────────────

Performing the Self

By 1990, any chronicler of documentary history would note the growing prominence of work by women and men of diverse cultural backgrounds in which the representation of the historical world is inextricably bound up with self-inscription. In these films and tapes (increasingly the latter), subjectivity is no longer construed as "something shameful"; it is the filter through which the Real enters discourse as well as a kind of experiential compass guiding the work toward its goal as embodied knowledge. In part, this new tendency is a response to the persistent critique of ethnography in which the quest to preserve endangered authenticities "out there," in remote places, is called into doubt. In his introduction to *Local Knowledge: Further Essays in Interpretive Anthropology* published in 1983, Clifford

Geertz suggested that the predilection for general theories in the social sciences had given way to a "scattering into frameworks." This meant a movement away from "universalist moods" toward what he called "a keen sense of the dependence of what is seen upon where it is seen from and what it is seen with."[10] It is not difficult to imagine observational cinema of the 1960s as a cinematic variant of the social scientific approach to which Geertz disparagingly refers, an approach in which generalizable truths about institutions or human behavior can be extrapolated from small but closely monitored case studies (e.g., *Primary* [1960], *High School* [1969], *An American Family*).

In the domain of documentary film and video, the scattered frameworks through which the social field came to be organized were increasingly determined by the disparate cultural identities of the makers. The documentative stance that had previously been valorized as informed but objective was now being replaced by a more personalist perspective in which the maker's stake and commitment to the subject matter were foregrounded. What had intervened in the years between 1970 and 1990 that might have contributed to this effusion of documentary subjectivity?

The cultural climate of this period, at least in the West, has been characterized by the displacement of the politics of social movements (e.g., antiwar, civil rights, the student movement) by the politics of identity. According to this scenario, the clarion call to unified and collective action came to be drowned out by the murmur of human differences. Instrumental to this sea change was the feminist movement, whose revaluation of the prior alternative political structures suggested that social inequities persisted, internal to the movement. Young men challenged the authority of their fathers to establish state policy but left intact gendered hierarchies. Women and the issues that mattered to them—forthright interpersonal communication; equal stress on the integrity of process as well as product; open and universally accessible structures for decision making; shared responsibility for the domestic and familial—received scant attention. The women's movement changed all that and helped to usher in an era in which a range of "personal" issues—namely, race, sexuality, and ethnicity—became consciously politicized (evidenced by the post-Stonewall gay rights movement as well as the intensification of racially or ethnically based political initiatives). In all cases, subjectivity, a grounding in the personal and the experiential, fueled the engine of political action. While some have seen the emergence of identity politics as an erosion of coalition, a retreat from meaningful social intervention, other cultural critics have argued loudly and persuasively for its efficacy. Stanley Aronowitz has suggested that the current emphasis on multiple and fluid identities (and the critique of "essential" identity as the underpinning for social collectivities) is entirely consistent with post-Newtonian physics:

> The sociological theory, according to which individuals are crucially formed by a fixed cultural system containing universal values that become internalized through the multiplicity of interactions between the "person" and her external environment, now comes under radical revision. We may now regard the individual as a process constituted by its multiple and *specific* relations, not only to the institutions of socialization such as family, school, and law, but also to significant others, all of whom are in motion, that is, are constantly changing. The ways in which individuals and the groups to which they affiliate were constituted as late as a generation earlier, may now be archaic. New identities arise, old ones pass away (at least temporarily).[11]

If indeed we now live in an age of intensified and shifting psychosocial identities, it should surprise no one that the documentation of this cultural scene should be deeply suffused with the performance of subjectivities.

While never considered a part of the mainstream documentary tradition, video artist Wendy Clarke has produced work that foreshadows current developments as well as echoes important discoveries of the past. Beginning in 1977, Clarke began experimenting with the video diary format, attempting to use the camera as a tool to plumb the depths of her own psyche. This concept evolved into the *The Love Tapes* project, in which individuals of all ages and backgrounds are given three minutes of tape time in which to speak about what love means to them. Each love tape, while identical as to length and subject matter, announces difference at the level of sound and image; Clarke renders each subject the metteur-en-scène of her own discourse through a choice of visual backdrop and musical accompaniment. Each individual is seated in a booth with only a self-activated camera, monitor, and the concept of love as a spur to performance. In all instances, those who might, in the interactive mode, have been the interview subject become the source and subject of enunciation; differences of experience, affiliation, and identity join with the unpredictability and variation of desire to make each of these monologues unique. Thousands of love tapes later, the project offers testimony to the absolute heterogeneity of the historical subject.

Some years previously, Jean Rouch, a prime shaper of the interactive mode in which the filmmaker-subject encounter takes precedence over externalized observation, had begun to explore the power of the camera to induce the display of subjectivity. Far from avoiding or disavowing the potential influence of the camera on its subjects, Rouch had from the late 1950s on employed the cinematic apparatus as a kind of accelerator, an incitation for "a very strange kind of confession."[12] Replying to an interviewer's question regarding camera influence in 1969, Rouch replied: "Yes, the camera deforms, but not from the moment that it becomes an accomplice. At that point it has the possibility of doing something I couldn't do if the camera wasn't there: it becomes a kind of psychoanalytic stimulant which lets people do things they wouldn't otherwise do."[13] The famous sequences with Marilou and Marceline in *Chronicle of a Summer* (1961) in which the subjects choose to probe memory and emotion *for* rather than *in spite of* the camera offer an apt illustration of Rouch's concept.

But *The Love Tapes* and the films of Rouch are only precursors for the new subjectivity on display in documentary film and video of the 1980s and 1990s. The work to which I refer may rework memory or make manifesto-like pronouncements; almost inevitably, a self, typically a deeply social self, is being constructed in the process. But what makes this new subjectivity new? Perhaps the answer lies in part in the extent to which current documentary self-inscription enacts identities—fluid, multiple, even contradictory—while remaining fully embroiled with public discourses. In this way, the work escapes charges of solipsism or self-absorption. In her recent book titled *Family Secrets: Acts of Memory and Imagination*, Annette Kuhn offers an eloquent rationale for the use of some of her family photographs as case studies for a work of personal and popular memory. In terms that echo the feminist precept, the personal is the political, Kuhn argues that memory work, when properly conceived, folds public and private spheres into one another:

> The images are both "private" (family photographs) and "public" (films, news photographs, a painting): though, as far as memory at least is concerned, private and public turn out in practice less readily separable than conventional wisdom would have us believe. . . . if the memories are one individual's, their associations extend far beyond the personal. They spread into an extended network of meanings that bring together the personal with the familial, the cultural, the economic, the social, and the historical. Memory work makes it possible to explore connections between "public" historical events, structures of feeling, family dramas, relations of class, national identity and gender, and "personal" memory. In these case histories outer and inner, social and personal, historical and psychical, coalesce; and the web of interconnections that binds them together is made visible.[14]

Kuhn's description of the coalescence of outer and inner histories offers an overarching characterization for the recent documentary works to which I refer.

In a number of instances, the maker's subjectivity is explicitly aligned with social affiliations. As in Kuhn's description, a network of familial, cultural, economic, and psychical forces converge and find expression in an act of historical self-inscription; but in these instances autobiographical discourse is conditional, contingent on its location within an explicit social matrix. A particularly rich example of this phenomenon occurs with works that explore exilic identity, films such as Jonas Mekas's *Lost, Lost, Lost* (1975), Chantal Akerman's *News from Home* (1975), Raul Ruiz's *Of Great Events and Ordinary People* (1979), Marilu Mallet's *Unfinished Diary* (1983), Meena Nanji's *Voices of the Morning* (1991), Rea Tajiri's *History and Memory* (1991), and Dick Hebdige's *Rambling Man* (1994). The exploration of displacement and cultural disorientation bridges the divide between the self and an Other who is specifiably kindred. In the first two of *Lost, Lost, Lost*'s six reels, Mekas focuses on the Brooklyn-based community of Lithuanians, the Displaced Persons, who in escaping Soviet persecution in the immediate post–World War II years experience profound dispossession—of land, climate, custom, language, and cultural context. The poets and statesmen of Lithuania find themselves without familiar mooring in a land whose size and world stature doubles that of the Soviet Union, reinforcing their sense of oppression at the hands of the "big nations." Although Mekas's magisterial film has most frequently been categorized as an autobiographical work of the American avant-garde, in fact it charts at least three histories over a fourteen-year period (1949–1963)— that of the Lithuanian exiles, the ban-the-bomb social protest movement of the late 1950s/early 1960s, and the emergent underground film scene of the same period. This filmic documentation takes as its pivot Mekas's own history and experience but envelops it in layers of historical documentation. Mekas's subjectivity is eloquently performed across decades of real time, three hours of film time, but his is an identity constituted, as Aronowitz has argued, by multiple and specific relations to institutions and significant others, all of whom are in motion.[15]

During the 1970–1995 post verité period, documentary explorations of gay and lesbian identities have exhibited a particular dynamism and vitality. In this category I would include such works as *Territories* (Sankofa Film and Video Collective, 1984), *Tongues Untied* (Marlon Riggs, 1989), Gurinder Chadha's *I'm British But . . .* (1989), Su Friedrich's *Sink or Swim* (1990), Sadie Benning's prolific output from 1988 through 1992—including *If Every Girl Had a Diary* (1990), *Jollies* (1990), and *It Wasn't Love* (1992)—*Thank You and Good Night* (Jan Oxenberg, 1991), Sandi DuBowski's *Tomboychik* (1993), and Deborah Hoffmann's *Complaints of a Dutiful Daughter* (1994). There is no template to which these works conform; only a few of them feature a coming out scenario, while those that do (*Tongues Untied,* for example) often discover ways to reinvent the form. Riggs's controversial piece may be the most outspokenly politicized of the group from its opening incantation ("Brother to brother, brother to brother, . . brother to brother, brother to brother") to its iconoclastic summary claim, "BLACK MEN LOVING BLACK MEN IS *THE* REVOLUTIONARY ACT." From the outset, Riggs puts himself and his body on the line. In an opening sequence, Riggs, undulating and unclothed, moves rhythmically against a black, featureless background, riveting us with his fiery gaze and dramatic narration. But the temptation to read the tape as an exclusively first-person discourse is undermined by the recurring presence of a black men's group, which functions as a rapping and snapping Greek chorus. It is this collectivity of black gay men (of whom Marlon is but one) that occupies the film's political and ethical balance point. Successfully fusing the personal with the social, *Tongues Untied* is both a germinal political manifesto of its epoch and a paradigmatic instance of the new documentary subjectivity.

Other gay- and lesbian-identified pieces take up the maker's sexuality less explicitly. Frequently, these works attempt to situate the artist-subject in the familial order, to witness or account for the difficulties of accommodation within rigid family structures to queer sensibilities and life choices. In these cases, identity comes to be constructed less in relation to the family as a relatively abstract institution than to particular, well-loved family members with whom the maker must nevertheless settle accounts. Often, this relative (the mother in Hoffmann's tape, a grandmother in DuBowski's and Oxenberg's pieces) is ill, dead, or dying. Sexuality and its sources or etiology are only occasionally the overt subject matter of such work. Instead, these films and tapes affirm the degree to which the (queer) identities of the makers are bound up with those of certain special (but straight) family members. These mothers and grandmothers, heterosexual but unerringly eccentric, have helped create the people the artists have become. Works such as these mourn and memorialize loss, yet they testify with equal force to continuity, to the intransigence of subjectivity, a process charged and revivified by contact with significant others in life and in memory. These works are perhaps the next generation of the new queer subjectivity on film and tape. Janus-faced, looking behind as well as ahead, personal yet embedded in the commonality of family life, these are works that bridge many gaps of human difference—those of generation, gender, and sexuality.

How can we account for the dramatic, even explosive appearance of new subjectivities on film and tape as the century comes to a close? Julia Watson has written about the historical conditions in which women have voiced their "unspeakable differences" through autobiographical discourses: "For the immigrant or multicultural daughter, naming the unspeakable is at once a transgressive act that knowingly seeks to expose and speak the boundaries on which the organization of cultural knowledge depends and a discursive strategy that, while unverifiable, allows a vital 'making sense' of her own multiple differences."[16] Such a statement well summarizes the circumstances in which this latest phase of documentary exposition has arisen. During the direct cinema period, self-reference was shunned. But far from a sign of self-effacement, this was the symptomatic silence of the empowered who sought no forum for self-justification or display. And why would they need one? These white male professionals had assumed the mantle of filmic representation with the ease and self-assurance of a birthright. Not so the current generation of performative documentarists. In more ways than one, their self-enactments are transgressive. Through their explorations of the (social) self, they are speaking the lives and desires of the many who have lived outside "the boundaries of cultural knowledge."

◆────────────────────────────────────

NOTES

1. Hans Richter, *The Struggle for the Film*, trans. Ben Brewster (New York: St. Martin's Press, 1986), 42–44.

2. Joris Ivens, *The Camera and I* (New York: International Publishers, 1969), 26.

3. Dziga Vertov, *Kino-Eye: The Writings of Dziga Vertov*, ed. Annette Michelson (Berkeley: University of California Press, 1984), 7–8.

4. See, in particular, Brian Winston, "The Documentary Film as Scientific Inscription," in *Theorizing Documentary*, ed. Michael Renov (New York: Routledge, 1993), 37–57; and Lisa Cartwright, *Screening the Body* (Minneapolis: University of Minnesota Press, 1995).

5. Raymond Williams, "Subjective," in his *Keywords: A Vocabulary of Culture and Society* (London: Flamingo, 1976), 308–12.

6. Bill Nichols, *Representing Reality: Issues and Concepts in Documentary* (Bloomington: Indiana University Press, 1991), 38–44. Nichols has chosen to update his fourfold typology in his more recent work by adding a fifth category, the performative mode, which corresponds rather closely to what I am terming the "new subjectivity" in documentary film and video. See especially the chapters "Embodied Knowledge and the Politics of Location—An Evocation" and "Performing Documentary," in Bill Nichols, *Blurred Boundaries: Questions of Meaning in Contemporary Culture* (Bloomington: Indiana University Press, 1994), 1–16, 92–106.

7. Winston, "The Documentary Film," 43.

8. Ibid., 51–52.

9. Stephen Mamber, *Cinema Verite in America: Studies in Uncontrolled Documentary* (Cambridge: MIT Press, 1974), 95.

10. Clifford Geertz, *Local Knowledge: Further Essays in Interpretive Anthropology* (New York: Basic Books, 1983), 4.

11. Stanley Aronowitz, "Reflections on Identity," in his *Dead Artists, Live Theories and Other Cultural Problems* (New York: Routledge, 1994), 197–98.

12. Quoted in Mick Eaton, "The Production of Cinematic Reality," in *Anthropology—Reality—Cinema: The Films of Jean Rouch*, ed. Mick Eaton (London: BFI, 1979), 51.

13. Quoted in G. Roy Levin, "Jean Rouch," *Documentary Explorations: 15 Interviews with Film-Makers* (Garden City, N.Y.: Doubleday, 1971), 137.

14. Annette Kuhn, *Family Secrets: Acts of Memory and Imagination* (London: Verso, 1995), 4.

15. For further analysis of Mekas's place within the documentary tradition, see Michael Renov, "*Lost, Lost, Lost*: Mekas as Essayist," in *To Free the Cinema: Jonas Mekas and the New York Underground*, ed. David E. James (Princeton, N.J.: Princeton University Press, 1992), 215–39.

16. Julia Watson, "Unspeakable Differences: The Politics of Gender in Lesbian and Heterosexual Women's Autobiographies," in *De/Colonizing the Subject: The Politics of Gender in Women's Autobiography* (Minneapolis: University of Minnesota Press, 1992), 140.

ALEXANDRA JUHASZ

[**4**] *Bad Girls Come and Go, But a*
Lying Girl Can Never Be Fenced In

We live in a culture of oblivion that perpetrates a kind of self-
induced denial in which the meaning of the recent past is
continually lost or distorted . . . much like feminist history was
always lost or distorted. The cultural history each generation
creates is immediately turned into waste: "That's old shit!"
Whereas my work is addressing issues involving 3000 years of
Western patriarchal imposition. So if I'm fighting with some
younger artist about the past 15 years—I'm already
suspicious: those are not the right stakes!
:: Carolee Schneemann, interviewed in *Angry Women*

I am a feminist in my early thirties; Carolee Schneemann is in her late
fifties. I have been making and writing about feminist and queer film and
video since the late 1980s; Schneemann has been making transgressive feminist art since the early 1960s. What are the "right stakes" for a discussion
about the recent feminist past? In an interview I videotaped with this "angry woman" for a documentary about feminist film history, Schneemann
let me know that her anger is not, in fact, directed only at three thousand
years of Western patriarchal tradition. She insists that our culture, my
generation, owes her a lot: recognition, a living wage, the ability to continue to make new work and preserve and archive past work. What are
the right stakes for conversation about the recent feminist past, and why
would we want to talk in the first place? In the interview, Schneemann
seems to suggest that successful dialogue with a younger artist would hinge
on that woman's *self-induced* recovery of and connection to past feminist
work, not as old shit but as live artifact. This is difficult; in our postmodern
condition, the past fifteen or twenty years are *history*: lost, forgotten, obso-
lete, "immediately turned into waste." Yet feminists have a need for the
recent past—history—to be alive, instructive, interactive, so as to be able to

perpetuate (the) *movement*. Living, working, and fighting in a perpetual present—a culture of oblivion—allow little opportunity to progress; there's nothing to build on.

By analyzing the video presented in two landmark, decade-defining feminist art shows (Bad Girls, 1994 and At Home, 1983), I will make a history from documents of the recent past to promote feminist dialogue and to better understand the present condition of feminism. Perhaps surprisingly, the documentaries in these two shows—separated by a gulf of ten to twenty years—share most fundamental qualities: small-format, inexpensively produced personal investigations of women's sexuality and gender roles that push boundaries about female propriety. Sometimes humorous, sometimes clinical, sometimes sexual, and often serious, what unifies this strain of feminist video are its transgressive content and form. Therefore, my historical survey of recent feminist video also becomes a recent history of women's transgression. What can we learn, in the present, from feminist video documents of women's transgression, from feminists' transgressive documentaries?

Bad Girls video demonstrates how women activists and artists are drawn to documentary and avant-garde form (and their hybridization) for similar reasons: these are accessible and adaptable sites of cultural production that allow feminists to mold a medium to the shape of their anger and desire. You could call the vast majority of this video work "documentary" as it is composed primarily of images of a videomaker's unscripted performance as she breaks rules of female propriety. Recorded on tape for later exhibition, these are documents of a politicized (usually autobiographical) self-expression: a woman performing and archiving her defiance against the rules of sex and gender. These transgressive documentaries record in something close to real-time the real words, real needs, and real anger of women. However, the transgressive content of the work demands that formal rules are broken as well. Women's defiant words and actions are expressed through amalgams of usually discrete generic forms: talking-head testimony is cut with scripted segments, voice-over narrates real-time recordings. Thus, I feel as comfortable calling this formally diverse work "art video." This largely semantic debate proves to be useful in that it reveals one reason why feminist video (like feminist history) is, as Schneemann argues, universally "lost or distorted." Slipping between the cracks of academic and art-world categorization, most of the tapes I will discuss here have gone unanalyzed and unremembered because they are neither straightforward documentary nor bona fide art. Needless to say, the consequences of this inattention are significant.

Because earlier feminist work immediately becomes waste, contemporary work is celebrated as anomalous and defiant rather than part of a larger movement. For example, in 1994 the New Museum in New York City and the UCLA Wight Gallery presented a bicoastal art show based on a "resurgence of activity around feminist issues in the arts."[1] The curators were quick to assure us that this work was special: it "has a distinctly different spirit from much of the 'feminist' art of the 1970s and 80s. It's irreverent, anti-ideological, un-doctrinaire, non-didactic, unpolemical and thoroughly unladylike."[2] The Bad Girls show promised to showcase a "new breed": "Those addressing feminist issues in an overtly funny way and, at the same time, operat[ing] outside the boundaries of propriety."[3] With great fanfare, the Bad Girls art show exploded into popular culture, daring to go where feminists had never been and do what feminists had never done. "Bad Girls make trouble by being honest, outrageous, contentious, wicked, and wanton," trumpeted the museum's press release.[4] The mainstream press bought the spectacle whole, behaving properly outraged, surprised, titillated, and even amused by this shocking turn of events: *feminists* acting sexy, funny, wanton—what a great gimmick. For as *Newsweek* reminded us, it is common knowledge that "feminist art created over the last 25 years is . . . dour, strident, dense and homely."[5]

And it was true that the work highlighted in the show was anything but *that*. In Bad Girls Video (nearly three hours of video programming that accompanied the show to much less media attention)[6] the curious voyeur could see the slick, wet, undulating images of women in water that had colored Diane Bonder's adolescent sexual fantasies (*Dangerous When Wet*, 1992), lots of beaver shots in Mary Patten's *My Courbet or a Beaver's Tale* (1992), and beautiful black lesbians eating bologna sandwiches (*I've Never Danced the Way Girls Were Supposed To*, Dawn Suggs, 1992). The pretty cheerleaders in *Love Boys and Food* (Lee Williams and Angela Anderson, 1993) chant "F-U-C-K-Y-O-U, that's the way to spell Fuck You," while in *Girl Power* (1993) lesbian pixel-vision wunderkind Sadie Benning presents images of her bobbing, whipping head as she slam dances to a Riot Grrrl sound track edited against cut-up letters spelling "F-U-C-K-Y-O-U-M-A-N," and "H-E-A-R-M-E-O-R-D-I-E." These nineties bad girls are angry, violent, and ready for action.

Yet you know what? Although certainly hot and even bad, such work is not necessarily new. For instance, take one of those "dour, strident, dense and homely" feminist art shows from a decade before—the Long Beach Museum of Art's 1983 At Home show, which, like Bad Girls, was organized as a retrospective of the previous decade of feminist art production. In the seventies and eighties feminists also acted sexy, funny, wanton. They used their portapaks to document themselves having sex with a boyfriend (*Excerpts,* Aysha Quinn, 1983), a chicken carcass (*Hey! Baby Chickey,* Nina Sobel, 1979), and a lamb shank (*Learn Where the Meat Comes From,* Suzanne Lacy, 1976). Susan Mogul recorded herself on the "casting-couch," pretending to hire actresses for a film and in the process provoking and teasing a room full of part-hungry women (*Waiting at the Soda Fountain,* 1980), and Martha Rosler allowed every one of her body parts to be clinically measured by a group of "scientists" in lab coats while she patiently endured the process in the nude (*Vital Statistics of a Citizen Simply Obtained,* 1977). In the seventies feminists emboldened by the women's movement turned the newly accessible videocamera on themselves (the personal is political) to investigate gender roles, gay and straight relationships, and female sexuality.

But you know what? From 1964–68 in the film *Fuses,* well before there was a videocamera or even a women's movement, Schneemann was documenting herself and her lover fucking, performing fellatio and cunnilingus: "I wanted to put into that *materiality* of film the energies of the body, so that the film itself dissolves and recombines and is transparent and dense—like how one feels during lovemaking."[7] In the fifties and sixties, Shirley Clarke was using the film camera to investigate countercultural activities like race relations, black, gay male identity, and drug use: "My subject and my style were a little bit—different. . . . No, more dangerous than that. Dangerous subjects—drug addiction—and not putting it down. Black people, for real, done in Harlem."[8] Before Clarke, Maya Deren used her film camera to explore and perhaps even promote her own sexuality. In her celebrated diaries, Anaïs Nin writes about Deren: "She has a need to seduce everyone. . . . We all live breathlessly, hoping she will find someone to pacify her so filming may go on. We may have to draw lots: Now you, Number one, go to Maya and make love to her and make her happy, for the sake of the film."[9] And in the twenties, Margaret Sanger produced a film about the effects of spermicide on sperm (*Biology of Conception,* 1920), establishing, with scientific rigor, the politics as well as the biology of heterosexual intercourse. From Sanger to Bad Girls lies a cursory history of women who have been "bad" by being funny, sexual, independent, lascivious, angry, and/or serious—and then recording and exhibiting documents of their wanton behavior on film or tape. It is both the doing and the taping of transgressive acts—the taping as proof that the doing occurred, the taping itself as rule-breaking activity—that make these documentaries dangerous.

Therefore, for the duration of this history critics have called female artists who use their cameras to seek dominance, freedom, and sexual independence "dour," "homely," or simply "women without humor"—that is, if they acknowledge or remember that the work existed in the first place. A brief review of the press coverage of feminist art proves that the easiest way to undermine women's work is to battle not over aesthetics or ideology but sense of humor. This is a gender-based tactic (that works!) to disregard the ideas, anger, and analysis of feminism. Just so, one mainstream reviewer of the Bad Girls show was pleased to note: "The show's satirical send up of feminism is refreshing: it's time for this subject to take on a little humor, already."[10] Although I will go on to emphasize that most of the tapes in the two shows surveyed here are actually quite funny, it is equally important to defend women's right to be serious against both mainstream reviewers as well as our feminist advocates. Bad Girls curator Marcia Tucker explains in an interview: "This isn't a new generation—the artists range from 20 to 60—but it's definitely a new attitude. The first generation of feminists didn't know how to harness their anger to humor, especially about sexuality itself."[11]

Try telling this to first-generation feminist videomaker Ilene Segalove. *The Mom Tapes* (1974–78), which was screened during At Home, is a compilation of video one-liners. In these short pieces, Segalove and her mom reflect on generational change in women's understandings of their world: the home, shopping, food, and sexual danger. In painfully funny scenes, Elaine Segalove plays the straight man to her daughter Ilene's bad girl. The following routine inserts both women's voices over the black-and-white real-time documentary image of a busy Los Angeles street. "Don't use underground crosswalks," cautions Mom. "They're terribly dangerous, filthy dirty, sometimes there are even men taking a leak down there." Mom says that good girls don't go underground, never expose themselves to putrid smells, smarmy bodily fluids, male lasciviousness; they skirt danger by passing over it. Yet after all Mom's careful cautionary advice, the documentary camera chooses to let loose as it takes on the point of view of the naughty daughter; it surveys the street, peeks at the underground crosswalk, and then . . . dives in. Ilene says: "I've never been down here myself. . . . So this is what it looks like." She emerges on the other side still alive to tell the tale: "Hey Mom, I made it. And I'm okay." Beat. Punch line from Elaine: "You were just lucky this time. I wouldn't try it again."

The daughter proves her personal independence and the forward-drive of the women's movement by breaking from her mother into the seething, sexy, stinky underworld. She knows that she lives because she is willing to cross this innocuous border of propriety. In her work on the abject, Julia Kristeva writes extensively about the relationship between identity and things grotesque: "These body-fluids, this defilement, this shit are what life withstands, hardly and with difficulty, on the part of death. There, I am at the border of my conditions as a living being. My body extricates itself, as being alive, from that border."[12] In 1974, the border that confirms existence for Ilene, the second-wave feminist video artist, is nothing more threatening than a well-lit, relatively clean cement tunnel. But this banal site proves to be the ideal place for her to disrupt the sanctions of her mother and come into life herself. Even though her passage is unmolested and lacking disorder, a break has been made. Kristeva explains:

> The one by whom the abject exists is thus a *deject* who places (himself), *separates* (himself), situates (himself), and therefore *strays* instead of getting his bearings, desiring, belonging or refusing. Situationist in a sense, and not without laughter—since laughing is a way of placing or displacing abjection. (8)

The joke is on Mom, about Mom: her fears are trivial, without warrant, at her own expense. Bad girls' work is funny because humor helps us displace our real fears. Laughter frames the border of the abject for the daughter; then Mom gets crossed over so that her daughter can move on. The sites of the mother's unsanitary fears are her daughter's gritty playpen, but this is much more than a messy game. "Where there is dirt there is a system," explains Mary Douglas in her seminal work on purity and danger.[13] The rules about dirt by which Mom led her life—where to buy raincoats and steaks, letting Dad make all decisions about money, never going underground—are proven to be part of an unfair system that serves to control both mother's and daughter's potential movement. The laughing but scared videomaker finds that she *is* by confronting her Mom's rules, testing them, and breaking through them into the dirt. It matters not at all that the tunnel proves to be clean; Ilene becomes a warrior by transgressing the system that her Mother's imagined dirt outlines. Again, Kristeva: "It is not the lack of cleanliness or health that causes abjection but what disturbs identity, system, order. What does not respect borders, positions, rules" (4). Women like Ilene access the abject by breaking the rules of their mothers; they do so with humor, but this laugh is at all women's expense.

Camille Paglia and Glenda Belverio's controversial *Glenda and Camille Do Downtown* (1993) is the Bad Girls show's direct descendant of this tradition. The Mothers to act out against may have changed (in this case "the mainstream feminist establishment" set in place by the very movement Segalove documents twenty years earlier), as have the Daughters (what Paglia calls "drag-queen feminists"), but the effects are remarkably similar. Camille and Glenda feel empowered—bad—by transgressing into the social and sexual spaces "their 'antisex' Mothers" told them were dangerous. They construe Greenwich Village, Gay and Lesbian Bookstores, and The Piers as virgin spaces to penetrate, all the while making sure their Mothers are noticing how naughty they are behaving. But look Ma, these places aren't so dangerous after all! Setting up establishment feminists as an easily slaughterable straw man (as Ilene did to Elaine), Camille and Glenda fail to realize (as did Ilene and Elaine) that some feminists have been going downtown, underground, or the many other "sleazy" places in between for a very long time.

To remember only the feminists who are afraid of dirt is to do all women a disservice; for every Mom afraid of sleaze there was another foremother fighting to revel in it. But instead of here dividing at the ubiquitous pleasure-danger fault line, as Paglia and Belverio taunt us to do, it is more useful to interrogate how the Daddies really keep us down. Otherwise, we miss a most convincing explanation for our amnesia about the bad girls who paved our way: we need mothers to serve as our straight men. Get this: mothers are the easy stand-ins for the signposts to the man-made margins that control us. Yet as I've been attempting to establish, this joke is really on both mother *and* daughter. The father's rules remain unscathed as we women triumphantly travel through his tunnel or walk along his downtown streets, all the while snubbing our noses at our timid (if not also righteous) moms who were never the enemy anyway.

Comparison between the shows demonstrates both repetition and progress. For there are three tapes from the Bad Girls show that do take one step forward and identify the dirt system as Daddy's. Their new site of transgression is the act of calling men (not mothers) on our fears of their whistles, leers, and urination in public spaces. The documentary *God Gave Us Eyes* (Elizabeth Beer and Agatha Kener, 1993) edits together into one long leer, without remark or interruption, the offensive comments of men on the street who explain why they harass women who walk by: "You say to her, 'Hey beautiful,' and all the things you can do to her. Even if she doesn't look, it's a big feeling that makes you sure that you're a man." *Bicycle* (Meryl Perlson, 1992) narrates images of city streets with a voice-over imparting a series of incidents of harassment that occurred to a woman on a bike as men in cars (including undercover cops) screamed insults or reached out to touch her. Although the narrator took down and then reported their license plate numbers, nothing happened to her harassers, and after two minutes of affect-free narration the voice drones forward, more stories to tell, nothing improved. *Street Walk* (Kimberly Stoddard, 1992) is a two-and-a-half-minute, black-and-white "documentary" film that turns the harassment table by following the butt and crotch of a man as he is propositioned, winked at, gestured to, and grabbed at by a series of lecherous women, including one who takes on that most offensive of male stances as she squats, pees, and jeers at him in one fluid movement. By quoting black-and-white, hand-held documentary style, these table-turning performances imagine a reality where women are sexual voyeurs.

A system is certainly challenged as women voice their anger at male violence and even act like lascivious men. In 1994 the humorous transgression of these bad girls is their insistence that men take responsibility for the inequitable doling out of sexual roles on the streets of this society. Yet this site of transgression, where contemporary women disturb "identity, system, order," is the demand for personal safety on the same city streets where in the recent past our foremothers took back the night (as well as other strategies) so as to map them as unsafe. In her introduction to the 1970 *Sisterhood Is Powerful,* Robin Morgan describes her initial break into a feminist consciousness:

> It makes you very sensitive—raw, even—this consciousness. Everything, from the verbal assault on the street, to a 'well-meant' sexist joke your husband tells, to the lower pay you get at work . . . everything seems to barrage your aching brain, which has fewer and fewer protective defenses to screen such things out.[14]

Decades later, to identify how your brain aches because of verbal assaults on the street is not movement, although it may still be personally liberating.

How can it be that this "new-wave of feminist art activity" breaks into consciousness at the exact same site that it did for a much-read feminist writer twenty-five years previously?[15] Perhaps feminist history slips through our fingers because transgression is itself an ambiguous foothold from which to build a movement. As Georges Bataille explains, transgression is fundamentally illogical because "there exists no prohibition that cannot be transgressed. Often the transgression is permitted, often it is even prescribed."[16] Bataille writes of how taboos are transgressed while still remaining within strict rules: in war (the taboo on murder), in religious sacrifice (the taboo on killing), in marriage (the taboo on sexual defloration and repetition). Therefore, the female transgression of calling men on sexual violence is, like all taboos, "as subject to rules [as] the taboo itself" (65). The social order women seek to outstep has already worked to contain them: the transgression demands permission, ritual. Thus, the Anita Hill/Clarence Thomas hearings, as well as these angry yet funny videos, are best understood as ritualized transgressions: the permitted and contained, if still briefly threatening, exposés by women of men's crimes of sexual harassment in public places. Because the society already acknowledges this site of trouble, it knows how to make safe the angry actions that occur along this illicit border. The joke, seemingly on the jerky male subjects of the tapes, is also on the bad girl makers who still don't get the bigger picture.

Sigmund Freud wrote that all taboos, primitive and civilized, "designate a particular kind of ambivalence,"[17] what Bataille calls their "illogic." According to Freud, "there is no need to prohibit something that no one desires to do, and a thing that is forbidden with the greatest emphasis must be a thing that is desired" (87). As I have established, there is a history to women's articulation through video of their desire to end the imbalance of sexual power in public settings: there is a taboo against it, and it feels "bad" when we do so. Railing at our mothers or even our fathers about the danger of city streets *does* break across a boundary of propriety (that's why these tapes continue to titillate), but this border is one that is already surveyed, mapped, and guarded. In a culture based on a system of taboos that serve to protect male dominance over women through establishing rituals around who has the right to perpetrate sexual violence and who does not, and then who inevitably fights such violence, the question must become, are there modes of transgression for women that are less ritualized, more radically disruptive?

Interestingly, whereas Bataille and other theorists concerned with taboo, transgression, and the abject list many illicit sites of action—from snot, to cum, to menstrual blood, and shit, from religion, to cruelty, murder, and orgasm—for our two generations of feminist video bad girls there is minimal play in the full array of potential transgressive fields. These artists, it seems, were not concerned with excretions, secretions, the repulsive. *Pretty, Fluffy, Cheesy, Bunny* (Alix Pearlstein, 1993) does seem, in title, to be the Bad Girls video that gets the closest to reveling in these sorts of prohibitions. But like the majority of feminist work I surveyed the video turns out to be concerned less with prohibitions around the sense of sleazy touch than those around sexual autonomy, period. The most provocative moments in the tape are images of a woman suggestively licking an index finger edited right up against her biting into a hot dog. Again, Freud in *Totem and Taboo*: "In the case of taboo, the prohibited touching is obviously not to be understood in an exclusively sexual sense but in the more general sense of attacking, of getting control and of asserting oneself" (91). Just so, for feminist video artists in the two shows, acts of transgression seem to be less about the want of a sleazy touch and almost exclusively about the threat of demanding rather than relinquishing self-control. Prohibited touching needs no nasty object, no slippery surface when touching in and of itself is against the rules for women. Feminist videomakers fight merely for the subject position from which to reach out.

In her chapter "The System at War with Itself," Douglas writes specifically about how social systems manage to control the internal dangers of gender distinction: "The whole society is especially likely to be founded upon contradictions if the system is one in which men define their status in terms of rights over women."[18] In a society like ours, where these rights are demanded in some spheres and then contradicted in others, Douglas believes that there will be a plethora of rules around "sexual pollution." In such societies, rules about what is right, wrong, dirty, and clean for women—sexual pollution—are where the contradictions of men's unnatural rights over women are controlled. "We find pollution ideas enlisted to bind men and women to their allotted roles" she explains (141). According to her theory, a society like ours, in a time of extreme contradiction about the allotted roles of men and women, would have many pollution ideas about women's sexuality. Therefore, it is in the realm of sexual pollution—signified through an array of representations of self-control—that transgressive art by women most often attempts to redefine and then storm the borders of gender distinction.

In the videos of the At Home and Bad Girls shows the most common forms of transgression are not enacted through depictions of assholes or farting, knife wounds or vomit, but through independent sexuality. Feminist videomakers do not descend to the bawdy orifices of the body, because as Angela Carter in her 1978 book on feminism and pornography explains, "Women do not normally fuck in the active sense. They are fucked in the passive tense and hence automatically fucked-up, done over, undone."[19] For a woman simply *to do,* as opposed to being undone, is to cross a boundary, to transgress into the polluted spaces where established patterns break down. As Douglas writes:

> Each culture has its own special risks and problems. To which particular bodily margins its beliefs attribute power depends on what situation the body is mirroring. It seems that our deepest fears and desires take expression with a kind of witty aptness. To understand body pollution we should try to argue back from the known dangers of society to the known selection of bodily themes and try to recognize what appositeness is there. (121)

With witty aptness (humor) women mirror the known danger of their own bodies—merely being active—to revel in a margin where power is at stake. In the videos from both decades body pollution turns out to be nothing more dirty than female self-autonomy. No wonder men so rarely find our work funny. And thus, one of the blind spots of Bataille's brilliant *Erotism,* his inability to differentiate modes of eroticism in light of difference (gender, sexual orientation, race) so that all sexuality is cast as a building, growing, swelling, spurting sort of activity, is corrected through the specific modes of badness found again and again in these videos by feminists. These women need not fuck and kill, they need not murder and explode, all they must do is be active. "A free woman in an unfree society will be a monster," says Carter (27).

The monstrous women in At Home and Bad Girls claim the erotics of active sexuality often by merely claiming activity alone. In *Waiting at the Soda Fountain* (Susan Mogul, 1980) and *I Am a Famous French Director* (Mira Gelly, 1993), the respective feminist videomakers, one from each generation, do just that—play at being male directors. The big laugh is that they get to pursue their actors, boss them around, subject them to sexist jabs, and pretentiously claim a unique, artistic vision. It is equally funny and threatening in 1980 and 1993 for a woman to claim such sexualized authority, even if there is no sex. And we see this particular joke again and again in feminist video. In *Pink Slip* (Hildegarde Duane, 1982) a female, white-collar businesswoman propositions and seduces a male, blue-collar repair man. She gets the pink slip, but it's okay by her: just like a horny man, she lets her hair down and exits out the window with her lower-class lover. Ten years later, *Grapefruit* (Cecilia Dougherty, 1989) and *Freebird* (Suzie Silver, 1993) allow women to play at that most virulent, adored of male aggressor/artists—the rock 'n' roll star. To be active—just like a man—is to be funny, bad, and polluted when performed by a woman's body. Thus, the at first more benign-seeming series *On Art and Artists* by Lyn Blumenthal and Kate Horsfield exposes what is really at stake in the ubiquitous "famous French director" genre of feminist tapes. By recording talking-head interviews with foremother feminist artists Judy Chicago (1974), Arlene Raven (1979), and Miriam Schapiro (1979), Blumenthal and Horsfield transgress the rules imposed both on female action through artistry, and on the passing on of feminist history: they pretentiously claim a unique artistic vision for themselves and their documentary subjects. This series of talking-head documentaries makes clear a condition relevant for all of the tapes under consideration: a woman's claim to an authoritative and permanent (taping) position is a transgression. With witty aptness, these very serious tapes mirror feminists' deepest desires. They act as (male) directors, and it is an offense.

Brains on Toast: The Inexact Science of Gender (Liss Platt and Joyan Saunders, 1992) serves as metadiscourse on all feminist works that grovel in ontological transgression. The tape focuses on the artificial constraints of activity and passivity built along gender lines in our patriarchal society. In send-up after send-up of scientific study bent on proving the biological basis of sexual difference, the tape challenges our society's fixation with the neat lining up of sex, gender, and sexuality. This is elaborated on in *Strut*

(Heidi DeRuiter, 1992), a silent film where a male is confronted by a lipstick-packing female in a woman's restroom. "What are *you* doing in here!" reads the title card. The woman's threat transforms into eager sexual pursuit upon the "man's" revelation of her breasts and therefore her status as butch which permits the "woman's" concurrent revelation of her status not simply as woman but femme. *Tomboychik* (Sandi DuBowski, 1993) and *The Fairies* (Tom Rubnitz, 1989) allow the male videomakers to dress like girls and be pretty, while *Love, Boys and Food* enables the most passive of girls, cheerleaders, to become aggressive and alter the traditional subject of their cheers from football heroes to cultural enemies like Jessie Helms, Mickey Mouse, and Clarence Thomas. Finally, *My Penis* (Lutz Bacher, 1992) is perhaps the most effective of all these humorous-but-serious gender-bending critiques. Bacher takes on William Kennedy Smith's masculinity by forcing him to repeat one phrase, through the editing and reediting of a sound blip first spoken as he sat on the witness stand charged with rape, "My penis." After the tenth or fifteenth repetition of "My penis," it becomes clear that Smith's penis is nobody's but Bacher's, whose video antics have turned his cherished member from phallus to farce. Mary Kelly, in one of the many (including this essay) decade-comparing "conversations" about feminist art during the past few years, discusses the connection between feminism, humor, and potency:

> Historically the avant-garde has been synonymous with transgression, so the male artist has assumed the feminine already, as a mode of "being other," but he does it, ultimately, as a form of virile display. So what the bad girl does that's so different from the previous generation is to adopt the masquerade of the male artist as transgressive feminine in order to display her virility. In zine speak you'd say: a girl thing being a boy thing being a girl thing to be a bad thing, or something like that.[20]

Bacher's boy-thing, girl-thing virility gets us back to two of the oxymoronic places where we started: feminist humor and the fixity of the women's movement. First, nearly every one of the tapes discussed so far is built on humor, and second, I can switch back and forth between feminist generations willy-nilly since their concerns so directly speak to and respond to each other. For the most part, both era-defining shows of feminist art video find active sexuality—his penis is my penis—to be something new, something dangerous, and something funny. Yet I continue to insist that the angry-if-humorous demand for an active female sexuality may be where we are, but it is no place new.

The areas of movement around active sexuality which I did uncover involved transgression in the terrain of sexual orientation and race. In the

Bad Girls show, African American lesbian curator Cheryl Dunye includes several tapes by lesbians, women of color, and lesbians of color, who insist that speaking their difference in a racist, homophobic society is transgression in itself. The At Home show includes no work by women of color in the screening series (although video installations by two Japanese feminists were included in the art show), and no work explicitly about lesbianism (although many of the artists are themselves lesbian, and Nancy Buchanan and Barbara Smith's tape *With Love from A to B* [1977] playfully enacts a girl-gets-girl, girl-loses-girl, girl-gets-back-girl romance between two sets of hands, both of them female). In Bad Girls videos, *Girl Power, Glenda and Camille Do Downtown, Grapefruit, Freebird, Dangerous When Wet, Strut, I've Never Danced the Way Girls Were Supposed To, War on Lesbians,* and *My Courbet or a Beaver's Tale* all assume an active lesbian sexuality. However, one need go back no further than the 1972 *Sappho Was a Right-On Woman* to find that although this might be movement in respect to our two representative video shows, it's not so far forward in terms of lesbian feminist history:

> Women's Liberation means independence. Feminists demanded control over their own bodies and over decisions that shape their lives. They demanded freedom from sex-role stereotypes. With independence foremost in their minds. It is now clear that the lives of Lesbians provide an example of Feminist theory in action.[21]

Similarly, the idea that to be nonwhite or non-American and also female is to be transgressive is the subject of *My American Friends* (Cheng Sim Lin, 1989), where Lin explains that her first three American friends—Tom, Dick, and Harry—eventually settled where they were supposed to (a banker, an aerobics instructor, a rock star), while she ends her piece uprooted, traveling, crossing borders: "I bought a Japanese car and became an American citizen." 'Nough said: this is transgression in itself for a girl. Then the idea that to be black and gay is transgressive in its own right is played with in Dawn Suggs's *I've Never Danced the Way Girls Were Supposed To,* where a narrator speaks to a presumed white or homophobic video voyeur who's just got to know what black lesbians *really* do in private: "This is a video about what girls do at home. Just another day in a black, lesbian household." The joke's on the honky or homophobe viewer—all these girls do is go about their business: eat sandwiches, shine their shoes, make love. "Sometimes I wonder what goes through straight peoples' heads when they think about gay people," ponders our narrator. Yet if that presumed white or straight viewer had read the 1981 anthology *This Bridge Called My Back,* perhaps Suggs wouldn't have had to assume that women continue to know so little of each other. Cheryl Clarke writes in 1981:

> For a woman to be a lesbian in a male-supremacist, capitalist, misogynist, racist, homophobic, imperialist culture, such as that of North America, is an act of resistance. . . . The black lesbian is coerced into the experience of institutional racism—like every other nigger in America—and must suffer as well the homophobic sexism of the black, political community.[22]

In the vast majority of feminist cultural production of the recent past, to actively be—female, lesbian, nonwhite, sexual, an artist—is an act of resistance, a site of transgression. However, when feminists continue to make work that remains lodged in the same sites of transgression (for instance, being a black lesbian as an act of resistance), the culture learns how to recognize, respond to, ritualize, and make safer this still real threat. Whoopi Goldberg's black lesbian character in *Boys on the Side* demonstrates just how palatable this one particular threat has become. Denied her sexuality and reworked into that most familiar role of mammy, Whoopi caters first to all the white girls on her road trip whose needs are infinitely more important than her own. Although the threat of being a black lesbian in a racist, sexist, homophobic culture may remain equally real over several generations, the transgression itself becomes defanged, already known, ritualized.

I insist that sexual agency for women—straight, gay, black, white, Chinese—like our desire to end male violence, is dangerous, but that danger is already known, prepared for. In *Fatal Women: Lesbian Sexuality and the Mark of Aggression,* Lynda Hart is concerned with how the representation of lesbian sexuality is displaced by images of female violence that usually take the form of female aggression. She argues—as our videos have also demonstrated—that it is less a crime for a woman to desire another woman than for her to desire, period: "If desire inevitably confirms masculinity, so does crime. Masculinity is as much verified by active desire as it is by aggression."[23] So what are the representational consequences when a woman not only acts like a man through claiming active desire, as we have seen in the majority of the videos from both decades but, more important, when she compounds this with images of actual criminal or aggressive behavior?

Bataille insists that "demolished barriers are not the same as death but just as the violence of death overturns—irrevocably—the structure of life, so temporarily and partially does sexual violence."[24] Is sexual violence, Bataille's transgression that allows man to "assent to life up to the point of death," equally liberating for woman? It appears not, for significantly in none of the transgressive videos that I viewed were there images of female violence, at least if we take this to mean murder or cruelty. For instance, the videos I've already mentioned, concerned with sexual violence *against* women, do not match it with violence of women's own. Women's violence instead takes the form of articulating the problem, not violating the violators (although *Strut* gets closest to this, as the fictive male character is forced to feel for himself the violence of voyeurism). Similarly, in other tapes from the two shows there is carnage, decay, and death, but never as a direct consequence of a woman's hand. In *Excerpts* (1983) Aysha Quinn has postcoital discussions about the relationship between sexuality and death: the lovers discuss the recent suicide of a friend who was only thirty. The man strokes her face: "Anyway, I'm not dead." "Try to kill me with sex," she replies. Her violence is her active desire and her ability to film it. Just as the tunnel need not be dirty for transgression to occur, the murder need not be literal. Whereas in the nineties American popular culture has been fixated with girls with guns—we see them everywhere, in movies, the nightly news, their own special magazines—none of the videos in these series presented this manner of bad girlism. As has been convincingly argued by both Carol Clover and Jeffrey Brown, these gun-wielding, muscle-bulging, women-cum-male-action-heroes are *male* fantasies about (the containment of) women's power.[25] Feminist video artists need not document such high levels of aggression. Even without the now standard pistols, steroids, and explosions of contemporary blockbusters, there is sexual violence in these tapes if we define that eroticism in terms specific to the boundaries placed on *women's* humanity and sexuality.

In the few works from these shows that actually include carnage and decay (four in total from a field of thirty-seven), the violence looks nothing like that enacted by male action heroes. Instead, feminists' bloody, murdered meat is bought at the grocery store, prepackaged, sealed, and stamped with the Board of Health's approval. For example, in *Learn Where the Meat Comes From* (1976), Suzanne Lacy frames her transgression in a manner similar to Segalove and Paglia. The tape begins from a position of matriarchal stability and sanction—a televised cooking show dedicated to "today's lamb, which means zesty flavors which challenge the wildest imagination." Lacy—ladylike, refined, poised—mocks what was perceived as transgressive for the mothers preceding her. She jokes that this earlier generation of women found transgression through "zesty flavor" and "establish[ing] a good relationship with the butcher. Learn to speak his language. Okay, let's see it in the flesh." However, as she begins and continues her clinical, butcher-like mapping of the flesh of a lamb shank, there is a progressive breakdown in order: a movement into her own coming into being. Her speech starts to slow and slur, she begins to touch the lamb meat suggestively. A jump cut in the video transforms our polite hostess into a monster with speech-impeding plastic vampire teeth. She's talking the butcher's language no more. "If all this seems too complicated, get down on all fours and imagine you are a lamb," she instructs. As the vampire-instructor begins to really feel up the shank, there is a cut to black: "Due to the adult subject matter of this program, it has been edited for TV."

Lacy has transformed from good girl to bad woman as she learns to speak the adult subject matter of both the butcher *and* the lamb. Her transgression is to break from the order of her mother *and* the law of the father. This is sexual violence for women: to learn and speak where the meat comes from but not to speak this as a man would. Carter subtitles the "Speculative Finale" of her 1978 *The Sadeian Woman and the Ideology of Pornography* "The Function of Flesh." She explains that flesh is human, whereas meat is "dead, inert, animal and intended for consumption" (137). Flesh becomes meat when a person is treated like an animal. "My flesh encounters your taste for meat. So much the worse for me," she writes (138). So much the worse for all of us lambs and women, Angela. She continues:

> The murderous attacks on the victims demonstrate the abyss between the parties to the crime, an abyss of incomprehension that cannot be bridged. The lamb does not understand why it is led to slaughter and so it goes willingly, because it is in ignorance. Even when it dawns on the lamb that it is going to be killed, the lamb only struggles because it does not understand that it cannot escape; and, besides, it is hampered by the natural ignorance of the herbivore, who does not even know it is possible to eat meat. . . . The relations between men and women are often distorted by the reluctance of both parties to acknowledge that the function of flesh is meat to the carnivore but not grass to the herbivore. (138–39)

Lacy bridges the abyss of the language of sexual violence and gender relations not through literal violence but through an aggressive breakdown of language. Also from the At Home show, Martha Rosler performs violence on (the language of) the kitchen. In *Semiotics of the Kitchen* (1975), she displays kitchen utensils from A to Z. But each signifier carries a hidden signified: with a (K)nife she (S)tabs, with an (E)ggbeater she (B)eats. She hurts no individual. There is no pool of blood, no ripped flesh. But there is violence nonetheless: she exposes the anger and danger signified just under the surface of the (signs of the) kitchen. In a sexist society, this is a violence specific to women's humanity and sexuality.

In *Hey! Baby Chickey* (1979), Nina Sobel also explores the difference between store-bought meat and flesh, again exposing the sexual violence underlying the sanctity of the home. The tape begins with a woman's hand opening a package of supermarket chicken. Performing her housewifely duties with the clear and capable movements of cherished routine, Sobel begins to prepare a chicken for dinner by pulling the neck from its inner cavity. But in the semiotics of this kitchen, the (n)eck is a (p)hallic (w)eapon, which this housewife uses to rigorously fuck the chicken's gaping orifice. Next, she pulls out the gizzards and gently rubs the chicken's other hole with them, then reinserts them so that they are again hidden inside only for her to sensuously retrieve them once more. There is a cut, and now our housewife is naked and dancing with the carcass. She cradles it like a child. Another cut. The chicken is suggestively reclining on a plate. Sobel's face enters the frame, accepting its invitation. She licks the chicken carcass. She bites it. She sucks the drumstick as she would blow a penis. Another in-camera edit. The woman lies naked on the ground of an outdoor chicken coop; she is held by a body-sized wooden picture frame. Live chickens move freely around her, and she attempts to draw them with pencil and paper. A baby cries offscreen and the tape ends. Joke's on Mom once again. Even if she can learn to speak the language of the carnivore, she's still stuck at home tending the lambkins.

From the Bad Girls show, only *The Scary Movie* (Peggy Ahwesh, 1993) makes sexual violence its explicit focus. In this truly scariest of movies, two prepubescent girls perform a macabre melodrama, complete with severed, bloody hand, repetitive sexualized stabs into the villain's back with a phallic tinfoil knife, and an agonizingly slow death scene suggestive of orgasm. Yet it is not the ritualized images of violence that make this a terrifying, transgressive film but, rather, the sexualized images of presexual girls performing them. The film ends with the girls, Martina and Sonja, doing a provocative MTV-influenced hip-hop dance. The taboo here is not violence, but female (adolescent) sexuality. "In common speech, a 'bad boy' may be a thief, or a drunkard, or a liar, and not necessarily a womanizer," writes Carter. "But a 'bad girl' always contains the meaning of a sexually active girl" (47). In the rare cases where women deal directly with sexual violence, the violence falls away to expose the sexual as the site of women's transgression.

Which is why I get to lying and back to documentary. For if it is true that to be a bad girl as a woman is only to be sexual, and that it also turns out that to be violent as a woman is also always to be sexual, then perhaps to become transgressive across borders where women are least expected is to be "a thief, or a drunkard, or a liar." In such places, women would not just claim men's activity but would then pervert and destabilize this stable identity. When men are thieves, drunkards, or liars, their perversion does not necessarily stem from their sexuality. When they lie, women seek the same freedom. And the hybrid art video/documentary is just the form through which to enact the particular violence that is the destabilization of truth. Instead of getting stuck demanding merely our fair share of men's hold on subjective authority (as evidenced in women's claim to standard documentary style), lying videos demand a flexible, mobile position from and style with which to speak about the complex self and her needs.

There are two videos from my selection, one from each show, that deal directly with the kind of transgression that occurs not within the women's sphere, which is sexual, but within men's borders of propriety—crime and truth. In *Nun and Deviant* (Nancy Angelo and Candace Compton, 1976) the artists continue the plea for individual artistic agency, which is articulated in all feminist tapes. Over the image of a cement court-yard where the two artists are dressing up respectively in wimple and cap to play their self-selected parts, Nancy Angelo whispers: "I am Nancy Angelo. I am an artist. Sometimes I am a nun. My work is about transfor-mation. My work is about being where I want to be, to say what I want to say, to be heard, to be seen, to be loved." It is the *transformation* part that sounds new; this sounds like that *movement* I've been looking for. Not just a demand for stable (male) agency, but a demand for agency-plus-nunnery, agency-in-flight. This is agency that moves beyond mere identity, identity that is so secure that it can risk change. Meanwhile, in long-take, Nancy's collaborator, Candace, approaches the camera as Nancy departs, and Candace says in extreme close-up: "I am a juvenile delinquent. I'm a de-viant. I've committed crimes. I've committed grand theft, and I've shoplifted." Do you believe her? Do *girls* do that? Candace—in drag as a boy delinquent—returns to the background to continue the tape's other naughty task of breaking a table of plates, and Nancy moves again to the foreground, but her story has switched: "Forgive me. I'm guilty. I'm bad. I'm wrong." Now the deviant's flip side: "I've never done anything bad. I'm not a bad person." And finally, Nancy again: "I am Nancy Angelo. I'm an artist. I'm a nun of my own design."

Both women demand at the same time artistry, nunnery, deviancy. They want to be good girl, bad girl, and in-between girl. Lying enables them to claim sites of transformation: places of change, mixed meanings, instability, places of multiple, contradictory, identities. For women in 1976, one space for such transformation is the newly accessible terrain of video. And the way to do this transgressive work best is by turning long-take, black-and-white, on-location video—(male) cinema verité's authorizing grip on veracity—on its head. Where I earlier noted that talking-head video in itself is transgressive for feminists in that it depends on a stable, permanent subject behind the camera, I now suggest that this too is another of our already ritualized transgressions: known, permitted, and easily defensible. However, to demand the stability of the documentary camera and then also to lie in front of it allow these seventies feminist artists a radical position of flight from which to record and perform. In this case, while the doing and the taping are transgressive, the doing and the taping become doubly transgressed because of the lying artist's disavowal of the permanence of both documentary and personal integrity. Lying documentary is dependent on both the security and flexibility of identity. Truth, rather than sex, becomes the currency of exchange.

This holds true into the nineties, where racial identity also enters the terrain of lying's destabilization. *Chronicles of a Lying Spirit by Kelly Gabron* (Cauleen Smith, 1992), a film with a style that looks nothing like the previous one's portapak, unedited, black-and-white video, nevertheless uses documentary film to create a dense, multiple, ambiguous, self-designed space where the feminist artist can be more than herself, where she can take (male) agency one step further. In her weaving of highly layered colored film stock, Kelly Gabron, the mythical author of an "autobiographical" piece about her life as black girl, proves to be lying, as we find out that she's been in places, times, and situations that are mutually exclusive. In this case, the artist takes on and then breaks from another authenticating (feminist) documentary discourse—autobiography—by claiming that her authentic voice is a multiplicity of voices. Gabron/Smith demands her own individual agency *plus* the authentic (if untrue because they are not "hers") voices of others like her. "Truth" is questioned as she gravitates between the veracity of an individual's self-knowledge and the weight of communal, identity politics.

We are told by two competing narrating voices, one male and one female, that Kelly Gabron has been sighted in 1983 in California, where she fell into "the surf, dread, punk scene." Daughter of a sharecropper, she was also seen in Texas in 1945, Philadelphia in 1961, France in 1927, and she died near the Bermuda Triangle in the Middle Passage in 1763. Kelly Gabron's life is nothing less than the history of all black women. Cauleen Smith lies and tells people that she is Kelly Gabron as a way to claim the truth of those many histories for herself. Like so many of her video foremothers she insists, "We will be seen and we will be heard," and that the way to accomplish these familiar goals is through making media. "The only way I'm going to get on TV is to make my own fucking tapes and play them," Smith explains. Therefore, the last entry in Kelly Gabron's life is "San Francisco, 1990: Cauleen purchases new technology. Sound out." Documentary—the technologies that allow the mimetic recording and exhibition of the black, female, artistic self—is not secondary to the transgressive acts it records. Rather, for Cauleen and Kelly the act of documenting makes them both real, even if this is a lie.

And if all this ends up sounding like a catalog of postmodern effects—unsettling identity, truth, singularity, race, history, autobiography—there is a decidedly feminist spin on these effects. The transgressions of criminality are already ritualized for men: we know they will be "liars, drunkards, thieves"—postmodern cowboys. However, for a woman to twist herself outside of her sexuality and into the male spheres of time, space, and truth allows her to move, at last, into unguarded terrain where the sentries are not yet expecting girls. Yet, needless to say, this is not the first time a feminist has made such work or drawn such conclusions. Here is Schneemann from a 1993 interview:

> [My work is] about transformation. Layers of metaphor are moving through any of the visual imagery that I am producing. It does not matter what the material or the materiality is, but there is the sense of the metaphor that recharges and is often visually disjunctive. In some sense this work is never symbolic; one thing does not represent something else. . . . Every construction or image I make has to do with the clarification of space as a time figuration.[26]

To be in dialogue with Schneemann, other feminist foremothers, and my contemporary sisters has taught me a great deal. I have heard echoes of current work in video from the past and I have seen the changes that are also possible across small increments of time. I have found that women's struggles for personal and sexual autonomy may be the most effective if we can dislocate the primary role of the body, so as to also claim space, time, material, and truth as our rightful transgressive legacy. When we lie, when "one thing does not represent something else," we are freed from the trap of individual subjectivity locked into the always sexed female body. If, as I have established, the women's movement has been founded on attempts to acquire human agency through sexual transgression, the reason why we may have been so politically immobile is that in the field of sexual danger it is easy to get caught. These are borders that are ritualized, monitored, sanctioned. Whereas transgression itself seems to be profoundly apolitical, about accessing spaces, if only temporarily, where one can abdicate control (those borders on the margins where you can't tell if you are alive or dead, in or out, solid or fluid), women seek these transgressive sites of instability for another reason: to gain self-control and therefore political power. Much of the movement's lack of movement may be the result of this fundamental contradiction.

Freud explained that "sexual needs are not capable of uniting men in the same way as are the demands of self-preservation. Sexual satisfaction is essentially the private affair of the individual."[27] I agree with him as far as *men* go: transgression seems exactly the wrong place to unite men and found a movement. But women can and must unite around the "individual" and "private" issue of "sexual satisfaction" because this is also how we demand "self-preservation" in the public arena. Thus, feminists' response cannot be to abandon sexual perversion (as has a prominant faction of the "movement"), but to complicate and dislocate it through simultaneous perversion within the fields of identity and documentary. This is not to abandon sexuality, history, or identity—as we see in Smith's tape, she tells her life story by lying about the stories of others—but to demand multiplicity, contradiction, and fluidity within the terrain of representation. As Schneemann explains, "The real dance is with the material."[28]

And this is not funny. The two lying tapes are also decidedly the most serious within the two shows. The transgressive videotapes in both shows use humor to gain permission to say the impermissible, and in the process they pin themselves down to a place where women in the struggle have already been fighting. This is why, despite technological change, the tapes of the two generations seem so eerily the same. Lying, however, proves to be the one transgressive site of unstable play, by definition always moving, always new, ever adaptive. Although shows from both decades include one piece about lying, Cauleen Smith's lie looks nothing, in form or content, like Candace Compton and Nancy Angelo's. While what women struggle for—agency—may stay the same from decade to decade, what we are willing to lie about is as flexible and unique as are any individual's dreams and desires about herself or video. Which leads me to speculate that while bad girls certainly do come and go, a lying girl can never be fenced in.

◆───────────────────────────────

NOTES

1. The New Museum, *Exhibition Fact Sheet: Bad Girls* (New York: New Museum of Contemporary Art, 1994).
2. Marcia Tanner, "Preface and Acknowledgment," in *Bad Girls Catalogue* (New York: New Museum of Contemporary Art, 1994), 10.
3. The New Museum, *Exhibition Fact Sheet*.
4. The New Museum, *Bad Girls Video Upsets Gender Conventions* (press release) (New York: New Museum of Contemporary Art, February 1994).
5. Peter Plagens, "Bad Girls for Goodness' Sake," *Newsweek*, February 14, 1994, 53.
6. Although video has been curated as a part of some museum and gallery shows since the seventies, it is rarely reviewed by the mainstream and art press that covers the events. If video portions of art shows are covered, it is almost always in film and video specific publications.
7. Carolee Schneemann, interviewed in *Angry Women*, ed. Andrea Juno and V. Vale (San Francisco: Re/Search Publications, 1991), 70.
8. Shirley Clarke, interviewed in Sharon Smith's *Women Who Make Movies* (New York: Hopkinson and Blake, 1975), 46.
9. Anaïs Nin, quoted in Ally Acker, *Reel Women: Pioneers of the Cinema* (New York: Continuum, 1991), 96.
10. Grace Glueck, "A Broader View of Feminism," *New York Observer*, February 7, 1994.

11. Quoted in Jonathan Napack, "*Talking 'Bout Bad Girls (Beep Beep),*" *New York Observer,* January 31, 1994.

12. Julia Kristeva, *Powers of Horror: An Essay on Abjection* (New York: Columbia University Press, 1982), 3.

13. Mary Douglas, *Purity and Danger* (New York: Praeger, 1966), 35.

14. Robin Morgan, *Sisterhood Is Powerful* (New York: Vintage Books, 1970), xv.

15. The New Museum, *Bad Girls* press release.

16. Georges Bataille, *Erotism: Death and Sensuality* (San Francisco: City Lights, 1986), 63.

17. Sigmund Freud, *Totem and Taboo* (New York: W. W. Norton, 1950), 84.

18. Douglas, *Purity and Danger,*149.

19. Angela Carter, *The Sadeian Woman and the Ideology of Pornography* (New York: Pantheon, 1978), 27.

20. Mary Kelly, "A Conversation on Recent Feminist Art Practices," *October* 71 (Winter 1995): 58.

21. Sidney Abbott and Barbara Love, *Sappho Was a Right-On Woman* (New York: Day Books, 1978), 136.

22. Cheryl Clarke, "Lesbianism: An Act of Resistance," in *This Bridge Called My Back,* ed. Cherríe Moraga and Gloria Anzaldúa (New York: Kitchen Table Press, 1981), 128, 130.

23. Lynda Hart, *Fatal Women: Lesbian Sexuality and the Mark of Aggression* (Princeton, N.J.: Princeton University Press, 1994), x.

24. Bataille, *Eroticism,* 106.

25. See Carol Clover, *Men, Women and Chainsaws* (Princeton, N.J.: Princeton University Press, 1992); and Jeffrey Brown, "Gender and the Action Heroine," *Cinema Journal* 35, no. 3 (1996): 52–71.

26. Quoted in Carl Heyward, "Interview: Carolee Schneemann," *High Performance* (January/February 1993): 13.

27. Freud, *Totem and Taboo,* 92.

28. In Heyward, "Interview," 13.

II Filmmaker/Subject: Self/Other

Filmmaker/Subject: Self/Other

This section of the book, "Filmmaker/Subject: Self/Other," borrows the name of that part of our introductory essay because the essays specify and extend the debates and dilemmas described therein. Two of the three essays, Susan Knobloch's and Ann Kaneko's, complicate matters by showing the applicability of feminist analysis to documentary films not specifically coded as feminist. (We thought about calling this section "Boy Docs.") Knobloch's essay, "(Pass through) The Mirror Moment and *Don't Look Back*: Music and Gender in a Rockumentary," soundly dispatches any vestigial notion that cinema verité could supply "uninterpreted data."[1] "Mr. Pennebaker's eye," Knobloch argues, composes a distinct vision, Oedipal in nature and therefore as subject to "Mulveyan logic" as a Hollywood classical film would be.

But if filmmaker-subject relationships are not neutral, then there are other possibilities for the filmic results besides the classically Oedipal, as the essays by Gloria Gibson and Kaneko illustrate. Gibson's essay, "Identities Unmasked/Empowerment Unleashed: The Documentary Style of Michelle Parkerson," highlights how black filmmakers and subjects can get together in the interest of consciousness raising and social change, and how the need to do so is particularly great in the face not only of gender prejudice but of racial and sexual prejudices as well. Specifically, Gibson shows how this impulse toward empowerment manifests itself in Michelle Parkerson's work as a fascination with black women's multiple identities and with the "performance frame" as a means of reinventing an abler self. Kaneko's essay, "Cross-Cultural Filmmaking, Japanese Style," is really "cross-everything." In frank detail, Kaneko discusses what it means to be sansei, the granddaughter of Japanese immigrants to the United States, having gone back to Japan to film new immigrants from around the world who come to Japan to earn money through manual labor. Moreover, she explores what it means to make a film in six languages, three of which you don't understand, in film and video both, and including as interview subjects men who are separated from family members and cut off by cultural practices from easy relationships with Japanese women. To characterize, but not to reduce, some of these differences, Kaneko brings in the concept *honne to tatemae*: to say one thing but think another.

In all of the essays of this section, saying, acting, and thinking are conceived as definite, though mediated, acts of agency on the part of documentary subjects-as-performers. Without denying the validity of the critique of the filmmaker-subject relationship as one in which power accrues to the filmmaker, the essays in this section suggest at the same time the productive liaisons among subjects, filmmakers, and audiences that can be discerned or developed in documentary films.

◆————————————————————————————

NOTE

1. The quotation marks around the phrase, placed there by Knobloch, indicate both that the phrase is Stephen Mamber's from his *Cinema Verite in America* and that the possibility promised by the phrase is an illusion.

SUSAN KNOBLOCH

[5] *(Pass through) The Mirror Moment and* Don't Look Back: *Music and Gender in a Rockumentary*

In D. A. Pennebaker's 1967 "rockumentary" *Don't Look Back,* Bob Dylan is shown laboriously tuning his guitar onstage three separate times, but the only time he is seen playing a song completely, from beginning to end, he is in a hotel room, not in front of a paying crowd.[1] Moreover, when music is performed offstage in the film, its affective and historical connotations are subordinated to the drama of scenes within which Dylan challenges and quiets other singers, whose bodies are concurrently fragmented or pictured slumped in defeat on the image track. This extreme denial of musical evocativeness and closure is unusual both for the rockumentary form itself—dedicated as it is to the exploration of the live onstage and "life" offstage performances of rock stars—and for Pennebaker as a prolific individual rockumentarian.

To explain why "Mr. Pennebaker's eye" (to borrow Dylan's later, self-absolving term for the film's editing structure)[2] so pointedly cuts into and away from Dylan's voice in song except when it is used as an interpersonal weapon, I suggest that Dylan, as a character within this film, balances uneasily on both sides of a divide that conventionally has been depicted in narrative film as gender based. On film as in life, Dylan's image edges toward the "feminine" when onstage: in his performative "to-be-looked-at-ness;"[3] in his submersion into music; and in his lyrics, used to express a willingness to shift places with others, across time, across gender, and across the gap between artist and fan. Offstage, on the other hand, the film's Dylan is a verbally aggressive, gaze-wielding, action-controlling music businessman. Since it spends most of its time with Dylan offstage, *Don't Look Back* thus creates a portrait of the young rock artist as a conventional male movie star. The song performances are worked into the narrative as mere by-products of the filmic Dylan's subjecthood and cultural power, which are represented as strongly Oedipal in nature—formed by fierce competition with other males and differentiation from/effacement of females. The more open and reciprocal types of subject-places offered by Dylan's songs and overall persona are not echoed but reshaped and limited by *Don't Look Back*'s narrative structure, and by Dylan's deployment of his body, eyes, and voice (his "screen acting") within it.

▶

Characterization: Dylan's Persona in Hollywood Form

By 1965, Bob Dylan had established himself as the most prominent and distinctive songwriter of the New York City folk music revival that took place in the early 1960s as a conscious parallel to the civil rights movement. He had released five albums' worth of innovatively wordy, if melodically derivative songs.[4] Even those few of his recordings that he had not composed were easily recognized as Dylan's by virtue of his cleverly phrased but precariously on-key vocal style and his reliance—until the album released just prior to *Don't Look Back*'s filming in 1965—on only his acoustic guitar and harmonica to accompany his singing. *Don't Look Back* offers footage of Dylan's last stage performances for a long time without a full rock 'n' roll band behind him. With each album as the '60s progressed, Dylan changed his musical style, lyrical preoccupations, and figurative and physical voices. In a 1967 article the rock critic Ellen Willis noted her impression of fan reaction to Dylan's persistent multiplicity:

> Bob Dylan as identifiable *persona* has been disappearing into his songs. . . . This terrifies his audiences. They could accept a consistent image—roving minstrel, poet of alienation, spokesman for youth—in lieu of the "real" Bob Dylan. But his progressive self-annihilation . . . conjures up nightmares of madness, mutilation, death.[5]

Don't Look Back, following a Mulveyan logic beneath its verité veneer, drives back the specter of such mutilation—of, in more psychoanalytically inflected terms, castration, femininity, loss of subjecthood—by situating Dylan as, more than anything else, an extremely competent and widely desired media professional among other (universally inferior) media professionals or would-be professionals. This characterization, not coincidentally, is the same one worked on the romantic leading men featured in a subgroup of 1940s women's films studied by Mary Ann Doane. As the "object of female desire," a fictional male is, Doane writes, "feminized" by his presence in the culturally discredited and female-oriented genre of the love story—a genre that depends even more than other Hollywood genres on music, under the androcentric cultural logic that consistently places emotion, femininity, and music together "in excess of the rational."[6] Doane argues that Hollywood love story heroes are very often written as professional musicians so that the supposed *over*emotionality of their films, expressed in Romantic scores, can be recuperated to a male agent's narrative control—and so that the male stars' "contaminated" masculinity may be linked restoratively to "the only culturally sanctioned and simultaneously 'feminized' activity: Art" (97).

An exploration of the title of *Don't Look Back* suggests that Pennebaker's film works to elide the "feminine" part of Dylan-as-artist in favor of the "culturally sanctioned" (read: 1965 hip) part. Taken alone, the title phrase may seem merely a studied and self-defined paradox: one has to "look back" to see the film's record of sounds and images past. Even at the time of its release, Richard Goldstein was able to write—echoing Ellen Willis's perceptions of Dylan's quick-change artistry—that "*Don't Look Back* is a finely wrought antique which offers no insight into Bob Dylan in 1967."[7] The title also echoes, however, "She Belongs to Me," a song found on the album Dylan released just prior to the film's making. "She's got everything she needs," the song begins. "She's an artist / She don't look back." Significantly, Dylan as songwriter positions him*self* as the singer of this song in a fan's or a less potent lover's place with regard to an(other) artist. The omission of the song from the film except as trace evidence fits the general treatment of such reciprocity in Dylan's work by "Mr. Pennebaker's eye."[8]

In coining this typically derisive yet evocative term, Dylan made it clear that he was, as I am, asking his audience to note a difference between Dylan's own authorial voice and the film's—that is, *Pennebaker's* eye. But the thrust of my argument is not to place all responsibility with D. A. Pennebaker for using filmic codes to deactivate the feminine potentials in Dylan's life story and musical corpus. It is the phallocentric filmic codes themselves, "the eye" as broad cultural construct in the wake of classical Hollywood, that demonstrate their own tenacity beyond the sphere of the fiction film in *Don't Look Back*—precisely because they fall into line with Dylan's publicly spoken and acted embodiment of (a side of) himself at the particular time and place filmed. (The collaboration was financial as well: since Dylan's manager Albert Grossman coproduced the film, Dylan paid Pennebaker to work for him, eye and all.) *Don't Look Back* is fascinating— and pleasurable, energizing—because it makes such a big show of playing on the tension between closure and fluidity, filmic codes and musical ones, dominant concepts of gendered subjectivity and repressed ones. It is convenient to call the film's enunciator "Pennebaker" and the film's omitted extratext "Dylan" to express the terms of the tension in shorthand, but the tension itself, of course, not only exceeds but constitutes both of those terms.

▶

Negotiating the Feminine/Extratext

"Mr. Pennebaker's eye" in *Don't Look Back* does, then, follow conventions of (fiction) film narrative to insist on its own ability to show and thus know Dylan more completely than other cameras and microphones can. And the offstage Dylan in the film also consistently speaks others' minds for them, telling them what they do and do not know about him and his art. However, a third pool of knowledge is again and again written—as though it were in invisible ink—into the film, both repressed and returned to by the other two (self-proclaimed) "superior" discourses. This third level of knowledge belongs to the dedicated Dylan fan, the spectator who has previously sifted and shifted through his records, his biographies, and the rock press, where the written, visual, and musical texts that establish Dylan's rock stardom outside of this documentary engender a wider range of both object choices and subject-places than sound fully in *Don't Look Back*.[9] The film's central strategy is to highlight certain details that buttress its hero's Oedipal subjecthood while muting less conventionally masculine elements from "outside," most fundamentally with regard to Dylan's performances of his songs—his relationships with his singing voice and his characters. The process is also at work in the film's selective representation of Dylan's relationships to other professional singers, his fans, and the press.

A specter haunting *Don't Look Back* is that Dylan's voice is in fact "contained" by all three of the devices through which Kaja Silverman contends that classical Hollywood films sonically confine female characters to the interior of the text while allowing male characters to subsume and embody the filmmaker's exterior power.[10] Like those of Hollywood's heroines, Dylan's onstage performances are clearly marked as performances for the pleasure of others; his singing voice, perhaps more than any previously successful white male pop star, is "scarred" by the "limitations" of his vocal cords/his body; and he is repeatedly forced, "for his own good," to speak his innermost thoughts at the demand of others (in interviews). In counteraction, Pennebaker's eye rigorously displaces away from Dylan all about performing music that classical Hollywood cinema conventionally ascribes to feminine bodies—or that rock 'n' roll records ascribe to male voices under a more open definition of the masculine. To take a small and odd example, Pennebaker includes enough of "The Lonesome Death of Hattie Carroll" for the viewer to understand that Carroll was a maid "slain by a

cane" hurled by a rich young man; Pennebaker does not include Dylan's final demand for his listeners' tears, in the face of the killer's six-month sen-
tence. In two other instances in the film, however, Dylan is presented as a
young man associated with a cane; in the very first line he speaks in the
film, he asks where his cane is, and later he walks on the preshow stage of
the Albert Hall, cane in hand. The film chooses details that open up the
possibility that the viewer will be pushed, in the opposite direction of the
record's listener, toward identifying Dylan not with his song's female victim
but with its male victimizer.

■————————————————————————————————————

Other Singers

Joan Baez's presence in the film allows for a similar displacement of the
feminine, and it too could not be presented as it is if Pennebaker did not
omit certain vital information about it. Pennebaker rarely frames Dylan-as-
singer above his shoulders.[11] Baez's face, in contrast, is filmed in extreme,
almost fuzzy, close-up when she sings "Percy's Song," a Dylan composition, not identified as such within the film. Pennebaker cuts to a wider
close-up of manager Grossman as Baez's voice continues, an irritating tap-
ping noise begins, and Pennebaker pans to show Dylan, his back to the
camera, typing something at his hotel room desk. He is the working media
professional, beyond the reach of the camera's investigative eye, his musical
product nevertheless pleasurably proffered to the viewer through a female
voice.[12] As Baez lets "Percy's Song" trail off, Pennebaker cuts to another
choker close-up of her, now singing "Love Is Just a Four-Letter Word."
Dylan inscribes his own authorship of this song into the movie by commenting, in a medium shot with his back to the camera, "I never finished
that song, did I?" Baez promises that if he finishes it, she'll put it on an album, but Dylan just mutters, "I could finish that," while rubbing his eyes.
Pennebaker here works to displace the sour-romance theme of this particular song onto an exposé of the behind-the-scenes mechanics of the music
business.

This displacement is especially remarkable in light of Baez's extratextual comments about the "true story" behind these particular filmic images. In an interview with Dylan's first major biographer, Baez says that
she accompanied Dylan on the British tour covered by *Don't Look Back*
in the hopes that he would let her share the stage with him, as she—in
America, the reigning "queen of folk" and of Dylan's heart—had let him a
few years earlier:

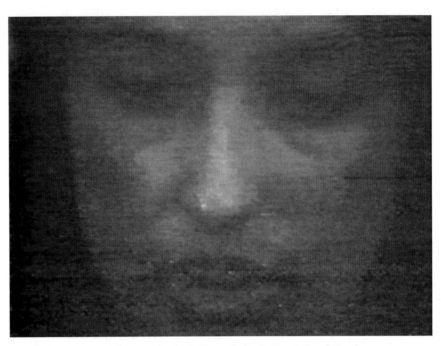

Joan Baez singing in close-up in D. A. Pennebaker's *Don't Look Back*.

> [But] Bobby was much more famous there than I was, so Bobby just took
> England. . . . He wouldn't ask me onstage to sing. . . . I was very, very
> hurt. . . . I should have left after the first concert. . . . When I walked out the
> door in the film, I never came back after that.[13]

None of this registers in the film at all. Baez is just another of the facts
floating around Dylan that Pennebaker never explains. This repression of a
woman's sensibility merely creeps around the edges of the sequence analyzed above, which actually proceeds to become something of an eclipse of
Baez's voice by Dylan's—an eclipse on which Dylan and Pennebaker seem
to collaborate.

Right after "Four-Letter Word," Pennebaker shows Baez singing
"Family Reunion," a song Tim Riley attributes to Hank Williams, one of
the first country music stars to earn a reputation as a genius songwriter,[14]
just as Dylan was one of the first rock stars. Dylan and his friend Bob
Neuwirth interrupt Baez to make unheeded requests—Dylan asks for
"Long Black Veil," recorded by Lefty Frizzell and also Johnny Cash, a musical ancestor with whom Dylan engaged in explicit dialogue on record and
TV a few years later. There is a cut across which Dylan takes control of the
guitar Baez has been playing, and it is now he who sits, albeit in unreveal-
ing profile, near the camera while Baez remains visible in the background.
Dylan then does some of "Lost Highway" and "I'm So Lonesome I Could

Dylan working in his hotel room as Baez sings.

Cry," two more Hank Williams–identified songs. The film does not identify the authorship or performance history of any of these songs, thereby
downplaying the debts and desires—the negative male Oedipality—seemingly in circulation between their previous famous singers and Dylan.[15]

While Dylan sings, Pennebaker zooms in for a close-up of Baez, her
chin in her hand, her fingers over her mouth. It is only after a long ten seconds that she uncovers her mouth and starts to sing a background part.
Her power to command the camera's attention is clearly determined as
much by the attraction of her (im)passive, marginalized visage as her feminine performance for others' enjoyment as a guitarist and singer. With such
visuals, Pennebaker defeminizes Dylan's own singing ability here by depicting it as a means not toward harmony—toward the exchanging of selves—
but toward dominance.

It is notable, however, that, while the film's editing contradicts Baez's
claim and shows her with Dylan even after she walks out of his hotel room
at the end of the Hank Williams songs, Baez is shown in two further shots,
asserting herself vocally in ways for which, Silverman argues, Hollywood
fiction films punish women.[16] In a car with Dylan, Baez sardonically twists
a line from his "It's All over Now, Baby Blue," so that it goes, "crying like
a banana in the sun" rather than "like a fire." And in a dressing room, she
repeats the title line of the band Them's "Here Comes the Night" twice,

screeching "Oooh!" at the end each time, until the laughing Dylan covers his ears. It is only after this scene that Baez vanishes from the film, her voice having been given not much, but some, room to express discontent to the viewer and to Dylan.

According to the logic of *Don't Look Back*'s editing, however, the main emotional conflict in Dylan's life at this time concerns not Baez but the up-and-coming Scottish folksinger Donovan. If, as Steve Mamber argues, many of the Drew Associates' seminal cinema verité films have a "crisis structure," which results in their persistent re-creation of a traditional American hero, *Don't Look Back* may be seen as having a "conflict structure," whose sole purpose is similarly to ensure the rigid boundaries of Dylan-as-the-One.[17] Pennebaker seems to have used all the footage in which Dylan mentions Donovan: first, Donovan is just a picture in the paper about whom Dylan asks (seemingly) mock-threatened questions. Later, Dylan says like a spy to his pal Bob Neuwirth, "Donovan. . . . He's our target for tomorrow."

Donovan evokes the published headline "Dylan Digs Donovan," another, "outside" medium's reflection of Dylan that does not jibe with the growing disdain for the Scottish singer shown in the film when, for instance, Dylan tells his manager to "give it to Donovan" after refusing to even see an award that an older Englishman wants to present to him. Earlier in the film Pennebaker cuts from a news photo of Dylan to a shot of the "real" motion-picture Dylan laughing at the paper and commenting, in an uncredited revision of Arthur Rimbaud, "I'm glad I'm not me."[18] But rather than showing the real Donovan behind the media's images of him, Pennebaker's later cut from a concert poster on Dylan's hotel wall advertising Donovan to Donovan's living (silent) face identifies the man with the headline. Margaret Horwitz argues that, in the case of the Beatles, such an equation feminizes the "poster boy."[19]

Indeed, in the hotel room when Donovan plays "To Sing for You," a pretty little ballad, in medium shot, Pennebaker pans to Dylan as he verbally overrides Donovan to say, "Hey, that's a good song, man," while Donovan is still singing. Dylan takes the physically active, visually controlling role attributed by Laura Mulvey to male Hollywood characters: his leg bounces nervously and the camera tilts down to get all of his restless shifting while a man on Dylan's left stares at the camera, but Dylan looks intensely off left, presumably at Donovan. Dylan's actorly gaze thus works with the camera's framing to mark the film's Dylan as looking, "(fourth) walled-off" subject more than seen, wide-open object. At the end of the song, Dylan takes the guitar from Donovan, and, in a muffled voice (with muffled command), Donovan asks him to play "It's All over Now, Baby

Blue" from his new, mostly electric album. "It's All over Now" is the title of a song written by soul singer Bobby Womack and successfully recorded and charted by the Rolling Stones in 1964; "Baby Blue" is a 1958 song cowritten and recorded by rock pioneer Gene Vincent, a song whose inspiration for his own later song Dylan directly acknowledged in a later interview.[20] The dialogue between singer-songwriters—spanning differences in era, nationality, race, and musical subgenres—that is apparent in the song title becomes a closed competition in the filmic Dylan's hands.

In a medium shot in the film, Dylan plays his song solo and acoustically with no mention of its electric rock parentage, but with a harder, more aggressive rhythm than he uses on record. The camera zooms in on his face, and he turns his head down and to his left, studiedly regarding his fretboard. However, on the couplet "Yonder stands your orphan with his gun / Crying like a fire in the sun," Dylan turns his full face to the camera and enunciates his words with conspicuous bite, smiling off to his right triumphantly; the viewer may almost be able to taste the pride he takes in his simile (and, perhaps, his "rescue" of it from Baez's mangling). Meanwhile, Donovan sits hunched in long shot, his right leg bent upward and held by his left arm, his right arm hugging his entire body. When the song ends,[21] Dylan smiles widely and asks, "You wanna hear—you wanna do another song?"

Pennebaker edits this scene so that Donovan is never shown singing along with Dylan, although he can be heard doing so at moments on the soundtrack.[22] Both Pennebaker and Dylan seem to want to see Donovan reduced to the status of "hearer" not "doer" (the same reduction worked on Baez, and, we will see, fans and interviewers). A little later, Pennebaker even cuts from a sign announcing that Dylan's upcoming concert is sold-out to a British promoter in the car with Dylan, answering Dylan's question about Donovan's tour with the snide comment that Donovan—and four other acts—could fill a hall for two hours. Seemingly, it is only by asserting that other singers are more visually and sonically contained—in Mulvey's and Silverman's terms, more feminized—than Dylan that the film is able to meet the desires for a triumphantly knowing and unifed subjectivity spoken (to) by its structure.

■──

Fans

Twin dangers arise along this path, however: if the viewer sees anyone except Bob Dylan inside the Lacanian mirror that Mulvey says the narrative cinema puts before him or (less easily) her, she or he will be put in the

Dylan wielding his gaze while singing.

uncomfortable position of identifying with either the already-feminine, which the film squelches, or the other-masculine, which the film vanquishes through feminization. It is true that, as long as Dylan's authority can ultimately be acknowledged, the position of the fan—the one who likes Dylan but, in the real world, cannot be him—is depicted as a happy enough one within *Don't Look Back*. In the film's one extended sequence of onstage songs, the representation of Dylan's performances is clearly controlled by Pennebaker, who separates each song fragment with a showy dissolve. Yet it is Dylan himself who changes the words of his "Talkin' WW III Blues:" Dylan recites the series of nonsense lines that begin, "Some of the people can be half-right part of the time" and then says, "T. S. Eliot said that." (On Dylan's 1963 recording of the song, it's Abraham Lincoln.) "I'll let you be in my dream if I can be in your dream," Dylan continues— and then with glee affirms, "I said that!" The interchange(ability) between (both Eliot and Dylan as) artist and (both Dylan and his listener as) fan— the same type of interchange latent in Dylan's and Baez's hotel room covers of Hank Williams, or Dylan's recombining of other songwriters' title phrases—is thereby celebrated in a way that the film overall never effects.

Both times that Dylan is shown talking to his admirers, in one case a group of Liverpool girls and in the other a young, all-male rock band, he ends by speaking for them. With the female fans, the camerawork allows

Donovan listening to Dylan sing.

room for a brief moment of resistance: initially, it feels as if Dylan's direct and friendly manner is formally reflected in the camera's even panning between the girls and Dylan in conversation. However, the first pan actually shows him talking to a girl close by him, even though another girl, located farther from him at the spot where the pan started, has been trying to tell him about her love of his acoustic protest songs. When the nearer girl says that some people think his recent shift from acoustic to electric music means he's becoming "commercialized," the camera stays with Dylan as he corrects her, "Well, you know different, though, right? As long as you know, you don't have to worry about anybody else." The camera pans back to the first girl, now silent and slightly frowning with her head bent down, as Dylan concludes, "All the people take care of themselves."[23] It is as if the camera here is both reinscribing and mildly critiquing Dylan's sentiments, showing Dylan's power—like that of Silverman's male Hollywood heroes—to set the terms of what is said or heard in the film, but also returning to the subdued posture of the unheeded and vicariously chastised girl (briefly held as it is: the camera on her, she turns to laugh with a neighbor).

The same pattern repeats with no implicit critique by Pennebaker's eye when Dylan chats with the anonymous, obscure all-male band that plays only cover versions of his songs. Pennebaker stops panning (or cutting, during pans) back and forth and holds on Dylan's face, not while Dylan is

The "unheard" fan of Dylan's acoustic music.

speaking as the band's equal about musical instruments but when Dylan explains to them that, whether they (as they say) "find it difficult to get people to listen to words" or not, "it's beyond me. . . . If I was booked to play, I just go out there and sing 'em. Not gonna try to get anybody to listen."

The Press

This purported businesslike lack of concern for others' response to his work—in direct opposition to the attitude Silverman finds expected of Hollywood's female singers—erupts from covert to overt hostility in Dylan's "conversations" with a young (male) British "science student" (Terry Ellis) and a middle-aged (male) American reporter from *Time* (Horace Judson).[24] Both of these sequences are very long: while Dylan's songs usually run about a minute, the Ellis interview takes more than eight screen minutes and the *Time* interview about six and a half. Ellis talks with Dylan in a dressing room, where it is striking that Dylan masculinizes his key stage prop, his acoustic guitar, by using it as a weapon on both the audio and video tracks. Dylan strums loudly while Ellis speaks but not while he himself does; and he now and then points the fretboard at Ellis like a gun, an action the camera emphasizes when it pans along (with) it as Bob

Neuwirth tries to hand Ellis a harmonica, another instrument turned into a marker of Ellis's inferiority (he can't play, he protests).[25]

For the majority of the interview, Dylan shifts from side to side in medium shot with his back to a mirror, within which the reporter's reflection is visible, sometimes caught between Dylan's reflected back on one side and his body on the other, sometimes obliterated altogether by Dylan's very mobile (within its very tight limits) form. "Why should I wanna know you?" Dylan asks snottily, and we cut to a close-up of the reflected Ellis, then zoom back out to the usual medium shot of Dylan. Only once does Dylan walk away from his spot, and then he hurries back, exactly in place again for the same symbolically charged shot of the other man's reflection. It seems that he is hitting an actor's mark, of his own or Pennebaker's making, with the intention of being able to construct the reporter's image as (a "fake," "feminine") image.

The film viewer, however, may find him- or herself identifying with the besieged interviewer as Dylan suggests acidly that he "be quiet and just watch and don't say one word," or as Ellis protests that "I'm a person!" and Dylan sneers, "So what? There's a million, thousand, billion—there's so many persons outside." Similarly, the possibility exists to feel very sorry for the quiet, mousy *Time* reporter in a later sequence.[26] Pennebaker pans from a profile shot of Dylan ranting through a class-based analysis of why he doesn't need *Time* to a high-angle, frontal close-up of the shorthaired reporter with bent head and uneasily shifting eyes. "I know more about what you do . . . just by looking, than you'll ever know about me. Ever," Dylan says, yet again destroying another man's authority in order to reinforce his own.

▶ ────────────────────────────────

Conclusion

Working from the notion that documentaries, like Hollywood movies, create places of pleasure for their viewers to occupy, I have demonstrated that *Don't Look Back* performs this function not by supplying "uninterpreted data"—as cinema verité (cl)aimed to do—but by fitting the real actions spontaneously captured by its camera into the same traditional Oedipal framework that structures most fiction films.[27] In Pennebaker's film, Dylan's music is narrativized as and marginalized by capitalist enterprise. The feminine—female bodies and voices, and male bodies and voices in such filmically unconventional masculine postures as self-display, song and speech production for and at others' pleasure, and reciprocity and submission toward others—is displaced by images (and sounds) of Dylan the star

Dylan before the mirror, with Terry Ellis reflected.

figure looking, singing, and speaking to silence fellow singers, fans, and interviewers. The huge amount of documentary detail (bringing into the film the pervasive specter of multiple and unstable subjectivities in Dylan's extratextual songwriting and recording, as much as the film works to re-press it) permits isolated moments of resistance to the very traditional gender representations thus effected: if a viewer's desires do not coincide with those of the heterosexual, male Oedipal trajectory, she or he can find off-hand pleasures in Joan Baez's screeching, Dylan's wiggling like a schoolboy at his typewriter, his rarely shown but sweetly androgynous onstage face. These subversive pleasures, however, are not highlighted within the main body of the film.

Several films follow *Don't Look Back* in a distinct strain of rocku-mentaries (including Dylan's own *Renaldo and Clara, No Nukes, The Last Waltz,* and *Hail! Hail! Rock 'n' Roll*), which, despite their countercultural rhetoric, assert the primacy of male star subjects as all-knowing Lacanian father figures. *Don't Look Back* makes the clearest case study inasmuch as these later films diverge from its virulence in also positioning their star fig-ures as lost sons, matched to an extent by sisters in elegiac, if energetic, song. Whether or not other documentaries of the past thirty years have consistently used music as feminist theorists (mostly of fiction films) such as Silverman and Doane have begun to suggest—that is, to represent the to-be-excluded-from-meaning feminine—these relatively widely distributed and popular rockumentaries do so in a manner all the more striking considering the oppositional political and psychosexual stances supposedly and sometimes actually typical of rock 'n' roll as a culture industry.

◆————————————————————————————————

NOTES

1. Dylan not only seems to spend more time tuning than playing onstage—the guitar needs work before "To Ramona," "The Lonesome Death of Hattie Carroll," and "It's Alright, Ma (I'm Only Bleeding)"—but Pennebaker also portrays his stage act as beset by other technical problems. The microphone fails during "The Times They Are A-Changin'," and Pennebaker holds a shot from the wings where sound technicians scramble around near the camera while Dylan keeps singing almost inaudibly in the background, tiny and half-hidden by curtains. Also, on two occasions Dylan's un-miked voice cannot be heard over his guitar or piano while he prepares for a show backstage. Dylan as stage performer is thus represented as possessing a "lack" that the properly functioning technology is needed to fill. However, Dylan's voice is always perfectly clear, often louder and more legible than others' around him, when he is using his songs or his speech offstage in veiled or open attacks on interlocutors' opinions and skills.

2. In extratextual interviews, Bob Dylan never speaks very fondly of *Don't Look Back*. One writer compliments him on the rough cut of a never-completed 1968 project shot by Pennebaker and edited by Dylan and Howard Alk but admits to never having seen their earlier film collaboration. Dylan says, "It's just as well. The difference between the two would be in the editing—the eye. Mr. Pennebaker's eye put together *Don't Look Back*." Dylan is quoted in John Cohen and Happy Traum, "Conversations with Bob Dylan" (1968), reprinted in Craig McGregor, ed., *Bob Dylan: A Retrospective* (New York: William Morrow, 1972), 265.

3. Laura Mulvey, "Visual Pleasure and Narrative Cinema," in *Narrative, Apparatus, Ideology*, ed. Philip Rosen (New York: Columbia University Press, 1986), 198–209. Mulvey invokes Jacques Lacan's conception of the mirror moment in order to explain the (male) moviegoer's fascination with the (male) movie star: the Lacanian infant's mis-recognizing his own image in the mirror as a "more complete, more perfect" self is echoed by the movie fan's identifying with his on-screen heroes as "ego ideals." The famous problem Mulvey finds is that the Oedipally defined ego ideals or subject-places offered by (fictional) narrative cinema are available only to male-identifying viewers.

4. There is a discussion of Woody Guthrie's advice that Dylan should follow Guthrie's own songwriting method ("I just pick up tunes I heard before and change them around and make them mine"). In Tim Riley, *Hard Rain: A Dylan Commentary* (New York: Vintage Books, 1992), 44.

5. Ellen Willis, "Dylan" (1967), reprinted in McGregor, *Bob Dylan*, 219.

6. All quotes are from Mary Ann Doane, *The Desire to Desire* (Bloomington: Indiana University Press, 1987), 96–97. Carol Flinn traces Western music theorists' long-standing linkage of these terms in "The 'Problem' of Femininity in Theories of Film Music," *Screen* 27, no. 6 (November/December 1986): 57–72.

7. Richard Goldstein, "Don't Look Back," *New York Times*, October 22, 1967, in McGregor, *Dylan*, 208.

8. Under the title credits, Dylan sings a few words from "She Belongs to Me" (not including the film's title phrase) in a soft, strangled voice that is buried by his acoustic guitar as he tunes up backstage.

9. A key example is Dylan's willingness to record songs whose first-person narrators are female ("North Country Blues," which he wrote and recorded in 1964; "Canadee-i-o," a version of which he released in 1992). Although Anglophone folk singers traditionally undertook such gender bending, and female rock singers since the 1970s have also done so, male rock singers almost never sing simply as a woman: though they do evoke conventionally feminine traits, it is usually in the service of a song about male sexuality, not (as in these two Dylan songs) about a female person's economic and emotional deprivation or her high-seas adventure.

10. Kaja Silverman, *The Acoustic Mirror* (Bloomington: Indiana University Press, 1988), 42–71.

11. When tight shots of Dylan are used, elements of framing or bodily deployment (a low angle, a turn to profile) stamp him (in patriarchal cinema's questionable terms) as heroic agent, not just passive object.

12. Dylan does bob his head from side to side,

nod, mouth syllables, and jiggle his near-camera arm and shoulder to Baez's beat, his body in that sense exceeding that of the contemporary "establishment" culture's traditional, buttoned-down entrepreneur. Baez's ringing, perfectly pitched soprano, legible phrasing, and stately, seamless guitar playing also distinguish her as a professional musician — by certain prerock conventions, more accomplished than he.

13. Anthony Scaduto, *Bob Dylan* (New York: Grosset and Dunlap, 1971), 196–97.

14. Riley, *Hard Rain*, 112.

15. Dylan on record and in extratextual interviews never seems shy about acknowledging the father figures, like Williams and Woody Guthrie, on whom his work builds. His persona is in fact founded on his taking an older man's name for his own: Robert Zimmerman changed his name in honor of Dylan Thomas. See Scaduto, *Bob Dylan*, and Riley, *Hard Rain*.

16. Silverman, *The Acoustic Mirror*, 42–71.

17. Stephen Mamber, *Cinema Verite in America* (Cambridge: MIT Press, 1974), 115–31. Mamber credits Drew Associates, the group for which Pennebaker served as cameraman from 1957 to 1963, with "defin[ing] American *cinema verite*" (3).

18. *Don't Look Back* never inscribes into its text the "I is another" quotation from Rimbaud that Dylan is probably paraphrasing. Instead, it encourages the assumption that the Dylan constructed not by the film but by news photographers and writers is the "me" whom he — the film's "I," Dylan the male star figure — "really" is not. While Rimbaud's quotation refers to the "I" within his poems, Dylan's refers to that within his publicity; but Pennebaker is no more willing to let Dylan's "true" self be defined by (the widely varying subjectivities within) his songs than he is to accept other mediamakers' conceptions of it.

19. Margaret Horwitz, "Persona and Spectacle in the Films of Elvis and the Beatles," Ph.D. diss., UCLA, 1990.

20. Dylan mentions Vincent's song in the liner notes on the record sleeves of the 1985 *Biograph* box set released by Columbia Records.

21. "It's All over Now, Baby Blue" is the only song in the film that begins and ends organically, with nothing elided by the film editing. However, Dylan switches certain lines and sings only two verses of the four that are on his recording of the song before strumming a rhythmic figure to conclude his hotel room performance.

22. During the first chorus, sung by Dylan and Donovan, the camera is on Dylan alone: he raises his eyes to frame right/Donovan but then turns to throw one swift glance directly at the camera, before nodding again at Donovan and then turning to smile (as he has before) at someone on his right off-screen. It is as if Dylan is skillfully using codes of screen acting to implicate both the camera and the person(s) offscreen in a joke at Donovan's expense.

23. Dylan does make reference to some of the only other male rock stars who equal him in importance and influence — with whom he has continued to engage in a relationship of reciprocal inspiration into the '90s — when he asks the girls at the end of the sequence, "Is this called Merseyside?" The extratextually informed rock fan cannot help but equate Merseyside and the Mersey sound with the Beatles; nor can she or he fail to recognize that Dylan (is said by rock historians to have) turned electric in 1965 under the Beatles' stimulus. Pennebaker inscribes none of this information into his text, cutting away from Dylan's question almost before the girls have the chance to say yes.

24. Neither name appears in the film or its credits, but Clinton Heylin gives them in *Bob Dylan: Behind the Shades* (New York: Summit Books, 1991), 118.

25. Dylan's exaggerated insistence on himself as a self-sufficient subject and Ellis as a dependent, and hence unimportant, object doubles back on Dylan's own careening and multiple identity, in that Dylan accuses Ellis of wanting friends who look and talk like he does, when it is Neuwirth, Dylan's companion, who talks and looks like Dylan. In 1989, Dylan wrote a bitter and paranoid rejection-of-affection song called "What Was It You Wanted?" — the same question with which he pounds Ellis here. As Tim Riley notes in *Hard Rain*, Dylan habitually addresses fans as (snarled) lovers and vice versa in his songs.

26. The sound recording and mixing make Dylan's speech very clear and loud but the reporter's is indistinct, positioning him more as quiet(ed) watcher than interlocutor.

27. The quoted phrase is Stephen Mamber's description of what cinema verité optimally should present (*Cinema Verite in America*), 183.

GLORIA J. GIBSON

[6] *Identities Unmasked/Empowerment*
Unleashed: The Documentary Style of
Michelle Parkerson

When you open and read something I wrote, the power you
feel from it doesn't come from me, it is the power you own.
:: Audre Lorde, in *A Litany for Survival*

If you're a filmmaker, you love risk. We love the whip of the
wind as we step off a cliff, not knowing where we'll land — on
a cushion or on the jagged rocks below.
:: Michelle Parkerson, in Jacqueline Bobo, *Black Women Film and*
Video Artists

Zora Neale Hurston, Madeline Anderson, Carroll Parrott Blue. These remarkable women took risks and established milestones in the history of
black women's filmmaking. For them, and many others, risk is the only option because complicity and silence are ultimately unacceptable and self-
destructive. Zora Neale Hurston was probably one of the first African
American women to film ethnographic images of her culture.[1] In 1928
with a camera supplied by her benefactor, Mrs. Mason (Charlotte van der
Veer Quick), she ventured to Florida to conduct fieldwork with both audio
recording equipment and a moving picture camera. Her silent film footage
includes children's game songs, men logging, a baptism, and images of
black women. Using anthropological camera techniques and styles of the
period initiated by Franz Boas and Margaret Mead, Hurston framed the
first images that could have served as material for a documentary or an
ethnographic film. What she hoped ultimately to construct with the
footage is still a mystery.[2]

From the 1920s, almost fifty years would pass before another black
woman, Madeline Anderson, once again took up the camera to investigate
the lives of her people. *I Am Somebody* (1970) provides a historical
overview of working-class black women who organize and fight for their

rights. Echoing the rhetorical chant of Jesse Jackson, Anderson's filmic acclamation mirrored the philosophies of the civil rights and women's movements. Themes of self-awareness and identity formation in her work would
coexist and reinforce the emerging racial consciousness swelling in urban
and rural areas across America. The need for empowerment in the black
community was real, and Anderson's film helped continue the momentum
that was initiated in the sixties.

Unfortunately, almost another decade passed before the cinematic
documentation of Carroll Parrott Blue. Once again, the thread of community, racial consciousness, and women's contributions emerges in her early
work. Her documentary *Varnette's World: A Study of a Young Artist*
(1979) assesses the artistic creations of Varnette Honeywood, whose work
was popularized on the television set of *The Bill Cosby Show* in the eighties and commands respect in community and national galleries. Blue has
continued to stress the importance of community in her subsequent films,
including *Conversations with Roy DeCarava, Eyes on the Prize,* and
Nigerian Art—Kindred Spirits.

With the advent of the 1980s several black women came into prominence as documentary filmmakers. Barbara McCullough, Debra Robinson,
Kathe Sandler, Camille Billops, and Jacqueline Shearer, to name just a few,
worked within their communities to discuss and make films about issues
pertaining to racial consciousness, intraracial prejudice, and the historical
contributions of African Americans. Their work sometimes focused on
black women and other times delved into the political and social turmoil of
being black in America. The individual strands of the work, however, can
be braided together to form an important ideological construct of black
feminist filmmaking that addresses oppression, resistance, liberation, and
self-affirmation.

Michelle Parkerson also began making films in the eighties, films that
highlight the identities of black women as performers and social activists.[3]
She documents women working in diverse professions and living in various
social classes. Additionally, her films embrace black women's sexuality. As
such, Parkerson's documentaries serve as a major contributor to the development of a black documentary style that seeks a holistic approach to
African American life.

This essay considers Parkerson's documentary films as they (1) thematically expose the diverse personal and social identities of black women,
identities presented within a framework that simultaneously incorporates
and examines the dynamic impact of black communities; and (2) figure a
"performance framing" structure that privileges the black woman, reinforces her messages, and at once interprets and reinterprets a wide range of

historical and cultural referents. I will argue that both theme and structure advance tenets of black feminism that serve to enlighten and empower.

Parkerson's documentary films to date are *. . . But Then, She's Betty Carter* (1980), *Gotta Make This Journey: Sweet Honey in the Rock* (1983), *Storme: Lady of the Jewel Box* (1987), and *A Litany for Survival: The Life and Work of Audre Lorde* (1995).[4] Each film focuses on the life and work of a black woman. On the one hand, the films are very different from one another because the women subjects represent various life experiences. These women engage in different forms of artistic expression, perform in different styles, reside in different social classes, possess various educational backgrounds, and are of different sexual orientations. On the other hand, these films are similar because they are all about black women who have encountered racist, sexist, and homophobic behaviors. Their artistic expressions, and the aesthetic essence that permeates each film, depict each woman's resistance to oppressive social and cultural forces, as well as her unrelenting desire to unmask and celebrate her identities, thereby promoting personal and community empowerment.

▶───────────────────────────────────────

Black Feminisms and Documentary

Scholars and activists such as bell hooks, Filomina Chioma Steady, Patricia J. Williams, Nellie Y. McKay, Barbara Smith, and Angela Davis, just to name a few, advance theoretical paradigms of black and Third World feminisms, or in the case of Alice Walker, a "womanist" perspective. At the core of their feminisms, which differ to some degree, is the *black woman*. She is the nucleus scholars study in conjunction with her relationships to family, lovers, friends, and communities. She is not relegated to an ancillary comparison to black or white men or white women. Moreover, the black woman is not viewed in isolation. Her empowerment is intensified by drawing dynamic connections to an African diaspora, which also simultaneously links her globally to other women of color.

In her chapter "Theorizing Race, Class and Gender" from the anthology *Theorizing Black Feminisms,* Rose M. Brewer states that black feminist critical thought places black women at the center of the analyses and "by theorizing from the cultural experiences of African American women . . . argue[s] epistemologically that experience is crucial to Black Women's ways of knowing and being in the world."[5] However, the everyday experiences of African American women encompass more than gender. Race and class are intimately intertwined in their identities. Therefore, gender alone is not the central component of most black feminist analyses and interpretations, claims Brewer. Rather, such analyses focus on the "simultaneity of these forces [gender, race, and class] . . . [and are] historically based and holistic" (27).

One additional element, however, also becomes crucial. Homophobia is alive and well in American society, but perhaps even more so in black communities. A holistic approach also considers sexual orientation. Black lesbians confront different experiences from those of heterosexual women, and they suffer an additional form of prejudice and discrimination. Their voices are crucial to understanding the diversity as well as the commonalities of black women's experiences. Black lesbian filmmaker Yvonne Welbon summarizes, "If we are not written about critically, and theorized by the institutional powers that be, we will not be 'legitimized' and will again be effectively rendered invisible by a hegemonic system that claims not to be one."[6] Therefore, a black feminist paradigm additionally interrogates the dialectic of blackness and homosexuality and challenges societally-based gender roles and expectations. Finally, a black feminist perspective, which centers black women, does not erase black men. While black feminist analysis calls into question male domination, it seeks a means by which both genders may coexist in a mutually fulfilling way.

As noted in the beginning of this article, black women have historically used the camera to document their lives and communities. The films unearth and explore actualities in the lives of black women. While documentaries seek to discover "truths," they are, of course, subjective truths. In her analysis of Camille Billops's *Suzanne, Suzanne,* scholar Valerie Smith reminds us that "no documentary is ever 'true' or 'objective'; 'the truth' is inevitably constructed."[7] The construction of black women's documentary privileges women's stories. Very often, the documentary filmmaker's objective is to use "the film medium to convey a new and heightened sense of what *woman* means or can mean in our society—this new sense of female identity being expressed both through the subject's story and through the tangible details of the subject's milieu."[8] Rather than debate the merit of "truths," it is perhaps more beneficial to acknowledge and to be sensitive to black women's memories and histories.

Telling women's untold stories to make previously invisible identities visible *is* Parkerson's goal:

> We tend to turn the camera on ourselves first because our story hasn't been told. It's only been recently that Black women have been making films; thus our story has only recently been told cinematically and realistically. I think there's an intuitive way we approach the subject, which is usually ourselves. There's a lot more humanity in the way we approach Black and female subjects in films and that is because we are that race and that gender.[9]

Given her philosophy to turn the camera inward, how does a scholar begin to discuss and/or theorize about the work of a black woman documentary filmmaker? How does that theory evaluate her work as documentary and as cultural product? The following analysis draws on tenets of a black feminist paradigm to understand and derive meaning from the documentaries of Michelle Parkerson. The goal of the analysis is to understand how elements of theme and structure, as theorized from a black feminist perspective, help unmask identities and unleash a sense of empowerment for black women, and perhaps for other women, regardless of color, class, or sexual orientation.

▶ ——————————————————————————————————

Thematic Prisms of Identity

Michelle Parkerson is a black lesbian writer and filmmaker. Each element of her identity is important because it is an inseparable part of a whole. Just as Parkerson acknowledges her identities, her work interrogates the various identities of black women so audiences might begin to understand the multiplicities of their own identity better. As Audre Lorde affirms, it is only when there is an acknowledgment of the "different ingredients" of one's identity that real empowerment can take place.[10]

One indisputable characteristic of Parkerson's films is that after viewing her documentaries, the audience knows the women featured in the films. Whether it is jazz singer Betty Carter, folk singer Bernice Johnson Reagon of Sweet Honey in the Rock, male impersonator Storme DeLarverie, or poet Audre Lorde, Parkerson builds a bridge from the screen to the audience that unearths the women's personal realities and artistic philosophies. Parkerson demystifies their identities, thereby contributing to their visibility as black women and as artists. This section considers the images and identities in Parkerson's four documentaries. Bernice Johnson Reagon, Storme DeLarverie, and Betty Carter are vocal performers; Lorde is a poet. As performers, they enjoy various degrees of recognition: most viewers probably do not know Storme; some may have heard of Betty Carter and Bernice Reagon; and most black women, certainly those in the academy and lesbian organizations, know Audre Lorde. Despite their levels of cultural popularity, Parkerson's documentaries demonstrate a similar goal of artistic communication intermeshed with social and political commentary.

Parkerson had met the group Sweet Honey in the Rock when she served as production coordinator for their second album. The relationship between filmmaker and subject, therefore, was not a sterile or strictly professional one. Because Parkerson and the women of Sweet Honey had shared aspects of life history resulting in a mutual trust or bond between them, the artists felt comfortable relaying political as well as personal information for the sake of the film. This relationship contributes to the development of a film that unmasks identities to present the total woman, not one who is viewed as simply filmic subject.

Sweet Honey in the Rock is composed of five singers and a deaf interpreter. Parkerson approached the entire membership of Sweet Honey to discuss the film project because it "is truly a collective entity and they approach all their business deals, as well as their music, as a communal experience."[11] For the purposes of this essay, however, only Bernice Johnson Reagon, one of the founding members who is still singing with the group, will be discussed. The interviews with her serve as a case study reflecting the technique the film uses to structure the biographies of all Sweet Honey's members. In fact, to consider Bernice Johnson Reagon is to consider two identities, that of Sweet Honey as well as her own.

Sweet Honey as an ensemble reflects and embodies the cultural history of African Americans. The music selected and their dynamic performance style recount stories from the past and encourage introspection and activism. As Angela Davis explains in her article "Black Women and Music: A Historical Legacy of Struggle," "Any attempt to understand in depth the evolution of women's consciousness within the Black community requires a serious examination of the music which has influenced them—particularly that which they themselves have created."[12]

The women of Sweet Honey created an a cappella ensemble that uses only percussion instruments or percussive sounds, very much in the West African performance tradition. The women's striking visual presence, also an assertion of identity, of natural hairstyles with beads, traditional African jewelry, colorful head wraps, and African cloth, exposes elements of individuality within diasporic cultural icons. Their repertoire includes love songs as well as song texts discussing racism, pollution, apartheid, and religion. However, before a song becomes a part of the repertoire, one member conducts research on the issues expressed in the song, the group discusses the issue, and they reach a consensus as to how it will be approached. Additionally, Sweet Honey encompasses more than meets the eye. In her interview segment Reagon explains that over the years the group has had eight former singers. While those women are no longer performing, in concrete and spiritual ways the presence of the former members remains a vital part of and influence on the ensemble. Sweet Honey's voices encourage audiences to think critically about their history and identity, their struggles and their means of resistance.

Sweet Honey in the Rock, from Michelle Parkerson and Joseph Camp, *Gotta Make This Journey: Sweet Honey in the Rock*. Photo courtesy of Women Make Movies.

In *Gotta Make This Journey,* Reagon is portrayed as African American performer, activist, mother, daughter, mentor, and curator through photos and film footage that capture images of Reagon with her children, mentoring other women musicians, and working at the Smithsonian Institution. Reagon's identities are not seen in isolation, but in relationship to her personal space and various communities.[13] We learn in the film that as an activist, she began singing during the civil rights era in the South. Even before the sixties, Reagon was a performer in a church choir. She speaks of her father's influence and her mother's strength. Through Reagon's voice as commentator and performer, the film encourages the audience to understand her interaction with the community and the place of the black church within the struggle for equality. The struggle did not end with the sixties but continues today. A historical bridge is presented from then until now.

The images of Reagon in her various roles, as powerful as they are, do not tell the entire story. Reagon has received criticism for pursuing so many interests, so many sides of herself. For her there is no single answer to the proverbial question, "What do you want to be when you grow up?" In her interview segment Reagon acknowledges she never listened to people who admonished her to decide what she wanted to be: "I'm always going to be in a state of being. I am what I am at this moment and that's sufficient, and the next minute will have to take care of itself." Reagon's personal testimony embodies the theoretical position of cultural critic Stuart Hall, who posits that cultural identity is a matter of "becoming" as well as of "being."[14]

Similar to Reagon, jazz singer Betty Carter possesses many personal memories of black music history and a sometimes problematic relationship with the music industry. Parkerson films Betty Carter on stage, at home, and with her family. Women's environments are an intimate component of women's identity, functioning as a physical manifestation of and conduit for the emergence of a particular self. On stage Carter is electrifying, dynamic, and engaging. While attending her son's graduation, her nurturing nature as a mother emerges. At home she relaxes in her garden, plays with neighborhood children, arranges music, and discusses her personal philosophy as an artist who has survived many years in the music business.

If Betty Carter had been asked directly whether she considers herself a feminist, she probably would have just acknowledged that she does what she feels is right. But in the filmed interview, it is clear that Carter is a black feminist, and someone who was a *feminist* long before the term was in vogue. Without a doubt, Carter's musical performance and life story as conveyed by the film indicate that she is a woman who has always known how to survive. Her feminism is clearly manifested in the agency of resistance and self-determination consistently registered in her voice (in performance and in spoken contexts). Carter recognizes and claims the histories, voices, and visibility of black performers. Consequently, her voice functions as a critique of patriarchy, race, and gender to question the past, and through performance style and subject matter it contributes to a woman-centered musical/political discourse.

Before she sings "Most Gentlemen Can't Take Love," Carter talks about the difficulty of maintaining a relationship and a career. Her explanation of "independence," as she describes it, sounds suspiciously like a form

Betty Carter, from Michelle Parkson, . . . *But Then, She's Betty Carter.* Photo
courtesy of Women Make Movies.

of feminism: "We didn't call it that; it was just hard work." This discussion
fades into the performance. In her very animated style, Carter sings a song
that reflects a familiar issue to many women who try to juggle a career and a
relationship. Almost inevitably, conflicts and jealousies arise. Black women
performers have historically used musical forms to express not only political
ideologies, but their sometimes turbulent relationships with men. Blues and
jazz ballads have historically functioned as vehicles to confront life on a personal basis as they explore intimate situations in detail. Rather than simply
"crying the blues," many songs provide a forum for women's examination
of self and their transforming consciousness. As Hazel Carby posits, in many
cases the lyrics and song structure represent a cultural icon communicating
sexual empowerment.[15] In this song and others, Carter acknowledges difficulties with men and life in general, but the story does not end there. As an
independent black woman, she continuously seeks strategies and methods to
improve both her professional and personal life.

Parkerson produced the film on Storme DeLarverie for a number of
reasons. As a child she remembers overhearing discussions between her
mother and a friend regarding the Jewel Box Revue. The women expressed
their enjoyment adding, "You couldn't tell the men from the one woman in

the show; you just couldn't figure out who was whom." When her mother closed the door, rather than dissuading Parkerson it piqued her interest. As an adult she remembered the engaging conversations and decided to look at impersonation in depth. As she explained when I interviewed her, "Some people are disturbed by impersonation and it's wonderful because it gets us talking and that helps dispel myths or at least it leaves room for those myths to be shattered and information to be provided. Media is a wonderful tool for that."

To dispel the myths, Parkerson takes the audience inside the history of the Jewel Box in Harlem. Much of that history is presented by Storme, who at sixty-six recounts her experiences as a male impersonator.[16] Storme was the emcee of the Jewel Box Revue, musical arranger, and mother to the chorus, having served previously as arranger and big band singer. Performance photos of her as a male performer throughout the film depict Storme as suave and debonair. With suit and tie, she was a forerunner of male impersonation long before female impersonation was showcased in films like *La Cage aux Folles* or *Torch Song Trilogy*. Even in her sixties, she is beautiful, her voice strong. While she still performs occasionally, her primary occupation is as a bouncer, a type of employment usually associated with men. The film investigates how Storme successfully takes on the persona of a man in regard to her occupation and as an art form, and in the process the film interrogates maleness.

The myths of maleness in *Storme: Lady of the Jewel Box* are stripped away as Storme explains how she becomes a man for her performances: "The boys are adding hips, busts, but I'm taking away." While on one level, she may be taking away to become a male—taking away curves, bust, and to a certain extent, facial perceptions of femaleness—on another level she is "adding to" by challenging the concept of masculinity. What does it mean when a woman becomes a man? In some ways, this is a problematic transition, especially for male viewers. As she changes visually, she calls into question the accompanying societal perceptions and social mores that privilege males. As Joan Nestle, curator of the Lesbian Herstory Archives, states in the film, "Male impersonators are more threatening than female impersonators; they pose a greater puzzle." To pass, to cross over, to cross-dress is to become the trickster; one temporarily possesses the power of the privileged gender or race. It is the audience that is transformed as much as the performer, as Storme adds, "They only see what they wanted to see, they believed what they wanted to believe." Simultaneously, the film privileges the authoritative male image and voice, only to frame them ironically to interrogate the arbitrariness of social valuation.

What do people see when they look at a black woman? Without a

Storme DeLarverie, from Michelle Parkerson, *Storme: The Lady of the Jewel Box.*
Photo courtesy of Women Make Movies.

doubt, they do not see the multiplicity of her identity. Audre Lorde is very
explicit about her identities as black, lesbian, feminist, warrior, poet,
mother. Moreover, she is cognizant of how diversity can be a tool to empower and strengthen. Her academic writings as well as her poetry signal

her as a woman who is politically motivated to unmask and explore identities.

Litany charts the growth of Lorde's personal and political consciousness. Through film footage and photographs, the audience is introduced to Audre Lorde as a child, young woman of nineteen, mother, lover, poet, activist, and teacher. The audience also understands Lorde's heritage as Caribbean via Africa and America. Her identity also reflects the war she wages with growing older and surviving with cancer. Perhaps most of all, the film captures Lorde's sentiments in her poem "Litany for Survival," acknowledging that it is better to speak, to act, to be—after all, "we were never meant to survive."

Much of the film is shot in Lorde's space, her home in the Caribbean. Parkerson integrates footage of her meditating alone at the shoreline, engaging in a heart-to-heart discussion with her daughter, and sharing time with Gloria, her partner. For Lorde, identities exude energy and power available to strengthen oneself and others. Parkerson explains, "One of Audre's operating tenets was to use one's differences and the many different parts of ourselves in the service of other people, the humanity of who we all are and in the environment that sustains us. She was about the use of one's identities as a base of power."[17]

One identity Parkerson explores that is generally neglected is Lorde's sexuality. She was an activist during the civil rights movement, the women's movement, and the gay/lesbian movement. Lorde made a conscious decision to come out because acknowledging her sexual orientation was central to her self-definition. Sensitive portrayals of black women's sexuality are mostly absent from mainstream cinema, and sometimes barely visible in black men's independent cinema. As Jacquie Jones notes, "The imaging of Black sexuality in mainstream film . . . continues to be the most denormalizing factor in the definition of the Black screen character."[18] The imaging of Lorde's sexuality is not included as an ancillary addendum, but as intrinsic to understanding the politicization of identity. Coming out and being out entail risk. As poet Sonia Sanchez explains in the film, "When she [Lorde] came out, she did so all the way. She explained to her children, her students, her friends and colleagues. Lorde's lesbianism was not easy. . . . Some people ran." By bringing visibility and a voice to Lorde's lesbian identity, Parkerson helps the audience to appreciate the bond between Lorde and her partner and hopefully begin to erase negative stereotypes of black lesbian women. The film achieves the normalization of black sexuality by framing an authoritative voice, and by placing sexuality central to identity and other spheres of being (work, artistic production).

Audre Lorde and her daughter, from Ada Gay Griffin and Michelle Parkerson, *A Litany for Survival: The Life and Work of Audre Lorde.* Photo courtesy of Third World Newsreel.

Performance Frames as Filmic Structure

The first section of this essay advances the concept that Parkerson centers the images of black women in her documentaries and thereby exposes the multiplicity of their identities. An appropriate question to also consider is, how are her documentary films structured? Is there a certain means by which the black woman is privileged by the way she is framed? Are there extracommunicative devices incorporated to advance different or additional levels of meaning?

In her article "Bakhtin, Language, and Women's Documentaries," Janice Welsch argues that in general women documentary filmmakers construct their films differently from the way male filmmakers do. For example, they replace the almost ever present traditional voice-over with woman-to-woman interviews and on-screen discussions. In addition, Welsch states, "feminist documentaries use language, including film techniques and verbal exchanges, narrative and visual discourses differently; they address issues of special interest to women and develop the new languages needed to discuss them."[19] Therefore, not only do the documentaries thematically address issues germane to women, within women-centered contexts, but the structures and techniques employed further punctuate and interrogate the feminist discourse.

Scholars theorizing African American documentary have advanced specific ideas about communicative filmic structures. For example, the use of performance as a documentary device has been well scrutinized in the work of Camille Billops and Marlon Riggs. In her analysis of *Finding Christa* by Billops and James Hatch (1991), Valerie Smith states, "The filmmakers interweave dramatic re-enactments, pantomime, and fantasy sequences with archival footage and interviews to question ideologies of motherhood and the adequacy of realist techniques of representation."[20] In *Tongues Untied*, Riggs "interweaves personal narrative with songs, interviews, dance, and performance pieces in an exploration of gay black male subjectivity in contemporary U.S. culture" (62). According to Smith, the results of these documentary structures are crucial. In regard to *Finding Christa,* the techniques "challenge the voyeuristic relationship between viewer and documentary subject," and in *Tongues Untied* they "deconstruct viewers' expectation of linear narrative and the authoritative voice-over" (61, 62).

In "Black Studies, Cultural Studies: Performative Acts," Manthia Diawara outlines a branch of black studies that he terms *performance studies*. Performance studies is compared to "oppression studies," which has "historically done much to uncover and decipher the exclusion of blacks from the inventions, discourses, and emancipatory effects of modernity."[21] The concept of performance, alternatively, "involves an individual or group of people interpreting an existing tradition—reinventing themselves— in front of an audience, or public. . . . such a performance is both political and theoretical" (7). Diawara further explains that performance "draws on existing traditions; represents the actor as occupying a different position in society; and interpellates the audience's response to emerging images of black people" (7).

A performance frame, a performance sequence within the film proper, is a recurring structural device inside documentaries by African Americans and a dominant structural device employed in the work of Michelle Parkerson. This structure sometimes functions to replace or reinforce the voice-over, but it always privileges the image of the black woman. The song/poetic text as well as the kinetic behavior heighten the communicative potential of the film. While this structure may occur at any point throughout the film, in many instances the final performance frame functions as a climactic, culminating device to reiterate not only the performer's message but the overarching themes of the film. While the performances do not necessarily shape the film proper in its entirety, they do tend to effectively mediate between film and interview text. In addition, audience response and interaction may be included in the frame to further underscore cultural identification, interpretation, and meaning.[22] The stage offers a forum for women to share their experiences in a cultural and politicized way. Each documentary film by Michelle Parkerson includes performance frame structures. This section will examine the final performance frame in Parkerson's documentaries.

For African Americans who lived through the civil rights era, music functioned as a significant vehicle to impart a political message and the spiritual essence of the historical past. Certain individuals, like Bernice Johnson Reagon, also personified the movement. The sixties will always conjure images of national turmoil but, hopefully, will also invoke memories of racial harmony. Many religious songs performed traditionally in black churches became theme songs for marches, sit-ins, and demonstrations. Just as some spirituals during nineteenth-century slavery incorporated metaphoric and symbolic meaning, so too did many of the civil rights songs. The vivid memory of thousands of people holding hands and singing "We Shall Overcome" after Martin Luther King's I Have a Dream speech electrified not only a movement, but a transforming country.

The final performance frame in *Gotta Make This Journey* is another familiar civil rights hymn, "Down by the Riverside." The song suggests parallels between the sixties and the present. While conditions are somewhat better in America for people of color, racism is still thriving, only sometimes in new permutations. The song text describes a world where weapons (sword and shield) will no longer be necessary and where one's time will not be occupied by "studying war," thereby resulting in "no more burdens." In the imagined utopian world everyone will be able to "join hands" and celebrate diversity.

The song text invites and encourages a spirit of reexamination and renewal. Furthermore, the placement of the song at the end of the film, its dynamic performance, and the strategically placed cameras combine to communicate an even more powerful message. Reagon sings the lead part, and the audience, already on its feet from the previous number, claps and sings along. As the song unfolds, Reagon's voice becomes more percussive and her body language intensifies. Her performance delivery further dramatizes and interprets the song by her kinesthetic behavior, which includes walking back and forth across the stage, kneeling, and vacillating between the group and the audience. Several cameras and tight shots are utilized to capture the excitement of the performance as affirmation swells from the audience. A camera behind the stage functions to capture the performer-audience dynamic, granting an authoritative voice to both. In addition, close-ups of audience members' face and body language symbolize a collective social consciousness embodying struggle and unity. In this performance frame, Reagon is simultaneously centered as performer, activist, and good-will ambassador. As the song references and symbolizes the historic and contemporary civil rights struggles, Reagon and the audience, in Diawara's words, "reinvent themselves" through the dynamics of performance.

Through performance and dress Storme literally reinvents herself and symbolically disrupts concepts of gender. The culminating performance frame begins with a panning shot capturing New York nightlife. The shot dissolves into Storme on stage at the Trivia! with a female band. The camera also includes the primarily female audience in the periphery as they give Storme an enthusiastic reception before she begins her number. She is dressed in her signature performance attire, a black suit and tie. As she sings, the camera moves closer and closer to focus on Storme. She sings a love song, "There Will Never Be Another You." Her smooth vocal style reflects a big band jazz tradition, unlike the sophisticated, syncopated vocal technique of Betty Carter.

This performance frame reinforces the images shown in photographs and discussed throughout the film. As she sings the love song, the issue of sexual orientation emerges, or in other words, the question of to whom is she singing the love song. Gender identity is foregrounded: is Storme a male singing to a woman, or a woman in drag singing to another woman or to a man? The female band and audience suggest a lesbian identity. At no point in the film does Storme discuss a lesbian identity, and nor does Parkerson. However, the context of the final performance frame and the discussions with Nestle, the Herstory Archives curator, function as mechanisms through which a lesbian subtext is communicated. In her article "Beyond Chiffon," Parkerson states, "*Storme: The Lady of the Jewel Box* is a coming out for me as a Black Lesbian filmmaker because the subject deals overtly with the Gay and Lesbian experience."[23] Paradoxically, while the filmmaker is out and suggests Storme's lesbian identity, an overt discussion never materializes.[24] The performance functions as the culmination of the film, simultaneously interrogating and embracing the image of male impersonator. The closing sequence questions gender difference as the performance engages both her maleness and femaleness. As she concludes the song, the audience provides thunderous applause. Storme bows and a voice-over proclaims, "The day I slow down they'll be sprinkling my ashes to the four winds." As a woman in her sixties, she openly rejects stereotypes of ageism, alludes to a lesbian identity, and thereby exerts authority over her filmic image.

Betty Carter expresses the same sentiment of independence in her final performance frame as she sings "Moving On." In her highly improvisational style, she dramatically and dynamically engages her combo and the audience. Reminiscent of the scat performance style of Ella Fitzgerald, Carter demonstrates her expansive vocal range, rhythmic sophistication, and her vast knowledge of the jazz tradition. The performance further demonstrates the inseparability of Carter the woman from Carter the musician. The fluidity of her vocal style mirrors the sense of freedom and independence conveyed in her interview. The interplay between her voice, her movements, and the combo parallel the polyrhythmic elements of her life.

The actual song text is sparse; only intermittently the words "moving, we're moving on" are heard. The meaning of the song is derived from the complexity of scat, body language, and Carter's interactions with the combo. The intensity of the performance serves as a vehicle for self-expression and power. Jazz, as other forms of black music, historically served to reflect the attitudes and values of the performers and was strategically linked to the resistance movement in black communities. During the sixties as soul music performers like James Brown affirmed their cultural identity, jazz performers like Miles Davis unleashed improvisational styles that mirrored the same need for affirmation and liberation. Likewise, Carter's performance style is free within the confines of improvisational structure, but it is simultaneously cultural and political. Most scholars affirm that "the purpose of black music is not merely to entertain but to articulate the definition, style, movement, and consciousness of the Black cultural community."[25] As a performer and as an individual, Carter expresses her artistic, personal, and communal ideologies, which are not static but constantly "moving on."

Meaning is further derived from how the final performance frame is edited. Parkerson uses montage, colorization, and a voice-over as Carter sings. The montage freezes various images of Carter in energetic poses. But rather than simply display the images as only photographs, Parkerson calls attention to them by coloring them gold, red, and blue. Additionally, in some sequences the photos move to the rhythmic sequence of the performance. Carter's free, improvisational style is also expressed in a voice-over: "Every time I come on stage, I know it's going to be different, it's off the top of my head—that's what jazz is, it's very spontaneous, it reflects that night. The next night I've totally forgotten what I did the night before, so the next night I have to do it again, but that's OK." The audience understands, appreciates, and expects the reinventive nature of jazz. When the performance concludes (for the first time), the audience gives Carter a standing ovation, and the clapping and cheers are thunderous. She in turn respects their acclamation and continues to perform. Once again, the importance of the performance lies not only in its inherent musicality, but in how it signifies and expresses Carter's personal and professional identities.

The excitement of the final performance frames in *Gotta Make This Journey, Storme,* and . . . *But Then, She's Betty Carter* are in stark contrast to the tranquility in Lorde's recitation; all four are expressions of individuality, but in very different ways. In *Litany,* Audre Lorde reads her poem "Today Is Not the Day."[26] The poem functions as a testimony of life as she speaks of her work, children, lover, illness, and impending death.[27] Yet death is not expressed as the Grim Reaper image, dark and ominous, but as feminine. The first line of the poem prelude states, "I can't just sit here staring death in her face." While Lorde realizes her death is imminent, she boldly announces, "today is not the day."

This performance frame is significant for a number of reasons, but perhaps most of all because it challenges our notions about illness and death. In the final frame Lorde appears physically weak. She is very frail; her voice is not as robust as it used to be. She is bald from chemotherapy. While she prolonged her life using homeopathic alternatives combined with medicine, it is evident from her physical appearance that her death is drawing near. Lorde's physical image has deteriorated, but her spirit remains empowered, her personality charismatic.

Aging, illness, and death are not subjects undertaken in many documentary films.[28] As Welsch's research confirms, women's health issues that are "often lost in patriarchally sanctioned silences or co-opted by a male medical establishment, [function as] another reality feminist documentarists have helped articulate and reclaim."[29] The final performance frame challenges the audience to think not only about breast cancer, but about the effect of social constructions of women's bodies. Especially in American society, the aged, wrinkled body or the sick, frail body becomes other, an undesirable, repulsive image.

In her article "Putting Herself in the Picture: Autobiographical Images of Illness and the Body," Jean Dykstra examines the relationship between women's illness, physical transformations resulting from illness, and the generally accepted viewpoint that the body is only a social construction. Examining the autobiographical photographs of several women with cancer, Dykstra shows that because the women

> represent a multiplicity of identities and images of bodies marked in specific ways by gender, disease, and class, they manage to resist the conventions of cultural imperialism that have constructed their identities for them. [The images] force us to reconsider our own assumptions about identity and the body, and the ideologies of gender, illness, and powers that are coded into images of the body.[30]

In much the same way as do the women photographers of Dykstra's focus, Lorde's reading challenges the equation of physical with mental fragility.

The film uses the camera to disrupt the myth of weak body/weak spirit, to demonstrate that at times the relationship between the physical and the spiritual essence may be, in fact, diametrically opposed. As Lorde reads the poem, the camera moves in closer and closer, until an extreme close-up is achieved with only Lorde's face filling the frame. She is centered, in control, and empowered. The poem text, its performance, and the camera movements are intimately intertwined to image Lorde as black, lesbian, feminist, warrior, poet, mother, but also as aged and dying. In acknowledging the multiplicity of her image, she re-creates her self-definition and a renewed sense of empowerment. Lorde encourages other women who live with cancer, who have undergone invasive surgery, or who feel their bodies are "old and unattractive" to maintain some level of control over their bodies and medical treatment. The poem, however, speaks to everyone because while "today is not the day," we ultimately realize that "we were never meant to survive." By using a performance frame at the end of the film Parkerson juxtaposes Lorde's physical image of a dying woman with her indomitable spiritual essence, which exudes a poignancy about life.

Michelle Parkerson possesses an unrelenting passion to stir human consciousness through documentaries that recognize and validate black women's histories and memories. Her visual documents contextualize black women's experience, thereby providing necessary critiques of the development, transition, and constant reformulation of identity. Parkerson is unwavering in unmasking the diversity and, in some cases, the irony in self-identification. Through it all, her goal remains clear—to use cinema, content, and structure to express personal and political implications of black women's identities.

Parkerson's documentaries, as those by many black women filmmakers, allow us to hear the inner voices of women discussing issues that are important to them. What is it like to acknowledge one's love for another woman? Yvonne Welbon's *Sisters in the Life: First Love* (1993) provides a sensitive portrait of two young girls cautiously expressing their feelings for each other. Or what about the impact of skin color and hair texture? Kathe Sandler's *A Question of Color: Color Consciousness in Black America* (1993) allows black men and women to speak openly about the effects of these elements on identity formation. Other documentaries by African American women detail historical accomplishments of black women, such as Ayoka Chenzira's *Syvilla: They Dance to Her Drum* (1979), which charts the accomplishments of dancer Syvilla Fort.

Black women filmmakers also give voice to the lives and accomplishments of black men, as exemplified by Jackie Shearer's powerful documentary *The Massachusetts 54th Colored Infantry*, or Pearl Bowser's *Midnight Ramble*, which surveys the contributions of Oscar Micheaux. Their films also embrace the African diaspora, as exemplified by Carroll Parrott Blue's *Nigerian Art—Kindred Spirits*. The issues explored by black women documentary filmmakers are, and will continue to be, as diverse and captivating as the women themselves. However, a constant remains: their films are a creative means to question dominant culture, to voice opposition to imposed identities and labels, and to celebrate the intersections of one's multiple identities. As a rapidly growing collective body of work, their documentaries can stimulate and empower. Seeing one's image centered rather than marginalized on the silver screen can potentially engage African Americans in constructive dialogues to "recall, recollect," and tap into the real power that comes from within.

◆──

NOTES

I dedicate this article to the memory of Dr. Ronald R. Smith, my teacher, mentor, and friend.

1. According to Henry T. Sampson's *Blacks in Black and White: A Source Book on Black Films*, 2d ed. (Metuchen, N.J.: Scarecrow Press, 1995), Peter P. Jones released a documentary film, "For the Honor of the 8th Illinois, USA," in September 1914. It showcased the dress parade of the Eighth Illinois black regiment being reviewed by the governor of Illinois. Sampson also credits C. E. Hawk with shooting and touring ethnographic footage at the turn of the century. Interestingly, he does not mention Hurston's footage.

2. Hurston's footage is now in the Library of Congress. *The African American Mosaic: A Library of Congress Resource Guide for the Study of Black History and Culture*, ed. Deborah Newman Ham (Washington: U.S. Congress, 1993), states that Hurston "shot ten rolls of motion pictures in the southern United States in 1927–1929 to document logging, children's games and dances, a baptism, a baseball crowd, a barbeque, and Kossula, last of the Takkoi slaves" (203). Additional footage that was either shot or supervised by Hurston during the 1940s in South Carolina is also available at the Library of Congress.

3. Parkerson has completed a futuristic science fiction film titled *Odds and Ends* (1993) and has also published a volume of fiction and poetry titled *Waiting Room* (1984). Most recently, she completed several performance collaborations including "DIVAS!" and "Women of Substance." She has also finished two feature-length screenplays and continues to teach at Temple University. Her first love remains writing, which she describes as the "connective tissue" because it is at the core of all her creativity.

4. *Litany* was initially a film project of Ada Griffin. Parkerson was brought in as director.

5. Rose M. Brewer, "Theorizing Race, Class and Gender: The New Scholarship of Black Feminist Intellectuals and Black Women's Labor," in *Theorizing Black Feminisms: The Visionary Pragmatism of Black Women*, ed. Stanlie M. James and Abena P. A. Busia (New York: Routledge, 1993), 15.

6. Yvonne Welbon, "Black Lesbian Film and Video Art: Feminism Studies, Performance Studies," *P Form: A Journal of Interdisciplinary and Performance Art* 35 (Spring 1995): 12.

7. Valerie Smith, "Telling Family Secrets: Narrative and Ideology in *Suzanne, Suzanne* by Camille Billops and James V. Hatch," in *Multiple Voices in Feminist Film Criticism*, ed. Diane Carson, Linda Dittmar, and Janice R.

Welsch (Minneapolis: University of Minnesota Press, 1994), 382.

8. Julia Lesage, "The Political Aesthetics of the Feminist Documentary Film," in *Issues in Feminist Film Criticism*, ed. Patricia Erens (Bloomington: Indiana University Press, 1990), 229.

9. Parkerson is quoted in Gloria J. Gibson, "Moving Pictures to Move People: Michelle Parkerson *Is* the Eye of the Storm," *Black Film Review* 3, no. 3 (Summer 1987): 16.

10. Audre Lorde, "Age, Race, Class, and Sex: Women Redefining Difference," in *Out There: Marginalization and Contemporary Cultures*, ed. Russell Ferguson et al. (New York: Museum of Contemporary Art, 1990), 285.

11. Gibson, "Moving Pictures," 17.

12. Angela Davis, "Black Women and Music: A Historical Legacy of Struggle," in *Wild Women in the Whirlwind: Afra-American Culture and the Contemporary Literary Renaissance*, ed. Joanne M. Braxton and Andree Nicola McLaughlin (New Brunswick, N.J.: Rutgers University Press, 1990), 3.

13. Reagon also briefly mentions how she met her husband. In general, discussion of Reagon and the other women's personal relationships and sexual orientations is conspicuously absent from the film. In my interview with Parkerson she mentioned that before *Storme*, "the sexual preference subtext in my films was not part of what ended up on the screen." The targeted PBS general audience for *Gotta Make This Journey* may have had an impact on how sexuality was handled. Furthermore, when *Litany* aired on PBS, it was a part of the POV series, which tends to include more "controversial" material.

14. Stuart Hall, "Cultural Identity and Cinematic Representation," *Framework* 36 (1989): 70.

15. See Hazel Carby, "It Jus Be's Dat Way Sometime: The Sexual Politics of Women's Blues," *Radical America* 20, no. 4 (1986): 21.

16. Storme is of mixed racial heritage, her father white, her mother black. There is little discussion of race in the film.

17. Gloria J. Gibson, "Michelle Parkerson: A Visionary Risk Taker," in *Black Women Film and Video Artists*, ed. Jacqueline Bobo (New York: Routledge, 1998), 181, 182.

18. Jacquie Jones, "The Construction of Black Sexuality," in *Black American Cinema*, ed. Manthia Diawara (New York: Routledge, 1993), 247.

19. Janice R. Welsch, "Bakhtin, Language, and

Women's Documentaries," in *Multiple Voices in Feminist Film Criticism*, 165.

20. Valerie Smith, "The Documentary Impulse in Contemporary African-American Film," in *Black Popular Culture: A Project by Michele Wallace*, ed. Gina Dent (Seattle: Bay Press, 1992), 61.

21. Manthia Diawara, "Black Studies, Cultural Studies: Performative Acts," *Afterimage* (October 1992): 7.

22. Yvonne Welbon's article "Black Lesbian Film and Video Art" discusses the applicability of performance studies, combined with feminist studies to theorize black lesbian film.

23. Michelle Parkerson, "Beyond Chiffon," *Black/Out: The Magazine of the National Coalition of Black Lesbians and Gays* 1, no. 3 (1987): 22.

24. In a phone conversation with me, Michelle Parkerson explained that during the filming of *Storme* she never openly admitted she was a lesbian, although many of her personal activities pointed to it. For example, she is very active in an organization for older lesbians and gays. However, since Storme never openly expressed her sexuality, Parkerson subsequently felt reluctant to discuss it in the film overtly.

25. Geneva Gay, "Expressive Ethos of Afro-American Culture," in *Expressively Black: The Cultural Basis of Ethnic Identity* (New York: Praeger, 1987), 12.

26. For the poem text see *The Marvelous Arithmetics of Distance: Poems 1987–1992* (New York: W. W. Norton, 1993), 57–58.

27. Audre Lorde died of cancer in 1992.

28. The following films tackle issues of age or illness: Camille Billops, *Older Women in Love*, which examines the stereotypes and societal myths associated with older women who choose younger male lovers; Ngozi Onwurah's semiautobiographical *Body Beautiful* juxtaposes the "beautiful" image of a young model with the "unattractive" image of her older mother who has undergone a radical mastectomy; Marlon Riggs's last film *Black Is . . . Black Ain't* (1995), which uses his impending death as a means to tackle issues of identity and representation.

29. Welsch, "Bakhtin, Language, and Women's Documentaries," 170.

30. Jean Dykstra, "Putting Herself in the Picture: Autobiographical Images of Illness and the Body," *Afterimage* (September/October 1995): 20.

ANN KANEKO

[7] *Cross-Cultural Filmmaking, Japanese Style*

In the fall of 1994, I embarked on the research for *Overstay,* a documentary about foreign migrant workers (*gaikokujin dekasegi rodosha*) in Japan. I had lived in Japan between 1986 and 1990, and when I returned to visit in 1991, I noticed a marked difference in the ethnic makeup of Tokyo. Over the past fifteen years, young men and women from other parts of Asia and Latin America have been flocking to Japan, the new Asian promised land. With the rapid growth of the Japanese economy, a shift to the service sector, and a labor shortage during the late '80s, known as the bubble years, fewer Japanese are willing to do manual labor—the "3K" work, that is, *kitsui* (hard), *kitanai* (dirty), and *kiken* (dangerous). Attracted by the strong yen, foreigners, often highly educated, have relocated to fill this labor need, working for substandard wages in urban and suburban Japan.[1]

I had the good fortune of receiving a Japan Foundation Artist's Fellowship, which enabled me to finance the first leg of the project in exorbitantly expensive Japan. I began this project with great trepidation since I was not current on the situation in Japan and was uncertain as to what I would find. Would I successfully find subjects who were part of this marginalized segment of Japanese society? Would they be willing to participate in a project like this one? Would I be able to communicate with them? Would I find a focus for a film? How would I be viewed by these *gaijin*? Except for spending time during the summer of 1991 with a young Iranian man, who spoke very little English or Japanese and who was most intent on seducing me, I had had little contact with the people on whom I intended to focus. Having been away from Japan, most of my knowledge of these new foreign residents came through TV news clips and articles I had read during 1991. I also knew that the tide of foreigners that had caused so much excitement in the early '90s was waning, and with the recession immigration authorities were cracking down. Many people had already left voluntarily or been deported.

I realize my anxieties were natural, given the ever-unfolding process of documentary filmmaking, yet somehow the stakes seemed higher since I was making a film in a foreign land about foreign people. Although I am fluent in Japanese and had already lived in Japan for more than three years, I knew that making a film would truly test my ability to artfully navigate social codes and cultural boundaries.

Given the array of circumstances I had to deal with, making the film was a very enriching and challenging process. I have tried to reflect on that process, shedding light on some of the choices I made and the circumstances under which I made them. As I comment on this film, I should mention that it is still a work-in-progress, so some of my textual analysis may pertain to sequences that may not be included in the finished film. Writing about the film while I am still editing it has made me reflect on some of the initial ideas that I had when I came to the project, and it has been an interesting process looking at how those ideas have evolved and how I have had to rethink their application in the film.

▶————————————————————————————

How I Am Perceived

Although I may feel like the same person in Japan, I am not who I am in Los Angeles. In a country where categories are particularly important, I am a *gaijin* and a woman—which mean different things from what it does here. In the United States, I cannot escape the features of my face that make me "Japanese" American, but I am still an American and another granddaughter of yet another immigrant. Like most Americans, I am a hyphenate. In Japan, where the notion of being a *gaijin*, which literally means outsider, is quite strong, I am *nikkei amerika-jin*, which means the American of Japanese ancestry, but a *gaijin*, nonetheless. In a land that claims homogeneity, I am a curiosity. At least it is an excuse for my accent and brash behavior, which would certainly not be acceptable if I were a "real" Japanese woman. Of course, these labels exist everywhere whether one pays heed to them or not. However, because I was making a documentary, I was more self-conscious about them; the relationships I formed with subjects would be based on how they perceived me.

In Japan, I was neither Japanese nor a member of the recently arrived immigrant communities, neither a member of the dominant group nor the underrepresented group. But I like to think of myself as being sympathetic to the new group of foreign workers in Japan because I had experienced

Hikari Yagi, Ann Kaneko, and William Higa (left to right). Photo courtesy of the filmmaker.

what it was to be a *gaijin* in Japan and because I am a grandchild of immigrants who had left the very country that was now hosting immigrants. This was my personal connection. Since I knew only one of my grandparents, I can only imagine their experiences coming to the United States years ago. But despite the passing of almost a century, somehow I felt I could get to know my grandparents through these new residents in Japan. I believed that there were common elements in the immigrant experience that I could learn about from these contemporary immigrants, bringing me closer to my grandparents. However, I was also well aware of the fact that my experience was quite different from theirs. I was visiting from a wealthy country and had chosen to come to Japan, not to work but to pursue intellectual interests. Did these considerations matter in Japan? I did not know and was curious to find some answers.

▶

Choosing Subjects and Establishing Trust

In order to meet possible subjects and get a sense of their working and living conditions in Japan, I began by contacting various nongovernmental organizations (NGOs) working to better the conditions of foreigners.

Making these contacts also facilitated getting the proper introductions, so important in Japan, to other organizations and individuals. Most of the organizations were known for serving specific ethnic or religious communities, but there is much crossover in Japan because of the small sizes of immigrant communities. Consequently, all foreigners are lumped into one big *gaijin* pot, and I found more intermingling among immigrants than I do in the United States, for example, where the individual communities are large and autonomous. Despite the vast differences in culture and language between South Americans and South Asians, Southeast Asians and East Asians, they all find a common bond in being *gaijin* in Japan.

As I met more and more people and got a sense of what stories I wanted to tell, I had to choose subjects for my film. I was looking for variations on the Japan experience. Aside from looking for different nationalities and genders, I was seeking a range of personalities and people, faced with different challenges. The subjects all have certain common attributes: they are young, have come to Japan to work and make money, and have overstayed their visas.

Under any circumstances, it is difficult to find people to be in a film because most people are not willing subjects. In fact, it might be safe to say that this reticence is even stronger among Asians because they are usually more concerned with saving face. They want to keep up appearances and often hide what they really think. Asians do not want to bad-mouth anyone and are less willing or interested in telling all or confessing than are Americans, especially if television talk shows are any indication.

The situation of my subjects is even touchier because they could face deportation if someone squeals on them. I have heard of other documentary filmmakers who conduct elaborate searches, similar to casting sessions, videotaping their prospective subjects and testing out how they express themselves and come across on camera. But given the undocumented status of my subjects, I did not feel as if this was an appropriate method; by pulling out a camera, I would probably scare away most of my prospects before asking even one question. Instead, I took a more intuitive approach. I knew that to ask people to let me into their lives to film them I had to get along with them and earn their trust. Consequently, I spent many hours hanging out with the four sets of subjects in my film. I never "tested" them on camera before I filmed them. I thought that if I found something compelling about them or their stories this would be reflected in the film. I was rewarded with amazing access to the worlds of my subjects, and I am not sure whether another approach would have granted me the same success.

As I edit the film, though, I realize the limitations of my methodology

From Ann Kaneko's *Overstay*, this is the office where illegal immigrants are detained and where some voluntarily surrender to go home. Photo courtesy of the filmmaker.

in choosing my subjects because there are those who are more articulate and who have more on-camera presence than others. By virtue of their personalities, the more outgoing subjects speak more freely and clearly in front of the camera, but they have different concerns from those of the more reticent ones. For example, Ashraf, a Pakistani subject who is one of the shyer characters in the film and who clearly has the most difficulty speaking in front of the camera, is in some ways more endearing and sincere because he is able to see the positive side to his experiences. He is less critical and negative about his life in Japan and provides a good balance to some of the others. Sally, a Filipina working as a hostess in Japan, is also quite shy and does not clearly articulate details about her work because she is ashamed of it. I hope that her modesty and ambiguity do not have the opposite effect of making her appear to be a prostitute.

Because I had found all of my subjects through NGOs staffed by people with whom they already had existing relationships, I think they tended to trust me more from the outset. They knew where my sympathies lay, and in general I found they were less guarded than their vulnerable position might suggest they would or should be. Although I was from the United States, being a *gaijin* worked in my favor because in their eyes I was still a *gaijin*, who knew somewhere else and was able to see beyond the idiosyncrasies of Japanese society. Perhaps in the same way that Japanese viewed me as a curiosity, they also were amused by the Japanese-looking woman who didn't act like a Japanese. Because of the prevalence of contracted second- and third-generation Japanese Brazilians and Japanese Peruvians working alongside other immigrant workers at factories and clubs, there was also a kind of understanding of how someone like me could exist. They could identify with me because they identified with the Japanese Brazilians and Japanese Peruvians who possess visas in Japan but are very much in the same class and vulnerable position as undocumented workers. These elements gave us a basis for forming a kind of camaraderie. And precisely because they had been living in Japan, they understood that there were those whom one could trust and those whom one could not trust regardless of nationality.

When one engages with the lives of his or her subjects, one wants to be sure that making the documentary is somehow a reciprocal arrangement. Documenting the situation of exploited individuals, I would be very distressed if power imbalances in their situation were mirrored in our filmmaker-subject relationship. Because they were giving to me, I felt it was extremely important that I somehow be able to reciprocate. This was not necessarily material or monetary. They were not interested in material remuneration, because we were friends and they would have been highly insulted had I tried to pay them. Among non-Westerners, money plays a different role and does not always settle accounts so definitively between people as it does in the West. Familial and fraternal ties are much more important than material payment, and because I was their friend and their guest, on many occasions, I had difficulty paying for anything—very different from in the West. The fact that I am a woman also made a big difference to my male subjects who came from more traditional societies, where women virtually never pay. Since I am roughly the same age as they are, in this respect also we were equals. Perhaps if I were older and richer and wielded more authority in society, this relationship might have been different. However, since I'm not and don't have any power and they knew it, they expected no more than my friendship and trust.

In light of the pressures of Japanese life and the isolation in Japanese society, I think it was enough that they could find a friend in me who was always willing to listen. I found that they were emotionally needy, and it served both of us if they confided and I listened. They had few close Japanese friends, if any at all, and their closest friends were other immigrants like themselves who spoke the same language. In the process of shooting the film, I spent hours listening to their trials and tribulations, clowning around with them, and becoming their friend. We became quite close. Because my subjects all work long hours in Japan (often ten to twelve hours a day and usually six days a week), their leisure time is limited, which also cut down the available time I could spend with them. Consequently, their free time is very special, which privileged the time we did spend together. Indeed, I remember Mujahid mentioning at a Japanese language speech contest how everyone in Pakistan always has time to *gup shup*, or "shoot the shit," as they say in America. At the end of his speech, he emphasized how Japanese are always working and never spend their time hanging out. Clearly, it was a pleasant change for him and the others to have someone so willing to *gup shup* with in a familiar Pakistani manner.

I can imagine how it helped them to share their frustrations with a disinterested party like me. Because of the closeness of the community, gossip also abounds, and that can make immigrants more hesitant to share anything personal with people from the same country. Consequently, they are trapped in a difficult situation, dependent on community members, against whom they also compete for the same jobs and resources and with whom they share an insular existence. This was true for Sally. I could tell that she felt extreme pressure from her Filipina coworkers, who did not empathize with her distaste for the work. Because the work (entertaining and serving drinks to male clients and occasionally being felt up by them) was degrading, it seemed that all of the women had become anesthetized to the unsavory aspects of the job. But Sally could not forget how the rest of society viewed her work or accept her everyday world as being the norm. Therefore, she could not confide in the other Filipina women, who spoke her language and knew best what she was experiencing, without being criticized and castigated for being so attached to her self-respect. Perhaps Sally's gripes cut too close to home. The other Filipina hostesses only consoled her by telling her that it was "just a job" and that it did not reflect on her real character. They advised her to go along with the game since she was in Japan to make money. In time, Sally resigned herself to these attitudes, and I began hearing her echo the advice she was given.

Although I would eventually like to show this film to the Japanese audiences for whom it is the most directly relevant, I anticipate that it will be shown in the United States and possibly Europe before it reaches Japan. This is better for my subjects. They were willing to participate in the project because they knew that I would be returning to the United States to edit and show the film there. If I were producing the piece for Japanese television, I am sure they would have had reservations about participating and would not have spoken as openly. Everyone in the film talks candidly about remaining in Japan illegally, and I do not want to jeopardize anyone's ability to stay there. Although it is unlikely that immigration officials would actually track down people in my film, I do not intend to show the film publicly in Japan until all of the main participants have returned home or have normalized their status.

Sally Abolos, a Filipina woman who worked as a hostess at an Ito club. Photo courtesy of the filmmaker.

Gender Roles

Gender played a distinct role in how I interacted with my subjects. Since there were both men and women in my film (all heterosexual, as I am), I was able to see how being a woman influenced my relationships with people of both genders. With the women, I was like a friend or a confidante. For the men, I was a love prospect, and my sexuality seemed to work as an important bait.

More than half of the foreigners working in Japan are men. In the South American, Chinese, Korean, Thai, and Filipino communities, there are almost equal numbers of women. However, in the Islamic communities, there are practically no women. Especially among these men, arranged marriages are commonplace, and one of the main attractions of Japan is the prospect of a love relationship. The reputation of Japan's sex industry has also spread to the rest of Asia, and many men had come in search of "free sex." Consequently, there are many young foreign men on the prowl in Japan, and the loneliness of their situation also prompts them to seek women for companionship. Although things have changed radically in Japan and intermarrying is not frowned on as it had been in the past, it is only with American or European white men that it is considered moderately acceptable. It is very much an issue influenced by class and status, and often dark-skinned Asian men, who come from Third World countries, have a difficult time finding a date unless they are willing to pay for it.

Under these circumstances, it is no wonder that I was so desirable. The reputation of American women that preceded me, thanks to Hollywood and the desirability of my citizenship, also made me a good catch. This certainly made meeting *gaijin* men easier, but it complicated the filmmaking process, to say the least. What in my mind was research for my film was for them a sexual advance. It did not take me long to realize that I was being misunderstood, and that because of the peculiarities of the circumstances of my subjects I would probably have similar experiences with whatever male subjects I chose. At one point, I seriously considered purchasing a fake wedding band to ward off some of the would-be suitors, but I decided that I could not lie to people from whom I expected the truth.

Although I was up front with everyone that I was not interested in them as they hoped, I realize that the possibility of a potential relationship seemed to have a great deal of power over them. It was obvious that they would volunteer information in hopes of getting my approval. Thus my sexuality did contribute to making me more privileged. No matter how strongly I tried to avoid manipulating them, I must acknowledge that I was taking advantage of the power I as a woman had over them in order to make them participate in my film. I do not explicitly portray these dynamics in the film, but Nasir and Mujahid, two Pakistani subjects, very candidly express their expectations of finding "girls everywhere" in Japan. Clearly, this is one of their primary concerns, so I leave room for speculation about how they view me.

With so many suitors, it was important for me to feel "safe," meaning that I was at least physically in spaces that would discourage my subjects from having the wrong idea about our relationship. I originally chose three Pakistani men living together because they also lived with a Brazilian woman when I met them. Since they lived with a woman, it made the environment safer for me, and I thought their living arrangement was unique to their experience in Japan. I avoided being with any of them alone so as not to mislead them. I never imagined that they could all get the wrong impression.

In jest, I often tell people that I could easily have made a woman's version of *Sherman's March* (1986). In that documentary, Ross McElwee sets out to make a film about General William Tecumseh Sherman's unforgettable Civil War march—destroying, pillaging, and killing—through the South, but the film becomes the story of his pursuit of romantic love after a breakup with a girlfriend. As he roams the South, he uses his camera as a means of approaching women and questioning them about love, romance,

Ashraf, Nasir, and Mujahid in their two-room flat. Photo courtesy of the filmmaker.

and his own failures. Almost all of his friends and family members seem intent on rescuing him from bachelorhood and become his matchmakers, introducing him to various versions of his "ideal mate." He gets tips about his appearance and how to be passionate. He follows the advice of his sister who suggests that his camera may be a way for him to approach women, since it is at least "a conversation piece."

A few parallels can be drawn between our experiences: McElwee was actively pursuing his women subjects in order to explore questions that he had about love, and his film was a vehicle for him to do so. People seemed to think that his marriage was long overdue. In my case, I was actively seeking out immigrant men to hear their stories for my film, and people seemed to think I was a very eligible young woman. A major difference was, of course, that McElwee was in search of a lover, and I was not. Whereas McElwee was chasing potential lovers, potential lovers were chasing me.

For both of us, our films were a means to meet and engage with people, and it is interesting to consider to what degree sexuality and the camera influenced these relationships. Each of my encounters seems to have been interpreted as a sexual advance, and my subjects were clearly more in-terested in me than in the camera. For Hassan, the Iranian participant in my film, I think that at times the film became an excuse for him to meet with me, but it was ultimately I he was interested in and not the film. This does not seem to be the case for McElwee. Some people around him who thought he should be getting married looked at the camera as a tool for courtship, but I am not sure to what degree all of the women were interested in him, and they were probably more interested in him with his camera than in him without it. In McElwee's case, women either tolerated him because of the camera or were attracted to the attention it lavished on them.

Traditionally, we are conditioned to believe that in male-female courtship, the man pursues the more passive female, waiting to be swept off her feet. According to McElwee's friend, Charlene, whom we meet in *Sherman's March*, this element of passion is precisely what he lacks and what is responsible for his failure with women. Even though I might have initiated conversation with my male subjects, they were compelled to pursue me, as is traditionally the case. Having come from the West where courtship is played out differently and dealing mainly with men who come from more traditional societies, I realize that these factors also have a great influence over our relationships. However, I wonder what my experience would have been if I were a man. I would most certainly not have had the same problems avoiding male suitors (or perhaps I would have if they were gay), but I wonder if my experience would have been the same with female subjects. If I were gay or vice versa, how would the dynamic have been different? Would they have interpreted any approach as a sexual advance, especially in a more traditional society? Or would I have had mixed results, as McElwee did? A heterosexual Japanese male photographer friend who was doing a project on the Iranian community in Japan mentioned his experiences with several gay Iranian men. It seems that some of his interactions paralleled my own and that the filming process became a means for his subjects to become closer to him.

Yet I also believe that because of isolation and limited contact with women, my subjects in Japan were more likely to share things with me as they would have done with their sisters or mothers and not just with their prospective girlfriends. One of the men in my film had broken up with his Japanese girlfriend, and he told me very frankly that there were certain subjects that were easier to talk about with women than with men. He couldn't see himself having the same conversations with his male friends that he had with me. Certainly, I will never know whether this was just a ploy to gain my sympathy or whether he was, indeed, being sincere. But I would like to give him the benefit of the doubt. Obviously, nothing was ever very clear-cut, and continuously hearing so many personal stories, I felt as though I were living a soap opera.

With the women, I did not have these complications; I was just a friend. Sally was isolated by her peers and her clients, so she really had no

Hiroaki Yamamoto (soundman), Ashraf (Sunny), Mujahid, Nasir, and Ann Kaneko (left to right). Photo courtesy of the filmmaker.

one to turn to. Unless she became intimate with one of her clients, it is highly unlikely that any of them would be very sympathetic or expect her to play anything but the part of the stereotypic, flirtatious, subservient Filipina woman she was hired to be. As I mentioned earlier, the other Filipina women did not empathize with her distaste for the work, and even her cousin, a former hostess, was not sympathetic. Consequently, even though I do not speak Tagalog, and her English and Japanese are not great, I sensed that she was able to confide in me more than anyone else in Japan.

There is an independently made student documentary called *Tsuma wa fuiripina* (My Wife Is Filipina), which gained notice in 1993 and 1994. In the film, Yasunori Terada, the Japanese filmmaker, focuses on his relationship with his wife, Teresa, a hostess he met at a Filipina pub. The filmmaker has said that he made the film to counter the media's sterotypes of Filipina women. However, the film furthers these stereotypes more than it destroys them. The perspective is mainly that of the husband/filmmaker, whereas the wife is quite guarded about sharing her views of Japan. Moreover, Terada never deals with his own obsession with Filipina women or the question of why Japanese men, in general, have commodified Filipina women. The film is problematic, and Terada seems to be oblivious to the politics of his relationship with Teresa. He is the more dominant figure in both their personal and social relationships, and this power imbalance is paralleled on camera.

In contrast, the filmmaker-subject relationship is much more explicit in *The Good Woman of Bangkok* (1995), Dennis O'Rourke's film about a Thai prostitute in Bangkok. To begin the film, O'Rourke "purchases" Aoi's services for 500 baht or about US $20 and directs her to tell the story of how she began doing this work, her trials and tribulations. O'Rourke is obviously sympathetic to his subject, yet as a viewer one cannot help but question his complicity in the system that exploits these women. He slyly acknowledges that he was no different from the five thousand other men who had come to Bangkok, only instead of purchasing Aoi's sexual services, he has "bought" her to make a film. Of course, on one level this is no different from a producer paying an actress to act in a film, but because O'Rourke's is a documentary film and Aoi a prostitute, it does raise questions about the propriety of his actions.

Hence, O'Rourke's film is in a sense about his manipulation of the client-prostitute relationship, and what makes it interesting is the filmmaker's involvement and acknowledgment of this manipulation. He includes in the film Aoi's comment about how she cannot help but distrust him and his motives and how her friends tell her that she is being manipulated. I wonder to what extent she is acting on her own accord or whether she is again pleasing her client as she must please her other male clients. She appears to be quite candid and sincere when she talks about her life, but she speaks less to the filmmaker than to herself. She uses the opportunity to confess that she has "never expressed this except to my tears." She is the most articulate and open when she speaks in Thai, which the filmmaker presumably doesn't understand.

The inequities in the relationship are vast, and she acknowledges that he will get far more benefit from her participation in the project than she will. She accepts these inequities but views the arrangement as being reciprocal. He no doubt is tipping her generously and promises to buy her a rice farm, which he does under the condition that she stop prostituting herself. In the epilogue of the film, he states that he returned to Bangkok a year later only to find her working in a sleazy massage parlor. She said that it was her fate to work there.

O'Rourke's blatant manipulation of the situation makes his film distasteful to me, but I credit his clarity in portraying the sordid, twisted nature of these relationships between men and female prostitutes. He also gives a voice to Aoi in his film at the same time as acknowledging his having taken advantage of her. In both Terada's and O'Rourke's films, their relationships with the women subjects are very much influenced by the inherent power inequities of being men interacting and filming women who are exploited by men. When a woman filmmaker directs women subjects, the power configuration is intrinsically different.

It is interesting to note that O'Rourke spends a great deal of screen time showing the women, including Aoi, at work, writhing, naked and disinterestedly, to disco music. In my film, you never see Sally at the club interacting with the men and serving drinks. I show her cleaning the club and getting ready to go to work, but I do not show her hostessing. I went to the club with two other crew members to try to record sound and take some stills, but I recorded nothing of her. Knowing that most club owners are aligned with the *yakuza,* the Japanese mafia, I did not want to risk her losing her job or cause her trouble. Perhaps viewers will wish for scenes explicitly showing her hostess work, but I will probably leave it to the imagination unless I insert footage from another club.

Sally is obviously embarrassed about her job, so I don't think she would have liked to have been documented working in a club. Since it wasn't a possibility, I never really broached the subject, but it does pose interesting questions about respecting the wishes of the subject and fulfilling the needs of the filmmaker. If there had been a possibility to film her and I had asked her for permission, she may not have objected, but it would have been because she could not say no to a friend. In Asia, one is more sensitive to those unspoken boundaries of what is acceptable, and getting her participation already seemed like so much. I don't imagine that Aoi liked to be filmed working either, but she probably never had a choice. There is an interesting moment when O'Rourke films her in bed, wrapped in a towel. She is extremely vulnerable and covers her legs with a sheet, which would suggest that she felt uncomfortable.

▶ ━━

Language

When I first went to Japan and was learning the language, many Japanese asked me whether I thought in English or Japanese. They think the true measure of fluency is whether a person actually thinks in the other language instead of going through a mental translation process. It is inconceivable to them that one may be able to formulate thoughts in a nonnative language. It is true that when one begins to learn a language, that translation process is very conscious. However, as a person becomes more fluent, one learns to express him- or herself with his or her limited vocabulary, and it simply becomes too slow to go back to the referential native language. People learn how to break down their ideas into simpler terms that they can express with the vocabulary they possess.

Language is also closely tied to culture so that our perception of the world is molded by the language we speak. When we speak another language, we adopt a little of that culture as well as bring a little of our own to the way we express ourselves in the foreign tongue. In short, we are constantly working through many filters when we communicate in other languages, and especially when we are communicating with people who are engaging in the same process.

For precisely these reasons, language played a pivotal role in our relationships. Although all of my subjects are conversational and spoke Japanese well enough to get along in daily life and at work, none of them is completely fluent in the language or can read or write it. All had learned the language by ear, using it at work. Those who do speak the language more fluently had been employed at the same small company for many years and have had long-term relationships with their employers and coworkers, which is very important in learning and practicing a language. They also watch many hours of television, which gives them immense amounts of language comprehension practice.

All of us are nonnative Japanese speakers, yet for the most part our common language is Japanese (or English, in the case of Sally). Except for the Peruvian couple, I was unable to communicate with any of them in their native language, and even in Spanish my limitations probably created more misunderstandings than I realized. Because of these language complications, there were always challenges in expressing ideas in terms we could both understand. Since I read and write Japanese, I occasionally used vocabulary that they did not know. They often did not comprehend what I could communicate by telephone to fluent Japanese or English speakers. They needed not only to hear my words but to see my body language. Consequently, I had to meet face-to-face with them regularly to keep abreast of their lives.

In documentaries, interviews are often one of the main ways of conveying information, and having people speak in English (if it is for an English-speaking audience) is usually most desirable. Although I hope that one of the audiences for this film will be English speaking, I do not want to cater solely to this audience. Actually, the main languages in the film are Japanese, Urdu, Spanish, Farsi, and Tagalog, and English only plays a minor role. For English-speaking audiences, almost the entire film will be subtitled. However, because of the number of languages in the film, I would also like to de-emphasize the spoken word and let actions speak more loudly.

I had to choose what language to conduct interviews in. Since I communicated with them in Japanese, Japanese would have been a logical choice. A Japanese audience also would be able to understand more of the film without subtitles. Yet I decided to let them speak in their native languages because I thought they would be more comfortable and could express themselves freely and fully. Moreover, I wanted the audience to hear another language and experience what the immigrants must have experienced when they first came to Japan (although the experience is necessarily different, since the audience will be reading subtitles). This transfers the power of expression to them so that they do not need to compromise their expression in a foreign tongue.

Another choice I made was not to show the translation process explicitly or involve viewers in it as *Shoah* (1985) so brilliantly did. When Claude Lanzmann revisits the Polish sites of the Holocaust and interviews local residents who recall the past, he speaks through an interpreter who translates what the Polish speakers say to Lanzmann. Lanzmann then asks his questions in French, and these questions are again translated. For an English-speaking audience only the French is subtitled, and the viewer must experience the laborious translation process along with Lanzmann.

My system had its limitations. My subjects roughly translated what they had said, but I was not able to understand exactly what they were saying at that moment. Consequently, I could not question them on specific points nor could I engage them in a conversation to make them more at ease. Essentially, I could not direct them. This was a gamble because I am supposed to be in control of the film. I was relinquishing my power in favor of giving them more control over their expression. I decided to take this risk and trust what I was understanding through a second language and a different set of codes about who they are and what they were saying.

For Hassan, this system was clearly limited. Having had his dialogue translated, I have found that he was extremely incoherent. He continually interrupts himself, trying desperately to sound educated and never finding the appropriate words. Fortunately with editing, I have made him coherent, but I cannot show him on camera because of the numerous cuts. He also comes across as being very dry. Because he was nervous, I am not sure what I could have done at the time of the interview. If I could speak Farsi, however, I might have been able to coach him better, making him more at ease. Still, if Hassan had been asked to speak Japanese, he would not have been able to convey his more complex intellectual ideas. I don't think I had ever clearly understood what he was trying to say about working in Japan until I read his translated interviews. For all of his incoherence in Farsi, his limitations in Japanese clearly curtailed his ability to express himself, which would have made interviewing him in Japanese a less viable option. As I edit and see how the film will take shape and how my viewers will experience it, I realize that language defines context. Since I know them in Japanese, I almost feel as though I do not know them when they speak in their own languages. Hearing them struggle in Japanese creates a filter that makes me more sympathetic to them regardless of the limitations of their remarks or the ambiguity of what they mean. When they speak in their own language, this filter is gone, and they become outsiders to Japan and that experience.

I have been editing the film with various friends who speak the native languages of my subjects. From this process, I get a glimpse of how the subjects are viewed by their countrymen and women. Nothing that they say surprises me, but the speed at which my friends are able to pick up on their personality types does amaze me. What took me a few meetings to figure out is immediately apparent to those who understand the spoken languages. Class, educational background, and personality are instantly revealed. Realizing that my audience will not necessarily speak the languages in the film, I am concerned about how apparent these details will be to them or whether they will be lost. The translations in the subtitles will be very important and will probably be one of the only ways to convey the subtle differences in the usage of language as well as when subjects are speaking in Japanese or in their native language.

▶

Interviews

One of the great challenges of interviewing is getting people to reveal what they think and feel on camera. Often, subjects are willing to share many of their insecurities and problems with you off-camera, but the minute the camera goes on, they fall silent. The person they "hated" a minute ago becomes someone with whom they "share differences." It is amazing how diplomatic they become. In contrast, some subjects get so caught up in performing for the camera or using it as a means of catharsis, that what they say does not ring true. For dramatic purposes, the juicy, candid, "true" confession is the payoff we look for, but it is rare that people are so revealing. Getting to know someone is to know the sum of his or her actions and words. Because of time constraints, interviews, voice-over, and narration are technically more efficient means of revealing and structuring information. For the most part, they are taken at face value—what is said is the "truth." However, people often tell a director what they believe she or he wants to hear and not what they really think or feel. Therefore, there are variations of this truth, and it often lies somewhere in the gray area between what they say, what they do, and what they think given the circumstances.

I decided to try to incorporate these considerations into my interviews. I thought it was important to conduct more formal interviews with my subjects filmed in 16 mm so that I could hear their responses to questions that they had had time to consider. Because the crew, lights, and equipment required by film as opposed to video are more intimidating, my subjects were stiffer. They were different from the people with whom I normally interacted. This is contrary to what one wants to achieve in interviews; one hopes that the subjects will feel comfortable with the camera, revealing their innermost secrets. Still, I could tell by their body language that they were expressing the same ideas, in much more serious terms, that I usually heard them joke about.

However, since I wasn't exactly sure what they were saying (because of the language difference) or how it was coming across in that language, I felt uneasy; on the other hand, I actually liked the tension that was created and hoped that the seriousness and deliberateness of their responses would balance the informal videocamera footage that I had also been shooting all along. Now that I have had their interviews translated, I find many of their responses quite truthful at the same time as being diplomatic. Since I know them well, I realize what is not being said, and that there is almost more conveyed in their silences and in the ways they have expressed their responses. I am trying to use these punctuated silences and their truncated responses to speak more about what is not being said, almost the antithesis of the way interviews are normally used in documentary. Yet I am uncertain as to whether I will be able to convey such subtleties in limited time and space.

One example of this occurred when I asked Sally on camera whether she feels close to her cousin. In fact, I already knew the answer: that although she got along with her cousin, she did not feel particularly close to her. She avoided my question, saving face, choosing not to say anything bad about her cousin. In the film interview, I also asked Sally if she could marry a Japanese, and she emphatically answered that she could never marry a Japanese. In this indirect way, she expressed what she thinks about her cousin, who married a Japanese client.

Two of my other subjects also have difficulty with their status, since one of them is really a political refugee and the other is in Japan using an alias. I asked Hikari to comment on her countrymen and women who must purchase false documents to work in Japan and I asked Hassan to give his views on political exiles. Although Hikari never admits that she did the same, nor does Hassan admit to his situation, discerning viewers will probably understand that they are talking about themselves.

My video interview with Sally took place upon her arrival at the apartment where she would be living to work at a new hostessing job in Yokohama. She talks about her utter hatred of the job and the men, and so on. I do not ask questions, and she volunteers her comments between cigarette puffs. The silences are long and tense. She is very different on film as opposed to tape, and she contradicts herself in the two interviews. On video, she says that she has never told her family about what she does, and on film she says that she keeps no secrets from her family. I realize that her responses could vary because they were shot at different times and that she might have disclosed more to her family after the first video interview and before the film interview. I find this contradiction very interesting and meaningful. It points to a truth that is dependent on the circumstances. I am sure she has reservations sharing her experiences with her family because she does not want them to be ashamed of her, but at the same time in the formal interview she does not want to say that she has kept secrets from her family, particularly her mother. Because it will possibly confuse the audience, however, I will probably not include this in the film.

With my two women subjects, I conducted video interviews as well as film interviews, and I found them to be much more candid and animated on video. Without a film crew and the large 16-mm film camera, they felt much more at ease. In each case, it was just the two of us and we were speaking the same language. These interviews were more like conversations.

With the Pakistani guys, I did a group session but did not conduct any individual interviews on video. Although the intimacy might have made for some juicier footage, I didn't feel safe alone with them and a camera. It is interesting to note that both McElwee and O'Rourke documented without a crew (although O'Rourke credits a few Thai soundpeople at the end). It is probably the intimacy of filming one-on-one that made their films more candid.

▶

The Video Diary

When I began researching this project, I was determined to not overshoot. Contrary to the notion that docs are made entirely in the cutting room, I believe that many decisions and choices are made in the conceptualization of a project. I wanted to limit the amount of footage that I shot so that I would spend less time cutting. Therefore, I gave myself plenty of time to think about what it was that I wanted to say and how I wanted to say it. However, after I had chosen my subjects, I realized that their lives evolved, whether I shot them or not, and that in this form of documentary, there are no second shooting chances. Consequently, I began shooting a kind of video diary. I was not always sure what would be useful or pertinent until later, so I shot everything I found vaguely interesting. I accumulated hours of footage and realized that it was not going to be easy to limit it. In retrospect, I realize that it would have been ideal to do the interviews earlier so that I could structure the piece around them, but I was forced to work backward because of the constraints on the availability of 16 mm equipment.

Shooting on Hi-8 was ideal for many reasons. It was cheap, small, and portable. Since I did not have the luxury of a crew, I could carry my equipment on public transportation (albeit with very sore shoulders) and shoot on my own. People also tend to be more accustomed to camcorders, which allowed me to be less obtrusive, and they saw the camera as my appendage. Subjects were much less self-conscious in front of a small camera. As a home videographer, I found that my camera was often a participant in the activities—people ignored the camera and would carry on conversations with me despite its presence. This is different from the way most news photography is shot because the cameraperson is supposed to be invisible.

As a cameraperson, I realized that my footage was very messy. Things were not very well composed. There tended to be a lot of movement because of the light weight of the camera, and I was not very disciplined in the way I shot many events because I was not sure what I would be using. Sound quality also was not good because I did not have a separate soundperson. I depended heavily on the videocamera's ability to shoot under low-light conditions, and much of the footage is not flattering or well lit. Usually, I could hardly concentrate on shooting when I was as much a part of what was happening as the people in my film. But I trusted that the footage would be read as a reflection of the way things unfolded and of my relationships with the subjects and would not be judged technically. In fact, my subjects do appear very natural and unaware of the camera, and in many ways, this footage is more candid and revealing.

Since video does not compare in resolution to film, I aim to use the juxtaposition of the two types of footage to help make a formal distinction. Hopefully, this will resonate with the distinction between how people behave and what they do or don't reveal in front of each respective camera. I am experimenting with intercutting between film interviews and video verité scenes to contrast the formality and the candidness of the two shooting formats. Although Hassan is stiff in his interview, he becomes much more likeable and human when you see him singing karaoke horribly. Nasir and Mujahid talk about going out with women, and then you see them going to a festival with their Japanese girlfriends. My intent to visually show these differences may not be so apparent in the final cut, because much of the interview material has become a voice-over with the video footage, but hopefully the spirit of juxtaposing these formal statements with their actions will still exist.

▶ ──

Honne To Tatemae

When Western students of Japanese culture are indoctrinated with its mysteriousness, they are introduced to the concept of *honne to tatemae*. This term describes the contradiction between *honne*, which is what people really think or feel, and *tatemae*, which is the rule and what people say. It literally means "to stand in front." Of course, these kinds of contradictions exist to varying degrees everywhere. But in the so-called land of ambiguity, this contradiction has become integral to the culture. The notion is fairly universal throughout Asia, and Westerners generally find this behavior to be perplexing and duplicitous.

I am trying to apply this idea of *honne to tatemae* to my film on several levels: in terms of public policy and practice, what Japanese society openly says but really thinks about *gaijin*; and what the subjects, themselves, say and do. As in the United States so in Japan the contradictions between public policy and practice are great, especially with regard to an issue like immigration. For example, the police are part of the Ministry of Justice and are supposed to enforce immigration policy, but they rarely deport anyone unless they suspect him or her of some other crime. Although all of my subjects (except William, Hikari's *nikkei* Peruvian boyfriend) are without visas and therefore at risk of deportation, they boldly lie about their status to police and apologize profusely if stopped, and they get away with it every time. The police generally know who is overstaying his or her visa, but if the person acts like a "good" *gaijin*, is respectful, and does not embarrass the police, they will let him or her go.

Probably the clearest example in my film of this kind of contradiction between public policy and its application is when the police appear at a gathering of Iranians (most of whom have no visa) to report a hit-and-run accident in which one of them was involved. The police arrive at a raucous (by Japanese standards) party of Iranians to discuss the matter with the legal owners of the vehicle, the Japanese employers of two Iranian brothers. When the Iranians begin dancing, the police leave, surprisingly, without checking anyone's documentation. Everyone knew that only a week before, more than twenty people had been deported from that town, and that officially the police are supposed to report anyone who is undocumented to the immigration authorities. But the policy is not enforced, and although immigration officials do not publicly condone people overstaying their visas, in practice the *honne,* the real message, is that undocumented foreigners can stay as long as they don't cause problems. The police in Japan generally do not want to function as fetching boys for immigration authorities, because they must maintain relations with the community. Arresting and deporting foreign employees would be unpopular with small-sector businesses that employ foreigners. Instead, the police closely survey where all foreigners work and dwell so that they can quickly locate a person if someone falls out of line.

I also juxtapose Sunny's *honne* to that of his employer's. (Sunny is Ashraf's nickname.) Sunny's boss frankly tells me that he is sure that Sunny has suffered a great deal but that Sunny would never complain to him because Sunny would not want to jeopardize his position by making waves. His boss acknowledges the boundaries of their relationship and knows that Sunny is silenced because of his vulnerable position in Japanese society, that is, having no visa. In Sunny's interview, he admits that he has had to struggle over the years but that he has had no choice, because he was there to make money. Consequently, both acknowledge the difficulty of Sunny's position in Japan, a fact that neither would admit to each other face-to-face.

Mujahid contradicts what he says about his boss, so we get a sense of his relationship to his employers. In his formal interview on film, Mujahid states how his employer has always treated him well and how the company is like a family. However, in a discussion I had with Nasir, Sunny, and him after the police had been chasing them in a nerve-racking case of mistaken identity, Mujahid reveals his *honne:* he emphasizes how his employer doesn't do anything when there are problems with immigration and expresses his disillusionment with his boss when he failed to visit a Pakistani coworker who had been detained for deportation.

In the above situation I was shooting video, so I hope that the tell-it-like-it-is video footage (*honne*) juxtaposed against the film footage (*tatemae*) formally underscores the differences between *honne* and *tatemae.* Another example of this contradiction occurs in Sally's interview, when she smiles and says that her work is just a job and that Japanese men are no worse than men anywhere else. Yet in the video interview, it is clear from her body language how much she detests her work as a hostess and her resentment for having to serve Japanese men. In another instance, Hikari states in her interview how insincere Japanese people are, but on video we see her interacting with a close, older Japanese woman friend.

Hence, my film is fraught with contradictions—immigrants contradicting themselves, contradicting what other foreigners say, what Japanese say about them; Japanese authorities contradicting their own policies; Japanese contradicting foreigners, and so on. I do not mean to show how duplicitous and chaotic Japanese society is but, rather, how complex this system of boundaries and protocols can be.

As I continue to view and shoot documentary films directed by other people, I always wonder about the intrinsic differences between my process and theirs. Recently, I was shooting second-unit camera on a documentary pilot about relationships. I had been hired because they wanted a mixed-gender crew. They anticipated that women subjects would not feel comfortable baring their souls to a room full of men. (How perceptive!) We interviewed ten couples. The director was a man, and I kept thinking what different questions I would ask and how differently I would ask them. The sound mixer (who also was a man) made a passing remark about how the director should be a woman because "she would know how to ask the questions better." I don't completely agree with him, because it also depends on the individual, but I couldn't help thinking that most women I know would have had a very different approach to interviewing the couples. The director's concept of relationships seemed almost foreign to me, and his questions heavily reflected his own biases. He did not seem very respectful of certain emotional boundaries. For example, he kept asking a reforming alcoholic, "Why not drink if you hide it so well?" and to the lover of someone with AIDS, "What will you do when he is dead?" He was extremely manipulative psychologically, almost abusing his power as filmmaker/therapist "Dr. Love." For me, this experience confirmed that there definitely are differences in a feminist approach to documentary.

When I began this project, I never anticipated dealing with the range of issues and situations that I have been forced to face. In a sense, the finished film will be only a glance at the many bridges that had to be crossed in order to produce this film. Since the film still has not been completed, I leave viewers the chance to speculate on how the ideas outlined above have been incorporated into the film and what significance they have in the context of the finished piece. It has been very challenging to write about the process of making a film that is still evolving. I have found that editing is about making clear the application of the ideas that had been incubating throughout the process of making the film, and because of the pure mechanics of conveying information to audiences sometimes these ideas must be abandoned. However, I hope that my experiences with the twists and turns caused by culture, language, and the gender of filmmakers and subjects provide insight and an opportunity to reflect on documentary process in comparative contexts.

NOTE

1. I might note that the economic climate in Japan has changed since the bulk of this essay was written. Japan's economy has been reeling from the effects of the Asian economic crisis, and the situation of foreign migrant workers has also changed. Now they are more vulnerable than ever and the gravity of their experiences is even more apparent, making many of the issues that this film raises extremely relevant.

III Going Back (with a Camera): Gender, Nation, and Documentary Returns

Going Back (with a Camera): Gender, Nation, and Documentary Returns

This section of the book is called "Going Back (with a Camera): Gender, Nation, and Documentary Returns" to accentuate the recursive subject matter of each of the essays in the section. These essays are about documentaries of return, documentaries that figure (whether as presence or absence) the desire for and/or the horror of homeland. Whether explicitly exilic or only "legacylic," as in the case of Shauna Beharry's video remembrance of her dead mother's sari (discussed by Laura Marks), these films are about women at a distance from the past and from a point of familial origin, which in most of these documentaries is non-European.

"Return, Transference, and the Constructedness of Experience in German/Turkish Documentary" by Silvia Kratzer-Juilfs introduces a wider audience to several documentaries about Turkish women exiles who immigrated to Germany to better their lives but who long for a homeland idealized by nostalgic memory. Islamic precepts about pilgrimage and travel are brought in to illuminate Kratzer-Juilfs's point that personal history and homeland are just as much a function of constructed memory as is identity itself. Anahid Kassabian and David Kazanjian would presumably concur when it comes to Armenia as a "misty figure of 'the homeland.'" In "Melancholic Memories and Manic Politics: Feminism, Documentary, and the Armenian Diaspora," Kassabian and Kazanjian discuss the documentary *An Armenian Journey* with reference to the historical context of the Armenian genocide and diaspora and with reference, as mentioned in our introduction, to Freudian notions of mourning and melancholia. The film, the authors argue, represents its female heroine's "work of mourning as a feminized melancholic affect, which is, in turn, productive of a masculinist manic politics." In "Fetishes and Fossils: Notes on Documentary and Materiality," Laura Marks uses fetishes and fossils as "two kinds of objects that condense cryptic histories within themselves" to get at documentary's transnational encoding effect. Shauna Beharry's *Seeing Is Believing,* Marks argues, exemplifies how documentary has the potential to reintroduce nonaudiovisual sense knowledge as a form of feminist knowing.

Deborah Lefkowitz's contribution to this section is an essay on her film *Intervals of Silence: Being Jewish in Germany.* Since the film originated when the Jewish and American-born Lefkowitz traveled to the hometown of her gentile, German-born husband, the essay abides in the "intervals" between the United States and Germany, World War II and the 1980s, Jew and gentile, female and male, silence and speech, departure and return, and history, given and withheld.[1] In her essay in this volume, "On Silence and Other Disruptions," Lefkowitz identifies a connection among Jewish discourses on the unspeakability of the Holocaust, the consistent communicative silence of some of the film's female interviewees, and the experimental formal pattern of the film.

Gender, nation, and the past, these essays argue, are conceptual terms whose constructedness may be suggested by certain filmmaking practices and/or illuminated by documentary analyses such as those presented in this section.

◆——

NOTE

1. The publication of Trinh Minh-ha's essay ("The Totalizing Quest of Meaning," in *Theorizing Documentary,* ed. Michael Renov [New York: Routledge, 1993], 90–107) from which Renov derived his meditation on the "interval" ("Introduction: The Truth about Non-fiction," in *Theorizing Documentary*), coincided with the release of Lefkowitz's film. We take the simultaneous use of the term as unintentional but apt.

SILVIA KRATZER-JUILFS

[8] *Return, Transference, and the Constructedness of Experience in German/Turkish Documentary Film*

The desire for a return to the past, a past that seems to be forever inaccessible and lost, figures prominently in many transnational and exile documentaries. And in fact, for some exiles, lost homes and former identities may not be entirely out of reach, as in the case of the temporary or voluntary exile or expatriate who may decide to repatriate. Still, the problem of return is fraught with complications and uncertainties; it is, in many senses, impossible. Using the examples of four recent German/Turkish documentaries about and (except for one film) by Turkish exiles in Germany, this essay will examine the intricate connections that can abide in representations of history, memory, return, and identity construction.

Each of the documentary films discussed here embarks on an itinerary that investigates an individual's memories of a former homeland and the implications of these memories for the exile's identity. But the films' probing of the past does not limit itself to the revelation of truths about the past reached by making the subjects' past experiences visible or by figuring identity as entirely stable. Instead, as this essay will argue, these films also point to the fluid and constructed nature of subjectivity. That is, in these documentaries the reemergence of the past and of past memories effects a rearranging of seemingly fixed subjectivities in favor of the realization of the fluid and fluctuating constructedness of all subjectivities.

In this way, these documentaries depart from more conventional documentary approaches to individual subjectivity and to the past. Traditional documentaries have often been concerned either with recording the present as events unfold before the camera, or with tracing the past to recover events long forgotten or suppressed by mainstream history. Even documentaries that trace counterhistories or set history in a new light by offering a new or overlooked perspective on a past event meticulously piece together evidence that bears witness to the veracity of the documentary account of the past. The evidence is gathered in a linear or a mosaic narrative that gives the spectator a new view of a previously unknown (or little known) truth about a period in time and its subjects' past reality. The documentaries examined here do present such a chronology of their subjects' unknown or overlooked pasts and histories, but these chronologies are simultaneously displaced by an archaeology of experience itself.

In her essay "Remembering Women," Mary Ann Doane points out that the past holds prominent explanatory value in the fields of historiography and psychoanalysis but figures very differently in each of them: "In historiography, the past is static, inert . . . in effect, more knowable." In psychoanalysis, by contrast, the past plays an aggressive role: "It returns, it haunts, it sometimes dominates the present." Where historiography "effects a 'clean break' between the past and the present," spatially isolating it (in museums, archives), "the past and the present" in psychoanalysis "are fully imbricated, locked in a struggle where 'forgetting' is no longer a simple accident but a defensive weapon aimed at the past."[1] Michel de Certeau, whose work Doane discusses, proposes a "renewal" of historiography through its encounter with psychoanalysis and its insistence on the interconnections between past and present. From a reverse perspective, Doane calls for a look at "psychoanalysis as a form of historiographical endeavor" (91). Extrapolating from these speculations, I propose that historiography traces the past along a linear, *horizontal* history while psychoanalysis conceptualizes a past that washes constantly into the present, leaving us with a perspective of history that one might call a *vertical* investigation of history.

Following this logic, I suggest that these documentaries by women filmmakers about the exile of Turkish women intertwine varying aspects of a historiographic past and a psychoanalytic one. In this respect they form a basis for realizing Doane's and to some extent de Certeau's respective projects of designating points of convergence and correspondence between historiography and psychoanalysis. These documentaries move along and lead down *both* axes: a horizontal, chronological history, and, written in and over it, a vertical one that guides the spectator along a temporality where past and present are no longer strictly separated but instead intersect and are superimposed. In this way, their double trajectories carry out, in documentary form, what Doane is calling for methodologically in her essay.

Each of the documentaries deals with an exile's return home, whether this is a little known and imagined home or a lost home long yearned for in nostalgic preoccupation. It is a return to the homeland of Turkish women who live as expatriates or *Gastarbeiterinnen* (guest workers) in Germany. The returns of the women may be imagined, fantasized, or actual, but in all cases they involve journeys across both time and space. Imagined returns occur when Turkish women remember their past homes or when relatives relate stories of the family's past. Actual returns involve physical travel across space to a geographical (rather than a remembered) home. The journeys across these dimensions, though, are frequently out of step or out of sync with each other. In the imagined return, the home exists exactly as it is remembered or as it is constructed in memory. By contrast, in the physical return the remembered home is often canceled out, since the visit transports the women to the actual space of the home, but the women no longer feel at home in the environment, and it is not as they remember.

In Muslim cultures the notions of home and return carry meanings that are altogether different from those of the Western context and culture, and they tend to be more complexly structured. In an Islamic context, the ideas of home and return, exile and migration, are never stable concepts but are always in flux. Muslim doctrine encourages certain forms of travel: the pilgrimage to Mecca, visits to local shrines, travel in search of knowledge, and the obligation to migrate from lands where the practice of Islam is constrained to those where in principle no such constraints exist.[2] Thus, migration and travel in Muslim cultures tend to be regarded as necessary and painful pilgrimages that separate one from a lost home but fulfill a religious obligation. As Dale Eikelman and James Piscatori explain in *Muslim Travellers,*

> All these [journeys] involve physical movement but also spiritual and temporal movement at the same time. One sense of *hijra* (emigration) is the movement of the soul from a state of corruption to one of purity, from unhappiness to happiness in this world and from damnation to salvation in the next. (xii)

Moreover, labor migration, as in the case of the Turkish guest workers in Germany, is from a religious standpoint just as much an obligation as is the travel to Mecca and Medina for the Muslim believer.

The obligation to travel is not divorced, however, from a desire to return home. "The very idea of travel," write Eikelman and Piscatori, "however much it may project the believer across spiritual space and time, and overcome barriers of gender and politics, cannot be separated from the anticipation of return to home" (xiii). Yet the concept of home is never one of a fixed place; it is neither geographically nor imaginatively constant or stable. Home can be the place of departure or "a new place of settlement as in the case of the Turkish *Gastarbeiter* in Germany" (xiii). Home and exile, point of departure, travel, arrival, and return are never stable ideas nor even polar opposites as in Western thought. Instead, "what seems clear is that travel and home—motion and place—constitute *one* process, and that in travelling beyond one's local time and space, one enters a mythical realm where home, the 'fixed point' of departure and return, is re-imagined and further travel inspired" (xiii). Thus, much as the memory of the past is a construction in psychoanalytic theory, home and return are constructions in Islamic thought.

Die Kuemmeltuerkin Geht (*Melek Leaves*; Germany, 1985) by the film-maker Janine Meerapfel investigates both the dynamics of memory and the constructions of home. The film records the departure from Germany of Melek Tez, a thirty-eight-year-old Turkish woman who has lived and worked for fourteen years as a *Gastarbeiter* in menial jobs in Germany. The preparations for Melek's return to her native Istanbul are interlaced with her introspections about her years in Germany.

In the film, Melek's identity is most visibly pronounced and powerfully apparent while she is still in Germany, where almost all of the documentary's scenes take place. Here she acts out different facets of her exile identity and the identity construction, that of the *Kuemmeltuerkin* (a racial slur in German), that is forced on her and that she rejects. Throughout the documentary, Melek ironically refers to herself as the *Kuemmeltuerkin*, subverting the racist discourse by maintaining an ironic distance from the negative stereotype.[3] Another form of Melek's resistance is her manner of dress. Melek usually dresses in Western clothing as do many Turkish women in Germany and in Turkey. One day, however, she dresses up with the head-scarf worn by traditional Turkish Muslim women, which act we take to be a dress game played to reverse and empty stereotypical notions of Turkish female identity. Such games with the identity of the *Kuemmeltuerkin* appear to be a form of defense for Melek against ethnic prejudice. Melek constructs her own identity as a counter identity, rejecting the derogatory connotations attached to the *Kuemmeltuerkin* name and appearance and reappropriating these marks of identity in a different context. In Germany she maintains an ironic distance and rebels against an imposed identity, defining and creating her own identity and individuality directed against racist and nationalistic stereotypes, male domination, and social and economic oppression.

In this film, as in others of its subgroup, various levels of return intersect. Melek's actual return to Turkey, though, is not documented in the film: we do not see her image in the footage of Turkey that does appear at the end. As Meerapfel depicts it, Melek's return occurs mainly in her anticipation and imagination of being back home in Turkey. In voice-over narration, she relates her fantasy of home to us as we watch her difficult preparations for her return. There, she is convinced, she will finally find the happiness and a sense of a wholeness that is denied her in Germany. At the end of the film Meerapfel reads in voice-over a letter she has received from Melek written in Istanbul. Melek relates her happiness that Turkey turned out to be just the way she had imagined it in every respect. However, while we hear Melek's letter, the film's selection and ordering of images and sounds of empty passageways in Istanbul, the streets where Melek now lives, appear on the screen, suggesting Meerapfel's skepticism of Melek's claim to be content at home there. Whereas in Germany, Melek's image and voice are present in almost every frame, in Turkey Melek is absent from the images, her voice silent. Thus, the void that Melek's absence leaves on the visual and audio level of the documentary introduces a doubt about Melek's claim finally to have found her identity as a Turkish woman, to have found "home."

The film's perspective seems to be that in Turkey Melek unquestioningly accepts her identity as that of a Turkish woman and this causes the loss of her individuality. She is portrayed as being subsumed under the fantasy of a unitary or uniform Turkish identity. Moreover, since the film opens with the voices of different Turkish returnees from Germany to Turkey lamenting their fate as former economic exiles, we are prepared to be suspicious of Melek's claims of contentment. The Turkish returnees of the opening explain that they have remained homeless even after their return from Germany to Turkey. Some feel they have lost their home instead of having won a second one during their years in Germany; others acknowledge that they don't know anymore if they are Turks or Germans; they don't know if they will ever feel at home again; they mourn their future, which they feel has been stolen from them. In this context, the almost defiant claims of Melek's letter appear as claims she only wishes were true. We are left suspecting that far from having won back the Turkish identity that Melek was longing for, her identity is split like those of the other returnees. Thus, through its structure the documentary leads us subtly to disregard Melek's own assertion in favor of that of the filmmaker's skepticism.

The film's skepticism does seem justified to a certain degree because Melek's letter is so thoroughly glowing. Melek indicates that she has closed the book on her past in Germany and found happiness in Turkey. She never once mentions any reverse culture shock or any problems she may have encountered adjusting to her new way of life. It seems doubtful that the problems that motivated Melek to leave Turkey to begin with—for one, the discontentment with life for a single woman in Turkey that Melek alludes to at the beginning of the film—have simply vanished during the years of her absence. And if they have vanished, one would like to know something about how and why and in what ways life in Turkey has changed so radically for her. Because of this absence of a rationale for Melek's contentment, her assurances of the fulfillment of her dreams appear utopian.

Whereas in Germany Melek freely offers and displays the various facets of her identity, her strengths, and her weaknesses, in Turkey she seems to shield and conceal her identity. We are led to suspect that Melek may be defending her happiness back in Turkey because of a lack of options. Her silence on the subject reads as a refusal to acknowledge that a perfect home cannot be captured, and that her utopian wish for an unfractured identity may be contingent on a return to an idealized past, an untainted memory. Her return home thus remains unreal to us as a result of her absence from the film and the fact that her memory is never tested against the reality of Turkey in the present time. Her Turkish identity, as presented to the film's viewers, is an identity frozen in an imaginary and invisible past.

And yet from another perspective Melek's letter might also be a refusal to allow the filmmaker to pry further into her life. Melek's denial of full access to her life may be part of a subtle tug-of-war between Melek's own assessment of her life in Turkey and filmmaker Meerapfel's skepticism about it. Melek's shielding herself from further scrutiny may in some ways be motivated by her sense that Meerapfel is superimposing her own autobiographical experiences onto Melek's story. As a child, Janine Meerapfel fled with her parents from Nazi Germany to Argentina, where she lived until her return to Germany in the late 1960s. And the harrowing experience of living in perpetual exile, unable to find a true home anywhere, is explored in *Malou* (1982), one of Meerapfel's feature films. The underlying debate between Melek and Meerapfel and Melek's final refusal seems, at least on one level, an assertion on Melek's part of the right to her own identity. It is as if Melek is rejecting an identity that is once again imposed on her by someone else, an identity projected onto her so someone else can use it for her own purposes.

In fact, Janine Meerapfel acknowledges that she sees Melek's story in light of her own autobiographical experiences. She sees *Die Kuemmeltuerkin Geht* as a continuation of her previous filmic work that dealt autobiographically with her and her parents' emigration from Nazi Germany and the subsequent search for her own lost roots, and her lost identity and homeland. This is why, toward the end of the film, the voice-over narration tells us that "today there are worse things in Germany than being a Jew." Meerapfel points out that "the Jewish people are no longer the scapegoats" in Germany today because "the Turkish people have taken over this function of the scapegoat."[4]

In a 1985 interview Meerapfel has indicated outright that she does believe that Melek idealizes her home in Turkey. But Meerapfel also downplays this aspect of the film's meaning by adding that Melek's supposed idealization is not intended as the focus of her film. Rather, the film "actually deals with the Federal Republic of Germany, and that which in this country is done to Melek, a Turkish woman, and a so-called *Gastarbeiterin*" (11). And Meerapfel intends to blame the Germans and not Melek for Melek's rose-colored view of her homeland: "The more illusionary the notions of these people [the Turkish guest workers] are about their homeland the more we in the Federal Republic of Germany have to ask ourselves to what extent we are responsible for this escapism, for these unrealistic notions of the possibilities [that await them] upon their return to Turkey" (11). Meerapfel believes that Turkish people who work in Germany "take refuge in illusions" because Germany doesn't offer them the possibility to "feel happy and taken care of in the reality of this country [Germany]" (11).

Therefore, written in and over the preparations for Melek's return to Turkey there is another level of return: a return to her painful past in Germany. The filmmaker encourages Melek to revisit the locations of her life in Germany and to narrate her life there. In a bitter journey we visit her first shabby apartment and the exploitative job situation connected with it. By immersing Melek in the sites of her earlier days in Germany, the film allows the past to impinge on the present. The sight of the dark, narrow, prison-like apartment triggers Melek to reexperience the claustrophobia and fear of her first years in Germany. The apartment has not been upgraded in all these years, and another *Gastarbeiter* tenant will have to live here again soon, presumably experiencing similar feelings of despair.

While Melek's returns to the scenes of her past in Germany are staged by the filmmaker, spontaneously occurring events also point to a past that keeps erupting into the present. As the documentary progresses, events unfold that are emblematic of all of Melek's past frustration, feelings of rejection, rage, and humiliation. On television Melek watches a German woman attacking a Turkish man for no other reason than that this is "our fatherland." In an interview, a German acquaintance of Melek comments on Melek's survival and business skills (Melek supplemented her income through selling homemade pillows): the habit of trading goods, the German acquaintance says, is a trait innate to the Turks that enables them to survive. The acquaintance declares that, due to their becoming civilized, the Germans have lost that skill. The acquaintance's racist hostility is thinly veiled behind her air of friendliness and seeming admiration for Melek's aptitude. These events are not recorded as singular or exceptional occurrences but, rather, as randomly selected samples of moments in Melek's life in Germany that point to a past where no doubt similar events were a habitual part of her everyday reality. It is precisely the ordinariness of these events that brings to the surface the weight of Melek's pain over the years.

In her article "Mirrors without Memories: Truth, History, and the New Documentary," Linda Williams discusses the postmodern documentary (using the examples of *Shoah* and *The Thin Blue Line*) not as a form charged with recapturing the (elusive) past, but as one charged with "finding [the past's] traces, in repetitions and resistances, in the present."[5] *Die Kuemmeltuerkin Geht* is shot through with "the past's reverberations with the present" (20). Everywhere Melek goes, she, and by extension the spectator, relives her past confronted as she is with often barely concealed, sometimes overtly expressed, xenophobic resentments. Through all this Melek struggles to maintain her rights while encountering endless bureaucratic problems, such as being forced to stand in line for what seems like hours to obtain her papers to leave for Turkey. The film's extended long take of her waiting in line forces us to experience some of Melek's frustration and anger (and by extension that of the other Turkish *Gastarbeiter* who stand in line with her) accumulated over years of similar mistreatment during her stay in Germany as a *Kuemmeltuerkin*.

While on the surface this documentary treats the present and the projected future as it records a Turkish woman's preparation for return to Turkey, on a deeper level it purposefully (in the case of having Melek visit the locales she frequented during her years in Germany) and sometimes accidentally (in the case of the bureaucratic red tape) engages the past as it is reexperienced in the present. At the end, the spectator not only understands Melek's need to leave but has experienced some of the bitterness that permeates her life as a foreigner in Germany.

In this respect, the trauma of the past is not merely remembered or recaptured but relived. Here, as in psychoanalytic transference, the past is reexperienced, and the past and present are not disjointed but, rather, superimposed. In being the catalyst of this transference, the documentary takes on an analyst's role for Melek and for Meerapfel. And through *our own* engagement with the film, the past seeps into the present where it can be observed and analyzed.

Toechter Zweier Welten (Daughters of Two Worlds; Germany, 1990) by the Turkish German filmmaker Serap Berrakkarasu traces the life of Meral, a Turkish woman in her early twenties. Where Melek was propelled by her (perhaps impossible) desire to return to the past and to a past identity, Meral is motivated by her desire to escape from the past, from the life it offered her and the identity it commanded. In interview form we learn the story of Meral's life: she was born in a Turkish village but was brought by her parents to live in Germany when she was still a child. She married the Turkish man her parents selected for her when she was very young, but during their marriage he raped, abused, and humiliated her. When she ran away from him, her parents were shattered but finally welcomed her back into their house.

Meral blames her upbringing for her inability to live the life of a Muslim wife that was expected of her. She feels that she could not endure her husband's abuse because she grew up in Germany, where women are granted more freedom and identities of their own, independent from their husbands' prescriptions. Her dilemma, she believes, is that of a split identity. She has grown up between two worlds and now cannot live in either one of them. A return to Turkey would mean the subjugation to a Turkish female identity, which is no longer acceptable to her, but a German identity does not fit her any better.

But between the lines of the chronology of Meral's history, presented by *Toechter Zweier Welten,* a second, "vertical" history emerges. Here, the dynamics of the past and the present are played out on an emotional level between Meral and her mother, Serbian. Meral's disobedience repeats Serbian's own disobedience as a young woman in Turkey. Serbian's narration of her own return to her past in Turkey weaves into her daughter's narration and contradicts the daughter's fantasy of an "authentic" or "originary" female Turkish identity she would have assumed if only she had been raised in one culture, that is, a Turkish one. The past in Turkey is far from idealized: the villagers in Turkey had watched Serbian's every move, keeping her like a prisoner. She had to escape secretly from the village to follow her husband who had left to work as a *Gastarbeiter* in Germany. Although her husband wanted her to join him, the villagers deemed it more appropriate for her to stay at home and wait for his return. Raised as a traditional woman in Turkey, she had no identity other than that prescribed by the Muslim community, and her act of self-assertion was perceived as an act of betrayal. The daughter's breaking out of the limiting lifestyle demanded of a Muslim woman thus mirrors that of the mother several decades earlier. Their lives, the remote past, and the more recent past and present, echo each other. The mother reexperiences her own pain in the past through the daughter's pain in the present. On the other hand, the daughter has little, if any, memory of Turkey except the memory "borrowed" from her mother. The borrowed memory from the mother becomes the daughter's own memory. The mother's place of origin and home of which the mother herself is critical becomes that which is fantasized about by the daughter.[6] Thus the memory bond established between mother and daughter in the documentary actually undermines, for viewers if not for Meral herself, the fantasy of a stable or unitary Turkish identity.

Furthermore, the documentary intercuts Meral's and Serbian's respective accounts at several points with scenes of the wedding of another young woman in Turkey who remains unnamed. This young Turkish woman's festive wedding preparations turn painful and may be seen as a commentary on Meral's own story when the Turkish bride breaks down in tears as she is married to a man she does not love. We learn that the man she loved was forced to marry another woman. Yet, as did Meral in the past, the bride yields to the demands imposed on her. Still, the documentary leaves open whether she will stay with her husband or whether, like Meral, she will eventually defy her role and the identity that this role dictates. The fact that this bride has grown up in Turkey and never lived in another culture does not seem to make it any easier for her to accept the role assigned to her by her community.

Although Meral desires an undivided self, a self not torn between two cultures and between two worlds, the documentary suggests the possibility, beneath the chronology of Meral's and Serbian's histories, not so much of a dual, conflicted self, but of an inevitably undecidable and fluid one. We can never be quite sure what might have been and who Meral might have been had circumstances been otherwise, but, ultimately, the identity the film presents is not a hybrid identity. We are presented with a fractured but not twofold subjectivity, a subjectivity constantly in the making and fluid, arising out of the struggle and the tension between memories (her own and those of Turkey borrowed from others) and the reality of her present life in Germany. *Toechter Zweier Welten* prompts Meral and Serbian to relive their past. But it also goes beyond that. It lays bare, at the interstices of its narrations of return, an identity constructed out of the diverging experiences of different cultures, different worlds, and different memories.

The constructedness of all subjectivity and of personal experience that transcends even cultural bounds is also the focal point of *Tekerleme* (Tonguebreaker; Germany/Turkey, 1985/86) and *Hayal* (Shadowplays; Germany/Turkey, 1989/90), two documentaries by the Turkish German filmmaker Merlyn Solakhan. In these documentaries, Solakhan returns to Turkey not only through the avenues of memory and fantasy but also through a physical journey back to the geographical place itself, her native Istanbul.

But in *Tekerleme,* despite the physical concreteness of Solakhan's return home, the return seems dreamlike. The past remains elusive and Solakhan's memory proves unreliable and changeable. Instead of experiencing a sense of recognition, the visitor experiences being a foreigner in her own homeland. Only the smells of the city, a song, and the view over the harbor seem to recall Solakhan's past. Everything else has changed: street names, friends, friends' addresses, and their whereabouts.

In a long take of almost fifteen minutes in duration, the city panorama slides across the screen as the camera pans so exceedingly slowly that its movement seems almost imperceptible. Parts of the city appear and then disappear as new views slowly drift into frame. Nothing lasts. By the time one gets oriented to a certain locale it has gradually glided away, so as to be accessible only in the memory as an incomplete image that meanwhile has been ruptured and overlaid by the other images that have drifted by our view. In the spectator's memory, everything—the panorama of the ever-changing city, its buildings, minarets, ships, the ocean—eventually seems to blur into one all-embracing impression of the cityscape. At the end of the long pan it is almost impossible to describe what came into view first and in what order. In the present time, we are left with a recollection of the city, different with every spectator, and a perception that is perhaps the most vivid when dusk begins to settle in and the long take finally fades into black.

Tekerleme, not unlike Chris Marker's *Sans Soleil* (1982) and *Koumiko Mystery* (1965), experiments with the limits as well as the deceptions of our memory. Yet in many regards these films operate in almost opposite ways. Marker's films overload the senses with a flood of images that make it impossible for the spectator or the visitor to ever fully capture or remember the places he visits. Solakhan's documentary works very differently. Instead of a rapid, staccato-like succession of images piled on images as in Marker's films, *Tekerleme*'s uncut pans linger on their subjects in a seeming attempt to savor each moment and connect each image to the following and preceding ones. Where *Sans Soleil* disconnects and juxtaposes its images, *Tekerleme*'s images change so gradually one barely notices any motion at all. The images float by, deliberately, slowly, as if the filmmaker were trying to urge the spectator to memorize the images' connections and links to each other. And yet, as the film seems to acknowledge, no matter how hard you try to linger on each image and imprint it in your memory, you will ultimately fail as its traces inevitably fade away. Moreover, while Marker's films investigate a foreign culture that remains inaccessible to him, *Tekerleme* is far from an ethnographic film. It attempts to capture the filmmaker's own past, her own childhood, and the receding layers of the memories of her own origin and identity in a place that is at the same time her own country and a country that has grown foreign to her.

Solakhan gradually seems to accept and explore her role as a visitor and no longer a citizen of her native city. She attempts to reestablish contact with old friends and with her own past. But communication proves to be full of obstacles and frustrations. Each phone call she makes and each house she visits seem to leave her more lonely, more out of place, a visitor who no longer belongs. The friends she is trying to reach have all moved away or are otherwise inaccessible. She finally manages to meet with one male friend, a journalist. At a lake, she and the friend recall a legend of two lovers who drowned here in the past. As they sit in a boat gazing into the depth of the lake, Solakhan and her friend hold a conversation in which they imagine the drowned lovers to live in a world below the water, a world that mirrors our world, but a world to which access is denied. To Solakhan, we realize, Turkey itself has become this world that she can gaze at but no longer reach.

At the end of the film we see Solakhan walking aimlessly along the streets of Istanbul, searching for friends who are no longer there. In voice-over she tells us, "I am Turkish," while children on the street sing the praises of the virtues of a Turkish child. Yet the very notion of a Turkish identity has become tenuous. Solakhan is Turkish only in the memories of her past; in the present she is an alien. Unable to connect with her own roots, she is alienated from the parts of her own identity constructed as Turkish.

Finally, Solakhan rents a hotel room in which, she tells us, a poet committed suicide years ago by jumping out of the window. She opens the window to survey the images of the bustling city. The camera follows her point of view, the same point of view held by the poet during the last moments of his life. This image opens up the possibility of assuming someone else's point of view, someone else's memory and identity perhaps, or, at the very least, of constantly re-creating one's identity over and against the past and an experience of the present that are constantly shifting and in flux. It is an image that erases the illusion of the fixity of one's own identity.

In *Tekerleme*, memory takes on unexpected and surprising prospects. That which is recalled is recalled in a falsified way (e.g., orientation in the city); that which is forgotten (e.g., smells and sounds of the city) unexpectedly erupts and demands recognition. It is the same, and yet it isn't (anymore). As such, this documentary may be as much about the way memory is structured like a palimpsest as it is about Solakhan's frustrated attempt to relive her own past. Her return to Istanbul yields more uncertainties than certainties about her identity and her past, unearthing previously forgotten layers of memories while depositing new layers that superimpose themselves over the old ones.

But where *Tekerleme* deals with the impossibility of recovering an autobiographical past, one's origin, and a sense of a stable identity, Solakhan's subsequent documentary, *Hayal,* is organized around an investigation of Turkey's past, a past that forms the background of Turkey's ethnic, national, and cultural identity. Before the appearance of the cinema in Turkey the *hayal* was a tremendously popular theater of shadow figures that enacted sexually and politically explicit folk comedies, the *karagoez* plays. In present-day Turkey, the tradition of the *hayal* is all but forgotten. As the film describes, without the work of Helmut Ritter, a German historian who lived in Istanbul in the thirties to record the *karagoez* plays, the history of the *hayal* would be even less accessible. Thus, in returning to this theatrical past, the film presents not an immutable Turkey that lags behind most Western countries, but a Turkey with a rich and evolving cultural history. And in bringing up Ritter's work, the film enriches and diversifies its own historiographic impulse: Turkish and German culture together are responsible for this historiography. The film's emphasis on Turkish history as an interlaced set of histories is also underlined when the history of Istanbul's cultural and ethnic diversity since the seventeenth century is reported by two other German scholars, and because the history of Turkish national identity is explored as a complicated proposition. The transformation of the word *Turk,* which once signified an uneducated peasant, received a revalorization during the 1920s and 1930s under the Turkish president Kemal Ataturk and came to signify an entire nation. As the documentary traces some of the innumerable threads of the rich fabric of Turkey's history, its national identity emerges much as Solakhan's own identity in her previous film: as a construction constantly in the making.

Die Kuemmeltuerkin Geht through its structures of absence and presence pierces the illusion that memory equals reality (whether past or present). *Toechter Zweier Welten* allows the memory of the distant past, of homeland, and of Turkish identity to resurface, but it proves to be unreliable and uncertain. *Tekerleme* and *Hayal* dissect memory only to find it endlessly layered and layering. Memory is unveiled as a palimpsest, and the attempt to find the origin of one's subjectivity leads not to an originary core but instead to its layered constructedness. And where *Tekerleme* traces the impossibility of uncovering the origin of one's personal identity and the structuring of subjectivity, *Hayal* reveals that even a national Turkish identity lacks an authentic core. Turkishness, like personal subjectivity, is shifting, interlaced with other identities and structured out of the varying layers of the past and out of what is remembered of it (even if that which is remembered is sometimes faulty and full of holes).

The reliving of the subjects' experiences in these documentaries functions through a process of transference in which experiences from the past resurface and are made visible. However, experience made visible cannot serve as a measure of truth. In fact, one could say, following Joan Scott, that these films show that "making experience visible precludes critical examination of the workings of the ideological system."[7] It is not enough to reintroduce past experience into the present, because "the evidence of experience [would then be] evidence for the fact of difference, rather than a way of exploring how difference is established, how it operates, and how and in what way it constitutes subjects who see and act in the world" (25). Experience itself has to be examined for the way it is constructed rather than as the origin of knowledge (25). In the documentaries I've been investigating, (past) experience is made visible, but its truth claim is rendered suspect and revealed to be unreliable and shifting. Instead of making visible the truth of other peoples' experiences, these documentaries make visible how subjects are constructed through experience.

In psychoanalysis the past reemerges in transference so that (infantile) conflicts can be rearranged. The goal, then, is an acceptance of a version of reality, a version of reality that is often the construction of the therapist. As Sigmund Freud in his essay "Construction in Analysis" asserts: "We [analysts] produce in him [the patient] an assured conviction of the truth of the construction which achieves the same therapeutic result as a recaptured memory."[8] But in the documentaries I have been discussing, transference functions not just as a recapturing and acceptance of the past, but also as a way of realizing the constructed nature of our subjectivity. The returning women produce their own memories and they test collective memories (e.g., what it means to be Turkish) and borrowed memories (e.g., the memories Meral borrows from her mother) that have been transmitted to them abroad or in exile. They also probe their own memories and point to their rewritings over time. In these documentaries, an increasing uncertainty emerges and with it a realization of the shifting nature of subjectivity, personal experience, and personal history.

In her analysis of *Golddiggers* and *La Signora Di Tutti*, Mary Ann Doane points out that "what is returned to the woman [in each film] is her memory through construction."[9] The cinematic convention to portray Woman as "Abstract," decontextualized and dehistoricized is "undone [in the films Doane discusses] through a laborious construction of a memory and hence a history" (94). The documentaries I have been examining do that as well, and they do it with an enhanced self-reflexive impulse. Instead of accepting, or attempting to uncover and attribute to a woman, one version of past reality, these films suggest that women's experiences and the histories of self are multiply and continually constructed. These documentaries help us scrutinize the various histories of selves and the various individual identities their subjects have constructed in relation to the secondhand histories (e.g., family stories or historical documentations) of selves and identities transmitted and attributed to them by others. In this respect, the films fulfill a function similar to that fulfilled by psychoanalysis only in its most radical form of reconstruction. That is, they affirm the fictional and provisional status of identity reconstructions.

The documentaries discussed here leave behind traditional documentaries' handling of history and histories. They present truths not only by bringing forth previously unknown experiences but by locating experience at the intersection and convergence of a vertical (eruptive) and a horizontal (chronological) investigation of history. The reexperiencing of the past in the present occurs at the same time that the constructedness of subjectivity and of individual experience (out of the layers of the past) is probed. Instead of constructing memories for women, these films perform the task that Doane is calling for in her essay: that of "produc[ing] remembering women" (93).

◆————————————————————————————————

NOTES

1. Mary Ann Doane, "Remembering Women," in her *Femmes Fatales* (New York and London: Routledge, 1991), 91.
2. Dale F. Eikelman and James Piscatori, "Social Theory in the Study of Muslim Societies," in *Muslim Travellers: Pilgrimage, Migration, and Religious Imagination*, ed. Dale F. Eikelman and James Piscatori (London: Routledge, 1990), 5.
3. In an interview, Meerapfel points out that Melek even calls herself *Kuemmeltuerkin* "to defend herself." Janine Meerapfel, *"Die Kuemmeltuerkin Geht,"* in *Catalogue for the 35: International Film Festival* (Berlin: Deutsche Kinemathek, 1985), 10. All translations from German are my own.
4. Ibid., 11.
5. Linda Williams, "Mirrors without Memories: Truth, History, and the New Documentary," *Film Quarterly* 46, no. 3 (Spring 1993): 15.
6. V. S. Naipaul in *The Enigma of Arrival* (Harmondsworth: Viking, 1987: 318) testifies to the power of the process of longing for an originary home when he speaks of "places doubly and trebly sacred to me because far away in England I had lived them imaginatively over many books and had in my fantasy set in those places the very beginning of things, had constructed of them a fantasy of home."
7. Joan W. Scott, "Experience," in *Feminists Theorize the Political*, ed. Judith Butler and Joan W. Scott (New York and London: Routledge, 1992), 25.
8. Sigmund Freud, *The Standard Edition of the Complete Psychological Works of Sigmund Freud*, ed. and trans. James Strachey (London: Hogarth and the Institute of Psychoanalysis, 1973), 5: 536–37. Quoted in Doane, "Remembering Women," 92.
9. Doane, "Remembering Women," 94.

ANAHID KASSABIAN
DAVID KAZANJIAN

[9] *Melancholic Memories and Manic Politics: Feminism, Documentary, and the Armenian Diaspora*

Stories of the Armenian genocide loomed large in our childhoods. In two very different families, we heard very similar stories about the Ottoman policy of exterminating Armenians that reached its peak in 1915 and ended in the deaths of some 1.5 million Armenians. Each of us came very early to understand how Armenians went into diaspora as a result of this history, forming large Armenian communities throughout the United States, Latin America, France, and the Middle East. Yet our respective relationships to this history are markedly different largely because of our families' different degrees of participation in Armenian culture and community: one of us grew up in a family rigorously assimilating to an idealized "Americanness" and knowing only carefully edited stories of a grandfather who was an immigrant genocide survivor, while the other has brought everyday practices of "Armenianness," as well as stories of familial survival and loss, from her childhood into the first marriage to an *odar*, or non-Armenian, in her immediate family's history. Growing up constituted in this complex history led us some years ago to begin working together on the articulation of Armenian identity in documentary films produced in the northern and western diaspora. Over the course of our ongoing collaboration, our intellectual and affective responses to the documentaries we have studied have converged on a number of questions.

In particular, we have been concerned about the persistence with which these films represent diaspora as a *problem* to be solved with the securing of reparations for and recognition of the genocide, and the stabilization of culture, history, language, and territory.[1] This vision of a secure and stable future is often held out as the just return of a past lost in the early part of this century during the violent instantiation of the modern Turkish nation-state. Magically named the Armenian Nation or the Armenian Spirit, this generalized and idealized lost past and just future tend to sweep away the strikingly uneven and rich complexity of diaspora, which, though not unconnected to discourses of nation, is nonetheless hardly exhausted by it. To us, the range of social and political questions that press themselves on the diaspora in its various geographic spaces can hardly be formulated, much less addressed, within the quite rigid and statist terms of the nation. As First World intellectuals and activists, in the face of these documentaries produced in the North and the West but claiming to represent a global diaspora, we feel a particular responsibility to interpret some of the vast changes the notion of an Armenian diaspora has undergone in the past decade. The questions raised by the shifts class and gender undergo across the geographic spaces of diaspora are particularly unthematized in the films we have studied and consequently are particularly pressing in our work.

We thus present this essay as an extended meditation on the following question: at this particular historical conjuncture, now that an Armenian nation-state exists, what does it mean for a First World intellectual to identify to a greater or lesser degree as "Armenian"? By *identify* we here mean something as specific as having the affective responses both of us had to *An Armenian Journey,* the documentary we will discuss at length in this essay. Though both of us found the film's attempt to represent into existence a global Armenian National Spirit profoundly troubling, we nonetheless found ourselves politically invested in the history of genocide and diaspora it was attempting to tell, and we found ourselves tremendously invested affectively in the sequences involving Mariam Davis, an elderly genocide survivor and one of the film's central figures.

We begin by giving a brief account of the genre of Armenian cultural production to which *An Armenian Journey* belongs. We then interpret the strategies of representing the work of mourning in texts of this genre by drawing on Sigmund Freud's essay "Mourning and Melancholia." Rather than simply applying "Mourning and Melancholia" as an ahistorical and unquestionable model to the historically saturated documentary, we first read the Freudian text itself as a parable about social and historical formations inflected by its own particular historical conjuncture. We then offer a reading of *An Armenian Journey* from the perspective of the Freudian parable of mourning and melancholia.

By drawing on the work of Sonya Michel and Judith Newton, Janet Walker and Diane Waldman argue in their introduction to this volume that "the same formal attributes (the use of 'talking heads' interviews, photographs, or voice-over narration) may serve very different functions in different films." We would like to push this insight even further; our reading of *An Armenian Journey* suggests that the same formal attributes may serve very different functions in the same film. Even in the midst of *An Armenian Journey*'s formal masculinism—during the talking-head interviews and the voice-over narration, for instance—images and sounds emerge, often quite subtly at the very edges of frames, that threaten formal masculinist control or containment. By attending to both the edges and the centers of *An Armenian Journey,* we pursue a reading that supplements a critique of masculinism with an attention to its internal, constitutive limits or fissures. This is not simply a voluntaristic call for resistive reading, because we are alerted to this supplementary reading of *An Armenian Journey* by our affective investment in, or identification with, the figure of Mariam—an affective investment that persists for us alongside the alienation produced by the masculinist form of the film.

Although *An Armenian Journey* condenses the affective work of mourning a lost homeland into a melancholic representation of Mariam Davis, and differentiates that representation from political and historical narratives grounded in a masculine authority, we suggest that the film also offers sites of identification that open up the work of mourning to a more complex and unstable ethico-political terrain. That is, the film offers sites of identification that undo its overt attempts to represent diaspora as nation by means of a rigorous regime of sexual difference. One possible strategy for a feminist approach to documentary films, we suggest, is to read for, or remain attentive to identifications with, figures that extend beyond the gendered boundaries films define for them. In our case, this involves reading Mariam Davis's work of mourning beyond *An Armenian Journey.*

▶

Hai Tahd as Genre

An Armenian Journey belongs to a genre of cultural productions we have begun to call *hai tahd*, which means "the Armenian case" in Armenian and which represents the history and consequences of the genocide in particularly juridical terms. The term is borrowed from the discourse of the Armenian Revolutionary Federation, or *Tashnagtsoutiun*, a socialist nationalist party formed in the 1890s, whose goal has been to establish a free and independent Armenia.[2] While there is no exclusive linkage between the *Tashnag* party and the term *hai tahd*, there is a logical linkage. After the 1915 genocide, the international Armenian community spoke mainly in terms of "the Armenian question," a turn of phrase still in use today. But after some complex developments in the diaspora in the 1960s, the *Tashnag* party spoke more consistently of the Armenian *case* and used the discourse of legal pursuit and redress in articulating their claims and platforms. Transformed from the Armenian *question* into the Armenian *case,* the history of genocide and diaspora came to be understood as a juridico-political history in which a single party (the Armenians) sought a conclusive and restitutive judgment on a legal and moral injustice (the genocide). While this transformation had strong tactical justifications in the 1960s, its costs and limitations have become too important to ignore today. The transformation of a question into a case telescoped the persistently open-ended, ethico-political texture of "Armenianness" into a bounded, calculable, empirically determinable event. Consequently, the northern and western diaspora was flooded by a discourse that seemed to forget the tactical character of the transformation. This discourse seemed to believe that the work of mourning the genocide could *finally* be completed, and the call to do the genocide justice could *fully* be answered, with juridical recognition and redress.

While what we are calling *hai tahd* films have no necessary historical or structural relationship to the *Tashnag* party's transformation of the Armenian *question* into the Armenian *case,* the films and the party share a juridico-political set of structuring assumptions and concerns. *Hai tahd* films consistently ground two generic features in the historic fact of the 1915 genocide. First, they posit a transnational Armenian identity based in the shared experience of genocide. They draw on other commonalities— blood, language, culture—that loom large in Armenian and other nationalist discourses but tend to subordinate them to genocide. Genocide survivors appear in every one of these films, often bearing affectively charged witness to the dismembered and mutilated bodies of family members. *Hai tahd* films suggest that, like the dismembered bodies of mothers and brothers, the Armenian national body was fragmented by genocide and insulted by the Turkish state's continuing policy of denial. Ironically, however, it is that very fragmentation, that shared experience of loss, on which they base a transhistorical, transnational Armenian identity. Second, the films embrace a discourse of a particular exchange: rights for victimization. Since Armenians transnationally share the identity of victim of genocide, the films propose, certain reparations must be due. The bodies and psyches of four generations of victims and survivors should be paid for with, in the farthest-reaching vision, an independent nation-state, but in all cases at least a special place in twentieth-century world history and an admission of guilt from the modern Turkish nation-state.

These two discourses—identity constituted in loss and the right to some form of reparation—are the minimal features of *hai tahd* documentaries. Though neither of us dismisses these political and cultural discourses and their consequent practices lightly or ungratefully, and in fact one of us counts them among her past affiliations, we suggest that they have boxed the notion of an Armenian diaspora into a tight corner. Because these documentaries, like the *Tashnag* party, consistently represent the history of genocide as the anchoring feature of Armenian identity, and because they almost exclusively answer the call to mourn and do justice to that history with demands for territorial reparations and political recognition, they tend to reduce the complexity of Armenian history to the fantasy of an eternally ethnically pure, territorially based nation-state. By naming this tendency *hai tahd,* and by historicizing its emergence, we hope to recall the forgetting that precipitated the powerful fantasy of final and full recognition and redress for the genocide.

The task of recalling such a forgetting and unraveling such a fantasy is not simply a historical one. Of course, we do need to remember that Armenian identity has long been a transgovernmental and heterogeneous phenomenon, with communities scattered across boundaries of empires and nations. In the nineteenth century, the lands historically occupied by Armenians were mainly governed by the Ottoman Empire, with a smaller section belonging to the Russian Transcaucases. The legal status of Armenians in the Ottoman Empire underwent constant changes: mid-century reform efforts, the 1874 constitution, the disappointments of the 1878 treaties of San Stephano and Berlin, the 1894–96 massacres in eastern Anatolia, and the elation of the 1908 *Ittihad* coup. But for most Armenians, eastern Anatolia remained a home with which they could politically, ideologically, affectively, and economically identify to some extent, even under these changing and often violent conditions. The 1915 genocide is the point at which that transgovernmental community became a vast international diaspora. Ottoman soldiers rounded people up, drove them out of their homes and villages, marched some to death, and executed others. Those who were fortunate enough to escape were often the sole survivors of their families. That violent loss of family and home, after centuries of uneven Ottoman policy, makes love of "the homeland" ambivalent, the process of mourning difficult, and the call of justice incalculable. *Hai tahd* films subject precisely this traumatic and ambivalent love to juridico-political calculation and thereby tend to suppress the complexity of this history. Yet the persistence with which they attempt to finally answer the call of justice and fully complete the work of mourning suggests that it took something more than historical inaccuracy to transform the Armenian *question* into the Armenian *case*. It is to that "something more" that we will now turn.

The Work of Mourning

Curiously, 1915 was also the year in which Freud wrote his crucial essay on mourning and its melancholic and manic forms, though it remained unpublished until 1917. The expressed purpose of "Mourning and Melancholia" is to "throw some light on the nature of melancholia by comparing it with the normal affect of mourning."[3] And yet, just as Freud almost immediately complicates the relationship between the normal and the pathological, he similarly nuances the relationship between the internality of an individual mournful, melancholic, or manic psyche and the externality of what he calls "the exciting causes [of melancholia and mourning] due to environmental influences" (251). Probably between February and May of 1915—when the first reports of Ottoman pogroms were filtering into Europe—Freud wrote the following passage in the second paragraph of "Mourning and Melancholia": "Mourning is regularly the reaction to the loss of a loved person, or to the loss of some abstraction which has taken the place of one, such as one's country, liberty, an ideal, and so on. In some people the same influences produce melancholia instead of mourning" (251–52). More interesting to us than any sociobiographical analysis that would tie Freud's writings on mourning to Armenian history, however, are the striking questions raised by Freud's introjection, with this passage, of a broad sociopolitical field into the drama of mourning, melancholia, and mania. How do we make sense of the contradiction between the claim that external "environmental influences" are "exciting causes" of an individual's mourning and melancholia, and the claim that a social "abstraction" can "take the [apparently internal, affective] place of" an apparently more primary "loved person"? It would seem that the volatile geopolitical scene of the 1915 conjuncture—which extended well beyond the Ottoman Empire—weighed on Freud's work during this period.[4] How, then, might we extend Freud's fleeting suggestion that psychic trauma is not simply an "internal" or individual affair?

Let us first recall Freud's manifest argument. He begins "Mourning and Melancholia" by arguing that melancholia is a more extreme, pathological, or dysfunctional form of the everyday affect called mourning. Both mourning and melancholia are precipitated by the traumatic loss of a loved object. In mourning, one resists accepting that traumatic loss by refusing to withdraw the libido originally invested in that loved object—that is, by refusing to accept the loss psychically. This causes one to experience "profoundly painful dejection, cessation of interest in the outside world, loss of the capacity to love, and an inhibition of all activity" (252). But eventually, "bit by bit," mourning gives way to the reinvestment of libido in other loved objects. In melancholia, by contrast, one gets stuck in mourning because one sets up a representation of the loved object under the guise of the ego. Thus melancholia involves a withdrawal of libido from the formerly loved object and the "internalization" of that libido. The result of this internalization of a representation of the lost object is an aggressive hatred of the self—one hates the part of the self that now stands in for the lost object.

"Internalization," strictly speaking, is a particular modality of identification in which intersubjective relations (such as conflicts or prohibitions) are transformed into intrasubjective relations. What is more, it is more idiopathic than heteropathic—that is, the subject identifies the other with itself more than that it identifies its self with the other.[5] But like any identification, internalization is not simply the action of a discrete external world upon a bounded internal psyche. It is a drama of the production of subjectivity, not a drama of the self's corruption or infection. As J. Laplanche and J.-B. Pontalis explain, identification is "the operation itself whereby the human subject is constituted."[6] The ego is just one part of this drama, not the central or the essential part. Consequently, the fact that in mourning as in melancholia the subject sets up a representation of the loved object under the guise of the ego has a *particular* meaning. Though Freud moved through a number of different conceptualizations of the ego, by 1915 he understood the ego to be more of a surface than a center or a source, and to be precipitated or developed rather than primordial. What is more, he believed the subject is often fooled into understanding the ego as its essence or primary agency.[7] Thus, mourning and melancholia involve the subject's representation of itself to itself. However, that representation is a highly selective and mediated one; it does not tell the subject the "whole story" of itself but, rather, an "edited" version of that story.[8]

The reason for the odd turn from common mourning to the internalization that precipitates melancholia is never precisely described by Freud, but it would seem to stem from what he calls an especially "ambivalent" love of the object before it was lost. That ambivalent love prevents one from accepting the loss of the object. Instead, one sets up a representation of the lost object under the guise of the ego, a representation that one can then punish with the extreme, even suicidal self-deprecation that characterizes melancholia. In other words, one punishes oneself as a representative of the ambivalently loved lost object. Self-punishment becomes a ritualized, psychic articulation of ambivalence.

Freud goes on to confront the frequent coupling of melancholia with mania, or what he calls the "regular alternation of melancholic and manic phases" (263). Oddly, he argues that "the content of mania is no different from that of melancholia, that both disorders are wrestling with the same 'complex,' but that probably in melancholia the ego has succumbed to the complex whereas in mania it has mastered it or pushed it aside" (263). That is, mania is also a response to the internalized loss of an ambivalently loved object. In mania, one feels a joy similar to the joy of emerging from a period of mourning; however, that joy is more intense and more fleeting. Mania is inevitably followed by a return to melancholia because it does not overcome the loss of the object; rather, it only partially overcomes the *melancholic representation* of that lost object in the ego. As Freud says, "Mania is nothing other than a triumph of this sort, only that here again what the ego has surmounted and what it is triumphing over remains hidden from it" (264).

Freud goes to great lengths to depathologize melancholia and mania, and to emphasize the formal and psychic features they share with mourning. In the essay's third paragraph he writes, "It is really only because we know so well how to explain [mourning, and know so little about melancholia] that this [mournful] attitude does not seem to us pathological" (252). Throughout the essay, he distinguishes mourning from the melancholic/manic constellation according to differences in degree and chance contextual history rather than differences in kind. In fact, Freud concerns himself much more with the similarities among mourning, melancholia, and mania as psychic structures similarly bound up with identification. In all three structures, an incorporative or idiopathic identificatory process takes over from the object-cathexis. Upon losing the loved object, a subject "wants to incorporate this object into itself," and "it wants to do so by devouring it" (258). Freud does suggest that, in the case of melancholia, this incorporative desire "regresses" to an obsessional narcissism (258), such that the subject unconsciously sets up a representation of the lost object within its ego, "splitting" the ego so that "one part of the ego sets itself over against the other" (256). And yet he repeatedly checks the tendency to simply oppose a pathologized, regressive melancholia to a "normal," developmental mourning by emphasizing that both hinge on a certain degree of narcissistic identification. The internalization of ambivalent love, or the process of turning into one's self that characterizes melancholia, seems to accompany normal object-love as a narcissistic process as much as it accompanies mourning and melancholia. The more important distinction between mourning and melancholia as prolonged internalizations of *lost* and *differently loved* objects would thus seem to turn on a certain form or force or modality of internalization. That is, the difference would seem to be a representational one, a difference in the form or force or modality in which the identification represents itself to the subject. In melancholia and mania, the form, force, or modality is particularly rigid, idiopathic, and tautological. What Freud calls the "work of mourning," on the other hand, seems more open to heteropathic identifications.

Though much of the essay addresses what seem to be individual psychic dramas, we have already seen how the process of subject (and particularly ego) formation is an aspect and effect of the identificatory drama of mourning, melancholia, and mania, not the frame within which that drama is conducted. What is more, the striking passage we quoted above from the second paragraph of the essay—"Mourning is regularly the reaction to the loss of a loved person, or to the loss of some abstraction which has taken the place of one, such as one's country, liberty, an ideal, and so on. In some people the same influences produce melancholia instead of mourning"—suggests that the lost object can take many forms, and that the melancholic response is as much precipitated by sociohistorical factors as it is by "a *real slight or disappointment* coming from [a] loved person" (257). The "internal" thus seems to lose all discreteness in this 1915 text, giving way to a much more complex interpenetration of social, psychic, and subjectival terrains.

We read "Mourning and Melancholia" as a parable about the representational forms and forces ambivalent loss can take, as a sketch of the affective lineaments of a drama that is very much social and historical, and that is irreducible to individual subjects or internalized psyches. That Freud often delivers this sketch in the language of individual psyches implies that, as in a parable, a wider social and historical set of arguments are being made in the highly symbolized form of a drama of individuals and internalized psyches. From this somewhat ex-centric perspective on the representational forms of the work of mourning, we would now like to turn to a particular *hai tahd* film.

▶

An Armenian Journey

Narrator and filmmaker Theodore Bogosian begins *An Armenian Journey* in Armenia, at the Martyr's Monument in Yerevan, without mentioning or representing the conditions of possibility for his being there, such as his access to capital and his U.S. passport. He also ends the film at the monument, not having found what he expressly set out to find, namely, irrefutable historical proof of the genocide. But at the end of the film he tells us that he did find something more valuable:

Theodore Bogosian stands before the Martyr's Monument in Yerevan in *An Armenian Journey.*

> For those who choose to deny the Armenian Genocide, I have come to see that there is no such thing as undeniable evidence. . . . The search I undertook for a truth no one could deny remains unfulfilled. But I did find in my search something greater. I did find the strength, the immortality of an Armenian Spirit that has endured despite all challenge and denial. In my search I found another truth that could not be denied. In a living people scattered across the globe, I found a Nation.

This symmetrical framing technique—beginning and ending the film in the "same place"—exemplifies the film's narrative structure, which is a nested set of three narratives: the sequences at the monument frame a story of Bogosian's quest for primary historical documents proving Turkish responsibility for the genocide.[9] In turn, the sequences of his search for the primary documents frame a trip he takes with Mariam and her daughter Joan to eastern Anatolia. This narrative technique is held together by the overbearing figure of Bogosian, who is everywhere in the film: he is director/producer/filmmaker, he is voice-off and voice-over, and he is physically in most scenes. He is the conductor of the narrative, the organizing principle, and the supreme voice of documentary authority. He travels the global Armenian nation-space single-mindedly and without serious hindrance. But perhaps most important, he can assimilate a multiplicity of discourses—Mariam's raw emotion, the old Turkish of the crucial document, the academic double-speak of Professor Justin McCarthy's refutation of the genocide—and translate them first into a historical narrative, and then into "an Armenian Spirit," and "a nation."

The rigidly structured and controlled form of the film takes on a desperate and furious air as the camera follows Bogosian across the globe—from Cambridge, Massachusetts, to southern Mexico to Yerevan to Arapkir and Egin—in search of the missing documents, Mariam, and Mariam's hometown. However, Bogosian's desperate and furious mobility is oddly undercut by his unbelievably consistent monotone voice. Whether he is discussing the brutalized bodies of genocide victims, addressing a tearful Mariam, recounting the distance he has just traveled on a particular trip, or informing us of Mariam's age, his voice maintains the same, flat measure. On first consideration these formal aspects of the film seem quite disparate. But in light of Freud's discussion of melancholia and mania, they emerge as a quite systematic oscillation between those two affective forms or modalities: the mania of Bogosian's global travels and of his single-minded quests on the one hand, and his persistent monotone accounts of genocidal memories on the other. The desperately controlled, rigidly constructed form of the film performs the obsessive work of a mania that labors to fix and focus attention on a task or an object in order to avoid noticing the traumatic site that is really motivating the mania—in Freud's terms, an ambivalently loved lost object.

If the film formally oscillates between melancholic and manic modes, what is its ambivalently loved lost object? This film struggles with a series of losses that are layered one on top of the other: the missing document, the irrefutable historical proof of genocide, the affective memories of genocide, and the bodies of genocide victims. Yet none of these objects is quite "lost enough" to precipitate the film's formally melancholic and manic features, since the film incorporates all of them into the diegesis, thus recovering them in the cinematic discourse. The misty figure of "the homeland," on the other hand, never quite materializes in the diegesis. As an internalized representation, a representation internal to *An Armenian Journey*, "the homeland" takes on the implicit form of a phantasmatic, transhistorical, ethnically pure Armenian national territory. The volatile, pregenocide, multiethnicity of the Ottoman Empire as well as postgenocide assimilation in the diaspora become the biggest threats to "the homeland" in the *hai tahd* sense, threats that can never be quieted in diaspora. It is the traumatic loss of this ambivalently loved figure of "the homeland" that induces *An Armenian Journey*'s melancholic/manic representations; the film's anxious call for the diaspora to internalize this figure is symptomatic of that melancholia.

This "homeland" of eastern Anatolia was not, of course, ethnically pure, nor was it national territory. In some areas of that "homeland" before the late nineteenth and early twentieth century, Armenians constituted a bare majority over Turks and Kurds, but for the most part they were only a plurality. Not only was the territory a shared space, but culturally and economically the Turkish and Armenian communities were as connected as they were separate. The Armenian identity Bogosian "finds" and recognizes as "Spirit" and "Nation" is thus not a transhistorical one born with Mesrop Mashtots's invention of the Armenian alphabet fifteen centuries ago and living on today across the globe. In fact, to the extent that it exists discursively, the most important origin of modern Armenian nationality can be located in that very conjuncture Bogosian represents as the moment of its near death: roughly the period between the Treaty of Berlin in 1878 and the establishment of the short-lived Armenian nation-state in 1918. This was the period of the 1890s massacres and the 1915 genocide, but it was also the period during which subjects of the Ottoman Empire were rationally abstracted into national citizens of Turkey. Both events contributed to a new formation of ethnicity and nationality in the territorial space of the Ottoman Empire. Armenians who had understood themselves as an Ottoman minority came to be understood and to understand themselves as an occupied people. Those occupied Armenians who then went into diaspora, as well as those who managed to stay in Turkey, had to understand themselves differently yet again.[10] We trace this history here (one of course much more complex than we have suggested) because it brings out the complicated genealogy of diaspora that *An Armenian Journey* tried to gather under the names *Nation* and *Armenian Spirit*, a genealogy the melancholic/manic form of the film seems desperate for us not to see. Nonetheless, markers of other genealogies that run counter to Bogosian's nationalist narrative do exceed the film's overt structure. What is more, those markers are consistently anchored to the figure of Mariam Davis.

An Armenian Journey stages a very predictable regime of sexual difference vis-à-vis Mariam. Bogosian finds Mariam in Mexico and takes her to eastern Turkey; he interrogates her about affective memories of the genocide and then reassembles those memories into a historical narrative told through maps, black-and-white stills, and his own voice-over. For example, the first sequence in which we meet Mariam begins with a montage of black-and-white stills of genocide victims—including the close-up of a girl child whom we are made to think of as Mariam by the voice-over, and a still of three bodies lying in a pit—which dissolves directly into a close-up shot of Mariam sitting on a sunny patio framed by lush vines, telling her story. She *is* genocide here, the fractured and brutalized bodies of genocide, which as a result of the dissolve spill into Mariam's image. She becomes a palimpsest over the pure brutality of genocide, giving that story of brutality a measure of coherence as a bodily form. Yet while she talks, she is interrupted by Bogosian's voice-over that fills in the facts—facts of geography, of time, all of which she presumably told Bogosian, but that talk over her, leaving for her the affect of genocide. The film incorporates her affect through repeated close-ups of her crying, followed by Bogosian's persistent monotone and his sadistic, interrogative attempts to narrativize her memories for her, to tell us how we are to understand her memories historically.[11] Mariam is often framed off-center, leaning out of the frame to take a drag of her cigarette, while Bogosian is shot perfectly centered in the frame, shoulders square, hands crossed in front of him.

Diegetically, Mariam is the most interiorized figure of the film, and as such is discursively impotent and lacking in control when compared with Bogosian's complete mobility and externality.[12] Her interview itself is interrupted by black-and-white stills of children and bodies, sometimes without voice-over, as if to remind us that there is a more substantive referent to which Mariam's memories refer, an outside to her interiorized affect—a history, a proof, a truth of which Mariam is just a part. Genocide is continually evoked and placed on her body (her leaning out of frame, close-ups of her crying, her struggling to find the words), and then immediately reinscribed in a bigger picture (the black-and-white stills, the historical voice-over of authority). As Bogosian says when he first introduces us to Mariam,

> I was drawn to Mariam's testimony for two reasons. Unlike most survivors, Mariam has photographs and documents that prove she lived in eastern Turkey during the deportations. But just as important, Mariam's tragic tale is typical of the horrifying stories that young Armenians, including myself, heard when we were growing up.

The desire into which Mariam is inscribed is one well suited to an often manifestly patriarchal Armenian American community: the reinscription of an incomplete woman, with a proper privatized place, interrogated by the accomplished man, who projects her into the bigger picture. It is through this masculinist regime that the film represents Mariam's work of mourning as a feminized melancholic affect, which is, in turn, productive of a masculinist manic politics. As we argued above, it is precisely the film's oscillation between melancholic and manic modes that sanctions the particular fantasy of a unified nation in diaspora.

And yet Bogosian has to work hard—and, we would argue, ultimately fails—to fully control Mariam and her memories. During crucial sequences

Mariam Davis in *An Armenian Journey*.

of the film, other representations of Mariam as a figure open up and escape the film's grasp. At one point Mariam recounts a horrific story of seeing dogs digging up the body of her little brother, who had been killed by Turkish soldiers. As she tells of finding her brother's body scattered in pieces and of gathering those pieces and reburying them, Bogosian interrupts as voice-off and asks, "How old was he?" to which she responds dismissively, "Oh, he must have been two-and-a-half, three—I can't remember the time element at all." Despite such persistent use of voice-over and voice-off to calculate Mariam's memories—to put them in the service of a historical narrative of objectively determinable and irrefutable fact, a narrative productive of a global Armenian nation—Mariam's dismissive response here begs the question of other memories and other narratives.

In another crucial sequence, Mariam violates what Bogosian calls "their agreement" not to tell anyone what they are really doing in Turkey and not to mention the word *Armenian,* an agreement ostensibly (and not completely without reason) reached so as not to draw the attention of Turkish authorities, but one that has broader effects in the filmic space. The sequence begins with Mariam's identifying the quarter of the city where she lived as an orphaned child, a city called Arapkir in eastern Turkey. She quickly becomes excited, and we get a shot of a street into which she walks and says, "Come on over here and I'll show you where

Director Theodore Bogosian in *An Armenian Journey.*

I learned to sew." Mariam leads us through streets and alleys, recounting her days in Arapkir, visibly happy over the familiarity. In fact, her familiarity and activity become so animated that she ventures something of a gibe at the camera: as they reach the top of the hill, Mariam says, "Shall we go back down?" to which Bogosian replies, "Sure, if this is the end of the street you remember." Mariam here interrupts him to say, "Oh, I remember *all* of it now. You can go on down." These are perhaps the only sequences in which Mariam directs her own action in the diegesis. It is not surprising, then, that the film works swiftly and effectively to prohibit Mariam's activity. Toward the end of this sequence, while the camera chases Mariam down the hill, Bogosian's voice abruptly cuts in as voiceover, blotting out the sound of walking and of the village, to say, "In the excitement of remembering Arapkir, Mariam forgot the need for caution." Then Mariam says, "Before, um, now these kids are walking around, before they were only Armenians, and children, hungry." This series of edits has the effect of retroactively catching Mariam in the act of a transgression. Bogosian inserts the voice-over to chastise Mariam for her enthusiasm, thereby regaining control of the narrative and interiorizing Mariam, pushing her back into place as an affective spectacle of memories within the narrative.

But these moments in which Mariam acts out also make her figure more complex, suggesting that the film's overt representation of her as the affective, melancholic figure for the Armenian Spirit encounters a certain resistance. That is, the figure of Mariam plays both a productive role for the film, as it figures the affect of genocide in a melancholic form so that the masculinist history of Armenia can be told and a manic nationalist politics can be conducted, and a defensive role for the film, as it suppresses or contains something that threatens the film's particular melancholic/manic narrativization of Armenian diasporan nationalism. In the Arapkir sequence we just recounted, Bogosian's prohibition against the word *Armenian* functions to keep Mariam's memories fixed on the affective horror of genocide and away from the complexities of her life among Turks. By keeping Mariam from uttering *Armenian* in Turkey, the prohibition seeks to keep memories of Armenians among Turks from surfacing in favor of retaining the singular memory of a Turkish space "ethnically cleansed" of Armenians by Turks. Mariam's violation of the prohibition thus brings into the frame of the film more complex histories—of, for example, Armenian-Turk coexistence, or of Turks who aided Armenians. It would seem that there is something about the figure of Mariam that threatens to stir the waters of the film's particular representation of the Armenian nation's work of mourning. We would argue that while much contemporary Armenian American cultural production is concerned with the work of mourning, *hai tahd* as a genre does the work of mourning in an incessantly melancholic and manic form. In turn, *An Armenian Journey*, as a particular example of *hai tahd*, offers a particularly masculinist representation of this oscillation. However, *An Armenian Journey* is also unique because Mariam Davis often figures the failure of this masculinist oscillation between mourning and melancholia. In other words, the film stages a struggle between the figure of Ted and the figure of Mariam. It is to this struggle that we would now like to turn.

▶──

Diasporan Ethics

Unlike in many classic masculinist representations of the nation, Mariam is not represented as the paradigmatic "mother of the nation."[13] In fact, she is actively dematernalized and desexualized throughout the film. By including only Mariam's childhood history and her immediate present as an elderly woman, the film excludes that entire part of her life from which she could be represented as a traditionally maternal and sexual being, even though her middle-aged daughter, Joan Davis, accompanies Bogosian and Mariam on their trip to Turkey. This is especially striking since the concept of *diaspora* carries with it a strong etymological connection to discourses of fertility and maternity/paternity, as it derives from the Greek *dia,* meaning "across," and *speirein,* meaning "to sow."[14] What is more, the images the film associates with the Armenian Nation are remarkably static, appearing consistently on the side of death: ancient crumbling ruins, old books and documents, black-and-white stills, even the Martyr's Monument in Yerevan. This particular narrativization of diaspora thus seems to posit a mutual exclusivity between the maternal, on the one hand, and the affect of mourning melancholically, on the other. We would argue that in a quite unique way *An Armenian Journey,* which labors so hard to prove the truth of the genocide and to establish the continuity and stability of the Armenian Spirit, sustains itself by systematically suppressing the thematic of reproductive labor. Though the figure of Mariam repeatedly begs the question of this thematic, its suppression is nearly absolute. Mariam's affect of mourning the genocide is put to work for the National Spirit in diaspora by means of this suppression, whose lineaments and implications can be gleaned from a careful reading of the shadowy figure of Mariam's daughter, Joan.

The film works hard to marginalize Joan, to keep her silent and off-screen, and thus to prohibit direct identification of or with her; never in the entire film does she utter a sound, nor does she occupy the center of the screen space, nor does Bogosian give us any information about her. Nonetheless, her marginal or shadowy presence begs a number of questions. As a daughter, Joan disrupts Mariam's assigned role as desexualized child victim of genocide. For example, at one point during her visit to Arapkir, Mariam excitedly addresses her daughter directly, pointing to the place where she polished brass as a child: "Look, Joanie . . ." she says. Though the film never represents Joan's response, Mariam's direct address suggests a personal exchange between mother and daughter that exceeds the camera's gaze. In particular, the diminutive *Joanie* marks a specifically U.S. childhood that raises questions about how Mariam acquired the *odar* surname *Davis,* and about Joan's own relationship to Armenian ethnicity. Further, the implicit exchange between Joan and Mariam raises the specter of an exchange between women, between mothers and daughters, an exchange unmediated by Bogosian or by the homosocial economy of diasporan nationality that dominates *An Armenian Journey.* Joan is thus herself a suppressed figure, actively and forcefully made to play an incidental role in Bogosian's narrative because of the threat she necessarily presents to the "immortality of an Armenian Spirit" that Bogosian claims to have found.[15]

From our reading of Joan's position in the film, one cannot ignore, as the film does, the histories of diaspora that constituted the white ethnicity of U.S. Armenians—histories radically different from those that

Mariam and Joan Davis on the way to Arapkir in *An Armenian Journey*.

constructed the ethnic and national identities of young Armenian children
in eastern Anatolia in 1915, or the ethnic and national identities of contemporary Soviet and post-Soviet Armenian immigrants in Los Angeles, or
the ethnic and national identities of Armenians living in Armenia or
Nagorno-Karabakh today. The film constructs an equivalence between
Mariam as an Armenian child in eastern Anatolia of 1915, Mariam as an
adult living in Mexico in the 1980s, Ted Bogosian living in Boston in the
1980s, and Joan living somewhere in New York in the 1980s according to
the general equivalent of an "Armenian Spirit"—an equivalence meant to
spur identification among northern and western Armenian viewers. Yet the
fleeting representations of Joan raise questions that break up that equivalence. We would suggest that, in Freud's terms, the questions raised by a
potential identification with the fleeting image of Joan carry out "the orders of the reality" of genocidal loss by giving the libido new objects to
which it can cathect. That is, were one to identify with Joan, one could begin the difficult "working through" of genocidal loss, not through masculinist and statist discourses of global Armenian Spirit but, rather,
through discourses of maternity, mother-daughter femininity, and biethnic-
ity. The work of mourning could thus become the occasion not for positing
a global diasporan nationality, but for coming to terms with the specificity
of contemporary First World Armenian ethnicity.

We would like to call attention to another moment in the film that suggests that the work of mourning the Armenian genocide can be completed without resorting to melancholic memories or manic politics. Bogosian, Mariam, and Joan are chauffeured on their trip to Arapkir and Egin by a Turkish cab driver, who, much like Joan, is persistently marginalized by the camera and by Bogosian's voice-over. There are three shots of him: one that begins with the image of an ornament hanging from his rearview mirror and then pans to his head, completely in shadow, as he drives the cab, during which the voice-over declares, "The Turkish driver of the taxi we hired spoke no English and knew nothing about our journey"; a second quick shot of him sitting in the back of the cab, his face obscured by the cab's open door, after the group has pulled to the side of the road to allow Mariam to walk in a field and remember her home village; and a third quick shot of him in the margins of the frame as he stands in the road waiting distractedly while Mariam walks along the side of the road. These shots and voice-over function to represent him as a potentially threatening, generalized, and racially other "Turk," a Turk somehow like those who ordered or carried out the murder of almost 2 million Armenians in the early twentieth century. In fact, the cab driver cannot be inscribed as a speaking or thinking subject here, because his very look or speech could threaten the film's entire project of constructing a global diasporan Armenian Spirit. The film needs present-day Turks as metonymic equivalents of past genocidal Turks in order to forge an equivalence between past Armenian victims of genocide and present-day Armenians around the globe. It thus cannot risk engaging with the cab driver, lest he prove to be something other than a murderous figure.

But we soon notice it is precisely the *film's* project, not Mariam's, that is threatened by the cab driver. If one listens to what Mariam says as she walks through Arapkir, one notices that she is mapping her integration as a marginal child laborer in the local Turkish economy of 1915: she tells of working as a seamstress, a brass polisher, and a helper for local shopkeepers. In addition, she recounts three stories of Turks helping her after she was orphaned. At one point, when a Turkish shopkeeper invites the three Americans for tea, Bogosian says in a voice-over, "The kindness of the shopkeepers surprised me, but not Mariam." After Mariam mentions the kindness of the Turkish merchants from the same town sixty-six years ago, Bogosian asks, "They were Turkish?" to which Mariam responds, "They were Turkish, but they were kind to me. I can't say they were not kind. It was the others who, up north, were not so kind." While for Bogosian, and for the film in general, Armenian is persistently equated with Christianity and the West, Mariam here remaps this East-West cartography according to an alternative, North-South one. In these sequences, as in the fleeting representations of Joan, glimpses of Mariam and the cab driver function as potential sites of identification that could turn the work of mourning in quite unsettling, but hardly melancholic, directions.

Who, then, might this cab driver be if not a metonymic equivalent of Ottoman government murderers? We suspect that the Turkish cab driver and the local Turkish shopkeepers belong to the class of laborers that has been the object of extensive bilateral labor-exchange agreements between Germany and Turkey since 1961. In those agreements, Germany paid the Turkish state to provide it with a surplus labor pool to work primarily in the manufacturing, automobile, and service industries. The so-called Turkish *Gastarbeiter* (guest workers) who went to Germany between the late 1950s and late 1980s—who today number about 1.5 million—have now, according to many Germans, "overstayed their welcome." Once highly sought after, these Turkish immigrants have been subjected to increasingly extreme neofascist violence in the past decade, violence justified in the name of purifying the German nation-state. As different as this anti-Turkish, neofascist violence in Germany is from the state planned and executed policy of genocide against the Armenians, both nonetheless materialize fantasies of a homogeneous, transnational, and transhistorical national identity. When *An Armenian Journey* puts the powerful affect of mourning the Armenian genocide to work constructing a phantasmatic equivalence between a young Mariam Davis as victim of genocide and an adult Ted Bogosian as First World Armenian American filmmaker, it paradoxically reiterates its own fantasy of timeless national homogeneity. Consequently, the cab driver disrupts the Mariam-Ted equivalence just as the *Gastarbeiter* threaten German nationalism. Beneath and beyond his shadowy, silent presence, the figure of the cab driver begs the question of a tactical equivalence or politico-historical analogy between a young Mariam Davis, as child laborer in Arapkir subject to genocidal violence, and present-day Turkish *Gastarbeiter* as paracapitalist laborers subject to neofascist violence. Putting that powerful affect to work to forge such a tactical equivalence would, we suggest, exceed the calculable terms of *hai tahd* and reopen "the Armenian question."[16]

Similarly, Mariam's tenuous structural position as a child laborer in the streets of Arapkir suggests a tactical equivalence or politicohistorical analogy between her childhood and today's underclass Soviet and post-Soviet Armenian immigrants in Los Angeles. Like Mariam, these immigrants found it necessary to leave their homeland because of global economic and political forces. Once in Los Angeles, however, many have found that the equivalence the film draws among all Armenians internationally does not

always operate: earlier generations of Armenian Americans who are finan-
cially secure resent the immigrants' participation in gangs and their drawing of welfare checks.[17] And yet it is precisely this equivalence of all
Armenians internationally under the name *Armenian Spirit* that the film
holds most dear. In its place, we are arguing that capital equates the child
laborer Mariam and the (post-)Soviet immigrants as mobile marginal laborers who present a constitutive challenge to nationalist discourses of
homogeneity.

These alternative equivalencies we have briefly sketched follow both a
certain deconstructive ethics and the logic of capital. We have traced how
capital exploits these subjects similarly by positioning them as mobile marginal laborers; by so doing, we keep the work of mourning open to potential redeployment in today's geopolitical scene. We see this as an ethical
process in particular because tactically equating Mariam with post-Soviet
Armenian immigrants in the United States on the one hand and Turkish
Gastarbeiter in Germany on the other involves, from an Armenian perspective, respecting subjects who have been represented as threatening others
both as *other*, in their irreducible otherness, and as *subjects*, in their similarities with Armenians.[18] In the case of *An Armenian Journey*, these ethical questions only became possible in the wake of a feminist reading of the
figure of Mariam. This kind of reading requires, we are arguing, a double
attentiveness: first, noticing figures that are pushed to the edges of frames,
which enables a critique of exclusionary and disciplinary representational
practices; and second, imagining identifications with those liminal figures,
which enables a reading out from under the representations at hand. Without the analysis of Mariam's interiorization and the suppression of her reproductive labor, it would not have been possible to suggest that her work
of mourning can lead away from the film's nationalist, melancholic memories and manic politics and toward a diasporan ethics.

◆————————————————————————————

NOTES

1. Some other documentary films we would
   place in this genre are PeÅ Holmquist's *Back
   to Ararat* (1988) and Michael Hagopian's *The
   Forgotten Genocide* (1975).

2. On the history of *Tashnagtsoutiun*, see Louise
   Nalbandian, *The Armenian Revolutionary
   Movement* (Berkeley: University of California
   Press, 1963).

3. *On Metapsychology: The Theory of Psychoanalysis*, vol. 11 of the Pelican Freud Library
   (London: Penguin Books, 1984), 251. All references to "Mourning and Melancholia" are

   from this edition and will be cited parentheti-
   cally in the text.

4. Similar references to wider socio-political
   scenes can be found throughout Freud's
   work on "internal" psychic processes. See,
   for example, "Claims of Psychoanalysis to
   Scientific Interest" (1913), "On Narcissism—
   An Introduction" (1914), and "Repression"
   (1915).

5. J. Laplanche and J.-B. Pontalis, *The Language of Psychoanalysis* (New York: W. W.
   Norton, 1973), 226–27, 205–8. For an ex-

tended discussion of idiopathic and hetero-pathic identification, see Kaja Silverman, *Male Subjectivity at the Margins* (New York: Routledge, 1992), 205–7, 264–70.

6. Ibid., 206.

7. For an excellent overview of Freud's complex and changing conceptualizations of the ego, see ibid., 130–43.

8. By *edited* we do not just mean that the story is missing crucial information but, rather, that the entire plot is reformulated. That is, information is also added and reorganized.

9. The phantasmatic character of this film, which we discuss below, is reinforced by the fact that Bogosian exaggerates the importance of this search for primary documents. In fact, the documents featured in the film had previously been known and at least partially translated.

10. See, for example, Christopher J. Walker, *Armenia: The Survival of a Nation* (New York: St. Martin's Press, 1980); Richard G. Hovannisian, "The Historical Dimensions of the Armenian Question, 1878–1923," and Helen Fein, "Transnational Defense of Minorities: The Movement for Armenian Rights (1876–1915) and the Contemporary Movement for Soviet Jewry," in *Genocide and Human Rights*, special issue of the *Journal of Armenian Studies* 4, nos. 1, 2 (1992).

11. For a discussion of sadistic interrogation as a masculinist trope in film, see Kaja Silverman, *The Acoustic Mirror* (Bloomington: Indiana University Press, 1988).

12. See ibid., chap. 2.

13. On this trope in the context of European nationalisms, see George L. Mosse, *Nationalism and Sexuality—Middle-Class Morality and Sexual Norms in Modern Europe* (Madison: University of Wisconsin Press, 1985).

14. For an interpretation of the classical relationship between the maternal body and fertility, see Page duBois, *Sowing the Body—Psychoanalysis and Ancient Representations of Women* (Chicago: Chicago University Press, 1988).

15. For us, the Mariam-Joan relationship calls forth the centrality of mother-daughter relationships in a number of other texts that do not fit the *hai tahd* genre, such as Arlene Avakian's autobiographical memoir *Lion Woman's Legacy—An Armenian-American Memoir* (New York: Feminist Press, 1992); Carol Edgarian's novel *Rise the Euphrates* (New York: Random House, 1994); Stina Katchadourian's *Efronia: An Armenian Love Story* (Boston: Northeastern University Press, 1993); and Nancy Kricorian's *Zabelle* (New York: Atlantic Monthly Press, 1998).

16. We would like to thank Khachig Tölölyan, whose comments prompted us to clarify our argument at the end of this essay.

17. Sonia L. Nazario, "Soviet Armenians Find New Foe Here: Their Countrymen," *Wall Street Journal*, 3 March 1989, A1–A4.

18. For an extended discussion of the ethical in these terms, see Jacques Derrida, "Force of Law: The 'Mystical Foundation of Authority,'" *Cardozo Law Review* 11, no. 5–6 (July/August 1990).

LAURA U. MARKS

[10] *Fetishes and Fossils: Notes on Documentary and Materiality*

Fetishes and fossils are two kinds of objects that condense cryptic histories within themselves. Both gather their peculiar power by virtue of a prior contact with some originary object. Both are like nodes, or knots, in which historical, cultural, and spiritual forces gather with a particular intensity. Fetishes and fossils translate experience through space and time in a material medium. In the following I would like to consider documentary cinema as fetish and as fossil, specifically with regard to the transformations that happen in the movement between cultures.

My use of the fetish and fossil metaphors relates to the materiality of film itself as witness to an originating object: to documentary's indexical quality.[1] To think of film as fetish or fossil requires an archaeology of sense experience and draws on an epistemology based on the sense of touch. Nonvisual, or nonaudiovisual, sensory knowledge has tended to be dismissed by major world philosophies, and feminist thought is one area that has defended the importance of these senses as sources of knowledge and identity. My exploration thus takes part in a materialist feminism and in feminist theories of perception. I wish to situate this work carefully, however, because the feminisms that echo through this writing are often changed in important respects. This includes the fact that my exploration of nonaudiovisual sense knowledge is related to the antiocularcentric theories of such feminists as Luce Irigaray and Julia Kristeva, but distinct in that I focus on how different cultures ascribe knowledge to the senses. I introduce the term *emergent senses* for nonaudiovisual sense experience in film: these are senses that are experienced by the filmgoer in the process of reception.

I also make arguments about the role of the fetish in subject formation that draw on feminist psychoanalytic work. Again, I want to temper this alliance because the approach I ultimately take is less psychoanalytic than phenomenological, as this latter approach seems more useful for dealing with bodily manifestations of cultural difference. When my argument turns to psychoanalysis, it is more to object-relations theory than to the Lacanian psychoanalysis in which much feminist work on cinema is grounded.

This essay uses the work of Shauna Beharry, a performance/ritual and video artist, to explore how a documentary film or video may function as both fossil and fetish. Beharry is a third-generation Canadian of Indian descent whose work focuses on the loss of language and of cultural reference that happens with displacement; the paradox that she still carries cultural references in her body; and sensuous or spiritual experiences that challenge translation. The stake of this exploration is to recognize the complexity of these fetishized objects that move between cultures, how they are created, how they are useful, and how they may self-destruct when their usefulness is ended.

▶ ───

Fetishes

A fetish is defined in terms of its *contact* with some original, powerful object. Of the many theories of the fetish that operate in anthropology, psychoanalysis, and Marxist analysis, I concentrate on those that explicitly attend to it in terms of a series of historical, intercultural displacements. I will argue that intercultural relations are necessarily fetishistic, although clearly fetishes are not necessarily intercultural. All fetishes are translations into a material object of some sort of affect; the fetish described by psychoanalysis is only one of these.

William Pietz's etymology of the word *fetish* turns out to be a long and complex history of colonization, appropriation, and translation.[2] In an impressive act of archaeology, he argues that the fetish is a specifically intercultural phenomenon. Briefly, Pietz traces the transformation of the Portuguese word *feitiço* from its use in Christian witchcraft law to the word *Fetisso* — also Portuguese, from the pidginization of *feitiço* — used by explorers in the part of West Africa that they called Guinea. In the later construction, "fetishism" was the sort of practice that invested lifelike powers in objects themselves, powers attained through physical contact. It came to be distinguished from idolatry because the objects concerned did not *represent* deities but in their very materiality held godlike powers. For example, the feather of a chicken is a sacred fetish because the chicken was sacred; the relics of saints, preserved fingers or scraps of cloth, gain their value as a fetish through contact with the saint. The fetishistic relationship is between two sacred objects, not a deity and an object. Fetishes, to European intellectuals' way of thinking, were stubbornly nontranscendental.

The notion of the fetish was mobilized during a period of imperial expansion. Pietz argues that this notion played a significant role in establishing European preconceptions about human consciousness and the material world, preconceptions on which the disciplinary human sciences that arose in the nineteenth century were founded.[3] For example, as he describes, the travelogues of Dutch merchants such as Willem Bosman portrayed African fetish worship as the perversion of the sort of rational self-interest that they saw as "the natural organizing principle of good social order." These writers' particular narratives were seized upon for general illustrative purposes by Enlightenment intellectuals, including Karl Marx.

Moreover, Pietz notes that the term *fetishism* was used by a particular stratum of Europeans to describe European peasants' superstitions, as well as Catholic ritual.[4] Only later did it come to describe the practices of Africans, in the coinage of Portuguese traders and colonizers. *Fetishism,* then, originated as a term used to separate the ruling Protestant, protocapitalist groups from others both outside and within the culture. The early use of *fetishism* to describe the practices of both European peasants and West Africans reaffirmed the emerging European powers' belief that, unlike themselves, these groups were irrational, incapable of abstraction, and mired in the body. Peter Stallybrass and Allon White argue in a similar vein that the rise of the European bourgeoisie necessitated a process of distantiation both inter- and intraculturally.[5] In order to consolidate an identity that was capable of "rising above" the merely bodily, the bourgeoisie projected its own unacceptable excesses elsewhere, separating itself from the grotesque and carnivalesque practices of the peasants. Colonial expansion exacerbated this process, as an even more primitive other became available for the disgusted/desiring projections of the European middle classes. Thus in some ways the forbidden object of desire is already an intercultural one, for the desire that the bourgeoisie had forbidden itself became embodied in primitivist fantasies.

It is important to note that intercultural fetishism is initiated both by the fetishizers and the fetishized: in this case, between the Portuguese traders and African middlemen who "explained" African spiritual practices to them. Pietz suggests that West African informants themselves used the term *Fetisso* to describe their practices to the Portuguese. This preemptive fetishism had the effect of shielding actual ceremonial practices from scrutiny. It is in this sense that the discourse of the fetish "has always been a critical discourse about the false objective values of a culture from which the speaker is personally distanced," always an intercultural product.[6] This view of the fetish as an object produced in the encounter between cultures strongly underscores Homi Bhabha's characterization of colonial stereotypes as fetishes—sites where cultural difference is fixed but in their very fixity reveal the instability of the encounter.[7]

The archaeological process of discovering the meaning of such historical fetish objects recognizes that they cannot be deciphered with finality but must be treated as keys to a particular historical moment. Fetishes, as Theodor Adorno wrote, are "objective constellations in which the social represents itself."[8] Pietz similarly describes the fetish in neo-Marxist terms as a historical nexus of different material discourses:

> The fetish must be viewed as proper to no historical field other than that of the history of the word itself, and to no discrete society or culture, but to a cross-cultural situation formed by the ongoing encounter of the value codes of radically different social orders. In Marxist terms, one might say that the fetish is situated in the space of cultural revolution.[9]

▶——————————————————————————————

Fossils

Fossils, like fetishes, acquire their meaning by virtue of an originary contact. A fossil is the indexical trace of an object that once existed, its animal or vegetable tissue now re-created in stone. Created in one layer of history, they get sedimented over, but instead of disintegrating they solidify and transform. So when some earthquake happens years later or continents away, these objects surface, bearing witness to forgotten histories. The fossil metaphor has been used by Gilles Deleuze to describe the unsettling quality of certain inexplicable but powerful cinematic images: "It is as if the past surfaces in itself but in the shape of personalities which are independent, alienated, off-balance, in some sense embryonic, strangely active fossils, radioactive, inexplicable in the present where they surface, and all the more harmful and autonomous."[10] To Deleuze, fossils are not cold, stone objects but live, dangerous things. These images, which should call to mind geological cross-sectional diagrams, refer to the power of memory images to embody different pasts. When an image is all that remains of a memory, when the memory cannot be "assigned a present" but simply stares up at one where it has been unearthed, then that image is like a fossil. It is possible to examine these images and learn the histories they have witnessed. The "radioactive" aspect of this sort of fossil is that it may arouse other memories, causing inert presences on the most recent layer of history themselves to set off chains of associations that had been forgotten.

Indexical Witness: Film as Fetish or Fossil

André Bazin described photography as an imprint of the world, a trace of material presence like a death mask.[11] This is the fetishlike/fossil-like quality that is at work in film: film bears the trace of another material object on its surface. This fact is what gives film its representational power, just as a fetish (in the religious sense) obtains its power by carrying the trace of another material object.[12] However, the essential qualities of photographic indexicality must be understood in the context of their historical use.[13] The use made of indexicality varies, to be sure, from evidentiary proof to mere ghostlike trace of the pro-filmic real. We can define documentary in the broadest sense as a cinema whose indexical relation to the real is of central importance. Any kind of cinema has this relation to the pro-filmic event, but only documentary claims this relation to the real as one of its defining qualities. By approaching the indexicality of film as a fetishlike or fossil-like quality, I mean to emphasize that this trace of the real on film is embalmed in layers of historical use and interpretation, which obscure and ultimately transform any original meaning it might have had.

The implication of this notion of contact that underlies both the fossil and the fetish is that representation and knowledge are not to be explained exclusively on the level of language but also participate in contact with the object represented. The objects I discuss here encode *material* conditions of displacement as well as discursive ruptures. Their substrate is not solely a referent but also a material touchstone. Clearly, then, in my use, the tropes of fossil and fetish operate on a fairly concrete level. Both can be used simply as heuristic devices based on a notion of contact with some original, powerful object. But I intend to use them as more than that. The notion of the fetish, in particular, I find epistemologically powerful because it requires a tactile, rather than purely mental, contact to take place between objects; it is not a metaphor.[14]

Fetishes and Fossils of Transnational Life

Fetishes and fossils encode material conditions of displacement; they are those historical objects that contain the histories produced in intercultural traffic. I want to stress that the intercultural space in which fetishes and fossils are produced is charged with power; it is not a neutral ground. Colonial power relations in particular, with their propensity for crossbreeding indigenous and imported meanings, are prime sites for the production of these objects. Where two or more material discourses crash together are formed any number of peculiar artifacts: consider the Korean peasant ceramics that got taken up as aesthetic objects in the tea ceremony of their sixteenth-century Japanese colonizers (and the aestheticized copies that ensued); national dishes such as mulligatawny stew (Britain) or *rijstaffel* (Holland) that translate the colonies' cuisine; or the very bodies of members of the Hauka cult in the Ivory Coast, as they became possessed by the spirits of the British colonial powers (documented in Jean Rouch's *Les Maîtres fous,* 1953).[15] These are some examples that tumble to mind of fetishlike objects that are the product of two- (or more) directional, power-inflected appropriation and retranslation.

Postcolonial history is necessarily an investigation of fossils. We are constantly discovering inexplicable factoids on the surface of represented history that invite us to cut through the layers and connect them to their source, cutting between private recollection and official discourse. More often than not, the investigator contracts their carcinogenic quality. The "piece of the rock" that contains our own lives, constituting them both in terms of and separate from dominant history, disintegrates into unstable, seething sands, and we have no choice but to sift through, looking for clues.

Deleuze's hallucinatory list of the qualities of the fossil, especially its potential to do harm, resonates strongly with Pietz's intimations that fetishes are rebellions just waiting to happen. Both fossil and fetish, in the senses I have described, carry within them histories that, once unraveled, make the fixity of the present untenable.

▶───────────────────────────────────────

Seeing Is Believing

Fetishes are produced not only in the course of built-up time, like fossils, but also in the disjunctive movement through space. Postcolonial life is producing these lateral fetishes at record speed as people become displaced, especially as they emigrate to the lands of their former colonizers. The interstitial space of the fetish produces meaning, lots of meanings, but they are often built on incomprehension. For example, the *bindi* that Shauna Beharry's mother, like all Hindi married women, wore on her forehead becomes in the West a signifier of exotic Oriental desirability. As she describes it in *Seeing Is Believing* (1991), Beharry's own skin takes on meanings over which she has no control. White people ask this brown-skinned Canadian woman where she comes from. If the response

"Moosejaw" doesn't satisfy them, then in order to answer, Beharry must undertake an excavation of the Indian heritage that set her apart. Her body, Beharry relates, is inscribed with a language she must laboriously learn to read. That is, she must learn to read for the purpose of translating back to people who assume the right to know things in their own language. When she finds, for example, that she is not "typical Indian," that her skin and eyes are different because her grandfather was Chinese (well, not exactly Chinese, he was from Hong Kong, and no, she doesn't speak Urdu, she grew up in Ireland . . .), the burden of explanation becomes overwhelming.

This burden of explanation is why people who are moving between cultures find that their luggage gets heavier and heavier. Their familiar objects are fossilizing. What was taken for granted in one culture becomes incomprehensible in another, and it becomes the immigrant's responsibility to build up and to excavate those layers of impossible translation.

Seeing Is Believing is a mourning piece about the death of Beharry's mother. The short tape evokes the closeness of daughter to mother expressed in terms not of vision, which would already imply a degree of distance, but of touch. Beharry is a ritual/performance artist, and *Seeing Is Believing* was her first work in a mechanically reproduced medium. The tape expresses Beharry's frustration over her inability to express in this medium, for, paradoxically, she is using video to show the limits of vision. It begins with Beharry's camera searching a still photograph over and over. It is a photograph of herself, wearing a silk sari. Her voice on the sound track is describing the anger and bafflement she felt when, after her mother died, she could not recognize her in photographs. Only when she put on her mother's sari, Beharry says, did she feel that she had "climbed into her skin." The disparity between the searching movements of the camera and her wistful voice on the sound track, between visual and audio, creates a poignant awareness of the missing sense of touch.

While Beharry tells her story, the camera has been looking ever more closely (*focusing* is not the right word) at the silk fabric of the sari in a detail of the photo. So when the tape keys in a smaller image of the portrait, superimposing it on the folds of the sari, the difference between these two ways of seeing is startling. I realize that the tape has been using my vision as though it were a sense of touch; I have been brushing the (image of the) fabric with the skin of my eyes rather than looking at it. Beharry says she wanted to "squeeze the touchability out of the photo," and she has: the difference between the senses collapses slightly. This experience of looking, together with Beharry's compelling words, makes us reflect that memory may be encoded in touch, sound, perhaps smell, more than vision. Walter

Benjamin's theory of the optical unconscious embraces a notion of seeing as touch, as involving oneself in the density of the image in a form of visual knowledge that is almost tactile.[16] Beharry's tactile use of the video camera evokes this form of seeing.

▶──

Is Seeing Believing? Cinema and Nonaudiovisual Sense Knowledge

Fetishes are sources of knowledge, especially knowledge of the nonaudio-visual senses. *Seeing Is Believing* calls on the sort of knowledge that can only be had in the physical presence of an object—or from the indexical witness of cinema. Touch is obviously a sense whose knowledge requires the physical presence of the object: Beharry makes this clear in her attempt to "squeeze the touchability out of the photo." To touch something one's mother, one's grandparents, or an unknown person touched is to be in physical contact, mediated by time, with the other person.

Similarly, consider how smell is an indexical witness. Failing direct neural stimulation (olfactory hallucination), we smell because molecules from the source of smell have reached the membranes within the nose. Smell requires contact, molecules coming into touch with receptors. A source of smell gradually diminishes over time as its particles disperse. To smell something, then, is to participate in its gradual destruction. But it is also to share the experience of the thing with others who smelled it before. Smell is the quintessentially fetishistic and defetishizing sense: it depends on the presence of the object, but it also destroys it.

Beharry is quite aware that the power of touch, smell, and taste lies in their transitoriness. She makes this a theme of her performance "Ashes to Flowers: The Breathing" (which I saw in Montreal in May 1993 at the appropriately named Gallery Burning). Participants smell incense and the food she prepares; at the end of the performance they walk on raw rice strewn in patterns on the floor, perceiving the image with the sense of touch at the same time that they disperse it. But to transfer this sense of the fleetingness of the senses to a recording medium, both its intensity and its evanescence, requires that the fetishlike quality of the audiovisual image be acknowledged. Film (like any mechanical reproduction) tends to fix and generalize its objects, but film is also capable of the fetish's volatility. Film as fetish is able to reactivate the presence of the fetishized object, as the (audio)visual image yields to the things it cannot represent; and in the process the image ceases to exist as a fetish. To move through this process acknowledges not just the fleetingness of time but also the fragility of culture in translation.

The artist's grief in *Seeing Is Believing* is colored by resentment of the Western cultural emphasis on visuality. The photographs of her mother seem to rob Beharry of actual memories of her. As such the loss she is trying to address is not only the intimacy between mother and daughter but also has to do with the regimes of knowledge that predominate in different cultures. Memory, she suggests, can be lost in translation, especially in the difference between cultures' regimes of sense knowledge. Beharry's use of video to critique photography is a pointed reference to the way visual records steal memories, precisely in their reified concreteness. Photography has a specific cultural history, which includes its ethnographic use as one of the technologies of imperial domination. Nevertheless, the Western snapshot has achieved ascendancy in most cultures, including the top echelons of "third world" cultures, as the way of coding private representation. Thus it is no surprise that, as Beharry has stressed, visuality is also the dominant mode of knowledge in Brahmin ritual, or the practices of the upper caste within Hinduism. It is no problem, or not such a great problem, to put a Brahmin ritual on tape, for instance. The rituals that get lost in the act of immigration and cultural translation are the non-Brahmin, the peasant rituals.[17]

Beharry's performances and videos carry out a feminist project in that they excavate a form of knowledge that patriarchal cultures routinely omit, namely, the sensuous knowledge that pertains to (diasporan) Indian women's daily lives. These are not experiences that would be immediately accessible to any woman. It is not possible to assert a feminine kinship with Beharry, or the women whose lives are implicit in her work, on the basis of identifying with some universal female experience. Her source of memory, the feel and smell of a sari on her skin, is quite specific to a particular group of women. However, though we the viewers may not be privy to the particular information Beharry learns from putting on her mother's sari, *Seeing Is Believing* does give us license to value other intimate, sense-bound experiences as sources of knowledge. Her mother's skin touched the sari, and now the sari touches her: knowledge is transmitted tactilely rather than visually. To be able to value this kind of knowledge, it is necessary to think of the skin as something that can distinguish, know, and remember.

To honor the knowledge of the senses has been the project of a number of feminist theorists, as well as critics of the rise of instrumental visuality.[18] Luce Irigaray, for example, privileges tactile knowledge as a feminine and primordial knowledge.[19] Irigaray argues that the sense of touch, because phylogenetically acquired prior to vision, is also the ontological foundation of vision. She infers this from the amniotic life of the embryo, the experience of wholeness or nondifferentiation that precedes the distinctions figure/ground, subject/object. Irigaray describes the sense of touch as a source of knowledge that does not require the separation of self and other that vision does.

It is quite possible to embrace Irigaray's description of tactile knowledge without accepting the ideal source to which she ascribes it. While neurophysiology and neuropsychology suggest that the senses of taste, touch, and smell are acquired earlier and located "deeper" in the brain than those of vision and hearing, this does not mean that these senses are outside the influence of culture. Thus when I appeal to the knowledge of the senses, it is not to call on a universal and primordial source of meaning. Tactile knowledge, while a form of knowledge that seems to be cultivated especially by women, is cultivated nonetheless. And with the cultivated knowledge of the senses comes a different quality of intersubjectivity. While knowledge based on vision tends to hold its object at a distance, the knowledge of the senses merges the knower with the object, however briefly. To touch, smell, or move in the presence of another is to experience that other in an intimate, embodied way. This tactile knowledge is mimetic, if we think of mimesis as an alternative form of knowledge to the instrumental knowledge that characterizes capitalism. As Michael Taussig describes it, "The sensuous moment of knowing includes a yielding and mirroring of the knower in the unknown, of thought in its object."[20]

It might seem appropriate to look to psychoanalysis for some account of how film creates impressions of touch, smell, and taste and stirs memories from them. Such an argument might explain tactility, smell, and so on in terms of excess: that which cannot be contained in a code. Excess is said to shatter meaning, simultaneously to threaten the unity of the symbolic order (and thus the subject defined within it) and to create a space of negativity in which the subject can be differentiated, however briefly. (I model this argument on Julia Kristeva's remarks on color, which she suggests extend to rhythm as well.)[21] Excess is what is individual in an otherwise universalizing code. I suggest, however, that nonaudiovisual information, even if it is difficult to pin down semiotically, has social meanings that make it part of large and fluid "codes." And even if this sort of information is fleeting, it extends beyond the level of the individual unconscious.

Finally, excess is said to be what threatens the symbolic order. The implication is that, even if we allow that the symbolic order is specific to a culture (which not all psychoanalytic theory permits), still the excess that pollutes it is of a more primordial and more universal character. Instead, I suggest that the seemingly extrasymbolic character of the emergent senses in film is actually informed by a wide range of cultural meanings.

▶ ─────────────────────────────────

Sense Knowledge and Embodied Perception

The knowledge of the senses is to a great degree learned, and it is learned differently in different cultures. It is commonly accepted that vision is schooled, as is hearing; it does not take too much stretch of the imagination to appreciate how touch, taste, and smell are cultivated as well. For example, the sense of touch and the ability to sense one's body moving through space are learned differently by construction workers, cooks, sculptors, lovers, dancers, and so forth. Anthropologists of the senses point out an astonishing degree of cross-cultural variation in how sense knowledge is educated. For example, the sense of smell is probably the sense least valued in the modern West as a source of information. It is, however, used as a distance and spatial sense by the native inhabitants of New Guinea.[22] The offering of perfumes is one of the most important forms of hospitality among many contemporary Arab people;[23] and in many other ways smell is cultivated as a means of communication in various cultures. In short, sense knowledge does not participate in a gulf of nonverbal meaning available to everyone; it is coded in particular ways depending on where it is learned.

But I do not mean that a culture's sense knowledge is innately inaccessible to outsiders, either. What Beharry gives us in *Seeing Is Believing* is not an introduction to the Indian woman's sense of touch, but an awareness of the importance of the knowledge of the senses in whatever our culture of origin might be. As we begin to seek our own sense knowledges, we can evaluate how our own cultures assimilate or filter out the knowledge of the senses.

▶ ─────────────────────────────────

Honoring Women's Sense Knowledges

Cultural transformation in diaspora is usually neither a full-blown assimilation nor an utterly random "hybrid," though of course both those patterns occur. More often, cultural practices pass through a selection process that, like the baggage scales at international airports, determines what is jettisoned and what is kept in the passage. What travels best is usually high class, intellectually powerful, and patriarchy friendly. It is the peasant practices, the women's practices, that go first—the bags of spice that spill from the overpacked luggage onto the waiting room floor. Diaspora intellectuals have usually already met the requirements for fitting into Western academic and cultural establishments, such as a cash base, a Western education, fluency in Romance languages, and membership in their indigenous elite. As Gayatri C. Spivak notes, when the Western intellectual establishment (which includes the art world) includes selected third worlders, it is doubly silencing others, namely, those who do not have access to elite education and international institutions.[24]

Shauna Beharry's excavations, then, are not just about finding the Indian "voice" silenced by generations of life in the West. They are also excavations of many histories that get lost in cultural translation, histories that are repressed at home as well. In "Ashes to Flowers: The Breathing," Beharry combines humble folk rituals with Brahmin ceremony, making carnival of Hinduism in a way that may be quite offensive to some people. When she makes chappatis with rose water and kneads rose petals into them, she is not only mixing peasant food with ritual offerings, but also allowing folk rituals and women's work to erupt into high Brahmin traditions. And in *Seeing Is Believing,* in the reading of the meanings fossilized in her own skin, she reveals the mixed legacy that includes a Chinese grandfather, undoing the myth of racial purity that matters both in cross-cultural "explanation" and in intracultural lineages.

▶━━━━━━━━━━━━━━━━━━━━━━━━━━━━━━━━━

Sensory Knowledge as Intellectual Knowledge

"Sensual abandon" is a phrase of Enlightenment subjectivity, implying that the senses (except maybe vision) dull the powers of the intellect. It implies that the Orientalist desire for the sense experience of other cultures is in part a desire to stop thinking, as though sensory knowledge is radically opposed to intellectual knowledge. But when in "Ashes to Flowers" Shauna Beharry lights incense, washes our hands with rose water, and encourages us to dance, she is not encouraging us to give up to our bodies but to respect our bodies' ways of knowing. These are knowledges that require just as much effort to acquire as intellectual knowledge. The "Oriental" trip she gives us is not an opportunity to breathe in the smells and let it all hang out, as she implies when shortly into the performance she changes from romantic Punjabi suit into a frumpy slip and housedress. Instead, it is a time to do a particular sort of work where bodies and minds work together. In short, stirring up the hierarchy of the senses is not a chance to play dumb: in fact, it's quite exhausting.

Fetishism as an intercultural relation involves a tremendous amount of translation, decipherment, and excavation. And ultimately there is no possibility of getting to a truth about either culture, for the fetish is produced only in the movement between cultures. As I noted before, fetishism as an act of preemptive translation protects an object from further scrutiny. Thus the intercultural act of fetishism seems to appeal to the desire for translation at the same time that it prevents further investigation.

Beharry's series of projects done under the "Ashes to Flowers" title addresses the difficulty of holding on to an ever heavier object inscribed with indecipherable meaning, and undertaking the burden of translation. In the ritual she performed at Gallery Burning, the earnest fetishistic translation of *Seeing Is Believing* gave way somewhat to an offhand dismissal of translatability. In the early part of the evening, Beharry attempted to recite a poem she had written in Urdu to the gathered group. The performer looked like a child trying to remember a lesson, stamping and tossing her head with frustration, her eyes wet with relief when she did manage to resolve a phrase. But she did not tell the meaning of the words to the group of friends gathered there, none of whom understood Urdu. It was only for us to experience the painful difficulty of excavation. (When Beharry performs this ritual for audiences of Indian descent, the reaction is no doubt quite different—sorrow, perhaps, at the cultural atrophy evident in her effort.) Such a renunciation suggests an acceptance of untranslatability as part of the intercultural experience.

Beharry's working process itself is built on a suspicion of the reification that happens when artwork enters discourse—which is quite different from fetishism. Fetishes are live things that can telescope back out to processes and relationships; reification reduces processes and relationship to things. One must obtain permission from the artist to write about her work, as I did when I first encountered it in 1992, and as I have in order to write this essay. She does not circulate images of her performances or stills from her videos but issues a single photograph, of her cupped hands holding a lily of the valley, to illustrate every event. Though she operates in the context of the Canadian art community, she has taken pains to work differently from most career artists. This course has been possible in part because of the relatively generous Canadian art-funding system, which enabled Beharry to pursue her practice in residencies and the like without being pressured to deliver discrete products. She refuses to

Shauna Beharry, "what my mouth forgets, my hands remember," from "Ashes to Flowers: The Breathing." Photo courtesy of the artist.

document her performances, preferring instead that information about her work be spread in the conversations of the people who have witnessed it. The statement she gives whenever required to represent herself in print is, "My work is small, simple, and travels by word of mouth. I trust in it."

Beharry's projects typically erase their own process but leave traces of the changes that have occurred. They may include burying objects, burning objects (including, to this critic's consternation, videotapes), scattering a pattern carefully traced on the floor, and otherwise ensuring that the record of the event remains only in the memory of those who witness it or hear about it. She is a curator's nightmare. When Beharry was asked to create an installation at the Vancouver Museum of Anthropology around its collection of First Nations artifacts, she proposed to surround the objects in their glass cases with chappatis cut into the shapes of hands. The museum curators were horrified because the bread would have attracted insects; but as Beharry points out, the little bugs are already in the walls and carpet of the museum, and her chappatis would only have made them visible! Her work is also necessarily a critique of the murderous potential of reification, the reduction of living things (in the sense that they are volatile actors in the spiritual life of a community) to dead objects.

Constance Classen notes that museums' practice of storing artifacts behind glass recontextualizes these objects as primarily visual and thus often misinterprets the sort of knowledge they provided in their traditional cultures.[25] She uses the example of a basket from the Desana tribe of Colombia, a culture, she demonstrates, that has a complex organization of knowledge based on symbolisms of color, odor, temperature, and flavor: "Though a Desana basket, for instance, is evidently a multi-sensory object, it would never occur to the ordinary Westerner viewing one in a museum that meaning might lie not only in its form and function, but also in its texture, taste, and smell."[26] Beharry's work carries out this critique by implying the smelly and gustatory processes that go unseen and disavowed in an ocularcentric culture, if only by appealing to the sense of smell of weevils and other bugs. Beharry's work, in short, is resolutely material in that it resists representation, and yet resolutely immaterial in that she erases its traces as soon as possible.

And interestingly, the way that these traces linger the longest is in the form of smell. Paper and flowers burned at one of Beharry's performance spaces leave their acrid fragrance for days after. Sites where she has worked retain the scent of incense that she buried in the walls, detectable even under a fresh coat of paint. Friends receive in the mail poems scented with rose oil, or envelopes full of ashes that burst onto their shirts.

▶

The Dissolution of the Fetish

Borrowing from Michel Leiris's beautiful essay on Alberto Giacometti, Pietz ponders the relation of fetishes—and successful works of art—to the body:

> The fetish is . . . first of all, something extremely personal, whose truth is experienced as a substantial movement from "inside" the self (the self as total-

ized through an impassioned body, a "body without organs") into the self-limited morphology of a material object situated in space "outside." Works of art are true fetishes only if they are material objects at least as intensely personal as tears.[27]

Pietz suggests that the movement from the inside to the outside—the process of concretization—is what makes a fetish a fetish. Tears are an example: they are a material expression of an internal state. The thing about tears, though, is that they do not remain a concrete object; they dissolve back into the body. Pietz's passing reference to the "body without organs" as the body that produces fetishes, or art, is provocative. Only a body that is not libidinally fixated in terms of particular parts can invest with desire something *outside*.[28] The body without organs produces fetishes galore, but it does not fixate on any one of them; they dissolve back into its undifferentiated surface. Similarly, the fetishes produced in the movement between cultures are only transitory markers of a brief relation that will probably change.

These notions of the fetish as produced on the body without organs find support in D. W. Winnicott's theories of the transitional object.[29] Is the transitional object—the comforting blanket; the TV that lulls the child to sleep; for that matter, the smell of a familiar food—part of the body or not? Certainly it's part of the body without organs, the body that makes itself anew by organizing itself with relation to an external object. The subject's identity comes to be distributed between the self and the transitional object. Yet it is the subject, not the object, that is in transition. The object remains the same, although it takes on layers of meaning that later, as the subject acquires some new sort of subjecthood, dissolve away. So it seems useful to suggest that *transitional object* might describe the fetish objects that occur in cultural translation and transcultural movement. The suitcase full of spices is a transitional object, and it becomes heavier as it condenses cultural meanings within itself.

But recall how fetishes are produced in the space between cultures. The transitional object is one not only for the person in transition from one cultural reality to another, but also for the one whose cultural reality is entered and changed. The object becomes a means of both of their projections about the other culture. As it moves, it is bound to become a lot heavier before it gets lighter. Here is the difference between fetishes and fossils, then. Fossils retain the shape of the cultural upheaval, perpetually inviting decoding even of past conflicts. Fetishes, although they are similarly dense with meaning, tend to dissolve away after the need for them has dissipated.

The function of transitional objects is decidedly not to aid assimilation. For they do not simply bring an aspect of their place of origin to a new site; they also make strange the place into which they arrive. Hence the radioactive character of these cultural fossils: they bring back lost histories in which both origin and destination are implicated. They reveal the radical hybridity already present at both sites.

By using these examples of a video work and performance by Shauna Beharry, I hope to have demonstrated a combination of qualities and practices that both materialize and dissolve the fetishlike quality of the moving image. The emphasis on the nonvisual qualities of the image in *Seeing Is Believing* turns our attention away from the kind of fetishism most commonly (and pejoratively) discussed in cinema, visual fetishism. At the same time, it calls attention to other material presences borne forth by the image, such as touch and smell. The life cycle of the fetish is also supported by Beharry's refusal to let her moving images circulate, often to the point of destruction. Her practices both acknowledge the dense aura surrounding the image and aid in its dissolution.

Let me make some generalizations about the fetishistic quality of documentary film. Beharry's work is a pointed example of how documentary can exploit film's volatile, fetishlike quality, but I would suggest that all documentary has the potential to act in this way. All documentary images are fetishes, insofar as they retain some indexical trace of an originary event. However, they do not transparently reflect it. Dense and crystallized documentary images function as transitional objects that encode the intercultural (or another transitional) encounter. When documentary is accused, as it often is, of fetishizing the people and events it represents, this is because it maintains the fetish in a state of fixity, in part by reducing the object to an object of visual knowledge. When the fetishistic quality of film is disavowed, its power remains, an exoticism attributed to some unknowable and distant source.[30] And when it is acknowledged but then maintained, the shell of exoticism remains as well.

In its privileged relation of indexicality to the object or event represented, documentary cinema is in a position to distribute the experience of the object across several senses. Documentary cinema has the same materiality as any other fetish, in that it brings the multisensory character of the originary object into contact with the body of the viewer.

Further, documentary cinema aids cultural transformation only when the fetish is experienced in all its density and then dissolved, untied like a knot. As the fetishistic relations these images embody are worked through, they are no longer necessary as transitional objects, and they cease to be fetishes.

Ending Story

Historically, the fetish seems to *fix* the value of a crisis moment, a moment of contact between incommensurable things. But in bringing these things together the fetish also volatilizes each one of them, renders both histories unstable. Like Shauna Beharry's chappati hands. Shauna Beharry makes chappatis, cuts them out in the shape of hands, two right, two left, smears them with the red paste used to mark a bindi on the forehead, and places them on an altar made of rice and vaguely in the shape of a woman's body. What shocks about these actions is the significance of the red hands. I had known that brides' hands are decorated with henna in Hindi weddings. But I only learned later that in the traditional practice of suttee or widow burning the last thing the widow does before she steps onto her husband's pyre is to dip her hands in henna, red like blood, and make the mark of two red hands on a stone. So the two sets of red hands Beharry made are not only about the tactile lineage of learning from her mother, and her mother's mother, how to make chappatis. Nor do they refer simply to the cultural dislocations that made the simple recipe, with all its concomitant responsibilities (as she tells us, "My father said, if you make nice round chappatis, you'll get a husband"), difficult for the third-generation daughter to learn. They also refer to the generations of women before her who have been forced to burn.

The force of this knowledge was physically nauseating for those of us watching the performance. Beharry could not and did not want to embrace her heritage uncritically, for it is a heritage of cruel subjugation of women. In her acts of excavation she cannot discover a lost history of women, for the women are gone for good. She can only cut through the geological layers, make inert histories volatile by crashing them into each other. It is only as a "Westernized" Indian woman that Beharry can carry out these investigations, because she is not the product of any one discourse but carries a number of irreconcilable histories with her. Her chappati hands are not the fragrant bread of nostalgia; they are radioactive fossils that destabilize everything that comes into contact with them. She says she is going to send them to me, and I am terrified.

◆————————————————————————————

NOTES

Heartfelt thanks to the people who have generously given their time to the thinking of this essay, including Shauna Beharry, Dick Hebdige, Akira Mizuta Lippitt, and my wonderful editors, Diane Waldman and Janet Walker.

1. See Bill Nichols, *Representing Reality: Issues and Concepts in Documentary*, esp. chap. 5 (Bloomington and Indianapolis: Indiana University Press, 1991); Maren Stange, "Documentary Film and Photography: Rethinking

Histories," presented at "Visible Evidence II: Strategies and Practices in Documentary Film and Video," University of Southern California, August 19, 1994.

2. William Pietz, "The Problem of the Fetish, I," *Res* 9 (Spring 1985): 5–17; "The Problem of the Fetish, II," *Res* 13 (Spring 1987): 23–45; "The Problem of the Fetish, IIIa," *Res* 16 (Autumn 1988): 105–23.

3. Pietz, "The Problem of the Fetish, IIIa," 107.

4. Pietz , "The Problem of the Fetish, II."

5. See Peter Stallybrass and Allon White, *The Politics and Poetics of Transgression* (Ithaca, N.Y.: Cornell University Press, 1986).

6. Pietz, "The Problem of the Fetish, I," 14.

7. Homi K. Bhabha, "The Other Question: The Stereotype and Colonial Discourse," in *The Location of Culture* (New York: Routledge, 1994), 70–75.

8. Theodor Adorno, quoted in W. J. T. Mitchell, *Iconology: Images, Text, Ideology* (Chicago and London: University of Chicago Press, 1986), 204.

9. Pietz, "The Problem of the Fetish, I," 10.

10. Gilles Deleuze, *Cinema 2: The Time Image*, trans. Hugh Tomlinson and Robert Galeta (Minneapolis: University of Minnesota Press, 1989), 112–3.

11. André Bazin, *What Is Cinema?*, ed. and trans. Hugh Gray (Berkeley and Los Angeles: University of California Press, 1967), 9.

12. Both the fetish and the film image correspond to Charles Sanders Peirce's category of secondness in the designation of a sign's degrees of removal from the object. See Peirce, "The Principles of Phenomenology," in *The Philosophy of Peirce: Selected Writings*, ed. Justus Buchler (New York: Harcourt, Brace, 1950), 77–80.

13. Stange, "Documentary Film and Photography: Rethinking Histories."

14. In this conception of the fetish I am suggesting a life of the object different from what Susan Stewart poses in *On Longing: Narratives of the Gigantic, the Miniature, and the Collection* (Durham, N.C.: Duke University Press, 1991). Stewart argues that the fetish, or souvenir (at least the "homomaterial object," Umberto Eco's term, evoked by Stewart, for an object that existed at the site of the event to be remembered), does not maintain any material relation to an event but is important precisely because it substitutes for an event: it elicits a stream of personal narrative that traces the trajectory of desire. In Stewart's account, any material connection to a primal scene of memory is necessarily effaced in the *narration* of a supposed connection to the remembered scene—a narration inward, toward the self. By contrast, I argue that the souvenir maintains a thread of material connection to the scene it remembers, and it is precisely in this materiality,

not in its willful forgetting, that the souvenir's significance lies—not narration, but physical connection across space and time. I am taking a position against a semiotics that replaces material presence with signs, with narratives.

15. A 1993 exhibition at the New Museum of Contemporary Art, "Trade Routes," examined some of these objects whose meaning is transformed in the movement between cultures. For example, an installation by Sowon Kwon, "From the Land of Porcelain," investigated the trade in porcelain from Asian countries to the West and its influence on Western art styles of *chinoiserie* and *japonisme*. See Laura Trippi, Gina Dent, and Saskia Sassen, "Trade Routes," exhibition brochure (New York: New Museum of Contemporary Art, 1993), n.p.

16. On the optical unconscious, see Walter Benjamin, "The Work of Art in the Age of Mechanical Reproduction," in *Illuminations*, ed. Hannah Arendt (New York: Harcourt, Brace, and World, 1968), 235–37.

17. To say that Beharry does something like "give voice" to peasant rituals has the danger of suggesting that, below the apparent exoticism of Hindu culture in general, another, even more exotic/authentic object has been discovered—a sort of fetishism *en abîme*. A number of scholars have alerted us to the danger of fetishizing lower-class "third world" women as the most authentic of them all: these include Rey Chow, *Writing Diaspora: Tactics of Intervention in Contemporary Cultural Studies* (Bloomington and Indianapolis: Indiana University Press, 1993), 112–14; Trinh T. Minh-ha, *Woman, Native, Other: Writing Postcoloniality and Feminism* (Bloomington: Indiana University Press, 1989), 79–117; and Gayatri C. Spivak and Sneja Gunew, "Questions of Multi-Culturalism," in *The Post-Colonial Critic: Interviews, Strategies, Dialogues*, ed. Sarah Harasym (New York: Routledge, 1990), 59–66.

18. This list is vast but gets smaller if we confine ourselves to those thinkers who not only critique visuality but explore other forms of sensory knowledge. These include Elizabeth Grosz, *Volatile Bodies: Toward a Corporeal Feminism* (Bloomington: Indiana University Press, 1994); Luce Irigaray, *An Ethics of Sexual Difference*, trans. Carolyn Burke and Gillian C. Gill (Ithaca, N.Y.: Cornell University Press, 1984) and *Speculum of the Other Woman*, trans. Gillian C. Gill (Ithaca, N.Y.: Cornell University Press, 1985); Martin Jay, *Downcast Eyes* (Berkeley and Los Angeles: University of California Press, 1993); Julia Kristeva, *Powers of Horror: An Essay in Abjection*, trans. Leon Roudiez (New York: Columbia University Press,

1982); Drew Leder, *The Absent Body* (Chicago: University of Chicago Press, 1992); Maurice Merleau-Ponty, "The Eye and the Mind," in *The Primacy of Perception*, trans. James M. Edie (Evanston, Ill.: Northwestern University Press, 1964); Elaine Scarry, *The Body in Pain: The Making and Unmaking of the World* (New York: Oxford University Press, 1985); C. Nadia Seremetakis, ed., *The Senses Still: Perception and Memory as Material Culture in Modernity* (Boulder, Colo.: Westview Press, 1994); and Vivian Sobchack, *The Address of the Eye: Phenomenology and Film Experience* (Princeton, N.J.: Princeton University Press, 1992).

19. See Irigaray, *An Ethics of Sexual Difference*.

20. Michael Taussig, *Mimesis and Alterity: A Particular History of the Senses* (New York: Routledge, 1992), 45.

21. See Julia Kristeva, "Giotto's Joy," in *Desire in Language: A Semiotic Approach to Literature and Art*, trans. Leon Roudiez (New York: Columbia University Press, 1980). I'm aware that these references to tactile knowledge, the hierarchy of the senses, and especially Shauna Beharry's valorization of a non-verbal, tactile relationship to her mother have strong resonances with Kristevan notions of the maternal semiotic and the abject. These are not connotations that I intend to pursue. My concern here is to discuss the material dimension of tactile knowledge and the intercultural base of fetishistic practices rather than to apply feminist psychoanalytic theories of fetishism. I believe that the universalism of Kristeva's psychoanalysis muffles vast cultural differences.

22. Constance Classen, David Howes, and Anthony Synnott, *Aroma: The Cultural History of Smell* (London and New York: Routledge, 1994), 98.

23. Constance Classen, *Worlds of Sense: Exploring the Senses in History and Across Cultures* (London and New York: Routledge, 1993), 125–36.

24. Spivak and Gunew, "Questions of Multi-Culturalism."

25. See Classen, *Worlds of Sense*. Diane Waldman points out that touching, smelling, and so on are encouraged in children's museums while they are prohibited in "adult" museums—as though one is expected to accede to a visual mode of perception and leave the childish senses behind.

26. Classen, *Worlds of Sense*, 136.

27. Pietz, "The Problem of the Fetish, I," 12.

28. I picture the Deleuze-Guattarian "body without organs" as something like a water balloon. You can willfully twist shapes onto its surface, play with them until they lose their fascination, and then undo them and make others. The appeal of this model built around desire rather than need is that, voluntaristic though it certainly is, it allows for the strange and contingent ways that subjects form attachments. The term is introduced in Gilles Deleuze and Félix Guattari, *Anti-Oedipus: Capitalism and Schizophrenia*, trans. Robert Hurley et al. (New York: Viking, 1977).

29. D. W. Winnicott, "Transitional Objects and Transitional Phenomena," in *Essential Papers on Object Relations*, ed. P. Buckley (New York: New York University Press, 1986).

30. This is similiar to Hamid Naficy's argument that Iranian exile television functions as a fetish of national identity. He argues that exile television must not simply recuperate a lost cultural experience in fetishized form but dissolve the fetish of nationality as it expresses the process of cultural transformation. See Hamid Naficy, "The Cultural Politics of Hybridity," in *The Making of Exile Cultures: Iranian Television in Los Angeles* (Minneapolis: University of Minnesota Press, 1993), 130–47.

DEBORAH LEFKOWITZ

[11]   *On Silence and Other Disruptions*

Much has been written by American Jewish authors about the silence they
encounter in Germany when the subject of their own Jewish identity comes
up in conversation. Susan Neiman, for example, in her memoir of the years
1982–1988 in West Berlin describes a conversation with the father of a
friend who inquired about any negative experiences she might have had.
Neiman answers him: "Perhaps the worst thing is the silence. I'm happy that
you asked me about it. . . . No one ever does."[1] Marc Fisher, Bonn/Berlin
bureau chief for *The Washington Post* from 1989–1993, makes similar observations about Jews in Germany: "Placed on display in German schools,
Jews meet a wall of nervous silence. . . . Germans, growing up in a country
without any significant Jewish presence, do not know where to begin."[2] And
Alison Owings, who is not herself Jewish, describes in the preface to a collection of interviews her amazement at the inability of a German woman she
met while vacationing in Spain to even utter the words *Jew* or *Jewish.*[3]

Having traveled back and forth to Germany since the early 1980s
when I met, then married, a (non-Jewish) German man, I have found that
my Jewishness often provokes oblique and unsolicited remarks. Once, for
example, during a visit to a friend's family when my friend stepped out of
the room for a moment, her mother blurted out at the breakfast table, "Of
course, you must realize, we simply didn't know." Or another example: I
was cutting vegetables in my mother-in-law's kitchen in preparation for a
family celebration. As soon as my husband was out of earshot, an older female relative turned to me and said, "Deborah, of course, we didn't know."

What hadn't these women known? I didn't ask, because I assumed
they meant the Holocaust: they hadn't known about Auschwitz, about the
explicit and horrible end to which the Nazi persecution of the Jews had
led. But this repeated—and truncated—insistence on not having known
(there was never any more to these conversations, in part because I never

could think of any reply) was so troubling that I had to consider what the subtext of such remarks might be. Addressed to me by older (non-Jewish) German women—and as I recall, only by women—I could only suppose they felt such declarations of past innocence to be a necessary prelude to our developing a relationship in the present.

But I also had to consider what was missing, what had been bracketed out by these remarks. Emphatically denying any knowledge of the concentration camps was also a way of avoiding a conversation before it ever got started, a way of suggesting there was nothing more to tell. In other words, this form of speaking was essentially a strategy for creating silence.

If my own experiences in Germany prepared me to listen for the silences, they also indicated that such silences were many and various. My documentary film *Intervals of Silence: Being Jewish in Germany* (1990) grew out of the private conversations I found myself drawn into long before I began to record them on audiotape. Exploring how Germans speak about themselves and each other, the film focuses on the aftermath of the Holocaust and contemporary relations between Jews and non-Jews—relations in which I was now also a participant.

I sought to encompass as broad a cross section of German society as possible in my interviews, including not only individuals of diverse ages and occupations but also with varying attitudes toward the subject of the film. By asking for suggestions and referrals at the conclusion of each of my interviews, I was able to speak with many people who would not have volunteered themselves and might not otherwise have come to my attention.

All in all I conducted approximately 150 interviews with residents—both Jewish and non-Jewish—of my husband's hometown.[4] The range of participants included high-ranking politicians and church leaders who publicly supported reconciliation and Jewish-Christian dialogue, as well as German high school students rehearsing for a production of *Fiddler on the Roof,* housewives studying English in adult education, history teachers and school principals, prominent local businessmen, journalists, self-proclaimed resistance fighters, and many "ordinary Germans" (to use Daniel Goldhagen's term).[5] Nearly sixty of these voices can be heard in the film.

Gender was not a category I consciously considered—either during the interviewing or subsequently during the editing. This was due, in part, to my own awareness of the chasms of understanding between communities defined in terms of being Jewish or non-Jewish, not male or female. I also cannot recall that any of the Germans I interviewed raised gender as a significant component of their postwar experiences.

Yet the notion of silence, so central to my film, has also figured prominently in feminist writings of the past several decades. Even more recently, the intertwined issues of gender and silence have begun to appear in writings about the Holocaust as well.[6] To what extent, then, are the "intervals of silence" in my film related to "the silences, the absences, the nameless, the unspoken, the encoded" that, in the words of Adrienne Rich,[7] define the reality of so many women's lives?

Several years after completion of my film, I am struck by the possibility that my interviews with women may, in fact, have influenced my thinking about the material I collected as a whole, as well as inspired some of the specific visual and structural ideas I employed in presenting this material. I wish now to consider the various meanings assigned to silence in my interviews, the relationships of Jewish as well as female voices to silence, and the resulting implications for the evocation of silence in my film.

▶

The Ebb and Flow of Conversation

It was my intention in conducting interviews for my film to ask open-ended questions at the outset, allowing each speaker to define both the scope and the length of the answer to be given. In most cases I began with a fairly standard list of questions (with four basic variations depending on the speaker's age and whether or not he or she was Jewish), then allowed the interviews to take their own shape as respondents became reticent, took an interest in my project, or chose to steer the discussion in other directions.

On the whole my interviews were shaped by question-and-answer patterns, with intervals of varying length between questions. What interested me, even at this initial stage of film production, was precisely the speech interval itself. Rather than attempting to fill in gaps or clarify inconsistencies, I was fascinated by the rhythm of starting and stopping points—a sort of verbal choreography—that resulted from each participant's engagement with me in conversation.

In the process of transcribing my interviews, I was struck by some remarkable exceptions to the general question-and-answer pattern—exceptions represented only by women speakers. Three interviews, for example, began with lengthy monologues unprompted by any question on my part. After ascertaining that my tape recorder was running, Frau D. began immediately with the following statements:[8]

> Let's see, my biography: I was born on October 16, 1911, as the second daughter to my parents Felix and Julia. My parents ran a tropical fruit and canned goods import business. My sister was still able to escape to Holland in 1938 with the help of the Dutch Red Cross, but she was later deported to Auschwitz. My parents and I were deported to the Riga ghetto in January 1942.[9]

Frau D. next related a story about those left behind in the Riga ghetto when she was transferred to a concentration camp and then proceeded to speak for twelve transcribed pages without interruption about her experiences after being released from the camp. Remarkable about this self-declared "biography" are the gulfs—the omissions of both chronological time and personal experience—between the sentences about her family's import business and her sister's escape to Holland, and again between her own deportation and the lengthy report of her return home. Struck at first by Frau D.'s talkativeness, I later became more attentive to what she failed to say.

Another interview with a Jewish woman, Frau E., also demonstrates how silence can be generated even while talking at great length:

> FRAU E.: Oh, oh, oh, where should I begin? At the beginning of 1933? When I was picked up, or before that?
> LEFKOWITZ: Before that.
> FRAU E.: Before that, okay. When I got married? Oh, my child, how long ago that is now. I got married in 1925. Yes, then everything was still pure sunshine, and it was not known what we would have to go through. And then came 1933. My mother died—thank God, I would say today—in '33. She was very ill with cancer. She died in October and thank God did not have to experience being picked up.[10]

In this interview, as in the previous one, the story begins with explicit references to a still intact network of family relationships, and to a rather fondly remembered time prior to the horrors of the Third Reich. Frau E. continued to speak for more than twenty-five transcribed pages, interrupted only three times by the interjection of requests for one- or two-word clarifications. She related the experience of her own deportation in 1942 and her non-Jewish husband's attempts to follow her. He succeeded in locating her before she was transferred to a work camp. Frau E. then jumped to the final days of the war and her long journey home.

A third interview with a Jewish woman, Frau J., again begins in the distant past:

> That must have been before 1933. I was then five or six years old, not yet of school age. At that time politics were discussed very apprehensively at home. And I know, I can remember my grandmother saying, "If Hitler comes to the helm, things will go badly for us." That was a metaphor that I did not understand at first as a child. I imagined a lake or a sea and a small row boat with men sitting inside it. And I absolutely could not imagine why men rowing so peacefully should mean such harm for us.[11]

Frau J. then proceeded to speak for more than thirty-two transcribed pages, interrupted only once for clarification. Unlike the preceding two women, Frau J. was not deported. She was able to "disappear" (with the help of friends and employers) in a large city almost until the end of the war. Her story ends rather abruptly with her return home—mostly on foot—to find her mother and father still alive:

> Yes, and that is also a scene that one cannot describe because, because it is too emotional. But everyone probably knows how such a scene was played out, when a family was reunited after such an ordeal and under such conditions. That was the point, the final point.[12]

In the first two interviews, deportation as well as the subsequent return home signal radical divisions in time. Although no deportation occurred in the life of the third woman, her interview demonstrates a similar disjunction. Covering the period before and during the war and ending with her return home, she comments on her life after "the final point" only in response to my further questions, and then only in summary form. There is clearly a distinction these women make between the broader brush strokes of remembrance and the fine-lined, personal rendering of details. For all three women—all Jewish, all survivors—my request for an interview unleashed lengthy personal narratives, yet even within the effusion of their speech reside the silences of what they chose not to say.

At the opposite end of the spectrum, there were a number of women who chose to remain more overtly silent. Some, when I approached them regarding the possibility of an interview, refused me outright. Others were present during an interview I conducted with someone else, but claimed they had nothing to say or allowed spouses and other family members to do nearly all the talking.[13] Of the thirty-six voices of women I recorded, twenty-six actively participated in interviews, while ten remained essentially in the background.[14] Consider the following excerpt from an interview I conducted with a seventy-nine-year-old woman and her adult daughter:

> LEFKOWITZ: Do you have any memories of Reichskristallnacht?
> FRAU P.: Of what?
> DAUGHTER: The Reichs—you know, when they set fire to the synagogues, that is the . . .
> FRAU P.: No, I'm sorry. The, uh, when I returned, I found out . . .
> DAUGHTER: No, mother, that was, that's not quite right. You know what it was, it has slipped your memory a bit. We woke up one morning.
> FRAU P.: Yes.
> DAUGHTER: And then we heard from others that Jewish stores had been smashed. They were chased out in their shirts, in their nightshirts. During the night they were simply put out in the street and . . .
> FRAU P.: Yes, that's right.
> DAUGHTER: . . . and the synagogue was on fire. That we knew. That we had

heard. And then we listened in utter horror. And then there was also your saying, "My God, Frau Jakobsohn, what will happen now?" Yes, it is . . .

FRAU P.: Yes, that's right. That's right.[15]

Throughout this exchange, Frau P. is barely able to utter more than a word or two at a time. She seems dominated by the daughter, who literally speaks her words for her. But this dynamic was established right from the start of the interview, and in large part due to Frau P.'s own wish for reticence:

FRAU P.: Well then, how should I begin?

DAUGHTER: You just say that you were friends with Jakob . . .

FRAU P.: Yes.

DAUGHTER: . . . during the Third Reich, or in general in the . . .

FRAU P.: He was . . .

DAUGHTER: Not only during the Third Reich, you were friends with him anyway. You say that you were friends with him and that during the Third Reich, . . . then in the Third Reich, because of course before the Third Reich you were, you were born in 1906, after all, you understand? [short pause]

FRAU P.: But I can't get it straight.

DAUGHTER: Oh, it really is difficult. It really is difficult. To speak in front of, into a microphone is terribly difficult.

FRAU P.: Yes, I just can't get it straight.[16]

As reluctant as Frau P. seems to speak on her own behalf, I have encountered at least eight other instances when women were present at an interview but remained almost completely silent. In fact, but for a chance remark recorded on tape, I would most likely have forgotten their presence altogether. Here is an excerpt from the end of an interview with a senior in high school. Turning to the friend who had accompanied the young woman, I asked:

LEFKOWITZ: Do you want to say something, too?

OTHER GIRL: I just came along.[17]

A similar exchange occurred at the end of my interview with Frau N., whose daughter in her early twenties had been listening for some time:

FRAU N.: [Long pause] Oh Andrea, this is all difficult, isn't it?

LEFKOWITZ: Would you like to say something, too?

FRAU N.: She doesn't have the nerve.

ANDREA: No, no.

FRAU N.: Well, I guess that is, that would be all then, okay?[18]

Once the tape recorder had been turned off, however, Andrea and I conversed quite easily. In fact, when her mother died two years later, Andrea wrote and asked me to get in touch with her again, which I did.

What, then, is the meaning behind the unwillingness demonstrated by so many women to speak "for the record"? Note that it was only women who demonstrated this unwillingness. Given the open-ended question-and-answer format of my interviews, I had anticipated that the length of answers would vary considerably depending on speaking style, rapport, and interest in the subject matter. But why are women's voices uniquely represented by the two extremes of this speech interval—unbroken monologues at one end, and no speech at the other?

Contrary to my own experiences, Alison Owings found that nearly all of the non-Jewish German women she approached (about fifty) were willing, even eager, to be interviewed: "Some spoke hesitantly, but most erupted like geysers. It seemed they had been waiting for decades for someone to ask them a question." She suggests a combination of reasons for women's need to talk, including "an urge to bear witness."[19]

This notion of speaking as an act of bearing witness appears in a number of feminist writings on silence. Tillie Olsen's words "We who write are survivors" convey her understanding that a survivor is "one who must bear witness for those who . . . did *not* survive."[20] Writing from the perspective of an entirely different "struggle against silence," Holocaust survivor Elie Wiesel perceives his role as a writer in similar terms: "I never intended to be a novelist. The only role I sought was that of witness. . . . I knew the story had to be told."[21]

For some women—and some Holocaust survivors—the urge to speak may be particularly strong. Yet the need to bear witness presupposes a backdrop of silence, a social environment in which this particular kind of speaking is not the norm. Thus the two extremes—speaking at length and not speaking at all—are intrinsically related, in some sense prerequisites for each other.

What, then, was my role as an interviewer in eliciting speech? For many, I provided an opportunity to articulate what would otherwise have remained unspoken. I have assumed that my presence along with my particular interest in listening—and perhaps my being Jewish as well as female, but not German—were all facilitating factors. But for the women who chose to remain silent, I also accepted their silence.

In some interviews, women explicitly referred to my presence as the motivation for their speech. Consider this excerpt (from a longer response) by a Jewish woman who decided to tell me about being raped by Russian soldiers at the end of the war:

> I have never told this before. It was not my first encounter with the Russians. The first encounter, I actually didn't want to say, but I'll say it. It was going to

America. I do not tell it here in Germany. The first encounter was during the night after we had been taken out of the bunker. We had hidden ourselves in cellars. . . . And in the night this cellar was combed by the Russians. And the Russians attacked every woman they found and raped her. And as I said, I had my response: "I am a Jewess." It was of no use to me whatsoever. No one believed it. . . . And this dreadful experience that up until this day you have been ostracized and persecuted, you were not a German, you didn't belong, you were an outsider. And now the Russians are there and you are treated no differently. Now you are blond, so now you are German. That enraged me so much, I absolutely cannot describe it.[22]

The condition for telling me this story—that it be made public in America but not in Germany—essentially precluded my using it in the film. But by respecting the speaker's wishes, in some sense I also perpetuated her silence.

Another woman not only entrusted me with a story but went to great lengths to find me for the purpose of telling it:

Yes. I called you up. I come from Pomerania. And we had a family doctor named Dr. Lefkowitz. Now I was very young at that time, but my sister, my brother, they will, or they can remember because they were always there a lot, because it was our family doctor, you know? And when I heard, or read, the name Lefkowitz, I remembered it again. . . . I made inquiries at several places . . . because I was interested in locating you, you know? I would have liked, uh, to find out where Dr. Lefkowitz ended up. We knew, of course, that he, uh, uh, emigrated to America before the Nazis came. But where and how and when, what became of him, that's in the stars.[23]

Although I was no relation of the Dr. Lefkowitz who had provided medical care to her family before the war, this woman hoped that by participating in my film there might yet be some possibility of communication with his descendants. Again, my presence was the catalyst for telling a particular story, and again, I did not include that story in my film.

Both stories illustrate the delicate balance—and my own understanding of that balance—between speech elicited in a private conversation and speech assigned to a public forum. On a personal level these stories meant a great deal to me; at the time I was making my film I chose to keep them personal.

Having considered some aspects of the speaking addressed to me during my interviews, I turn now to the speaking that occurs between Jewish and non-Jewish Germans and the social dynamics implied by these spoken encounters. As I explore in my film, it is through their speaking—as well as through their silences—that Jewish and non-Jewish Germans define each other.

The silence with which I began this essay, the silence of Germans not knowing what to say to Jews, is only half the picture. The other half involves what Jews say—or don't say—in return. Silence, as linguist Deborah Tannen points out, "is always a joint production."[24] For example, when I asked Jews how openly they speak about their Jewish identity, I received the following responses quoted in my film:

> I don't make a secret of it. If someone asks me, I say that I am Jewish and expect that it will be accepted.

> But, of course. I am proud to be a Jew. Everyone who knows me in Germany knows that I am Jewish.

> The people I know also know I belong to the Jewish religion. But I don't advertise that I am Jewish.

> I have no choice. People ask me where I'm from. I have to say I am from Israel. "Well, then, you are a Jew." One can see that I am a foreigner, that I don't belong.

> It still costs me an effort to say that I am Jewish. There are not really any natural reactions here in Germany. Many people do you special favors or treat you with kid gloves, which I don't think is right. So I no longer have any desire to say it, and for the most part I keep it a secret.[25]

In grouping these remarks together in my film, I am clearly interested in observing—and having the viewer observe—the relationships of different voices to the same experience.

Reading the above comments in text form, we can see the range of attitudes they convey. Hearing them spoken in my film, we can also discern the gender identity of the speakers. In this group of comments, the split between forceful and qualified assertions of Jewish identity occurs along gender lines: it is the women who speak of not wanting to "advertise" their Jewishness, or of not having "any desire to say it." Edited to begin and end with the idea of Jewish identity as a secret—denied by the first speaker, admitted by the last—this section of my film explores self-imposed silence as one end of the spectrum of Jewish responses to living in Germany.

While these remarks are spoken on the sound track, a black-and-white image depicts two silhouette figures standing at the edge of what appears to be a precipice. After many moments of stillness, these figures begin to walk slowly forward, dissolving into the whiteness of the surrounding sky. The figures' disappearance occurs just after the words "for the most

Speaking about Jewish identity in Deborah Lefkowitz, *Intervals of Silence: Being Jewish in Germany*. Photo courtesy of the filmmaker.

part I keep it a secret" have been uttered, suggesting a linkage between silence and invisibility.

But given the knowledge that Jews (literally) disappeared in smoke in the gas chambers of the concentration camps, this image implies a connection between the legacy of the Holocaust and a reluctance to speak about Jewish identity. Note that it is specifically the response of a Jewish woman—a response not shared by all speakers in this section—that provides the clue to the linked meanings of text and image, namely, the erasure of Jewish identity from the landscape.

As I consider other sets of image-text relationships, I realize that the influence of women's voices on my image choices was entirely disproportionate to their representation in either the interview sample as a whole or in the sound track of my film. This reflects, perhaps, the fact that I found the metaphors and figures of speech—those of both Jewish and non-Jewish women—particularly evocative.

In attempting to address silence visually, I worked not only with single images, as in the sequence above, but also with layered images achieved through optical printing and matte photography. In creating this layering—high-contrast black-and-white mattes superimposing dark shapes over color images—I wished to suggest one of the intrinsic conditions of silence, namely, its dual existence in relation to both an implied speaker and an implied listener.

The silence of not wishing to speak is related to the many silences of not being heard.[26] Again, it is a Jewish woman who most clearly makes this connection. In two separate remarks recorded in my film, she complains about her perceived inability to speak critically in Germany on the basis of her Jewish experience. In the first, she refers to her powerlessness to refute anti-Semitic utterances:

> It is revealing that people basically accept the fact that such remarks are made. If we raise any objections, people get this pitying look on their faces as if to say, "It's obvious you would say that."[27]

In the second, she suggests that any criticism of Germany by a Jew is unlikely to be heard:

> Even a good acquaintance once said to me, "Why don't you go back to Israel if you don't like it here?" Basically, we are not permitted to speak critically. At some point, this reproach is bound to come: "You have nothing to say anyway because you don't really belong here."[28]

Both of these comments point to a troubled communication between this woman and her non-Jewish acquaintances. However, this insight is not one they would necessarily share with her. Compare the above remarks, for example, with the following statement by a non-Jewish German woman:

> I don't know any Jews. But the fact that people hardly speak about them anymore makes it obvious that our living together is now normal.[29]

In another section of my film I explore Jewish speakers' perceptions about their relationships to non-Jewish Germans and their ability to speak within these relationships:

> My parents' former neighbors are no longer alive. Even their children have now grown old. And with the children of these people I no longer have any contact.

> Those whom we knew have died. The people outside are all foreign to me. All foreign. We simply don't come into contact.

> I have many contacts here. I don't feel self-conscious with them except if they notice that I live as a practicing Jew. Then they grow uncertain, and we don't know how to talk to each other.

> With the older generation when one said, "I am Jewish," one got the unsolicited response, "I had a Jewish friend," or something like that. I don't then say, "Oh, what a good person you are!" I feel uncomfortable when I hear such remarks. I ask myself of course what that person has to hide. But I feel no urge to talk about it with them.

> I don't think it is our job to settle this issue for the people here. And when we try to open our mouths, we are stifled at once. People do hear what we say,

but it has no impact at all. And in this respect, the Final Solution really was a final solution. We actually no longer exist.[30]

The experiences conveyed by these Jewish speakers range from total isolation (no speaking) to relationships in which some things can be said, but not much about Jewish identity. Of the five speakers, only the last is a woman, and it is her voice that most clearly indicts other Germans for her own speechlessness. She uses the metaphor of being stifled (or literally reduced to silence through gagging) to connect the idea of her silence with the extinguishing of her existence, thus in part fulfilling the Nazi designs for Jewish obliteration.

While these comments are spoken on the sound track, a stark black-and-white image shows the shape of a cross above a small mound. This image was seen just a few moments earlier in full color and identified (through my voice-over narration) as the location where all four of my husband's grandparents are buried, a place frequently visited by my mother-in-law for the purpose of tending their graves. After the first two voices in this section have spoken, the shape of the cross turns red, the mound green. Shortly after viewers hear the final words "We actually no longer exist," the black-and-white layer of the image fades out, revealing an underlying image with red and green colors: a close-up of a hand planting flowers (presumably on a grave).

Again, as in the image/text sequence discussed above, the final comment by a Jewish woman is crucial to understanding my juxtaposition of spoken texts and images. The meaning she assigns to not speaking—no longer being in existence—in conjunction with the literal representation of Christian burial grounds further develops associations suggested by the earlier sequence. The two figures disappearing into thin air, mysterious as a black-and-white negative image, appear again in full color at the beginning of this second sequence. Originating, in fact, in the footage I shot in the cemetery containing the graves of my husband's grandparents, the color version is quite innocuous: two women wearing white coats disappear around the bend in a path behind some greenery. From my voice-over narration it can be inferred that these women have come to the cemetery for the same purpose as my mother-in-law, namely, to tend the graves of deceased family members.

These two sequences—linked together not only through verbal references to disappearance and death, but through a shared film image as well—suggest a relationship between the visual presence of Christian dead and the visual absence of Jewish dead. (Those Jews who died in the Holocaust have no graves to be tended, no grave markers to be seen.) Or

Speaking about Jewish and non-Jewish relations in Deborah Lefkowitz, *Intervals of Silence: Being Jewish in Germany*. Photo courtesy of the filmmaker.

consider the further discrepancy between the visibility of Christian dead compared with the relative invisibility of Jews still living in Germany.

This is not to deny the presence of Jewish cemeteries in Germany. In fact, I was frankly shocked by how many Germans took me to visit Jewish cemeteries with the suggestion that I might find motifs for my film. I did, as it happens, shoot footage in several old Jewish cemeteries, and I did incorporate some of this footage. But most of my images evoke absence and invisibility obliquely and without explicit references to either cemeteries or concentration camps. And when I do make these references, it is to underscore a different set of relationships regarding speaking and silence, and the intervals that open up between them.

▶ ────────────────────────────────

Framing Disruptions

In addition to the "intervals of silence" that I made visually palpable, there are the omissions of time—both narrative time and chronological time—that I recorded in my interviews. Hayden White points out that "every narrative, however seemingly 'full,' is constructed on the basis of a set of events that might have been included but were left out."[31] As George Lakoff and Mark Johnson explain, "Normally, when we construct life stories, we leave out many extremely important experiences for the sake of

Two women strolling through a Christian cemetery in Deborah Lefkowitz,
Intervals of Silence: Being Jewish in Germany. Photo courtesy of the filmmaker.

finding coherence."[32] Thus no matter how exhaustively detailed, any interview provides only a partial picture. The question, then, for editing is
whether coherence requires that the omissions be obscured.

In structuring my film, I paid attention not only to where omissions
occurred within individual narratives, but also where narratives failed to
take shape at all. Given the prominence of silence and fragmentation in the
stories of lives spanning, but irrevocably severed by, experiences of the war
years, I chose an editing approach that would similarly disrupt the apparent seamlessness of narrative continuity.

But why call attention to the disruption rather than the continuity, especially in cases where lengthy narratives exist in my interviews? As discussed above, the stories told by Holocaust survivors divide into two parts:
before the war (before deportation or exile), and after the war (or after
their return). Of their own accord (and it was not my intention to probe if
this information was not volunteered), Holocaust survivors related extremely little about the time between their deportation and their return to
Germany. The significance of these narratives thus lies in the very fact of
disruption. What remains unsaid cannot be simply pieced together, or
adroitly bridged.

The most pronounced interval of silence—both visually and aurally—
occurs near the middle of the film: an image of smokestacks with white
smoke billowing in extreme slow motion. With no accompanying sound

(not even ambient sound), this image remains on the screen for almost sixty seconds. Photographed in the industrial landscape of postwar Germany, these smokestacks also, of course, conjure up the gas chambers of Auschwitz. But as this image is contextualized in my film, the absence it connotes is not the deaths of Jews in the camps. Rather, it is the absence of Jews who were deported, survived, and later returned to Germany.

The image is sandwiched between two stories told by the same Jewish woman. The first of these stories is as follows:

> Being taken away, that was not the worst of it. For years one had been wait-ing, knowing it would happen. Every time the doorbell rang, one thought, now they are coming to take you away. One evening I was preparing dinner and was about to slice some tomatoes. And my husband said to me, "Why are you trembling? Why are you cutting the tomatoes so thick?" And I said, "Please, you cut. I can't anymore." I was waiting for the things which were to come. The next morning at five the doorbell rang. My husband jumped up and said, "What is this? Who is ringing the bell so early? Who is there?" I didn't say a word. I was just waiting for the things which were coming. I knew then that I would be taken away.[33]

The second story immediately follows the smokestack imagery:

> How happy we were—just knowing that we were coming home. And then I was given a big welcome. I could lie down on the couch, shoes off, socks off. The women were delighted and had already opened a bottle of wine. And I thought, dear God, where have you ended up? The loud talking and laughing and merrymaking—and they were happy that the war was over. But they really didn't have to go through much, just a few nights in a bunker. Then I said, "Please." I folded my hands and said, "Please, leave me to be alone."[34]

The visual silence between these two stories accentuates a consider-able omission of time from the narrative. More than simply reflecting a pause that was already present, I have purposefully replaced portions of the recorded interview with silence. My insertion of silence into this woman's narrative at just the moment when deportation is about to occur thus marks the subject matter—as well as the time frame—that has been collectively omitted from conversation.

The division of narrative time into before and after with a missing sec-tion in between was not only true for the Holocaust survivors I inter-viewed. It was also true for non-Jews of the same generation when speak-ing about Jews. Consider this rather peculiar story told by a non-Jewish woman about her mother during the Nazi years:

> Well, my mother, she was friends with a, uh, Jewish family, especially with the wife. . . . She was horrified to discover that they were also haunted by the persecution of the Jews. And she had to watch helplessly that they had to

wear the Jewish star. And in spite of the fact that my mother was employed by the police, that is, in public service, she, uh, did not allow herself to be forbidden to maintain contact with them. She spoke openly with them on the street. She visited them. And afterward when it happened . . . that they had to leave their apartment . . . the woman wanted to give her a key from an apartment she owned so that we could move in. But my mother didn't take it. And then she gave Mother as a token to remember her by, because it was to be the last time, because she said, "We are going to be evacuated," she gave her a candelabrum. . . . And then we were ourselves, uh, evacuated to East Prussia. And when we came back after the war, after we had been bombed out, gone through the entire flight experience, then we would have liked to know where the Jakobsohns ended up in order to get in touch with them again. Since Mother was at a loss what else to do, she went to the cemetery and thought, let's see first what's there, because we had heard in the meantime what had happened to all of the Jews. And then she was able to read on the plaque that they had also died in a concentration camp. Then Mother cried bitterly and said the Lord's Prayer.[35]

The first part of this story occurs just prior to the Jewish woman's deportation, and the second, at some point after the war. Between these two periods of time there is a gap during which the thread of the narrative—and the fate of the Jewish woman—gets lost.

Although I ended up including only part of this story, the relationship suggested here between silence and the omission of narrative time inspired the editing of another sequence in my film. Emerging from the fade-out of the previously discussed sequence of the Christian cemetery, printed English text appears over a black screen while a voice explains in German:

> We have mounted a commemorative plaque on the site of the former synagogue, which was destroyed during Reichskristallnacht. We also have a Jewish cemetery here that is tended by the city, where you can find evidence of the strength of the former Jewish population.[36]

Two subsequent shots reveal the Jewish cemetery, graves mostly overgrown with greenery but some of the names and dates still legible. The following shot is a composite of two image layers: a black-and-white mask of a window opening through which the city-employed gardener can be seen raking. During this shot the voice of a Jewish man is heard:

> It really annoys me that when Judaism is depicted, they always show cemeteries. You ask about Judaism here and you are taken to the cemetery. This probably even prevents people from coming into contact with the living Jews here. We are not a cemetery culture, nor cemetery trustees. Our Jewish congregations are not institutions for cemetery maintenance.

Then a Jewish woman's voice adds:

When Germans relate to Jews, they can think of them only as victims. And in this respect, we have really reached a turning point. We can now present ourselves differently.[37]

As if in response to her words about a turning point, the scene shifts dramatically. A black-and-white image of a slowly turning ferris wheel fills the screen. The next shot is another composite image employing the same black-and-white window mask as before. But now in the window opening, in place of the gardener, a whirling carnival ride is visible. A German voice, heard over background carnival noise, announces:

We take your imaginative powers to their limit. With the most enchanting magic, we take you far beyond your rational thoughts. Enchanting! Marvelous! Wondrous! Unparalleled! Unimaginable![38]

With a dissolve, the image of the carnival ride is removed from the window opening, leaving an empty frame throughout the next section of voices. The first of these, a woman's voice, counters the barker's invitation to stretch her imaginative powers with the following comment:

We must visualize something but our imagination has certain limits. One can never fully feel someone else's pain. Never fully feel it. One can only say, it was terrible.[39]

Clearly, the context in which the imagination is to be set in motion has shifted, as signaled by the dissolve and the removal of the carnival image from the window frame. But a strikingly similar use of language carries over the dissolve into the next set of statements. These statements, each by a different speaker, parallel the barker's superlatives:

Dreadful! It was dreadful, say what you will.

Horrible! A horrible time. Horrible!

Unimaginable! Unimaginable! Simply unimaginable!

Such madness, such a holocaust! It is not conceivable. What was done to the Jews, that was the most terrible thing in the whole world.[40]

Only in the final excerpt is the reference to the Holocaust made explicit. And at the completion of this statement (by a non-Jewish woman), the window on the screen begins to move slowly from right to left, followed by another window, and then another in the succession of windows that reveal the movement of a passing train.

As one window comes to a standstill at the left side of the screen, the voices resume:

A carnival barker's pitch in Deborah Lefkowitz, *Intervals of Silence: Being Jewish in Germany*. Photo courtesy of the filmmaker.

> And then I saw for the first time that they had numbers on their arms. They said the numbers had been burned in and would never come off. And then no one said anything else about it—until they saw the pictures. It's incredible.

> The first discussions about the extermination of the Jews came when we saw the films of the camps. I can still remember how many people staggered out and got sick when they saw those gruesome images. I still have gruesome images in my head.

> That was so horrifying! I immediately turned off the television and wept bitterly. I have never turned on such a program again and I never will because they just upset me so much. I simply cannot see such things.

> If these films were not shown all the time, then maybe grass would grow up over some of this.[41]

Again, as if in response to the spoken words, a dissolve reinserts an image in the window opening: the green leafy branches of a tree. The overlying window matte disappears, revealing a full-frame image of tree branches, followed by a long shot of a playground. After a few moments of silence, I explain in voice-over narration that I had been told there had been a Jewish cemetery on this site before the war. Thus, at the conclusion of this sequence a rather crude figure of speech has been given a direct visual equivalent: grass really did grow over this site covering up not only Jewish graves, but the Nazi act of converting a cemetery into a playground.

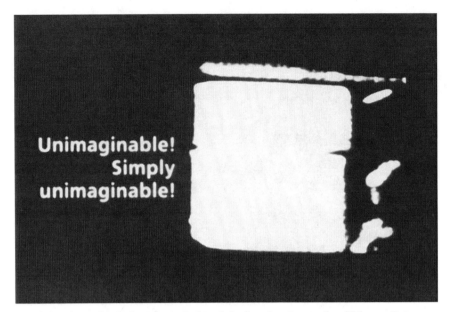

Speaking about the Holocaust in Deborah Lefkowitz, *Intervals of Silence: Being Jewish in Germany*. Photo courtesy of the filmmaker.

This sequence, nearly symmetrical in construction, begins and ends with a framed green space seen within the full film frame. The first of these framed green spaces depicts a surviving Jewish cemetery, no longer in use, but restored, labeled with the appropriate "commemorative plaque," and cared for by the city gardener. On the sound track a Jewish speaker complains about the constant focus on Jews in relation to cemeteries. At the end of the sequence, as the framing reveals the green foliage surrounding the site of a former Jewish cemetery, a non-Jewish voice also complains—albeit for very different reasons—about constant reminders of the Jewish dead.

The symmetry points to a cyclical, as opposed to linear, progression of time but also emphasizes the silence contained in the middle of the sequence during the slow movement of train windows across the screen. Before this silence, non-Jewish voices are referring to the Holocaust. Afterward, when voices return to the sound track, they are speaking about the period following the war. The insertion of silence into this stream of voices serves to separate speaking about the Holocaust from speaking about images of the Holocaust (in films and television programs produced sometime later). Thus silence again marks the interval of time from the early war years to the end of the war, the interval during which Jewish voices were— literally—not present in this city, because Jews had been deported.

Thinking about the relationship of narrative to historical time and perceiving silence as an apt metaphor for ruptures in this relationship, I find resonances with other writings about the Holocaust. "The Nazi past," writes historian Saul Friedländer, is simply "too massive to be forgotten, and too repellent to be integrated into the 'normal' narrative of memory."[42] Primo Levi in his account *Survival in Auschwitz* remarks that "for living men, the units of time always have a value. . . . For us, history had stopped."[43] Pointing also to discrepancies between the time in which—and of which—Holocaust survivors write, Ida Fink begins an autobiographical short story: "I want to talk about a certain time not measured in months and years. For so long I have wanted to talk about this time . . . but I couldn't, I didn't know how."[44] And R. Ruth Linden, cognizant of the inability of words to do justice to the experience of the Holocaust, reflects: "Can deliberate silence be the only alternative to the narrative that belies itself?"[45]

But silence as a response to experiences incommensurable with narrative can be found not only in the writings of Holocaust survivors. Irma Garcia perceives silence in the relationship of women, and women writers, to time: "Memory intervenes and . . . dislocates the linear train of thought." Referring to "the 'times-outside-time' . . . where silence treads," Garcia maintains that "these moments . . . form holes in the narrative," and that women have "a predilection for these blanks and these spaces" in their writing.[46] Referring more specifically to the writings of German women, Marie-Luise Gaettens discusses strategies for narrative disruption such as "remembering in anecdotes," a form of self-imposed silence that serves "to avoid confronting the ambiguities and the disturbing aspects of the [Nazi] past . . . when the process of memory seems too painful."[47]

While *Intervals of Silence* partakes of these other meanings of silence, the film also maintains its own meanings: it represents my attempt to speak into the silences, perceived or actual, of the film's viewers. By juxtaposing statements of Jewish and non-Jewish Germans, I wish to overcome the silence inherent in non-Jews speaking and listening only to non-Jews, Jews only to Jews. Superimposed over the collective identity—Jewish or non-Jewish—is the individual experience, and my film urges viewers to hear all speakers on their own terms and without labels.

Yet there is a relationship between how I wish my film to speak and how I insist that it not speak. My refusal to label speakers, for example, is one silence I have created. I do not identify voices heard on the sound track either by name or by title; I do not even correlate voices with images of the speaker. Instead, I am continually redefining the congruity between words and images.

Some images in my film, for example, consist only of printed words— white letters against a black screen. Others, accompanied by silence, have no words whatsoever. In some sequences images replace words—or vice versa—either literally in terms of graphic placement on the screen, or figuratively in terms of metaphoric connotation. And, as all four of the film sequences discussed in this essay demonstrate, verbal and visual evocations of silence are often interchanged. Thus, silence about Jewish identity is represented by the disappearance of two figures from the screen, and the historical disappearance of Jews from the city is twice heard as a prolonged silence on the sound track.

In formal terms, my film repeatedly makes use of dualities: two sets of voices in the sound track; two layers of images, black-and-white and color; two forms of language, one spoken (German) and one written (English). These dualities suggest that silence is inherently a function of relationships. But the relationships I establish between two image layers, or an image and its accompanying spoken text, allow multiple meanings to coexist. Ultimately, then, silence is the space in which to contemplate the harmonies and dissonances of such meanings.

◆————————————————————————————————————

NOTES

1. Susan Neiman, *Slow Fire: Jewish Notes from Berlin* (New York: Schocken Books, 1992), 260.

2. Marc Fisher, *After the Wall: Germany, the Germans and the Burdens of History* (New York: Simon and Schuster, 1995), 211.

3. Alison Owings, *Frauen: German Women Recall the Third Reich* (New Brunswick, N.J.: Rutgers University Press, 1993), x.

4. This town is located in northwestern Germany near the Dutch border and the industrialized Ruhr Valley. However, in order to guarantee Jewish speakers (far fewer in number and therefore more easily identifiable) the same anonymity allowed non-Jewish speakers, the town remains unnamed in my film. For the same reason it will remain unnamed here as well.

5. See Daniel Jonah Goldhagen, *Hitler's Willing Executioners: Ordinary Germans and the Holocaust* (New York: Knopf, 1996). Compare Goldhagen's notion of "ordinary Germans" with the definition provided by Thomas Heydrich, nephew of Gestapo head Reinhard Heydrich, in an interview conducted by Israeli psychologist Dan Bar-On. Prompted by Bar-On to explain what he meant by describing his mother as an "average German," Thomas Heydrich said, "What I call a 'normal' citizen is someone who knew exactly what a burning synagogue meant, who knew that people were constantly disappearing.

And who didn't ask, 'Who set the fire?' or 'Where are they?'" See Dan Bar-On, *Legacy of Silence: Encounters with Children of the Third Reich* (Cambridge: Harvard University Press, 1989), 146.

6. For example, Joan Ringelheim points out that anti-Semitism treats men and women very differently. Ignoring these differences "creates blind spots in the memories and reconstructions of the Holocaust." See Joan Ringelheim, "Thoughts about Women and the Holocaust," in *Thinking the Unthinkable: Meanings of the Holocaust*, ed. Roger S. Gottlieb (New York: Paulist Press, 1990), 145. Although survivor narratives by male writers are generally considered representative accounts of the Holocaust, Myrna Goldenberg argues that women's survivor narratives portray significantly different experiences. See Myrna Goldenberg, "Different Horrors, Same Hell: Women Remembering the Holocaust," in *Thinking the Unthinkable*, 150–52. Carol Rittner and John K. Roth reiterate that since much of the most widely read and most easily accessible scholarship on the Holocaust fails to address gender differences, the particularities of women's experiences have been disregarded. See *Different Voices: Women and the Holocaust*, ed. Carol Rittner and John K. Roth (New York: Paragon House, 1993), xi. Similarly, Marlene E. Heinemann contends that little attention has

been paid to either gender issues or women writers in the study of Holocaust literature. See Marlene E. Heinemann, *Gender and Destiny: Women Writers and the Holocaust* (New York: Greenwood Press, 1986), 4–5. Claudia Koonz, investigating the role played by German women during the Third Reich, comments on the virtual absence of women's voices in the historical record: "Public man had left an archival trail, but where might I find the voice of private woman?" See Claudia Koonz, *Mothers in the Fatherland: Women, the Family, and Nazi Politics* (New York: St. Martin's Press, 1987), 8.

7. Adrienne Rich, *On Lies, Secrets, and Silence: Selected Prose 1966–1978* (New York: W. W. Norton, 1979), 245.

8. Note that last names and some place names have been omitted or changed.

9. Deborah Lefkowitz, interview typescript D-12a (1985), 1. Here as elsewhere when I quote from the unedited interview transcripts, the translation from the German is my own.

10. Lefkowitz, interview typescript D-9a (1985), 1.

11. Lefkowitz, interview typescript D-54a (1985), 1.

12. Lefkowitz, interview typescript D-54b (1985), 33.

13. My interviews were mostly recorded with individuals one-on-one, in the interviewee's home or place of work. If conducted in the home, there were often other family members present and sometimes they participated in the interview as well. A few interviews were conducted in the context of larger groups, primarily with students in a classroom setting.

14. Of the twenty-six active participants, thirteen were recorded in one-on-one interviews, nine participated in joint interviews with another female speaker, and only four in joint interviews with a male speaker.

15. Lefkowitz, interview typescript D-35a (1985), 7–8.

16. Ibid., 1.

17. Lefkowitz, interview typescript D-22b (1985), 44.

18. Lefkowitz, interview typescript D-11a (1985), 19.

19. Owings, *Frauen*, xv–xvii.

20. Tillie Olsen, *Silences* (New York: Delacorte Press/Seymour Lawrence, 1978), 39.

21. Elie Wiesel, *From the Kingdom of Memory: Reminiscences* (New York: Summit Books, 1990), 14, 21.

22. Lefkowitz, interview typescript D-54a (1985), 22–23.

23. Lefkowitz, interview typescript D-11a (1985), 1–2.

24. Tannen, "Silence: Anything But," in *Perspectives on Silence*, ed. Deborah Tannen and Muriel Saville-Troike (Norwood, N.J.: Ablex Publishing, 1985), 100.

25. Lefkowitz, typed transcript of the complete text from *Intervals of Silence: Being Jewish in Germany* (1990), 7. Here as elsewhere I am quoting the English titles that appear in the film.

26. Underscoring this relationship between speaking and being heard, Elie Wiesel has written: "It's not because I don't speak that you won't understand me; it's because you won't understand me that I don't speak." See Wiesel, *Kingdom of Memory*, 144.

27. Lefkowitz, *Intervals of Silence* transcript, 17.

28. Ibid., 20.

29. Ibid., 4.

30. Ibid., 13.

31. Hayden White, *The Content of the Form: Narrative Discourse and Historical Representation* (Baltimore: Johns Hopkins University Press, 1987), 10.

32. George Lakoff and Mark Johnson, *Metaphors We Live By* (Chicago: University of Chicago Press, 1980), 175. Note in this regard German filmmaker Wim Wenders's contention that "narrative involves forcing the images in some way," and that he has "never yet been involved in a story with a beginning, middle and end." See Wim Wenders, *The Logic of Images: Essays and Conversations*, trans. Michael Hofmann (London: Faber and Faber, 1991), 53, 54. Based on her twenty-two-year study of women's lives, psychologist Ruthellen Josselson maintains that "any effort to draw a life in linear language inevitably distorts it." See Ruthellen Josselson, *Revising Herself: The Story of Women's Identity from College to Midlife* (New York: Oxford University Press, 1996), 14.

33. Lefkowitz, *Intervals of Silence* transcript, 10.

34. Ibid.

35. Lefkowitz, interview typescript D-35a (1985), 3–4.

36. Lefkowitz, *Intervals of Silence* transcript, 14.

37. Ibid.

38. Ibid.

39. Ibid., 15.

40. Ibid.

41. Ibid. Note that the text has been shortened here.

42. Saul Friedländer, *Memory, History, and the Extermination of the Jews of Europe* (Bloomington: Indiana University Press, 1993), 2.

43. Primo Levi, *Survival in Auschwitz*, trans. Stuart Woolf (New York: Collier, 1973), 107.

44. Ida Fink, "A Scrap of Time," in *Different Voices*, 41.

45. R. Ruth Linden, *Making Stories, Making Selves: Feminist Reflections on the Holocaust*

(Columbus: Ohio State University Press, 1993), 18.

46. Irma Garcia, "Femalear Explorations: Temporality in Women's Writing," trans. Eva Goliger Reisman, in *Taking Our Time: Feminist Perspectives on Temporality*, ed. Frieda Johles Forman with Caoran Sowton (Oxford: Pergamon Press, 1989), 171, 177.

47. Marie-Luise Gaettens, "The Hard Work of Remembering: Two German Women Re-Examine Nationalsocialism," in *Taking Our Time*, 77.

IV Innovative (Auto)biographies

Innovative (Auto)biographies

Being both retrospective and autobiographical, Deborah Lefkowitz's contribution in the previous section provides a good transition to this last section of the book, "Innovative (Auto)biographies." By foregrounding unconventional self-expression through film and video, the essays in this section carry on the feminist tradition of validating women's histories while at the same time interrogating the forms through which those histories get represented. Michelle Citron's essay, like that of Lefkowitz, is about her own filmmaking practice used as a springboard for thoughts about the cultural and social dimensions of filmic confessions and silences. "An autobiographical work," writes Citron, should be seen for the political act it is and not denigrated as a "trashy 'true confession.'" "An autobiographical work," she continues, "risks exposing that which the culture wants silenced." In a candid essay about the ethical choices that face a documentary filmmaker, Citron "confesses" where she has fled into fiction and how that flight may be seen to reveal as much as it obscures.

Chris Holmlund's essay, "From Rupture to Rapture through Experimental Bio-Pics," begins with the insight that the term *bio-pic,* normally used to characterize Hollywood feature filmmaking, can be redefined as a rubric under which traditionally disparate feminist film practices can be brought together. Extending Julia Lesage's 1978 perception that early feminist documentaries "show the unshown" by portraying the lives of ordinary women,[1] Holmlund suggests that avant-garde and experimental works also can be construed as "showing the unshown," from an innovative and (auto)biographical perspective. The feminist bio-pic, she therefore proposes, is elastic enough to include early movement documentaries *and* avant-garde or experimental works. Under Holmlund's analysis, Leslie Thornton's tape *There Was an Unseen Cloud Moving* (about the extraordinary life of the explorer Isabelle Eberhardt) exemplifies the experimental incarnation of the bio-pic in which the viewer is "put on the spot to invent, along with the film, a way of reading."[2]

The collection ends with a new essay by Julia Lesage. We place the essay last to honor Lesage's twenty years of writing on feminism and documentary, from her timely yet prescient "The Political Aesthetics of the Feminist Documentary Film" to the present. In "Women's Fragmented Consciousness in Feminist Experimental Autobiographical Video," Lesage sets out an ambitious taxonomy of feminist autobiographical video work, which she exemplifies with detailed analyses of Vanalyne Green's *Trick or Drink* and Lynn Hershman's *Electronic Diaries*. But, generic differences apart, these tapes are linked, argues Lesage, by a common "fractured, disjunctive, nonteleological narrative style" that expresses a psychological dynamic shared by "groups of oppressed people, including men." In reconsidering decades of creative expression (in this case videomaking, but it could as well be history writing) and in connecting gender inequities to the politics of race and class, Lesage's essay reiterates the profound concerns of the editors and contributors to this volume.

◆───

NOTES

1. Julia Lesage, "The Political Aesthetics of the Feminist Documentary Film," reprinted in *Issues in Feminist Film Criticism*, ed. Patricia Erens (Bloomington and Indianapolis: Indiana University Press, 1990).

2. Here we are quoting Holmlund quoting Thornton cited in Trinh Minh-ha's "Which Way to Political Cinema?" in *Framer Framed* (New York: Routledge, 1992), 258.

MICHELLE CITRON

[**12**] *Fleeing from Documentary:*
Autobiographical Film/Video and
the "Ethics of Responsibility"

In documentary film or videomaking every shot is charged with ethical implications and choices. That is why early on in my career I made the decision to create fictions with actors who were paid to deliver the words that I wrote. I thought I'd just avoid the ethical quandaries. But this fiction didn't wholly solve the problem either. For there, at the end of the production process, at the moment of exhibition lurked another set of ethical issues— my responsibilities in relation to my audience.[1]

Bill Nichols articulates this distinction well: interactive documentary texts acknowledge the encounter between filmmaker and subject and thus foreground their ethical relationship; reflexive documentary texts, and he includes my own film *Daughter Rite* here, question representation and foreground the relationship between the filmmaker and audience.[2] I evolved my filmmaking style to flee from the problems of the first and engage in the issues of the second. What I want to do is take a second look at both spaces of responsibility, particularly as shaped by the autobiographical film.

▶ ─────────────────────────────────────

My Family

With the autobiographical act the personal moves into the cultural, the private becomes the social. Acknowledging this, John and Judith Katz defend autobiographical filmmaking "in terms of the public's right to know. Private life at the end of the twentieth century is surrounded by a high degree of secrecy. . . . We compare ourselves to myths, not reality. . . . The value of knowing, in more realistic fashion, about other people's interior lives is unquestionable."[3] Autobiographical films and videos bear witness to our lives in all its variation, and these lives are untidy and contradictory: we have passions, both creative ones and destructive ones; we betray each other and do surprisingly heroic things; we experience profound joy and almost crushing emotional pain; we are both cruel and compassionate. All these experiences and feelings fuel the autobiographical act. Because of this, the autobiographical film or video can break a silence and by doing so lessen the isolation and despair that we often experience, both personally and culturally.

The comfort that comes from knowing other peoples' lives is an important function of many autobiographical films and videos, from the white middle-class observational documentaries of the seventies (Joyce Chopra's *Joyce at 34*; Amalie Rothschild's *Nana, Mom, and Me*) to the more multicultural, mixed-mode autobiographies of recent years (Wei-Ssu Chien's *A Woman Waiting for Her Period*; Rea Tajiri's *History and Memory*; Aarin Burch's *Spin Cycle*).

The honest autobiographical film or video publicly speaks about the socially hidden: gay sexuality (Jennifer Montgomery's *Age 12: Love with a Little L*); being disabled (Jacqui Duckworth's *A Prayer before Birth*); or violence against women (Margie Strosser's *Rape Stories*). This is the implicit threat that autobiography poses to the status quo. As a culture, we have been little able to tolerate the truth of the variety of lived experience: that truth threatens the social order.

The autobiographical act is historically significant for women, and all others, who have traditionally lacked either a voice or a public forum for their speaking. Françoise Lionnet in writing about women's autobiographical novels notes that women are "consumed by need to find their past, to trace lineages that will empower them to live in the present, to rediscover histories occluded by HISTORY."[4] It is in this sense that the autobiographical act is a political act, something we risk losing sight of when women's autobiography is labeled confessional. This label denigrates, as in the trashy "true confessions" magazines of the fifties, or the 1–900 phone numbers of the nineties. There is a class as well as a gender dimension here. The middle class thinks it rude to air dirty laundry in public; social decorum requires that secrets remain hidden.

The confessional label dismisses autobiographical film as being inappropriate for public display, at best self-indulgent, at worst narcissistic. One male critic was overheard telling another at Amsterdam's 1990 World Wide Video Festival that Vanalyne Green's *A Spy in the House That Ruth Built* was "impressive but awfully confessional."[5] Compare this to J. Hoberman's praise of Ross McElwee's *Sherman's March* for its "delirious excess of libido that makes life worth living."[6] *A Spy in the House That Ruth Built* has as much libido as *Sherman's March*; Green finds a pleasure in men's derrieres that is equal to the pleasure that McElwee has for women's breasts. Green's crime is that she dares to be the female voyeur in a territory claimed by men. Her exploration of female desire isn't missed by female critics, who praise the video for revealing that which has remained private for too long.[7] Is this simply a case of each critic defending his or her own? I suspect that power still follows the male: on the issue of self-disclosure, the female is criticized for her narcissism, while the male is lauded for his courageous vulnerability.

To confess means to disclose something damaging or inconvenient to oneself. Confession implies guilt. A criminal confesses and pays the penalty for doing so. With women's autobiographical film just what, precisely, are we guilty of? And who, exactly, pays?

An autobiographical work risks exposing that which the culture wants silenced. I completed *What You Take For Granted . . .* , a film that speaks explicitly of harassment toward women in the workplace, in the year of my tenure review. I feared that the perfect punishment a disapproving Father could enact on an indiscreet Daughter was the denial of her tenure. This particular fear was not realized, though, at an institution that had not yet fully embraced women's studies or awarded many women tenure; neither was it unreasonable. Others have been less lucky. As history has shown us, when a film is too threatening funding can be withheld, exhibition denied, voices silenced.[8]

There is a personal dimension of risk at work here as well. The autobiographical film or video is intimately bound to the filmmaker's psyche, a site where guilt and projection lurk. When I completed *Daughter Rite,* I didn't show it to my mother for many years. My guilt for making it was fueled by a fear that she would withdraw her love upon viewing the film since it spoke the secret of a daughter's anger toward her mother. Here my fear was more expressive of my guilt than of my mother's character, as she is one of the rare nonjudgmental people I know. When she finally viewed the film, her actual reaction was something I could have never imagined. But that's a story for later.

An autobiographical work is connected to the preexisting tensions in a videomaker's or filmmaker's life. This makes the issues surrounding autobiographical media complex because the life that exists outside the piece is as important, if not more so, than the piece itself. It is in this dynamic relationship that exists between the media work and the artist's life that the ethical dimension dwells.

Autobiography can be dangerous to others, particularly those on whom the video or filmmaker turns her camera. Lovers, spouses, children, parents, and friends can find themselves suddenly appropriated as subjects into the autobiographical artist's celluloid or tape presentation of "self."

An autobiographical artist uses her own life *and* the lives of others in the service of her art. Immediately an ethical responsibility arises. It is one thing for me to be an exhibitionist, quite another to turn my camera voyeuristically on those close to me, exhibiting their lives for the pleasure of strangers.

I was first confronted with this ethical dilemma in my documentary film *Parthenogenesis.* At the time, I was transitioning from the field of psychology to that of media and was in the process of redefining myself as a filmmaker. As a woman it was a lonely and isolated struggle. This chaotic moment in my life motivated *Parthenogenesis,* a film about three women artists: my violinist sister, Vicki Citron; her concert violinist teacher, Rosemary Harbison; and my filmmaker self.

The film, shot over the course of five consecutive days, shows the process of Rosie teaching my sister Bach's Double Violin Concerto in D Minor. Cut into these sessions are conversations between Vicki, Rosie, and myself on the various problems we encountered as women in the arts: working with men who trivialized us, the shadow of the virtuoso tradition, the ways in which institutions limited our visions and actions, and our own self-censors.

This was an intimate shoot comprising only the three of us. I taught my sister how to mic a shot, and everyone lugged the equipment. At those moments when I entered into the discussion, I would lock down the camera, come out from behind, and sit down with the other two women at the table. But acknowledging my presence by actively participating in the discussions was not enough. Fully committed to both Marxist and feminist politics, I was acutely aware of the power relationship that was created between the filmmaker and her subjects in the making of documentary film. Determined to subvert that relationship, I designed the following scheme.

Parthenogenesis was shot on the now ancient and crude half-inch open-reel video format and later transferred to film for editing and exhibition. This technology allowed for a broader conceptual control among all the participants. Every morning I would tape Vicki and Rosie learning and rehearsing the concerto. And each afternoon was spent with the "subjects" watching the previous day's rushes, collectively discussing the issues they raised, and taping whatever conversation we decided to have in response. Each successive morning's shoot was shaped by the previous afternoon's group discussion in which we all equally participated. This would, I believed, give my sister and her teacher power over their representation.

The two women, especially my sister, were also involved in the film's editing. They watched successive cuts and their input greatly influenced the final film's structure and meaning. Much later, of course, I understood that this complicated process was successful at the level of the content and the aural track only. The conversation in front of the camera was mutually agreed on through long discussion among the three of us. As musicians, Vicki and Rosie both had expertise on the musical content of the film; in these matters I followed their lead. However, they were not as sophisticated about images; being behind the camera, I controlled the film's visualization. And, it is Rosie, and not my sister, whom my camera favors. The two are positioned in such a way that in order for Vicki to talk to Rosie she must turn toward her and away from the camera; for most of the film, it is Rosie's animated face and my sister's back that the viewer sees.

The production process for *Parthenogenesis* had a second benefit as well. Because my sister and Rosie were so intimately involved in the process, I believed the issue of consent was nullified. Voluntary and informed consent is perhaps at the heart of the video or filmmaker's ethical responsibility to the subject in documentary.[9] And although one can endlessly question whether or not subjects can ever really have informed consent, this is at least one ethical issue with both a long history of debate and well-developed procedures.[10] With an autobiographical piece, however, informed consent becomes quite murky.

Most autobiographical films and videos are about the family.[11] And as John and Judith Katz argue, levels of intimacy, trust, as well as the specific dynamics within families greatly complicate the ethical issues. Katz and Katz make the case that in autobiography, the maker has a greater responsibility toward her subjects because using family subjects, the artist usually has undue influence. After *Daughter Rite* I made *Mother Right,* a documentary video of my mother discussed below. In my most cynical moments I know this tape was easy to make because my mother would do almost anything for me: I am her daughter and she loves me.

Love, guilt, desire to help—all the convoluted feelings that infuse familiar relationships—influence the maker-subject dynamics in most autobiographical films and videos. This is because the film or tape enters into the already preexisting relationship between the artist and her family subjects. And this can have an unpredictable, and often unknowable, influence on the film being shot. In *Parthenogenesis* Rosie is the seasoned performer, aware of the camera, and in control of her persona. My sister, much younger, seems vulnerable in her unfolding formation. Early in the film Vicki admits to having doubts about her talent, her drive, and her goals. She tells Rosie, "Finally, it's just come down to me confronting myself. And I don't know if I can do it." Now watching the film, I suspect that I unconsciously used my big-sister influence to convince Vicki to participate; I needed a stand-in to work through my own insecurities as a woman artist. And I suspect that my sister's eagerness to play with the older women artists made her vulnerable, in turn, to that influence.

In autobiographical video or filmmaking, the artist can't just walk away from her subjects when the project is finished. The relationship extends beyond the moment of shooting; both the maker and her family know this. Whatever happens in front of the camera must be lived with, by the artist and her family, for the rest of their lives together. What kind of subtle censorship shapes the autobiographical work for this reason alone—an answer hedged, a feeling unexpressed, an experience left unspoken? At the other extreme, what type of hyperbolic moments occur in these works precisely because of the camera's presence and a desire, by at least one of the participants, to act out for the camera what can't be acknowledged behind closed doors?

All of these concerns played a major role in my flight from documentary into fiction film. I created fiction because of the ethical discomfort experienced in exhibiting someone else's life, despite his or her willingness to do so. I created autobiographical fiction because of a driving need to use my life as a case study and, unable to flee from my subjects once the filming was over, was protective of both them and myself. Fiction was the escape hatch.

Over the years, I've steadfastly maintained that *Daughter Rite* is not autobiographical. After all, I told myself and anyone else who asked the question, I had interviewed many daughters prior to writing the film and later hired actors to speak the text. The film was about mothers and daughters in general, not my mother and her daughters specifically. Through this semantic sleight of hand, I let myself off the hook. Of course, the reality of the film's verisimilitude is more complex.

Daughter Rite contains different approaches to the autobiographical act, both documentary and fictional. The taxonomy plays out this way. At one end lie the autobiographical references that have fidelity to the details of my life. In *Daughter Rite,* these are the documentary images represented by actual filmic documents shot by my father—the home movies. Historically, most film or video autobiographies are cinema verité and fit into this category.

A second category exhibits fidelity to the details of other women's lives: the stories told to me by the thirty-five daughters I interviewed for the film. These stories are clearly not autobiographical, yet they could have remained as documentary interviews surrounding the more autobiographical elements of the film. Instead, I transformed these interviews into material that is scripted and acted. I think of this material as being true to the details of women's lives in general (mine included), however reworked. The scene where Stephanie tells of the rape by her stepfather is an example of this. The story, told to me by a sixteen-year-old woman, is faithful to both that woman's life and the interview she gave. The only changes were made in order to fit the story into Stephanie's character and the film's narrative line. Given the highly charged nature of the material, I felt more comfortable having an actress, rather than the young woman, speak the story.

Finally, there is the material that is totally imagined: the scene where Maggie and Stephanie make salad; the sisters rifling through their absent mother's bureau; the narrator describing her mother's depression.

Yet this taxonomy is misleading; the film is untidy in a way that my categorization belies. In *Daughter Rite,* there is no predictable relationship between the above categories and the various aesthetic elements of the film. For instance, the mother's reading the daughter's mail as well as her divorce from the father and move to Hawaii are all details from my own life. Yet the first appears as a story related by the sisters in one of the faux documentary scenes, and the latter is told by the narrator. And the dreams, visually represented through the most manipulated images in the film, are as authentic as the home movies, in that I actually dreamed them.

Ultimately, however, these categories insufficiently express the autobiographical nature of the film, for it is in the emotional texture that the film is truly autobiographical. The passive-aggressive power struggle that threads through Maggie and Stephanie's relationship resonates off my own family experience. And the daughters' anger toward their mother is an emotion I must own. The film represents only a narrow band of the full feeling spectrum that is my relationship with my mother. Yet a core of my lived experience fuels the fiction in a way similar to that real bit of sand that precipitates the pearl—though, as with the sand and the pearl, at first glance their relationship isn't self-evident. The fictional form of these broadly defined autobiographical elements situates my personal experience in a larger cultural context and simultaneously lets me off the hook.

Viewers of *Daughter Rite* assume that the mother character portrayed in the film is my own mother. This audience response caused me much guilt over the film. I felt that I had betrayed my mother, both by allowing my anger toward her to show in the film and by implying that the depressed mother in the film represented her. My guilt was further exacerbated since I knew that I encouraged this response with the use of a first-person, filmmaker, narrator. Perhaps this narrating device was a way to clue the audience into the autobiographical nature of this fictional work. Perhaps it was my strategy to have it both ways: I could make an autobiographical film, while at the same time denying its autobiographical nature.

Mother Right was made to assuage my guilt over *Daughter Rite,* to enable my mother her voice. My working-class mother is a straight talker, some would say alarmingly direct, and as such, she is a lively and compelling film subject. After divorcing my father, she moved to Hawaii and spent the next fifteen years working in a prominent gay restaurant and bar in Honolulu. She herself is straight.

In *Mother Right* my mother talks frankly about her existence in this gay environment: what attracts her to it, why she finds it emotionally satisfying, and how her straight friends react. The tape, shot in the early pre-AIDS eighties, shows my mother at work in the bar and restaurant, socializing with her straight friends and planning the annual Gay Pride party with her gay friends, the party itself complete with strippers. My mother is proud of her life and wanted very much to make the tape. As she tells a bar patron and friend of hers on camera: "You know when she shows *Daughter Rite,* people question her, 'Is that what your mother's really like?' She's gonna prove to them that's *not* what I'm really like."

My mother was emotionally involved with the gay men she came into daily contact with as coworkers and customers. They were also her friends. Once AIDS hit the gay community, she became very active in fighting the epidemic. She raised consciousness in the straight community, raised money for the local AIDS foundation, and, sadly, helped her friends die. My mother became the adult who parented these men, deserted by their own mothers, through their final days: feeding them homemade soup, listening to their fears, visiting them in the hospital, attending their memorials. I believe my love and respect for her informs *Mother Right.*

I rarely show this video since I lack releases from some of the people who talked, sang, and danced before my lens. Yet on those rare occasions when it has been screened, I've been surprised at viewer response—many were critical of my mother as portrayed in the film. This negative response is usually made up of different threads: outright homophobia focused on my mother; covertly expressed discomfort toward the male gay life explicitly portrayed in the tape; and anxiety created by a woman who left home and family to follow her own desires and, as a heterosexual woman, spends much of her libido on what is considered an inappropriate object—gay men. My loving point of view toward my mother, carefully inscribed on the screen, is inconsequential. *Mother Right,* meant to express the mother's point of view, leaves her vulnerable to criticism despite my conscious intentions. My mother, I know, would find this reaction confusing and upsetting.

Paradoxically, *Daughter Rite,* made exclusively from the daughter's point of view, permits a significant amount of criticism of the daughters as

The filmmaker's mother at home, in Michelle Citron, *Mother Right*. Photo courtesy of the filmmaker.

The filmmaker's mother being playful with a customer at work, in Michelle Citron, *Mother Right*. Photo courtesy of the filmmaker.

The filmmaker's sister interviewing their mother at a picnic with friends, in Michelle Citron, *Mother Right*. Photo courtesy of the filmmaker.

self-absorbed, and viewers often defend the mother against these ungrateful offspring. Thus, audiences often read into the films the opposite of what I intended.

Obviously, audience response to any video or film is both multivariable and unpredictable. This uncertainty, however, takes on ethical weight in documentary pieces where real lives are exhibited. Unless a subject is media sophisticated, and few people including my family are, what significance does informed consent really carry? And what right do I have to display them to audiences in often unpredictable ways? These questions are further intensified for me in autobiography, where I'm intimately attached to the people being filmed and taped. The tension that exists between respecting the rights of others and speaking the unspeakable, what is often labeled the right to privacy versus the right to know, is solved by fiction.

The question arises, what compels a filmmaker or videomaker to create an autobiographical work? The autobiographical impulse is obviously motivated by multiple sources. Briefly, my own work is fueled by a desire to understand my life in relation to larger cultural forces, as well as a yearning for a presence in the world. Why, for me, these needs take the form of the autobiographical act, and not some other equally appropriate form, is not my subject here. What is of interest is the function of fiction in my choice:

fiction gives me distance on a subject—myself—that I often have precious little distance on.

The Canadian videomaker Lisa Steele writes, "To convert one's life into a process is the process of autobiography."[12] By turning one's life into such a process, new possibilities for self-understanding open up. Françoise Lionnet in describing women's autobiographical fictional writing says it this way:

> The narrator's process of reflection, narration, and self-integration within language [and I include film and video here] is bound to unveil patterns of self-definition (and self-dissimulation) which may seem new and strange and with which we are not always familiar. The self engendered on the page allows a writer to subject a great deal of her ordinary experience to new scrutiny and to show that the polarity fact/fiction does not establish and constitute absolute categories of feeling and perceiving reality. The narrative text epitomizes this duality in its splitting of the subject of discourse into a narrating self and an experience of self which can never coincide exactly.[13]

Lionnet calls the gap created by this split a "space of possibility where the subject of history and the agent of discourse can engage in dialogue with each other" (193). I am particularly interested in the dialogue set up in this "space of possibility," this space that opens up both at a personal and an interpersonal site.

Fiction gives voice to my unconscious, allowing me to have a dialogue between that which I know, and that which I don't even know that I know.[14] From this dialogue, insight springs. At the end of *Daughter Rite* the narrator relates a dream about her dying sister, which reads in part:

> I go home to Mom. Nancy is there and asks to be killed. She says to set her on fire. I do, and she melts very slowly. It is terrifying to watch, especially her face melting. Mom is wonderful. She really helps, talking to Nancy as she burns, stoking the fire. . . . Finally, I cannot take it any longer . . . I leave. Nancy is dead, but not totally burned up. I know I should stay till the very end, but I just can't. . . . I need to be alone. I am scared and upset . . . I go home, hoping Nancy's body is gone. It is gone. Mom waited until it burned completely, then smashed it up and buried it in the marsh. She has done this terrible task so that I wouldn't have to do it. I am very grateful. I wander over to her, she holds me in her arms, and I start to cry.

In the images that play under this narration, the mother looks almost heroic. She struts down the walk, pivots at the end of a pier, and moves toward the camera, over and over in different shots filmed at various locations. This mother owns the environment through which she moves; the montage is made of images from the mother's point of view. She is alone in the frame, independent of the daughter, whose film this has been. The last shot in the sequence is the one exception. In it, the mother puts her arm around her daughter, and in long shot they walk together across an empty field. Placed as the final shot in the mother's montage, this image allows the filmmaker daughter to project her desire for mother love onto the mother, while pretending these feelings are from the mother's point of view.

I wrote this segment to illustrate the daughter's belief in her mother's willingness to care for her: a fantasy of sacrificial mother love. But the scene hints at a darker desire as well—my murderous competition with my sister for my mother's affection, a wish I was not consciously aware of at the time. In the fiction, created through the free play of imagination, that which was hidden is made visible. In the words of Adrienne Rich, the film allowed me "to remember what it has been forbidden even to mention."[15] In this fictitious moment the possibility for knowledge, and thus change, opens up before me.

Interpersonally, a different space of possibility is created through autobiographical fiction. As mentioned above, my mother didn't view *Daughter Rite* until years after the film's completion. The day after the screening, my mother took me aside and altered our lives forever. She disclosed a painful secret that I had never known and that she had never revealed to anyone else before: the ongoing sexual abuse she had experienced as a child. This revelation, driven, she said, by the viewing of *Daughter Rite,* significantly changed my relationship with my mother and my own sense of place in the world. In that moment a "space of possibility" opened up: a place of dialogue between my mother and me that gave a new degree of consciousness to both our relationship and our individual lives.

Fiction provides a much needed space of denial that my family and I can inhabit when it's psychologically necessary or convenient to deny that what I speak is referential. No one is fooled, but this trick we play with each other is essential. It allowed my mother to hold her secret until she was willing to disclose it. A documentary film might have confronted my mother to speak before she was ready, and furthermore, it would have put me in control of the moment of confrontation. Perhaps she never would have spoken. *Daughter Rite* motivated the telling of secrets; fiction allowed my mother to choose her own time and place. The process was one of illumination, not accusation.

Autobiographical fiction presents a paradox. It allows for more authenticity by giving voice to that which we both consciously *and* unconsciously know. Yet at the same time, it works by deception, which ironically, by opening up a space of safety, may ultimately lead to honesty and truth.

Making autobiographical fiction shifted my ethical responsibility away from the subjects in the film and toward the audience. This was enhanced by my use of fiction, disguised as cinema verité, to deliberately confront the audience with their assumptions of documentary verisimilitude and the expectations that flowed from that belief.

Documentary films and videos, which present a historical subject up on the screen, often push the audience away. For example, I react differently when I know that's an authentic dead body I'm seeing and not just an actor pretending to be dead—hence my great distress and difficulty in sitting through Stan Brakhage's film *The Act of Seeing through One's Own Eyes,* a film in which autopsies are recorded by the unflinching camera.[16] The authentic dead bodies in this film produce shock and distancing for me the viewer. The dead bodies performed by actors in the latest Hollywood blockbuster, on the other hand, can allow for an easier play of identification since there is always the awareness that these bodies aren't really dead.

Documentary potentially sets up a dichotomy between us and them; we sit in the audience as voyeurs and watch someone else's life unfold. It is all too easy to think, "It's just their problem, it's goddamn for sure not mine. I've never been raped, or have AIDS, or . . . [fill in the blank]." Ironically, a fictional character potentially allows for greater identification because our knowledge of their fictional nature makes such identification safer. The character is not "real" so we can experience the overlaps without having to actually be too much *like* them.

I once screened *Daughter Rite* in a class I was teaching for non–Radio/ Television/Film students at Northwestern University. I started the discussion by asking them what they felt after viewing the film. One woman said that the film made her angry, especially the moment where the character Stephanie talks about being raped by her stepfather. She said that she had never been raped herself so her response wasn't "personal." Rather, she believed that she empathized with a real woman and felt betrayed when she discovered otherwise. This student invested her empathy in what she believed was an authentic woman and felt betrayed when she found out Stephanie was a fiction performed by an actress. Part of this betrayal might lie in the investment the student had in experiencing herself as someone with empathy and largesse toward another. *Daughter Rite* evoked that feeling, then deprived her of it. Part of her reaction might simply be a wounding of her sense of herself as a sophisticated film viewer. By manipulating the codes, *Daughter Rite* broke the filmic contract, and this student might have felt foolish that she fell for it. Even though there is a social reality to the scene, in its referentiality to both an interviewee's life and a statistical fact of our culture,[17] it was the filmic reality that held importance for this woman.

Audiences have a psychological investment in the aesthetic codes and contracts of a film's reliability.[18] They want their media to be accurately labeled. They want truth in advertising: this is a real woman telling them a real story in an authentic documentary; or, this is fiction; or, this is autobiographical fiction; or, these are clearly inscribed documentary scenes within fiction.[19] They feel safe because what they see matches what they're told they're seeing; to be told otherwise is to feel crazy. We all want to feel this safety, allowing, of course, for those moments of pleasure we find in roller-coaster rides. *Daughter Rite* violates this safety, particularly since it is not a cool and detached text; it is an emotional look at the mother-daughter relationship rife with the feelings experienced by many families. The film's emotional intensity might make a viewer feel particularly vulnerable, increasing her desire and need for safety, making the betrayal felt even deeper.

I tried to obviate this betrayal of the audience in *What You Take For Granted . . .* by deliberately designing the film to deconstruct its aesthetic in a more obvious way. Starting with the transcripts from forty interviews, I scripted a film about women, both working class and professional, who labored in jobs traditionally held by men. The film begins with six characters who talk in direct camera address about their experiences on the job. Ten minutes into the film two of the talking heads, the truck driver and the doctor, start interacting in a story shot in a somewhat conventional narrative fiction style.

I anticipated that this contrived narrative, populated with two characters who were also seen in sequences coded as documentary, would make the film's aesthetic strategy easy to read. The two short montage sequences of women working that open and close the film make up the only authentic documentary footage in *What You Take For Granted . . . .* I hoped that the existence of this authentic documentary footage (unique in the film in both its visual style and what it depicts, different women from those depicted in the talking heads sequences—women actually laboring) would bring the fictitious nature of the rest of the film into even greater relief.

Audiences have had different and creative ways to read the construction of the film. Some saw what was true: that all the characters and the entire film, except for the opening and closing montages, are fiction. Some believed that the four characters seen exclusively in the interviews were historical subjects in authentic documentary sequences while the truck driver and the doctor were actors, both in the narrative and the interview scenes. Yet even others believed that all the women were authentic documentary subjects and that a genuine truck driver and a genuine doctor were persuaded to act out narrative scenes for me in front of the camera.

Whatever reading strategy the viewer chose, however, there was a clear message that the film was highly constructed. The manipulation by this film is more clearly inscribed in the frame than in *Daughter Rite*. In my experience, audiences do not feel betrayed by *What You Take For Granted . . .* to the extent that they do with *Daughter Rite*. The conscious way in which they engage in figuring out the aesthetic puzzle of the film allows them to feel more active as viewers and thus less manipulated. When the trick of the film's construction is revealed, they usually just laugh off their missing the answer to the puzzle.

With *What You Take For Granted . . .* identification is spread among a greater number of characters, who themselves are quite diversified in terms of age, class, race, and sexual orientation. The range of job experiences they describe are quite broad, too, both in the actual work performed and the emotional tone of the experience. This allows for dispersed identification, deintensifying the viewing experience. Furthermore, the emotional stakes for the viewer of this film are not as high as in *Daughter Rite*; *What You Take For Granted . . .* is almost sociological in its approach. This makes for a more emotionally cool film that mediates against such deep feelings of betrayal as those experienced by viewers of *Daughter Rite*.

What You Take For Granted . . . is an ethical success. Yet that success is bought with a much subdued emotional tone. For an autobiographical work, this is a high price to pay. As an artist I'm concerned with the personal *and* the social, the emotional *and* the analytical. My current autobiographical film work is exclusively fiction and clearly coded as such. This resolves my ethical responsibilities toward both my subjects and my audience. However, there are many reasons that fiction compels me beyond ethical considerations. But that is a subject for another time.

NOTES

1. In the title of this essay I am borrowing the phrase "ethics of responsibility" from Bill Nichols, *Representing Reality* (Bloomington: Indiana University Press, 1991) and bending it to fit my own argument here. Ideas for this chapter were developed in nascent form in "The Unreliable Aesthetic," presented at the Documentary Fictions Conference, Luxembourg, 1993.

2. Nichols, *Representing Reality*, 44–68.

3. John Stuart Katz and Judith Milstein Katz, "Ethics and the Perception of Ethics in Autobiographical Film," in *Image Ethics: The Moral Rights of Subjects in Photography, Film and TV*, ed. Larry Gross, John Stuart Katz, and Jay Ruby (New York: Oxford University Press, 1988), 128.

4. Françoise Lionnet, *Autobiographical Voices: Race, Gender, Self-Portraiture* (Ithaca, N.Y.: Cornell University Press, 1988), 25–26.

5. Mandy Farber, Video Data Bank, private communication.

6. J. Hoberman, "I Sync Therefore I Am," *Village Voice*, September 9, 1986, 52.

7. This point is persuasively made by Laura Kipnis in "Female Transgression," in *Resolutions: Essays on Contemporary Video Practices*, ed. Michael Renov and Erika Suderburg (Minneapolis: University of Minnesota Press, 1996), 333–45.

8. One only needs to look at the recent history of the National Endowment of the Arts and its defunding of individual artistic works for examples.

9. Much has been written about the responsibilities of the filmmaker in relation to the subject: the nature of consent; the participants' often competing needs; and the implications of technical choices, such as focal length of lens and composition, in carrying meaning. See Gross, Katz, and Ruby, *Image Ethics*, as well as Nichols, *Representing Reality*, for extended discussions of these issues.

10. See Nichols, *Representing Reality*, and Gross, Katz, and Ruby, *Image Ethics*.

11. A random sampling of just a few of the autobiographical films (and tapes) available through the Women Make Movies catalog include: *She's Just Growing Up, Dear*, Julia Tell's film about childhood incest; *Trick or Drink*, Vanalyne Green's tape about growing up with alcoholic parents; Su Friedrich's *The Ties That Bind* and *Sink or Swim*, respectively, about her relationship with her mother and with her father; and Deborah Hoffmann's *Complaints of a Dutiful Daughter*, about her mother's descent into Alzheimer's disease.

12. Lisa Steele, quoted in exhibit catalog, *Autobiography: Film, Video, Photography* (Toronto: Art Gallery of Ontario, 1978), 94.

13. Lionnet, *Autobiographical Voices*, 92.

14. Adrienne Rich writes, "Poems are like dreams: in them you put what you don't know you know." "When We Dead Awaken: Writing as Re-Vision," in *On Lies, Secrets, and Silence: Selected Prose 1966–1978* (New York: W. W. Norton, 1979), 40.

15. Ibid., 13.

16. For an extended discussion of the ethical space in documentary film see Nichols, *Representing Reality*, 76–89. See also Vivian Sobchack, "Inscribing Ethical Space: Ten Propositions on Death, Representation, and Documentary," *Quarterly Review of Film Studies* 9, no. 4 (1984): 283–300.

17. Current estimates are that in the United States one in four women have been raped. Diana Russell, *Sexual Exploitation: Rape, Child Sexual Abuse, and Sexual Harassment* (Beverly Hills, Calif.: Sage, 1984), cited in Judith Herman, *Trauma and Recovery* (New York: Basic Books, 1990), 30.

18. This is particularly important in documentary or news footage—for example, the outcry over Janet Cooke, who faked her *Washington Post* story about a young boy on drugs for which she won, and later lost, the Pulitzer Prize, or NBC *Dateline's* faking an explosive crash of a GM truck, for which the network's news director as well as three producers were fired.

19. For example, Warren Beatty's film *Reds*.

CHRIS HOLMLUND

[13] *From Rupture to Rapture through Experimental Bio-Pics: Leslie Thornton's There Was an Unseen Cloud Moving*

> *When documentary boundaries grow permeable, there is the possibility of looking again, with new questions in mind.*
> :: Leslie Devereaux, "Cultures, Disciplines, Cinemas,"
>   in *Fields of Vision*

Since the early 1970s, feminist documentaries have often been framed as biographies. Though the term *bio-pic* is usually associated with Hollywood feature films, many early movement documentaries might, I believe, usefully be reconsidered as activist bio-pics, for by focusing on ordinary women, they intentionally recast both Hollywood bio-pic and portrait documentary standards of fame. Using linear narratives, direct interviews, and/or monologues, many of these early films provided portraits of exemplary but ordinary women, designed to raise consciousness and build feminist community. Others investigated the contributions of precedential but more exceptional women to history, art, science, and politics through compilation footage and narrative voice-over.[1] Emphasis in these early feminist documentaries was on "showing the unshown": in Julia Lesage's words, they were intended as "a critique of and antidote to past cinematic depictions of women's lives and women's space."[2] As most of the women who directed these early feminist bio-pic/documentaries were socialist and/or radical feminists, "showing" and "the unshown" were, not surprisingly, thought of in a realist and materialist sense, as manifesting an "embodied knowledge."[3] Both makers and audiences typically assumed that this "embodied knowledge" could be simply, transparently expressed; few thought to examine the conventions through which these life stories were told.

Another set of early feminist films, customarily described as avant-garde or experimental rather than as documentary, was also interested in "showing the unshown" from biographical or autobiographical perspectives.⁴ Though not always reflexive, films such as *Fuses* (Carolee Schneeman, 1965–68), *Schmeerguntz* (Gunvor Nelson and Dorothy Wiley, 1966), *Kirsa Nicholina* and *My Name Is Oona* (Gunvor Nelson, both 1969), *Unfolding* and *Holding* (Coni Beeson, 1969 and 1971, respectively), *I Was/I Am, Double Strength,* and *Women I Love* (Barbara Hammer, 1973, 1974, and 1976, respectively) all imagined showing in poetic rather than realist terms and frequently foregrounded "the sensuous properties of the art work itself."⁵ Some, Richard Dyer argues, were influenced by "cultural feminism" and therefore conceived of "the unshown" as encompassing the spiritual as well as the material world, at times referring to mythical or mystical female figures, at times using layered editing structures to, as Dyer puts it, "question the appropriate boundaries of things."⁶

The majority of feminist biographical documentaries made since the mid-1980s continue to deploy a realist film language. A significant minority fluidly mix fact and fiction, biography and ethnography, often through performances. Yet though overtly concerned with the limits and lies of realist representation, most of these recent works and most current documentary theory as well continue to conceptualize knowledge as embodied and/or existential. This materialist predisposition leads Bill Nichols, for example, to argue that contemporary documentary still operates within "a domain of *social* subjectivity and *historical* engagement," and Alexandra Juhasz to urge of autobiographical and biographical work that "the body . . . be specified back into existence, acknowledging the material effects of race, class, gender, weight, disease, and other body rooted indices of privilege."⁷

Unfortunately, the emphasis in contemporary documentary theory and practice on the "real," decidedly material world implicitly excludes spirituality not only from definitions but also from debates. A secondary omission in recent critical work, especially curious given the continuing prevalence of conventional and unconventional portrait documentaries, is an assessment of biography per se. In this essay, therefore, I want to focus squarely on the category of biography, using Leslie Thornton's experimental bio-pic *There Was an Unseen Cloud Moving* (1987) to test the limits of documentary theory and to highlight how feminist bio-pic practice is changing. For my purposes, Thornton's choice of Isabelle Eberhardt as the subject of her tape is ideal. A cross-dressing, cross-cultural, turn-of-the-century explorer and mystic, Eberhardt has fascinated biographers since she died at age twenty-seven in a flash flood in the Algerian desert. Thornton's tape further intrigues me because it synthesizes what were disparate approaches in 1970s feminist work: like the realist portrait films, it revolves around one woman "at a particular time, . . . whose changing status has made her identity problematic";[8] like the avant-garde personal films, it is concerned with spirituality, nature, and subjectivity, highlighting by example how inadequate a purely material approach to biography and documentary can be.

At the same time, however, *There Was an Unseen Cloud Moving* differs from 1970s work. Unlike most early activist documentaries, Thornton's tape returns to earlier Hollywood bio-pic standards of fame, choosing a celebrity as subject without holding her up as an example. Instead, like other experimental bio-pics made from the 1980s onwards,[9] *There Was an Unseen Cloud Moving* uses staging, performance, editing, and the like to question the assumption that a composite of photographic images and sound recordings could ever transparently translate the truth of a life. And where some "cultural feminist" films used "images and symbols from colonized cultures as markers of an authentic otherness,"[10] Thornton's tape refuses to reify and romanticize "other" images and "other" voices, preferring relentlessly, if fitfully, to undermine fixed identities and exotic representations.

Originally a painter who shifted to film and video, Thornton has recently started painting again after a twenty-year hiatus. Her interest in diverse visual arts makes her part of an avant-garde that "challenges accepted forms and the divisions between forms" as *a* "way to political cinema."[11] Interested in experimental cinema since she was a teenager, Thornton studied film at SUNY-Buffalo with Stan Brakhage and Hollis Frampton while majoring in painting, then worked with Richard Leacock at MIT. Now a professor in the semiotics department at Brown University, her work typically explores "the outer edge of narrative,"[12] employing reflexive techniques to rupture linear logic and refuse closure. Some of her films and videos, including *There Was an Unseen Cloud Moving*, also move beyond rupture to rapture, envisioning the end of life and the possibility of other lives, afterlives.

The better to bring out how, to paraphrase Leslie Devereaux, Thornton's tape enables me to look at and listen to biography and documentary again, "with new questions in mind,"[13] I first compare Thornton's de- and reconstructions of Eberhardt's life story with several prose biographies and a 1992 mainstream bio-pic. My aim in this section, which I call "What Was This Life, Anyway?," is to highlight how Thornton troubles notions of stable identity, which most biographies take for granted. In a second section whose title, "Whose Life Is It, Anyway?," I take from an article by Christine Tamblyn,[14] I discuss Thornton's work with photography, film, and video in *There Was an Unseen Cloud Moving* in light of her 1983 film *Adynata* and the ongoing film and video series *Peggy and Fred in Hell*

(1987 to the present). I concentrate here on how Thornton emphasizes "-graphy" in order to expose clichéd representations of the Third World (the Near East) and of other worlds (geographically, the moon; temporally, nineteenth-century Europe) as "constructs of our own cultural vision."[15] I weave my reflections in the third section, called "Which Life Is It, Anyway?," around Eberhardt's diaries and short stories and Thornton's recent color video *The Last Time I Saw Ron* (1994), exploring how *There Was an Unseen Cloud Moving* articulates what Thornton there calls "the overflow of ecstasy into speech." In conclusion, I ask one final question, "What Kind of Life Will It Be, Anyway?" Threading my observations around Thornton's most current work in progress, another experimental bio-pic about Eberhardt called *The Great Invisible,* I seek to involve readers in the political issues that underpin Thornton's twistings and unravelings of fiction and history, rupture and rapture, through experimental bio-pics.

▶

What Was This Life, Anyway?

For Isabelle Eberhardt, cross-dressing, both cross-culture *and* cross-gender, was the staple of existence and the key to writing: as Marie-Odile Delacour and Jean-Rene Huleu argue, Eberhardt took Arthur Rimbaud's visionary maxim "Je est un autre" (I is an other), quite seriously, deploying fiction in the service of both truth and life.[16] From an early age Eberhardt's gender identity was fluid. The illegitimate child of a Russian mother (her father was probably her tyrannical tutor), Isabelle was raised in the French-speaking part of Switzerland. Taught several languages, she knew some Arabic already as an adolescent and often affected female and male Arab dress.[17] At age twenty she finally traveled to North Africa with her mother. Most of the rest of her life was spent roaming the desert or exploring the cities, usually dressed as an Arab man. Attracted to Islam as a teenager, she became increasingly devout as she grew older and was even initiated into the Quadrya order, according to Ursula Kingsmill Hart, as a man.[18]

Beginning with the memoirs of Eberhardt written by her friend and fellow journalist Robert Randau, print biographies describe Eberhardt's physique in the most unflattering terms. Most point out, moreover, that by the end of her life she had lost all her teeth and was probably suffering from syphilis. Randau himself is quite derogatory, writing "with a protruding forehead, sallow skin. . . . she had none of the physical attributes or sentimental charms which attract and retain lovers."[19] A few literary biographies try to explain why Eberhardt's cross-dressing, tobacco and

Photograph of Isabelle Eberhardt, used in Leslie Thornton's *There Was an Unseen Cloud Moving* and *The Great Invisible*. Photo courtesy of the filmmaker.

hashish smoking, and multiple lovers were tolerated, even accepted, among Arabs though not most French colonizers. Cecily Mackworth, for example, maintains that "the delicate courtesy of the Arabs admitted that, as she wished to pass for a man, she should be treated as such," especially because "Arab mythology contains a long tradition of female marabouts, several of whom had scoured the desert disguised as men."[20]

All prose retellings of Eberhardt's life do, however, contextualize her cross-dressing in some way, and all conclude that certain aspects of her life are inexplicable. Mackworth writes: "Neurotic . . . adventuress . . . artist . . . mystic. Isabelle was all of these in turn. . . . It is useless to look for a logical thread on which to hang so chaotic an existence."[21] Lesley

Blanch similarly, if more deliriously, accumulates hyperboles and antitheses at the start of her treatment of Eberhardt, titillatingly titled *The Wilder Shores of Love*:

> Everything about her was extraordinary. She was a woman, dressed as a man. A European turned Arab. A Russian . . . whose untidy mystical torments . . . found peace in Islam's faith—and flesh. . . . She adored her insignificant [Arab] husband, but her sensual adventures were without number. . . . Her death was strangest of all, for she was drowned in the desert.[22]

In contrast but like most mainstream bio-pics, Ian Pringle's 1992 feature film *Isabelle Eberhardt* assumes that Eberhardt's life is both explicable and representable. Though the film is peopled with scores of secondary characters, Eberhardt is without question the central character of the movie. Scene after scene emphasizes her fondness for cross-cultural cross-dressing and her appetites for sex, drink, and drugs. At the same time, makeup, costuming, and framing consistently highlight her femininity: even in Arab robes, actress Mathilda May always wears lipstick and eye makeup, and she is often shown in profile so her breasts appear beneath her robes.[23] Shot on location in North Africa, the Pringle film uses the desert primarily as an exotic backdrop and refers only schematically to the complicated political and religious climate in turn-of-the century colonized North Africa.[24] No explanation is offered of the Arab reaction to "Si Mahmoud Essadi," Eberhardt's name for her masculine Arab persona.

Thornton's experimental bio-pic is, like Pringle's film, largely unconcerned with the original sociopolitical contexts in which Eberhardt moved. Unlike Pringle's film, however, Thornton's tape questions contemporary reframings of a variety of historical events. In addition, Thornton portrays Eberhardt's identity as performed and variable rather than as fixed and unchanging: in the space of sixty minutes, seven different amateur actresses play Isabelle. Visual and verbal references are made to Eberhardt's cross-dressing. One actress appears as an Arab woman; another as an Arab man; yet a third, a punk, combines Cossack and Arab headgear with hiking boots. But nowhere does Thornton find Eberhardt's transvestism or numerous heterosexual love affairs as tantalizingly transgressive as Pringle's film does.

Yet though, as Linda Peckham argues, only a "minor portion of the tape is preoccupied with verisimilitude,"[25] and though most spectators would not know it, Thornton's tape follows the chronology of Eberhardt's life more faithfully and, in some senses, more completely than Pringle's more obviously linear bio-pic: Pringle concentrates only on the adult Isabelle, but Thornton alludes to Eberhardt's unorthodox childhood; her

One of the Isabelles (the punk) in *There Was an Unseen Cloud Moving*. Still by Leslie Thornton; photo courtesy of the filmmaker.

wanderings in North Africa; a return to the deserted, decaying family villa; a trip to France to solicit funds; the assisted (by Eberhardt) suicide of her tutor/father, stricken with throat cancer; a politically and religiously motivated attack on her life by a young Algerian; a meeting with Randau; and, finally, her own mysterious death in the desert.

However, Thornton's representation of even these "real-life" episodes is far from realistic. All of the re-created sequences are shot on location in and around Providence, Rhode Island, and New York. Some episodes are recounted through intertitles, others through voice-over narration and/or photographs. All, whether reenacted or recounted, are interrupted. Thornton thereby insists on the many ways biography can be told, making it impossible for spectators to regard "biography" as *the* truth of a life à la 1970s feminist portrait documentaries. Instead, we are encouraged to ask, not just "what *was* this life, anyway?" but also "whose life *is* it, anyway?"

▶

Whose Life Is It, Anyway?

There Was an Unseen Cloud Moving approaches the problem of "whose life is it, anyway?" from many angles, always without offering a singular or final solution. Less concerned with providing answers than with prompting questions, Thornton's tape casts its excursions into what Nichols calls "anthropology's own unconscious" as forays into biographical form.[26] Like the ethnographies Nichols describes, however, it is very much concerned with "who has the responsibility and legitimacy (or power and authority) to represent others, not only in the sense of rendering likenesses but also in the sense of 'speaking for' and 'presenting a case'" (64).

Other works by Thornton confront similar issues without tackling biography head-on. The 1983 *Adynata* most closely resembles *There Was an Unseen Cloud Moving,* but its improvisations around Orientalist images and sounds center on a single photograph, a formal portrait of a Chinese Mandarin and his wife taken in 1861. Though as in *There Was an Unseen Cloud Moving* reenactments are crucial, in *Adynata* they often focus on a single gesture or pose rather than on a sequence of actions, let alone an entire life.

The currently four-part *Peggy and Fred in Hell* series builds its investigations into the wasteland of American culture around two children (Peggy and Fred), but these children never emerge as characters or social actors with "lives" of their own.[27] Like the seven Isabelles of *Unseen Cloud,* Peggy and Fred frequently perform—usually incomprehensibly and unpredictably—but as children they embody an indeterminate, floating identity, which Thornton describes as "not quite us and not quite other. They are becoming us, or they are becoming other."[28]

There Was an Unseen Cloud Moving, in contrast, is presented as a biography almost from the start: a few shots from a 1950s travelogue of cars pulling men on skis over sand dunes are quickly followed by intertitles that present Eberhardt's life story. Throughout the video these intertitles and not the many narrators who speak in direct address and voice-over are responsible for moving the biographical narrative forward. Quickly, Thornton undermines our confidence in their authority by insisting on their *written* dimension. Typefaces and handwriting styles vary constantly. Sometimes a title card is shown being typed or written. The sources of these title cards are never identified, but it is obvious that they differ, for some are lyrical, some factual, some rhetorical.[29]

Thornton underscores how much "-graphy" shapes "biography" in other ways as well. Early on, an offscreen female narrator (Thornton herself) recounts "the story" of Eberhardt's childhood over a slide show of still photos. For a time, only the whir and click of the slide projector in the background distinguish Thornton's "lecture" from the feminized "voice-of-God" narration used by many conventional feminist portrait documentaries. Some of the images that illustrate the lecture are photographs of the young Eberhardt; others are photographs of people and places that the voice misleadingly identifies as Eberhardt or members of her family. Thanks to what Roland Barthes calls the "what has been" of photography,[30] all of the photographs lend a patina of salvaged authenticity to the lecture until a title card appears, which reads: "With the emergence of Photography as a technology, the Victorians lost no time both documenting themselves, and bringing home the spectacle of other cultures through images. The parlor became the repository for all of the bric-a-brac which were the spoils of colonialism, each house a small museum."[31] In retrospect, this intertitle reframes the photographs, undercutting the idea that photography "authentically" preserves the past for the present, and positioning nineteenth-century Europe as well as Arab cultures as the object of contemporary fascination.

As she does in the various parts of *Peggy and Fred in Hell,* moreover, Thornton intercuts snippets of documentaries throughout *There Was an Unseen Cloud Moving,* intentionally raising what Hayden White terms "the spectre of the fictionality of the historian's own discourse."[32] But where the documentary segments in *Peggy and Fred in Hell* revolve around the West,[33] with few exceptions those in *There Was an Unseen Cloud Moving* revolve around North Africa or the moon. Ethnographic footage of an Arab woman puncturing her wrist with a large needle is punctuated by television coverage of an American astronaut happily singing "We're off to see the Wizard" as another plants a U.S. flag on the moon. Lengthy sections of a *National Geographic*–style documentary titled *The Moslem World: Part 1 — Lands of the Camel* are followed by satellite footage of the desert. A fragment of the same 1950s travelogue seen at the beginning of *There Was an Unseen Cloud Moving* ends the tape. Now, however, a line of girls in knee socks traipse over desert dunes as an offscreen male narrator pontificates about the "desert glory that it is our additional privilege to see." (Though *There Was an Unseen Cloud Moving* does not mention the fact, the girls in the original film are blind, according to Thornton.)[34]

Clips from two feature films (Josef von Sternberg's 1930 *Morocco* and Julien Duvivier's 1936 *Pépé le Moko*) are cut in to further blur distinctions between fiction and documentary. At certain moments historical and fictional times seem to coexist within the space of a single shot/reverse shot figure: toward the end of the video, for example, the captain from *Morocco* exchanges looks with one of the seven Isabelles. Genres collide on the sound track as well, for, like *Adynata, There Was an Unseen Cloud* plays quite literally with what Linda Peckham calls the question of "fidelity to and recuperation of history."[35] In *Adynata,* however, no character/actor ever speaks, whereas in *There Was an Unseen Cloud Moving* dialogues and monologues spoken in English are intercut with voice-over narration, snatches of dialogue and narration spoken in other languages, and patently found sounds and songs from different countries and eras.[36] The narrators of the various documentaries and fiction films all construct *their* desert as *the* desert, *their* casbah as *the* casbah, even as they largely concur in painting desert peoples as vermin, fakirs, and freaks.

Because, as in *Adynata,* Thornton multiplies voices and constructs "the relation of sound to image [as] . . . contentious rather than supplementary, [she] produc[es] ruptures and disjunctive moments which force the discourse of Orientalism to stutter and falter."[37] Unlike earlier cultural feminist work, moreover, both *Adynata* and *There Was an Unseen Cloud Moving* insist on the ways in which North American feminists consciously and unconsciously collude with Orientalist visions. In *There Was an Unseen Cloud Moving*, Isabelle no. 1, played by Su Friedrich in an Arab veil, is the first to playfully intone *The Wizard of Oz* theme. Near the end of the tape her wonder at the fact that people actually live in the desert is repositioned as the passing amazement of the tourist:

> A little Tuareg girl . . . sells you a piece of grilled cheese and then turns and starts walking back across the desert. As far as you can tell for about three thousand miles there's nothing, but it's her home. . . . [Isabelle no. 1/Friedrich looks at her watch and shrugs in response to a barely audible question from offcamera.] Well, it's four minutes to three, I think we should go, don't you? Let's go. . . . Any tiny questions that you really care about? [Fading out.] You want me to say what was scariest?

At another point an earnest young punk speaks at length about what Eberhardt means to her, painting her as a hell-raiser whose autobiographical writing was "like a morbid Victorian version of Harlequin Romances but much more violent." Gleefully, she suggests that to play Isabelle she should "maybe be, like, dirty and pee."

Disjointedly but relentlessly, Thornton thus investigates "history . . . through the refractions of desire and identification."[38] As in earlier cultural feminist and other avant-garde work, coherent representation is rejected, and instead the sensual and physical qualities that make up each segment are emphasized. Color, for example, stands out because some of *There Was an Unseen Cloud Moving*'s footage is shot in black and white and vice versa.

To the extent that we try to make sense of the chunks of complementary and competing narratives that Thornton offers up for visual and aural consumption, we necessarily find ourselves asking with her, "whose life is it, anyway?" and reflecting on how much our own desires, not just her desires, are at work in shaping biographical life. As Peckham says, "this biography of Eberhardt is . . . very much a contemporary portrait, a narrative that unravels the limiting notion of 'the true story' and writes along the traces of Eberhardt's legend, so that she is not reduced to another occupied territory but becomes known as an enigma."[39] Peckham's formulation "known as an enigma" is apt, for in *There Was an Unseen Cloud Moving* Thornton is concerned not only with life and rupture but also with death and rapture. Behind "what life was it, anyway?" and "whose life is it, anyway?," then, shimmers a third, usually unasked question: "*Which* life is it, anyway?"

▶ ———————————————————————————————————

Which Life Is It, Anyway?

For Eberhardt this was a question with a religious answer: life, she came early to believe, was so caught up with death that it could only be lived in the conviction of a life after death. As the actors and intertitles of Thornton's tape intermittently attest, two older brothers, her father, and a niece all committed suicide.[40] Fragments of Eberhardt's poems and diary entries that convey her obsession with death and dying are included as well:

> The world moves
> towards death
> As the night
> towards dawn
> 3/20/1894

> I say what I think
> I should do.
> You say Die

> 9/21/98
> You speak and I start laughing.
> Corpses come to life
> I'm trying not to talk gibberish today
> though totally lost and wandering

> 6. The wind from the Sahara is coming with a vengeance. Its breath has the pure flame of the furnace. Now in the sun it is 142 degrees F.
> 7. Only the tomb can take this richness from me.

In many ways, of course, Eberhardt's "morbid, hysterical, and eroticized fascination with the *idea* of death" was typical of nineteenth-century Victorian attitudes.[41] Twentieth-century Western cultures, in contrast, avoid visual or verbal representation of death. "Indexical in code and function," documentaries in particular, Vivian Sobchack argues, "observe the social taboos surrounding 'real' death."[42] In *There Was an Unseen Cloud Moving* as also in her most recent video, *The Last Time I Saw Ron,* Thornton would seem to agree with Sobchack that "non-being is not visible. It lies over the threshold of visibility and representation. . . , forever off-screen, forever out of sight" (287–88). Unlike the majority of the documentaries Sobchack describes, however, Thornton tries in her two videos to envision a space and time that may be beyond visibility but not entirely beyond representation.[43]

Thornton describes *The Last Time I Saw Ron* as more speculative than *There Was an Unseen Cloud Moving.*[44] A brief but poignant meditation on loss, love, destruction, and creation, *The Last Time I Saw Ron* weaves together footage shot for a play titled *Philoktetes Variations* (of explosions, the ocean, a solar eclipse, naked bodies floating superimposed "in space," and more) with found sounds from nature (bird cries, waves), music, and Thornton's voice-over meditations about the death of her friend and collaborator Ron Vawter from AIDS. Opening intertitles inform us that Philoktetes was bitten by a snake on his way to Troy. The wound will not heal, and his terrible moans and the smell of the wound compel Odysseus to abandon him to die on an uninhabited island. Vawter's actual dying in the role of Philoktetes transformed the production for cast and crew alike. The play became the "rehearsal of [Ron's] death," "the staging of his own funeral." Far from abandoning him, all sought with him the connections between death, birth, and rebirth. Off-screen, Thornton says slowly, "During rehearsals, he was surrounded by people who loved him. When he had to use a wheelchair sometimes, we tried to see right through it and into the universe. The play felt so big and it bound us so tightly in this landscape of death that we could walk right through it together." Superimpositions, focus shifts, sound overlays, and silences hint at the different dimensions that exist in, around, and even after life.

There Was an Unseen Cloud Moving similarly experiments with how sounds and images might translate transfiguration. Following a path Eberhardt blazed in her fiction, Thornton seeks in the wonder of nature something that would wordlessly speak to the nature of wonder. Eberhardt "looked for [a] reflection of the divine in simple people, in stories she lived wherein her look captured the incident, 'which falls softly like a leaf on the carpet of life.' A look, a face, a song, a meeting, a promenade. . . . All these nothings from which fiction unfolds."[45] Thornton inscribes these "nothings" as close-up inserts of a leaf, a tree branch, a crack in a wall. At times, as in *The Last Time I Saw Ron,* these images move in and out of focus, as if to admit that visual clarity is neither possible nor really the point.

Ron Vawter performing in *Philoktetes Variations*, from *The Last Time I Saw Ron*. Still by Leslie Thornton; photo courtesy of the filmmaker.

Unlike *The Last Time I Saw Ron,* however, *There Was an Unseen Cloud Moving* is also concerned with the possibility of cross-cultural transmutation, for Eberhardt's longing for the otherworldly was intimately, inextricably linked to her fascination with other worlds, especially Islamic worlds. Though she inherited a number of racist and sexist views of North Africa from writers like Pierre Loti, Théophile Gautier, and Charles Baudelaire,[46] the numerous short stories and articles that she wrote about everyday life in Algeria represented feverish attempts to communicate her love for the desert and solidarity with its peoples. Invariably, the principal characters of her short stories are those whom Europeans most despised: landless fellahin, convicts, prostitutes, mystics, and madmen.[47] Many of her short stories center on Arab women, though her decision to dress as a man probably restricted her actual contact with them.[48] Often she rails against forced marriages and oppressive gender roles.[49] In her diary entries as well, she frequently objects to the limitations placed on women, by women as well as by men: "Women cannot understand me, they consider me a strange being. I am far too simple. . . . When woman becomes man's comrade, when she ceases to be a plaything, she will begin a new existence. . . . Woman could be anything one might wish, but . . . a slave or an idiot is all [men] can love, never an equal."[50]

Midway through *There Was an Unseen Cloud Moving* a passage from Eberhardt's diary appears that suggests how fanatically she felt about freedom for all:

> The most difficult of all things, the only difficult thing perhaps, is to enfranchise oneself and even harder to live in freedom. Anyone who is in the least free is the enemy of the mob, to be systematically persecuted, tracked down, wherever he takes refuge. I'm becoming more and more irritated with this life and the people who refuse to allow any exception to exist.

For Eberhardt, life on the open road, in good health, represented both "the essence of freedom" and "the path to spirituality," a "deliverance."[51] Thornton's tape reenacts Eberhardt's wanderings in video form, traipsing deliriously through different genres, times, spaces, and tones.

On the whole, however, Thornton is less interested in Eberhardt's writings about this life than she is in her writings about the next life. One of the last "facts" presented in the biographical intertitles informs us that Eberhardt gave "herself entirely to Islam, penetrating some of its most recondite mysteries, [becoming] in the eyes of many tribes of Algeria and Tunisia, a kind of saint." Yet *There Was an Unseen Cloud Moving* condemns most Western versions of this mystery as implicitly imperialist, juxtaposing, for example, a worn recording of "Ave Maria" over a black-and-white world map with drawings of camels, and intercutting contemporary color footage of Moslems praying with "grotesque ethnographic footage of religious frenzy and self-mutilation."[52]

Suspicious of works wherein "A Meaning" is pregiven in the desire for meaning,[53] wondering whether it is "possible to 'know' difference differently,"[54] Thornton turns toward poetry and song. In a section titled "The Overflow of Ecstasy into Speech" a turbaned Isabelle recites a lengthy and highly ornate passage (from the Koran) as unidentifiable video images flicker and roll behind her.[55] Shortly thereafter the punk Isabelle chants a song that begins, "And I'm hungry," modulates into "I'm fucking everybody. . . . I'm fucking everybody," and finally ends with an off-key rendition of "Amazing Grace."

Meaning of a kind remains, but fractured and multiplied, dehistoricized, deterritorialized, dematerialized. Julia Kristeva might well have been describing Thornton's "trial/process" (*proces*) of Eberhardt's biography in *There Was an Unseen Cloud Moving* in "Psychoanalysis and the Polis":

> Within the lucidity of contemporary discourse another path, post-hermeneutic and perhaps even post-interpretive, opens up for us. . . . Breaking out of the enclosure of the presentness of meaning, the *new* "interpreter" no longer interprets: [she] speaks, [she] "associates," because there is no longer an object to interpret; there is, instead, the setting-off of semantic, logical, phantasmatic and indeterminable sequences. As a result, a fiction, an uncentered discourse, a subjective polytopia come about, canceling the metalinguistic status of the discourses currently governing the post-analytic fate of interpretation.[56]

Like waves on a shore, Thornton's musings on "what was this life, anyway," "whose life is it, anyway?" and "which life is it, anyway?" meet and merge, leaving in their wake still another question: "What kind of life will it be, anyway?" I turn to this question in conclusion, viewing it in light of Thornton's most recent work in progress, another experimental bio-pic about Eberhardt begun in 1990 and titled, most appropriately, *The Great Invisible*.

▶
_____

What Kind of Life Will It Be, Anyway?

In choosing a female explorer and mystic as the principal subject of her biographical musings, Thornton has, of course, already suggested the need for more inclusive answers to the question, "what kind of life will it be, anyway?" Like the 1970s feminist portrait documentaries that chronicled women's lives, Thornton's focus on Eberhardt flies in the face of Hollywood bio-pic tradition. As George Custen notes, mainstream bio-pics create public history by "build[ing] a pattern of narrative that is selective in its attention to profession, differential in the role it assigns to gender, and limited in its historical settings": only 1.1 percent of films about women are about female explorers (most center on entertainers and paramours); two and a half times more films are made about men than about women; and only 3 percent of all films are set in Asia or Africa.[57]

Thornton's avant-garde distortions, fracturings, and embellishments of biographical authority further frame formulations of and responses to the question of "what kind of life will it be, anyway?" by demonstrating that supposedly objective and definitive accounts of History are instead marked by patriarchal methods of analysis and styles of representation. Where some avant-garde works were and are blind to the ways feminists participate in Orientalist fantasies, Thornton pointedly explores such complicity through the seven Isabelles, contemporary settings, and fictional and documentary footage she uses. The bric-a-brac of colonialist collection is, as a result, redefined as detritus, and Orientalism is repositioned as, in Mary Ann Doane's words, "a kind of continuous misreading which does not, however, presuppose a 'correct' or 'accurate' reading."[58]

We cannot afford to forget, however, that modernist and postmodernist strategies of reflexivity and rupture often speak primarily to and for certain segments of society, about other individuals and groups. Supposedly surpassed and outdated, the presumptions of salvage ethnography continue to shape perceptions in our "postcolonial" world. Thornton's tape may be primarily concerned with Western images and imagination, but the fact that the voices of Arabs, and especially of Arab women, are largely missing inadvertently reinforces an us-versus-them mentality. Along the same lines, some viewers may find problematic Thornton's juxtapositions of Orientalist clichés culled from different media, produced in different countries and at different times, because they obscure the historical and geographical specificity of Orientalist thought. To cite Emily Apter, the danger here is that the use of "theoretical signifiers in an internationalist context . . . [will] blind the [spectator] to cultural and class difference."[59]

Yet simply to counter with the demand for local analysis, as contemporary feminist theorists often do, would be to ignore the fact that we urgently need to build coalitions around provisional generalizations; carving a new fetish around particularity will not advance political struggles.[60] Even though "Truth" cannot be definitively, completely shown or seen, it may be partially and provisionally represented.

Thornton herself today admits that *There Was an Unseen Cloud Moving* conveys a sense of blindness and distance that, she says, she is re-

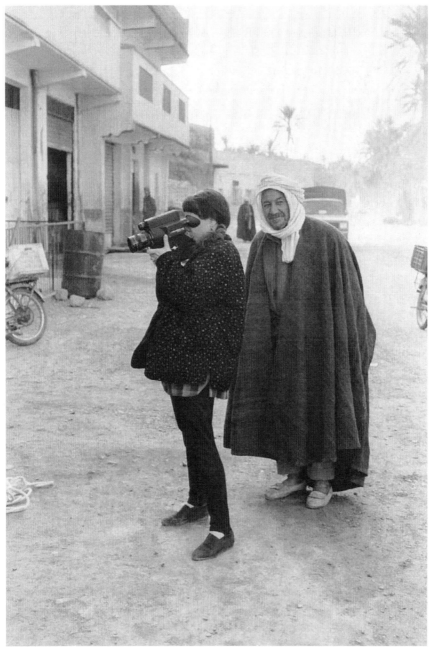

Leslie Thornton filming *The Great Invisible*. Photo courtesy of the filmmaker.

jecting in her current experimental bio-pic about Eberhardt, *The Great Invisible*. This latest, now film, version of Eberhardt's life story is, like *There Was an Unseen Cloud Moving*, preoccupied with performances of Eberhardt's life: all the actors simultaneously play themselves and a role. Now, however, Thornton is shooting on location in North Africa, and she is conducting more extensive research than she did for *There Was an Unseen Cloud Moving*. Though she recognizes that even this latest film may still be seen as "a claim to cross over," she insists that her goal is not to explain a woman traveler's imaginary experiences or even to speak them with authority: one of the final points of tension to emerge from this most recent work will be the question of "what Isabelle Eberhardt's possible transformation could be."[61]

Since *The Great Invisible* is a work in progress that will probably not be finished until summer 1998, it is, as I write this essay, truly "the great invisible." In a sense I prefer that this be so because, as I consider the questions around which this article revolves, I find most telling the fact that Thornton continues to contemplate the scandalous questions Eberhardt raises "of love, death, the force of desire, the fatality of destiny, faith, and the idea of God. Questions without definitive answers and which one is today embarrassed to take up for fear of ridicule so long have they been repressed by 'modernity.'"[62] I imagine that *The Great Invisible*, like *There Was an Unseen Cloud Moving* and Eberhardt's own writing, will engage not just with materiality and rupture but also with spirituality and rapture, offering a different kind of ethnographic realism that "blend[s] documentary description with poetic, metaphysical evocations of the emotional violence aroused by the desert landscape."[63]

Certainly, by making experimental bio-pics that, she says, "drif[t] back and forth between reason and the unfamiliar," Thornton offers another approach to biography, wherein "the 'Self' is not that interesting, . . but what flows through it can be," and the viewer is "put on the spot to invent, along with the film, a way of reading."[64] Significantly, too, and as in the ongoing *Peggy and Fred in Hell* series, by returning to Eberhardt, Thornton revises conceptions of "completed work" and "work in progress," gesturing toward and questioning, simultaneously, a political cinema that features "slowness—you give yourself, and your work, and your audience time. . . . Nothing in our culture is organized around slowness—another site for resistance?"[65]

Thornton's journeys via Eberhardt's travels thus provide ample indication that bio-pics are not just portraits of past lives. As feminists who make, critique, and watch video, television, and film, we must recognize that there are no, can be no, should be no definitive answers to the ques-

One of the Isabelles in *The Great Invisible*. Still by Leslie Thorton; photo courtesy of the filmmaker.

tion, "what kind of life will it be, anyway?" For our "mission," should we choose to accept it, is instead to explore, in the present and in the future, how we, as spectators and critics, actors and authors, piece and patch, will piece and will patch, the crazy quilt of lives, indeed of life itself.

◆————————————————————————————————

NOTES

Thanks to Leslie Thornton for talking with me about her work and to Women Make Movies, Video Data Bank, and Drift Distribution for providing preview copies of her films and tapes.

1. On early portrait documentaries, see Patricia Erens, "Women's Documentary Filmmaking: The Personal Is Political," in *New Challenges to Documentary*, ed. Alan Rosenthal (Berkeley and Los Angeles: University of California Press, 1987), 554–65; E. Ann Kaplan, *Women and Film: Both Sides of the Camera* (New York: Methuen, 1983), 125–41; Annette Kuhn, *Women's Pictures: Feminism and Cinema* (London: Routledge and Kegan Paul, 1982), 147–55; Julia Lesage, "The Political Aesthetics of the Feminist Documentary Film," in *Issues in Feminist Film Criticism*, ed. Patricia Erens (Bloomington:

Indiana University Press, 1990), 222–37; and Jan Rosenberg, *Women's Reflections: The Feminist Film Movement* (Ann Arbor: University of Michigan Research Press, 1983).

2. Lesage, "The Political Aesthetics of the Feminist Documentary Film," 223. As many feminist critics pointed out at the time, "women's lives and space" were absent and distorted in fiction films as well.

3. On "embodied knowledge," see Bill Nichols, "Embodied Knowledge and the Politics of Location: An Evocation," in his *Blurred Boundaries: Questions of Meaning in Contemporary Culture* (Bloomington: Indiana University Press, 1994), 1–16.

4. Rosenberg makes a point of recognizing that these works often offered portraits that expressed the "private moods, feelings, and interior experiences" of their makers. See Rosenberg, *Women's Reflections*, 48.

5. Richard Dyer, *Now You See It: Studies on Lesbian and Gay Film* (London: Routledge, 1990), 193.

6. Ibid., 193. For a more complete discussion of lesbian "cultural feminist" films, see 174–210.

7. Bill Nichols, "Performing Documentary," in *Blurred Boundaries*, 106, emphasis added; and Alexandra Juhasz, "Our Autobodies, Our Selves," *Afterimage* 21, no. 7 (February 1994): 14.

8. Rosenberg, *Women's Reflections*, 21.

9. Compare Steve Fagin's *The Amazing Voyage of Gustave Flaubert and Raymond Roussel* (1986), Woody Vasulka's *The Commission* (1983, about Niccolò Paganini and Hector Berlioz), and Mark Rappaport's *Rock Hudson's Home Movies* (1992).

10. Dyer, *Now You See It*, 190. In this passage Dyer is referring to Janet Meyers's *Getting Ready* (1977), but his comment could be applied to some of Barbara Hammer's early, admittedly nonbiographical, work as well, for example *Moon Goddess* (1976) and *Machu Picchu* (1981).

11. Leslie Thornton cited in Trinh T. Minh-ha, "Which Way to Political Cinema?," in *Framer Framed* (New York: Routledge, 1992), 244.

12. Ibid.

13. Leslie Devereaux, "Cultures, Disciplines, Cinemas," in *Fields of Vision: Essays in Film Studies, Visual Anthropology, and Photography*, ed. Leslie Devereaux and Roger Hillman (Berkeley and Los Angeles: University of California Press, 1995), 329.

14. See Christine Tamblyn, "Whose Life Is It, Anyway?," *Afterimage* 15 (1987): 22–24.

15. Linda Peckham, "Not Speaking with Language/Speaking with No Language: Leslie Thornton's *Adynata*," *Discourse* 8 (Fall/Winter 1986–1987): 104.

16. Marie-Odile Delacour and Jean-Rene Huleu, "Le Jeu du je," in Isabelle Eberhardt, *Ecrits sur le sable. Oeuvres completes II* (Paris: Bernard Grasset, 1990), 10 (my translation). Rimbaud biographer Pierre Arnoult imaginatively posits that Rimbaud was Eberhardt's father because (1) the two looked alike; (2) Rimbaud was in the region when Isabelle was conceived; and (3) Isabelle was the name of Rimbaud's much-loved sister. See Michel Tournier, "Isabelle Eberhardt ou la métamorphose accomplie," in *Le Vol du vampire* (Paris: Mercure de France, 1982), 212. In her brief introduction to an abridged edition of Eberhardt's diaries, Rana Kabbani finds other, more prosaic reasons to compare Eberhardt and Rimbaud: both fled to North Africa to escape oppressive familial situations and "though . . . affect[ing] to despise the privileged world of the *colons*. . . , both still functioned within and ultimately served the design of colonialism." Rana Kabbani, "Introduction," in Isabelle Eberhardt,

The Passionate Nomad: The Diary of Isabelle Eberhardt, ed. Rana Kabbani, trans. Nina de Voogd (London: Virago, 1987), viii.

17. Eberhardt's fondness for Oriental fashion was common: "After the conquest of Algeria, . . everyone smoked a *nargileh*, hashish replaced champagne. Young people wore a *burnous*." What was unusual was Eberhardt's love of male Arab dress. Denise Enslen, "Isabelle Eberhardt et l'Algérie," Ph.D. diss., University of Southern California, 1979, 26 (my translation).

18. See Ursula Kingsmill Hart, *Two Ladies of Colonial Algeria: The Lives and Times of Aurélie Picard and Isabelle Eberhardt* (Athens: Ohio University Center for International Studies, 1987), 89.

19. Robert Randau, *Isabelle Eberhardt: Notes et souvenirs*, cited in Elise Nouel, *Carré d'as . . . aux femmes!* (Paris: Guy le Prat, 1977), 93 (my translation). The only features that biographers praise are Eberhardt's "aristocratic hands" and "lovely eyes." See, for example, Nouel, *Carré d'as*, 65.

20. Cecily Mackworth, *The Destiny of Isabelle Eberhardt* (New York: Ecco Press, 1975; originally published 1951), 116, 47. Mackworth was the last of Eberhardt's biographers to interview people who had known her. See also Hart, *Two Ladies of Colonial Algeria*; and Kabbani, "Introduction," ix.

21. Mackworth, *The Destiny of Isabelle Eberhardt*, 228.

22. Lesley Blanch, *The Wilder Shores of Love* (London: John Murray and the Book Society, 1954), 273.

23. Some of the more salacious sequences shot but cut from the final film version read like erotic fiction: "In the smoky darkness of a small alcove at the back of the [kif den], a naked arm bends and the young man raises himself, arching his back in a sexual frenzy to thrust even harder amidst the clothes and blankets covering the bed. Isabelle, her own face twisted with lust, lifts herself and scratches her fingernails down his side, drawing blood. A second man, also naked, suddenly kneels up and points his crotch at Isabelle, who greedily buries her face in it. The young man is pumping harder, and Isabelle arches her head back in a look of pain or sexual ecstasy as she comes." Stephen Sewell and Ian Pringle, "Isabelle Eberhardt: Scénario intégral bilingue," *L'Avant Scène Cinéma* 420 (March 1993): 24.

24. In the early 1900s, the coastal regions of Algeria were under civilian control with native representation while the southern regions were administered by the military. Although the French constructed railways and hospitals and hence were considered preferable to the former colonizers, the Turks, they were nevertheless regarded by many as infi-

dels invading a holy territory. Insurrections and assassinations fueled by religious confraternities were common. For further discussion of the various political and religious groupings around Eberhardt, see Mackworth, *The Destiny of Isabelle Eberhardt*; Hart, *Two Ladies of Colonial Algeria*; and Annette Kodak, *Isabelle: The Life of Isabelle Eberhardt* (New York: Alfred A. Knopf, 1989).

25. Linda Peckham, "The Overflow of Ecstasy into Speech: Leslie Thornton's *There Was an Unseen Cloud Moving*," *Cinematograph* 4 (1991): 92.

26. Nichols, "The Ethnographer's Tale," in *Blurred Boundaries*, 65.

27. The series consists of *The Peggy and Fred in Hell Prologue* (21 minutes, 16 mm film, black and white, 1985), *Peggy and Fred in Kansas* (11 minutes, video, black and white, 1987), *Peggy and Fred and Pete* (23 minutes, sepia, video, 1988), and *(Dung Smoke Enters the Palace)* (16 minutes, black and white, 16 mm film and video, 1989). According to Thornton, a complete presentation involves shifting back and forth between the two media. For further on the series, see Linda Peckham, "Total Indiscriminate Recall," *Motion Picture* 3, no. 1/2 (1989/1990): 16–18.

28. Thornton cited in Trinh, "Which Way to Political Cinema?," 256.

29. Thornton combines passages from Mackworth's biography with her own retellings of Eberhardt's biography, a quote from the Koran, and selections from Eberhardt's writings. The credits do not mention Mackworth, however, an omission Thornton told me she now regrets. Telephone conversation of August 11, 1995.

30. Roland Barthes, *Camera Lucida*, trans. Richard Howard (New York: Hill and Wang, 1981), 85.

31. Peckham makes a similar point: "[These photos] give the effect of documentation but are entirely a fiction. . . . *There Was an Unseen Cloud Moving* resists the 'parlor' model of history—that the past can be salvaged and displayed in the halls of our period or that the past speaks from a place that is distinct from the present." Peckham, "The Overflow of Ecstasy into Speech," 92.

32. Hayden White, "Historiography and Historiophoty," *American Historical Review* 93, no. 5 (December 1988): 1195.

33. The *Peggy and Fred in Hell* prologue builds on a science film of vibrating vocal cords. *Peggy and Fred in Kansas* incorporates documentary images of a storm, shown as if in rough cut with a time code counting away on the side of the screen, and NASA footage. *Peggy and Fred and Pete* includes found footage "introducing Pete the Penguin" and found footage of water flowing. *(Dung Smoke Enters the Palace)* includes Edison footage shot in a foundry and NASA footage of a moon landing.

34. Personal communication of November 14, 1996.

35. Linda Peckham, "Not Speaking with Language/Speaking with No Language," 104.

36. The sound track includes a Herb Alpert selection, scratchy recordings of Arab songs, Arab and Western instrumental music, running water, chirping birds, a chugging train.

37. Mary Ann Doane, "The Retreat of Signs and the Failure of Words: Leslie Thornton's *Adynata*," in *Femmes Fatales: Feminism, Film Theory, Psychoanalysis* (New York: Routledge, 1991), 179.

38. Kaja Silverman, "White Skin, Brown Masks: The Double Mimesis, or With Lawrence in Arabia," *differences* 1, no. 3 (1989): 4.

39. Peckham, "The Overflow of Ecstasy into Speech," 93.

40. Eberhardt also lost her mother when she was in her early twenties, though *There Was an Unseen Cloud Moving* does not mention this fact.

41. Vivian Sobchack, "Inscribing Ethical Space: Ten Propositions on Death, Representation, and Documentary," *Quarterly Review of Film Studies* 9, no. 4 (Fall 1984): 283.

42. Ibid., 286, 282. While documentaries do record war deaths and executions, Sobchak argues that there are not many film records of individuals dying of natural causes.

43. Sobchack's description of Franju's *Le Sang des bêtes* and Resnais' *Nuit et brouillard* at the end of her essay is comparable, though these films show many dead bodies: "The most shaped and structured films of death tend to be poetic elegies which speak less of the deaths they contain than of death's unspeakability" (299).

44. Telephone conversation of August 11, 1995.

45. Delacour and Huleu, "Le Jeu du je," 12.

46. Kabbani is especially critical of Eberhardt's racism and sexism, charging that Eberhardt "became a mouthpiece for patriarchy." Kabbani, "Introduction," ix. See further v–xii. See also Emily Apter, "Female Trouble in the Colonial Harem," *differences* 4, no. 1 (1992): especially 215–22.

Racist and sexist metaphors appear less frequently in Eberhardt's writings than Kabbani claims. The following passages stand out, however: "There is an Arab beauty about the women. The expressions in their large languorous and melancholy jet-black eyes is resigned and sad like that of wary animals"; "All I want is a good horse as a mute and loyal companion, a handful of servants hardly more complex than my mount, and a life as far away as possible from the hustle and bustle I happen to find so sterile in the civilized world where I feel so deeply out of place." Eberhardt, *The Passionate Nomad*, 3, 59.

47. According to Randau, Eberhardt felt a strong affinity for the poor and the downtrodden: "She was not at all repulsed by filth, vermin, or the lack of hygiene. . . . She considered this poverty to be a part of herself. She urged the men to tell her their stories. . . . In return, she counselled them to be vaccinated, sent them to the doctor, watched over women in childbirth. Sat at the bedside of the sick," Randau, cited in Nouel, *Carré d'as*, 96. Denise Enslen notes further that Eberhardt "devotes only a few lines, often critical, to colonists, intellectuals, and officers," while Hart comments that Eberhardt spent more time with common soldiers than with officers. See Enslen, "Isabelle Eberhardt et l'Algérie," 162, and Hart, *Two Ladies of Colonial Algeria*, 106.

48. According to Mackworth, for the cross-dressed Eberhardt, "all Arab women must remain . . . mysterious and apart. It was inherent in her equivocal position that she might have no dealing with them. Here she must never abandon the role of Si Mahmoud, for whom it would be a sin to regard the face of a woman." Mackworth, *The Destiny of Isabelle Eberhardt*, 216. Kabbani charges that this state of affairs "suited [Eberhardt] perfectly, since she hadn't the slightest desire to associate with women, for whom she felt only dislike and hostility." Kabbani, "Introduction," ix.

49. In "Achouara," for example, Eberhardt is uncritical of what she paints as her abandoned heroine's only option, prostitution: "Like all the women of her region, Achouara considered the sale of her body the only escape from want that was available to a woman. She had no desire to be cloistered again by marriage, nor was she ashamed to be what she was." Isabelle Eberhardt, "Achouara," in *The Oblivion Seekers*, trans. Paul Bowles (London: Peter Owen, 1988), 32–33.

50. Isabelle Eberhardt, *L'Ombre chaude de l'Islame*, cited in Nouel, *Carré d'as*, 103–4. A similar passage, dated August 17, 1901, reveals Eberhardt's rage at the denial of sexual and sensual pleasures to women: "Stupid and revolting as it is, young girls are hitched to a husband for life, and he is a ridiculous figure in the end. The woman's physical virginity is all his. She is then expected to spend the rest of her life with him, usually in disgust, and suffer what is known as her 'marital duty.'" Eberhardt, *The Passionate Nomad*, 79–80.

51. Eberhardt, *The Oblivion Seekers*, 68.

52. Peckham, "The Overflow of Ecstasy into Speech," 95.

53. On the oppressive implications of "A Meaning," see Julia Kristeva, "Psychoanalysis and the Polis," in *The Kristeva Reader*, ed. Toril Moi (New York: Columbia University Press, 1986), 303–4.

54. I take this formulation from Sarah Williams, "Suspending Anthropology's Inscription: Observing Trinh Minh-ha Observed," *Visual Anthropology Review* 7, no. 1 (1991): 12.

55. To achieve what she calls "a sense of absence" and to mask the fact that this reading is "already a derivative reading, a Western reading of an Islam image," Thornton "recorded the text and then, through a hidden earphone, [the actress] heard it for the first time as she spoke it. . . . What she recites is actually an interpretation of the Islamic conception of paradise, as interpreted by a nineteenth century English man. It appears as a footnote in . . . the first English translation of the Koran." Thornton cited in Trinh, "Which Way to Political Cinema?," 261.

56. Kristeva, "Psychoanalysis and the Polis," 306.

57. George Custen, *Bio/Pics: How Hollywood Constructed Public History* (New Brunswick, N.J.: Rutgers University Press, 1992), 3. See further 66, 92, 257. *Calamity Jane* has thus far been the only Hollywood bio-pic about a female explorer.

58. Doane, "The Retreat of Signs and the Failure of Words," 180.

59. Apter, "Female Trouble in the Colonial Harem," 206.

60. Increasingly, theorists note the limitations of local analysis per se. Ernesto Laclau and Chantal Mouffe, for example, warn that we risk moving "from an essentialism of the totality to an essentialism of the elements." Ernesto Laclau and Chantal Mouffe, *Hegemony and Socialist Strategy: Towards a Radical Democratic Politics*, trans. Winston Moore and Paul Cammack (London: Verso, 1985), 103. Francis Barker, Peter Hulme, and Margaret Iversen extend Laclau and Mouffe's point: "A commitment to particularity is not, *ipso facto*, a rejection of the very possibility of any totalizing knowledge and of the grounding of a politics in that knowledge . . . The local must be valued for something other than its 'localness.'" Francis Barker, Peter Hulme, and Margaret Iversen, ed., *Colonial Discourse/Postcolonial Theory* (Manchester: Manchester University Press, 1993), 11.

61. Telephone conversation of August 11, 1995.

62. Delacour and Huleu, "Le Jeu du je," 11–2.

63. Apter, "Female Trouble in the Colonial Harem," 216.

64. Thornton cited in Trinh, "Which Way to Political Cinema?," 250, 256, and 258.

65. Ibid.

JULIA LESAGE

[14] *Women's Fragmented Consciousness in Feminist Experimental Autobiographical Video*

Toward the beginning of Margaret Stratton's 1994 videotape *Kiss the Boys and Make Them Die*, she describes in voice-off narration that she wears her grandmother's "simple . . . sweet" wedding ring. As she says this, we see a tight close-up of barbed wire glinting in the sun. A few sentences later, when she describes the hard physical labor that the ring on her grandmother's hand saw, the camera pans down a close-up of many strings of rosary beads hanging together, pauses at the crucifixes at the ends of the strands, and then tracks back up the beads. Connotative links between the images are not offered; rather, their disjuncture lets them convey their ordinary emotional power as rosary, ring, or barbed wire without the viewer's having to articulate discursively what they "mean." *Kiss the Boys and Make Them Die* enacts in its stylistic ruptures and subject matter—an artist's reflection on her womanly inheritance—a sensibility often found in women's experimental autobiographical video as it expresses women's fragmented consciousness.

Literary scholar Jeanne Braham finds that moments like this scene occur frequently in women's autobiography, where they elicit a resonance between the autobiographer's experience and the reader's own. More precisely, details such as the juxtaposition of ring, rosary, and barbed wire set up a profound resonance between the text and the reader's response. According to Braham, such moments "incorporate" the reader into the text, inviting her to enter it on emotional and analytical levels. Braham summarizes autobiography's formal workings and the political and psychological reasons why women are compelled to tell their story artfully and why other women are compelled to listen:

> If the story of one woman's life provides a script the reader enters and resignifies, and in some collaborative sense makes her own, then contemporary

women's personal narratives chart rich new possibilities for the ways that women may want to live their lives. They present forms at once fragmentary and "contextual" enough to satisfy postmodern ideas about the "self" and powerful enough to link a reader's consciousness to an author's testimony.[1]

My topic in this essay is women's autobiographical video, which for the past twenty years has frequently taken as its theme and used as a major structuring principle women's fragmented consciousness. Such a fragmentation results from women's labor in the domestic sphere, the dynamics of the family, the institution of heterosexuality, women's social devaluation, male control of key social institutions (including industry, finance, law, the military, the mass media, information gathering and diffusion, medicine, and religion), and ideology's dependence on manipulating and controlling the representation of gender and sex. As feminist scholars worldwide have analyzed these issues in depth, over the same period of time feminist videomakers have been tracing women's fragmented consciousness in art, a project that asserts the vitality of women's consciousness at the same time as the art often explicitly condemns the social forces shaping women's lives and minds.[2]

Although women share many psychological dynamics in common, subcultural and ethnic inflections in the art dealing with women's consciousness trace how psychic fragmentation exists among groups of oppressed people, including men.[3] For example, lesbians, gay men, and transgender people may have unique relations to the psychosexual structuring of the nuclear family and its consequent effect on adult sexuality. In particular, key feminist experimental autobiographical videotapes deal with issues of fragmented consciousness from the viewpoint of women of color. Such tapes include *Who's Going to Pay for These Donuts, Anyway?* (1992) and *Memories from the Department of Amnesia* (1989) by Janice Tanaka, *History and Memory* (1991) by Rea Tajiri, and *Measures of Distance* (1988) by Mona Hatoum. These works trace the effects of racism and imperialism in the fragmented consciousness of both men and women, with a special emphasis on women's unique subjectivity. What I posit as common among women, fragmented consciousness, appears as a motif in these and other narratives by women of color—in fictions and autobiographies, in particular—where it is seen as deriving from material oppression, especially colonialism and racism, and from the structures of women's lives as women.[4]

In general, avant-garde film and video have not been widely embraced by progressive literary or media scholars. For example, little of this work is written about in feminist academic journals or left cultural journals. Partly this has to do with the institutional nature of the avant-garde and its intellectual role within elite culture under capitalism. Partly it has to do with avant-garde media's emphasis on formal innovation, especially when received in a mass-mediated culture where mainstream film and television usually rely on closed narrative forms with all the connotations supporting a single conclusion or a climax. Among the artists whose tapes I discuss here, to work in experimental video means to inherit the legacy of modernism, delighting in playfulness and using the art medium itself as a tool of discovery. These autobiographical video narratives play off the fact that in most narratives, both fictional and "real-life" ones, the protagonist, the person with agency, the one everyone wants to identify with is a white man. The diffracted narratives that feminist video autobiographies forge, in contrast, assume that women have multiple subject positions, identify with and stand apart from male protagonists, and accept and resist dominant cultural institutions at the same time. And those works are made by women mediamakers who function professionally in both mainstream media culture and in women's culture, especially in the domestic sphere; and if the videomaker partakes of another subculture as a woman of color, a lesbian, a disabled person, or a mother, the complexity with which she understands women's modes of identity formation may be visibly layered into her work.

Aware of feminist ideas, the videomakers I discuss here understand how hegemonic discourse refuses the reality of women's fragmented consciousness. Unlike social-issues documentarists working over the same twenty years in a realist mode, most of these women artists do not presume to represent a continuous stable identity or a cohesive self. Rather, they pursue an epistemological investigation of what kinds of relations might constitute the self, using as a laboratory their own consciousness. For these videomakers, to shoot and edit an autobiographical work entails their conceptually reformulating relations between women's mind, body, emotions, and history—especially family history. For such an ambitious exploration, conventional verbal and visual language is hardly adequate to the task. For this reason, these experimental videomakers also take as their subject matter verbal and visual communication. They create new connections among established discourses, and they reshape the video medium, both in terms of process and aesthetic technique, more adequately to represent women's daily lives.

▶──

Stylistic Characteristics

In this essay, I consider first stylistics, in a formalist sense, and then thematics—as related to genre issues and to women's subjectivity. In terms of stylistics, experimental feminist video autobiographies are usually structured in one of four ways, and each structure also represents a different approach to the video production process.[5] In the first kind of work, the videomaker crafts an interpretive, prose narration, usually spoken primarily in voice-off in the tape. She approaches the writing of the narration knowing that certain key visual or textual materials await her use. She often draws on family photos, perhaps also diaries or letters from family; on the larger cultural scale, she may take advantage of photos, magazines, or popular film footage from an earlier historical period. She also may do research on a related subject and plan to incorporate text from published sources into the video, either as visual text or spoken narration. She has heard certain stories and anecdotes from family, school, and work that she is determined to retell and contextualize within her own autobiographical piece. She may plan to create drawings, charts, or construct special sets for dramatized tableaux, or have photos taken of her in certain locations, in street dress or in costume. This image material created just for the video is often ironic or witty. In general, the image track serves primarily to illustrate the verbal narration. It may connotatively reinforce it, obliquely reflect another take on it, or contest it—in what Sergei Eisenstein calls an "intellectual montage" that leads to a new concept from the clash of two conflicting ones. For a tape in which the videomaker structures the narration first, the editing stage is crucial; it is the point at which she forges specific sound/image inflections and links.[6]

In the second structure for experimental video autobiography, here more closely allied with the diary or home videomaking, the camera becomes a tool for the visual and social exploration of daily life, seemingly in real time. Primacy is placed on the moment of shooting, on the artist's skill or wit in visual composition, or on capturing significant, impromptu social moments. These works contain internal evidence that they were made with a passion for the present moment.[7] In some cases, this home movie–like format records a process, even becomes a daily confidante that the maker talks to not only to "hold herself together" but to use the act of shooting (and re-viewing and editing) to construct a self or to seize or "fix" life in process. In terms of narration, the videomaker may speak her interpretations or explanations to the camera at the moment of taping, film written or graphic material as a visual insert, and/or insert her voice over images as glue in the editing process. In this mode of production, editing becomes a task largely of condensation, of deciding what to choose from the large amount taped, of understanding the value and wit of ellipsis, and of knowing where to place emphasis. Both very long and very short works have been edited from this kind of work; the maker faces a major decision about the length of the work to present to the public. While editing, the videomaker compiles the tape with a respect for chronology or with an aim to bring out some quality that was there at the time of filming. Although the editing strives to highlight the processual aspect of the footage, self-censorship often occurs since so much material must, in fact, be left out.[8]

The third kind of autobiographical experimental video, one usually made by a woman more experienced in her craft, is autobiographical fiction. When the maker moves from behind the camera and becomes a director of videography and actors at the same time, she finds other ways to have a voice than just through writing a narration, which sets up a rigidly fixed sound/image relation. Editing becomes a process of crafting a final product from the most technically polished and emotionally convincing footage, and it is oriented usually to executing, tightening, and polishing the original concept that the maker first worked out in the dramatic and shooting scripts. Fatal errors, often seen in a director's first fiction, occur with bad acting, lighting devoid of dramatic emphasis, camerawork not intuitively in tune with the director's project, or blocking that does not enhance the image's connotative quality. If verbal eloquence and wit characterize the most successful voice-over-narration autobiographies, skilled direction of actors and cameraperson characterizes the best autobiographical fiction. Exemplary in this genre are Vanalyne Green's *What Happens to You?* (1991), Cecilia Dougherty's *Coal Miner's Granddaughter* (1991), Lynn Hershman's *Seeing Is Believing* (1991), and Cheryl Dunye's *She Don't Fade* (1991).

Finally, it is important to note the conceptual advantages and structural possibilities of a newer form. That is, electronic media makes possible a close tie between video production and computer animation or manipulation of the image in editing, especially with layering and fragmentation. Videomakers who use computerized animation for autobiographical explorations usually take up some of the more traditional themes of film animators, especially that of metamorphosis. Along with manipulating the image track, these artists also creatively manipulate the sound track or forge one electronically. The effect is that the video as a whole often has a musiclike temporal construction, often for a lyrical effect. Among experimental feminist videomakers, Annette Barbier in particular has used computer animation for autobiographical expression.[9] Because of the relatively inexpensive extension of this kind of production into the computer format of CD-ROM, we can expect to see more women artists taking advantage of this kind of self-exploration.

Women video artists have used these four production styles in an autobiographical way, sometimes playfully, sometimes seriously, to explore the social and psychological context of women's everyday lives. One theme surfaces over and over—that of women's consciousness. The rest of this essay will focus primarily on the work of two exemplary video auto-biographers, Vanalyne Green and Lynn Hershman, who document their subjectivity. Their work serves as a platform from which to explore genre issues related to autobiography, documentary, and experimental media— particularly to discuss the status of the referent in video, which simultaneously belongs to all three genres. Furthermore, these two artists use an open-ended, diffracted form to elaborate a theme that is personally important to women and that functions as an aesthetic structuring principle for many other women artists—that of feminine masochism.

▶ ───

Textuality and the Body in *Trick or Drink*

Trick or Drink (1984) is an example of a work in which the narration is primary. It was first developed as a performance piece by director Vanalyne Green, spoken in the first person along with projected, illustrative images. From that performance, Green wrote the video's narration about her growing up in an alcoholic family, enacting addictive behaviors—compulsive eating, bulimia, jealous spying on her lover—and coming to terms with her past through the help of other supportive adults, especially through Al-Anon, the organization for adult children of alcoholics.

The image track and the concrete, imagistic narration that Green speaks from a finely wrought script provide a good example of how auto-biography's *textuality* allows the artist to conduct an epistemological investigation into the components of selfhood and indeed recuperate that self by reconstructing the social, historical, and emotional context in which self is embedded. Eliciting a particular resonance among women viewers is the tape's opening, which conveys the texture of a teen girl's preoccupation with appearance as well as the anomalies and ruptures of a girl's thought processes and feelings. Green first gives words to girls' ordinary craziness and then proceeds to demonstrate the extraordinary psychic and physical violence in an alcoholic family.

In the first section of *Trick or Drink*, Green reads from a document from her adolescence, "Your Beauty Diary," a log of weight and complexion problems that she kept at age fourteen. As presented in the tape, the diary chronicles elaborate examples of compulsive eating and crash dieting, and it finally mentions her family. We also see her "progress chart" for the "beauty plan," with repeated notations of "no picking." The audio track is obsessively concerned with eating, while the image track shifts to a diary entry, "Dear Diary, I HATE THEM [scrawled large]. They're driving me crazy. I HATE THEM." A grainy photo depicts a couple outside a California home in which the man and the woman each have a drink in their hands, and Green's voice ends the section with these words: "April 26. . . . I'm so confused about my parents. Mom was drunk."

The visual and verbal opening to this tape has a great resonance for women audience members remembering their teen years—the beauty and self-improvement plans from girls' magazines or photos from high school that depict an attractive girl and belie the obsessive worrying about appearance hidden behind her smile. Of particular significance in the opening is the way it presents the girl's rituals and "failures" in the areas of eating and skin care. In fact, these are stress-related problems often related to living in a dysfunctional family. As Green puts it, this is something the girl cannot fathom until she is the narrator-adult, since girls are led to think that "beauty" problems are something each individual must deal with alone and get under control.

In feminist autobiography, according to Sidonie Smith, personhood, ideology, desire, and culture collide in the narrator's body; the autobiographer evokes images of the body as "the site of heterogeneous axes of signification."[10] In the opening section of *Trick or Drink*, as in many of the videos I discuss, still photos are interrogated for the discourses that produced the bodies in them. In particular, glamour pictures manipulate an image of female sexuality to sell products with models' come-hither glances.[11] High-school photos of teenage girls often imitate that pose and have the same goal, a face that begs, "Let my looks make you want to approach me." At the same time, the makeup and costuming for these photos—at the prom, for the yearbook, and so on—draw on a standardized register of femininity, marked by its historicity in photos taken decades ago. The feminine pose becomes a disguise.[12] For a teenage girl, to perfect that disguise is to achieve a self and gain validation and self-esteem. The connotation of these photos in the context of the verbal narration is that the photos hide the reality of a girl's life within an alcoholic family. And because of her family situation, her desperation to "get it all together" in terms of feminine self-presentation is all the more intense and all the more fraught with difficulties in its execution.

The beauty diary may have served Green as a memorable object triggering personal recollections to incorporate into her art. Her use of the beauty diary is fascinating for the layers of textuality it sets up in the tape and the various "measures of distance" it establishes in relation to the girl's body.[13] First, the girl writes a text about her body in the framework of a commercial beauty diary available from an outlet like a teen magazine. Then she tries to sculpt her appearance like a text and in this way also implicitly

Vanalyne Green, *Trick or Drink*. Photo courtesy of Video Data Bank.

get control over her life; finally, the diary logs the chronicle of her failed attempt. Green uses this past text in her present-day art to redeem that wounded child and affirm continuity with her past self and also to demonstrate how far she has moved beyond the girl's constricted mental categories and limited use of language that affixed her within an alcoholic family.

The teenager was policing her body to create order in the midst of chaos; as Julia Kristeva would put it, she was abjecting the body to exclude baseness and unruliness.[14] For most teenage girls, the rituals of selecting and putting on makeup, shopping for clothes, and dieting have the social and psychological function of ordering sexuality. The rituals around physical appearance allow them to construct a version of self that both invites sexual approach and polices the parameters of desire. By concentrating on the physical, these rituals focus attention on achieving "beauty" and thus reduce any conscious awareness of the structural nature of heterosexuality as a social force. In Green's case, the girl's diary reveals how little she feels at home in her body. It shows how she tries to use her body to achieve a satisfying predictability and define boundaries, something denied to children in alcoholic families. She eats uncontrollably to establish a nurturing relation with herself, an oral reunion with a better mother, and a familiar, readily available, sweet surround. In Freudian terms, not just her family environment becomes terrifying and *unheimlich*, her relation to her appear-

Vanalyne Green, *Trick or Drink*. Photo courtesy of Video Data Bank.

ance, her exterior protective shell, becomes *unheimlich*, too.[15] The beauty diary has a terror lurking underneath, and the connotations that link "body" to "alcoholism" are anchored in the sequence's final shots: the diary's filmed scrawl, "I hate my parents," the photo of the girl with the sad smile, and the grainy, blurred image of the parents with a drink.

▶ ───

The Status of the Referent

Trick or Drink's second section begins with the intertitle "1982." We see a long shot of a contemporary interior, a study with a bright patch of sunlight on the floor. The narrator's voice discusses how difficult it is to articulate her family history publicly:

> The thoughts locked in my throat don't come from self-pity. Had I known there were other children like myself, for whom no one intervened, other children who saw things that shouldn't have been seen, perhaps my life would be different.

The key words here are *things that shouldn't have been seen*. To present to the public kinds of details that have not been previously articulated and are therefore denied public existence, the narration moves into a concrete, imagistic mode, one characteristic of survivors' dreams following trauma—

such as the dreams of combat veterans about battles or of car crash victims—in which they compulsively rehearse the smallest details over and over at night while they are asleep. A detailed, concrete, imagistic mode of narration is also one that a witness rehearses for a jury trial or a sexual harassment adjudication at work, where she is expected to report all the relevant details in concrete terms (as a sexual harassment officer must have counseled Anita Hill, for example).

In this section of *Trick or Drink* the image track consists of magazine drawings of a California-style yellow house, its domestic objects, and then the windows seen from the outside, shown in grainy close-up and panned across over and over again, as if the exterior of a house should reveal to passersby what goes on inside. On the audio track, Green gives dense lists of details proving the evidence of alcoholism in her home. She calls on the senses of vision (lists of places where liquor bottles were hidden), sound (the clinking of ice in a glass warning her to avoid that place), and smell ("the smell of stale smoke, mixing with the aroma of vomit and whisky and urine didn't leave the house even in periods of recovery").

Verbal narration like this, which uses concrete images to evoke all the listener's senses, characterizes the best performance art and also the best voice-over narration in documentary or autobiographical media. In some autobiographical videos, such narration comes through interviews, tying the work more closely to traditional documentary video forms.[16] One such work, straddling both the experimental and documentary modes, is Mindy Faber's *Delirium* (1993), which has a similarity to *Trick or Drink* in that it analyzes her mother's mental illness within the context of family life. The concrete verbal evocation of a past moment most aptly comes when the mother, Patricia Faber, demands to have the camera and turns it toward her daughter Mindy, demanding, "What do you think I took out on you, anyway? What did I do?" Mindy had very carefully planned a tape that would not be about victimization or filled with recrimination, but at this point she tells what happened: with each example that Mindy gives, the mother declares, "You must be kidding," and says she does not remember any of that. However, we, the audience, need to hear these details in order to understand the maker's childhood and feel the passion invested in making this tape: "You used to tear up my room. . . . You used to throw pots and pans at my head."

This kind of concreteness of the referent plays a very important role in autobiography. It makes the narrated history *feel* verifiable, as does the incorporation of cultural icons from the past such as magazine pictures of domestic life. Concreteness lends the narration psychological verisimilitude, a sense that we know or feel the past, and it provokes empathy with the child/young person/adult's varying relations to her lived experience. Something that happened in the past, considered from the perspective of the present, was a "contingent" event depending on context and precipitating factors or interpreted as fate or chance. It's done. But narrating such events, which comprises much of daily discourse, is always tinged by a present desire to discover or tell. In everyday life, we constantly re-create our subjectivity as we use the word *I* to make experience intelligible, to place it in a familiar framework. We fabricate small narratives about our past and present experiences, and we address these to the ever present "me" in our heads or to others in conversation.

Incorporating this very common mental construction, the need to tell, good video narration combines a sense of present urgency with the narration's presumed basis in referential truth, conveyed through concrete, sensorially evocative detail. The concrete description of past events gives us a sense of the teller's sincerity and current engagement, which the audience evaluates in terms of the texture of the details that the speaker remembers and the emotional inflection with which these details are expressed. Furthermore, since autobiography relies on the genre convention that the author is sincere, we listen to an autobiographical video narrator's first-person voice as an authoritative statement attempting to re-create and interpret the past and to testify to an inner life that only she could know.

In autobiography and documentary, it is the genre convention or "pact" with the audience that establishes intentionality.[17] In these feminist autobiographical videos, the narrator is a woman speaking in her own voice and under her own name who is granted the attribute of sincerity, even though she may be deceiving herself or unable to tell the whole truth.[18] However, it is in our judgment of whether or not she tries to tell the whole truth, whether she looks hard at herself without self-pity, that we judge the *good* autobiographer. And there are even other qualities that make an autobiography something we want to read or watch.

One of the qualities that viewers of autobiographical video enjoy the most is presentness. We want past events to have a quality of presentness, and we want indications of the artist's current emotional engagement in the videomaking process. We enjoy the speakers' colloquialisms, their personal and subcultural specificity, their use of everyday expressions, and their wit. As people tell stories about the past, especially about their daily lives in days gone by, listeners gain new insights into how the past can be structured and thus thought. "Remembrance," William James wrote, "is like direct feeling: its object is suffused with a warmth and intimacy to which no object of mere conception ever attains."[19] Autobiographical video, with its emphasis on the word *I,* teases our desire for immediate discourse and pure presence, a desire that the television monitor on which we watch video teases us at other moments with its mundane televisual discourse. Yet in contrast to television's presentation of an uncomplicated, unitary subjectivity expressed by its speakers who address us with the word *I*, experimental autobiographical videomakers deliberately complicate and draw on the television viewer's desire for presentness. In a complicated dance around reference, feminist experimental autobiographical video maintains a commitment to truth, especially to telling the truth of one's personality, one's own existence. However, as *experimental* video, drawing on an older tradition of modernism, it can rarely embrace the notion of a fully constituted self or use a teleological narrative with a decisive conclusion toward which all the connotations point.[20]

Because of its status as autobiography, this kind of video shares the commitment to historical truth that documentary has. In *Trick or Drink,* Green articulates her subjectivity as a social phenomenon in terms of alcoholism's effect on the family. To call such work "experimental documentary" is to uncouple the prevalent assumption that documentation of one's own past or of social process requires a realist aesthetic. Feminist autobiographical art comes from the artist's fierce need to tell. The autobiographer seeks to document publicly how women live their lives while using an aesthetic most appropriate for conveying ordinary aspects of women's subjectivity, a task that a realist aesthetic often cannot fulfill.

▶───

The Child's Voice

One of the ways that feminist experimental autobiographical video reveals how truth is more complex for women than a realist aesthetic could easily depict is by presenting versions of an internalized child's voice shaping adult women's perceptions, self-image, and experience. The videos do not depict the kind of "inner child" theorized by transactional psychology but, rather, an interior voice specifically related to women's experience in the domestic sphere, sex-role socialization, and sometimes childhood sexual trauma.

In *Trick or Drink,* for example, at certain points the narration moves into the voice—and age—of the narrator as she was living through the event, which may mean regressing to a child's mode of expression. After telling several anecdotes about her parents, one in which they almost killed each other but were too drunk to do it successfully, Green says in voice-off:

> This is about a living surrealism. Pretend you are dreaming. [This sentence is frequently repeated]. Everything is a blur. . . .

The scenes move from one to another for no logical reason. Why are they laughing at you? Why are they mad? Don't you have the right to be thirteen? Don't you have the right to buy a new dress? . . .

Where is Aunt Irma, Aunt Theta, and where are the next-door neighbors? . . .

You are a good child, you have a good family, you will wake up, and this will end.

Evocation of the narrator as a child occurs frequently in these videos. Such a regressed voice or point of view cues women viewers to identify with the work. Reduced in pop psychology to the inner child, the internalized child's voice is a hallmark of women's fragmented consciousness. Sometimes the voice is that of a discrete child persona(ae), most often stemming from dissociations that result from the experience of childhood sexual abuse. (I will discuss this kind of child's voice later when I present *First Person Plural* by Lynn Hershman, a videomaker who uses the video diary and the moment of taping to construct a self.) The child's voice may have its source in all-too-common trauma within a dysfunctional family, but as a persistent presence in many women's psyches it has other sources, and it is reinforced by major social and psychological structures. As Nancy Chodorow has pointed out, domestic life consists of an intergenerational community where women most often do the child rearing. Especially in an infant's early years, when it responds to the mother's voice and presence emotionally and not conceptually, mothers often—usually unconsciously—project backward into their own infantile experience, identifying with their child's emotions.[21]

Furthermore, girl children are taught by example the necessary, unpaid, psychological labor carried out by their mothers in the domestic sphere—that of ego tending, a role that Helen Hayes immortalized on Broadway in the 1918 James Barrie drama *What Every Woman Knows* (my mother's favorite play). While still children themselves, girls learn to be aware of and tend to the child in the adult, especially in the man. For example, in colloquial terms, women understand that cooking skills appeal to the family's need for oral gratification and that getting a good meal is one of the reasons a man needs a wife: "Can she bake a cherry pie, Billy Boy?" Or as the subtitle to my mother's 1936 *Settlement Cook Book* (23d ed.) put it, cooking is "The Way to a Man's Heart." Another aspect of women's domestic labor that makes women constantly aware of the child within the adult is the fact that the domestic sphere is the site of another kind of unpaid work, that of caring for the sick and the very old. Both these states induce dependency and are frequently accompanied by personality regression, which the woman of the house must explicitly deal with.

An autobiographical videomaker who is a mother, such as Annette Barbier in *Women's Movements* and *Domestic Portraits, 1*, may incorporate into her tapes the real-life problems that a woman videomaker faces when she has a young child making claims on her attention at the same time that she wants to create video art within the domestic sphere. Or she may create wonderfully humorous images to express a socially taboo desire, that of the mother to regress, as do Mindy Faber in *Delirium* and Sherry Millner in *Womb with a View*. The importance of the child's point of view to women artists is, however, very different from Wordsworth's romantic vision for artists, echoed by experimental filmmaker Stan Brakhage: "The child is father to the man." Wordsworth and later Brakhage assume that the artist [male] must strive to keep the freshness of vision and presentness to experience that he had as a child. For these women autobiographers, however, the child's voice elicited in their works is far from Wordsworthian—not a tabula rasa or simple, naive, or innocent.

Working against ideological notions about the innocence, freshness, and naïveté of the child, which are well-established assumptions in our culture, Vanalyne Green in her 1989 autobiographical videotape about her obsession with baseball players and their masculine world—*A Spy in the House That Ruth Built*—provides a more complex meditation on the child in the adult and its relation to heterosexuality.[22] Green investigates and plays with the ties between her desire, conventional masculinity, oedipality, domestic memories, and her need to enter public space. In the way that Green represents what the world of baseball means to her, she circles around her obsession, juxtaposing sequences and images that offer seemingly incompatible interpretations of it. She enters the inner sanctum of pro baseball's all-male world as a press photographer. She is then shown maladroitly interviewing players, one of whom asks her out. Surprisingly, she turns him down, even though earlier she had expressed an acute, unfulfilled desire to date baseball players. As she and her friend Becky Willis drive home from the game, they discuss Vanalyne's refusal and offer each other an entire psychological interpretation in just a few words: "This is so deep, Vanalyne," Becky says. "Do you know how deep that is?" Vanalyne answers, "Daddy." The visual footage shows a father in the baseball stands holding his little girl who hugs him with one arm, puts both arms around his neck, and kisses him, and then, after looking directly in the camera, turns and cuddles him again.

As if to clarify how her adult obsession is related to childhood sexual desire, Green playfully and impudently takes advantage of her photographer's press pass to do sexual image making at a safe distance from the men filmed. She tilts her videocamera wittily down to the level of the players' buns and crotches. At the same time, she complains that as a woman press photographer, she has to dress in a sexless way in long-sleeved white blouses "while 6′5″ gods stride the field spraying their sex in all directions."

She concludes the tape by tracing the metaphorical connotations of the word *home* in baseball. "I took the way men had fragmented my body and turned sex into my enemy," she says in voice-off, "and I used it against them in baseball." She remembers her "teenage anathema"—high school boys' asking each other, "Did you go all the way, reach home?" The word *home* is a revealingly domestic word for sex. Green uses a graphic of a woman's thighs spread apart, and into the space between the legs, she keys a baseball diamond with home plate located at the woman's crotch, creating a joke about stealing home as metaphorical intercourse. She discusses in voice-off how the world of men inspired in her a fear that she had since childhood, "which I understand only as a sense of damage having been done." This world, the "daddies'" world, is both desirable and seemingly off-limits or unsafe.

Then the tape shifts tone. We see Green in her own domestic space, her study, where she talks about the way the stadium had become a kind of maternal home, "a shimmering configuration of female solace with the words *danger* and *man* said in one breath." She talks about her constant need to reassemble a family: "No theory will ever diminish the child's landscape within me, composed of images of my father and my mother and rendered beyond my comprehension by a mysterious and unknowable sexuality." The visuals accompanying these words are shots of the stadium intercut with shots of a small girl (easily interpreted as images of her from home movies) being tended by her mother brushing her hair; she leans into the comfort of the mother's belly, and the arm of the mother casts a shadow over her face.

Green captures in this tape women's layered sensibility about entering public space while desiring domestic security. The fluid, circling structure of *A Spy in the House That Ruth Built* places a primacy on impressionistic subjectivity and shifting desires. It is a humorous piece with a dark shadow underneath.

▶

First Person Plural

If *A Spy in the House That Ruth Built* takes a witty look at a woman's heterosexual desire, Lynn Hershman's *Electronic Diaries* documents her adult reckoning with childhood sexual abuse and consequent psychic

Vanalyne Green, *A Spy in the House That Ruth Built*. Photo courtesy of Video Data Bank.

shattering. The *Electronic Diaries* are a project that has occupied much of her artistic career, having been shot over the past ten years. This series features Hershman's direct address to the camera, in which she presents her thoughts and an analysis of her life. Shooting in innumerable sessions, usually at home or in her office at work, Hershman usually speaks to the camera alone, without a cameraperson present. This is an example of video autobiography that places a primacy on the moment of shooting, in the process of which the diary is used to establish a sense of self. In conversation, Hershman told me that she very carefully respects the time order of what she shoots and never interferes with that chronology in the editing. She does, however, insert additional visuals to accompany her voice, or she manipulates her own taped image ingeniously on the computer. One of her most common uses of the image processor is to insert a small box or wipe of herself speaking, sometimes doubling the image, sometimes taking over the screen. I do not know if she scripts out written or verbal material to speak into the microphone on a given day; the tapes offer no internal evidence to indicate that might be the case. The voice in which she speaks to herself, delivered in private to the camera in order to forge a self, has a serious intellectual tone, and she often incorporates historical and philosophical reflections to explain herself to herself.

In the *Electronic Diary* series, Hershman quite explicitly elaborates a model of women's consciousness and its relation to historical process. In numerous other videotapes, mostly fictional, and in computer installations, she deals with the same issues, but in a more refracted, disjunctive way. Interestingly, the *Electronic Diaries,* with their blunt explanation of her own psychological process, offer a direct aesthetic explanation of her other work. As a result of incest, she experienced fragmented personae or levels of her personality in a dissociated way.

Here, I am concentrating on one of Hershman's tapes in the *Electronic Diary* series, *First Person Plural,* the title of which refers to these multiple personae. In the tape, Hershman also describes self-destructive behavior as an adult and her own feminine masochism. *First Person Plural,* like the whole *Electronic Diary* series, consists primarily of talking-head shots, keyed differently or framed for emotional emphasis, but, as will become evident in the course of my analysis, the piece also uses some fictional elements to link modes of consciousness and unconsciousness, and it experiments with the repertoire of electronic media.

First Person Plural begins with Hershman talking about the Dracula myth and her attraction to it. We see inserts from *Nosferatu* and a man in a red cape coming up a flight of stairs. She says how hearing footsteps in the hall at night when she was a child provoked the Dracula fantasy, making her feel both excited and repelled. Then, as she does at various points in the tape, she whispers in a child's voice, "You're not supposed to talk about it." In her adult voice, she says that these unspeakable things recur in her head to remind her where she came from and who she is: "It helps to talk about it, but I know it's painful to listen."

She describes how she would escape from thinking about assault by pretending to be other people, ones she made up or characters from a story. Later, as an adult, this behavior continued: "In my closet I had wardrobes of several people and also several sizes, since my weight would fluctuate." Not described in the tape is how fruitful Hershman's capacity for dissociation and projection has been for her artistic career, often enacted in the avant-garde art world in site-specific environments depicting violence against women and in her own performances of adopted personae in the public sphere.

In *First Person Plural,* Hershman refers concretely to the kinds of family violence that led to her dissociative personality and self-destructive behavior. She recounts the beatings she received almost daily, sometimes with a belt and other times with a broomstick. She had her pelvis and her nose broken and almost lost her hearing. She asks, like Vanalyne Green in *Trick or Drink,* why no teacher at school ever noticed her bruises or

Lynn Hershman, *Electronic Diary* series. Photo courtesy of the filmmaker.

fainting. She returns to the theme of the "sexy" Dracula, and she notes how she was attracted to destructive people, particularly men:

> I'd be drawn to them like a magnet, as if I was trying somehow to re-create those episodes but not know it. But they knew it. I'd be drawn to people who would impose the silence and continue the nonmemory of not talking about it and continue the guilt.

In turning inward to probe the lower depths, Hershman is heir less to modernism than to the romantic tradition of looking into the self to express one's innermost, unarticulated feelings, especially to express the wounds, loss, and incompleteness that occupy the soul. From Jean-Jacques Rousseau's *Confessions,* that foundational text of European and North American autobiography, to present-day canonical art video, this kind of self-exploration has been the prerogative and often goal of the petit-bourgeois white male intellectual and artist. The male romantic hero's quest, however, has always been one of melancholy and restlessness. His pose is usually that of the wounded and self-destructive outsider who strives to enhance his knowledge and creativity by exploring his senses and articulating his unique sensibility. He often behaves as if he is stirring out of a state of semiparalysis and cultural ennui to create something in a self-destructive way, like a moth to a flame.

Women have taken up the romantic artist's quest, arising out of culturally induced paralysis to look inward and express themselves, with a

whole different tenor. Their motives, tactics, and results are completely different from those of their male forbears or counterparts. Heirs to the romantic tradition of using art as a tool for psychic expression, women and
artists from dispossessed groups have used the tactics of the romantic artist
to give voice to what had been voiceless in their environments, to provide
especially for their group the open and public articulation of other subjectivities that the dominant culture systematically denies and silences. This is
how, at the end of *First Person Plural,* Hershman describes the romantic
project—as a recuperative act for herself and her daughter:

> We're all born with a history, with scenes that took place before us but yet af-
> fect us. We inherit our role. But like any good actor, we learn that we can
> transcend that role by feeling it more deeply. And how we do that can affect
> the legacy for the next generation.

▶──

Feminine Masochism

Hershman's work, indeed most of the tapes I describe in this paper, circle
around the issue of feminine masochism, as does the very thesis I posit,
that the tapes take as their theme and use a structuring principle, women's
fragmented consciousness. The tapes themselves conceptually deal with
many issues about women's self-destructive behavior, painful memories,
and subordinate position, but cumulatively they raise an important theoretical question. Why are women readers and viewers so often drawn to
narratives (often presented in a confessional form) that relate stories of
family abuse, rape, battery, and the torture and murder of women? Furthermore, when women hear a personal narrative about rape or incest, which
they may not have experienced, they often identify with the teller's life and
especially her psyche as somehow very similar to their own. What establishes that resonance?

In terms of the work discussed here, experimental feminist autobiographical video has a very self-conscious relation to mainstream images
of and narratives about women and has many resources to escape conventional modes of depicting violence against women. However, these videomakers still often focus on women's pain, even on women's embracing pain
or cultivating a masochistic fantasy life. In this way, I have to ask myself, in
its formal aspects, in the way it deals with self-exploration and in the way
it evokes a response in an audience, what does the genre of feminist autobiography have to contribute to our potential identification with, pleasure
in, or psychic use of such stories of violence against ourselves?

As women, we are all vulnerable to rape and sexual harassment. If the

Lynn Hershman, *Electronic Diary* series. Photo courtesy of the filmmaker.

boy's route to maturity, according to the oedipal narrative, is to expunge the feminine from himself and become the heir to culture and a future mom/wife as he enters into the symbolic realm, the girl is heir to rape culture and the domestic sphere. Girls learn about rape threat as early as age three to five. It may not be taught in explicitly sexual terms, but girls are taught very young about the dangers of public space. The boy who denies the feminine in himself not only wards off a fear of castration, he also never has to feel the fear of rape in the way that all girls are taught to feel it. Boys and men are aware of homosexual rape as a remote possibility, but for every woman, rape is always a real threat, and thus rape threat stays with her as a permanent mental structure. In a dissociated way it remains in the background of her consciousness but springs forward as lively fear as soon as a shadow crosses hers or a footstep comes up behind her in public space. We identify with stories of battery and rape because of rape consciousness, which is an integral part of our lives.

Women and girls fantasize about the threat that lies in parents, especially fathers' abusing children, in going out on the street, especially "unprotected," and in all heterosexual relations, especially if, as Hershman says, a woman who was abused may make bad sexual choices over and over again.[23] If, in contrast, I get a good man, I know that is just luck, just winning the lottery. Fifty percent of marriages end in divorce, but not usually because of battery. So I must ask myself why the story of a battered woman signals to most female viewers, "There but for the grace of God go

I." It is because it depicts in graphic detail the end-of-the line case of "bad" marriage—although marriage is held out to women as the heterosexual prize. In fact, beyond telling cautionary tales about women's place, stories of battery and rape provide the female viewer the masochistic frisson of heterosexuality itself, heterosexuality as an institution. That is, as long as my sexual object choice has more social valorization or income or strength than I do, and this is a systematic aspect of the structure of desire, feminine identification with stories of abuse makes sense.

In her *Electronic Diaries,* Lynn Hershman lays out the answers to some of these formal and personal questions so bluntly that I think her very completeness is why she has been neglected by feminist cultural theorists and activists. Her work is also interpreted by art-world critics in a way that consistently overlooks what she so emphatically tells us in the *Electronic Diaries* in a direct-address mode—that women's consciousness itself is shaped by our living in a violent world, and that there is an ever present connection between the abuse of women and our perceptions, behavior, and art.

Hershman's work has always been ahead of its time. In *Binge,* the *Electronic Diary* tape that comes before *First Person Plural,* for example, Hershman deals with a forty-pound weight gain she went through after her husband walked out on her with no previous warning. She loses, then gains, then loses weight again in the course of this diary tape, mostly composed from the head up, sometimes doing a computerized manipulation of the image to make her look thinner. Her honesty and political reflections on fatness are as uncomfortable as they are illuminating. Because her treatment of fat would speak almost universally to women, even skinny and "medium-sized" ones, the tape presents another very common example of women's fractured body image and its genesis, offering an explanation akin to that in "The Beauty Diary" section of *Trick or Drink.*

In *Binge* Hershman gives an often-quoted summary statement of much of the art that she has produced in her career:

> I think that we've become a society of screens, of different layers that keep us from knowing the truth, as if the truth is almost unbearable and too much for us to deal with, just like our feelings. So we deal with things through replication, through copying, and through screens. Through simulations, through facsimiles, through fiction, through faction.

As Hershman speaks those words and is seen speaking on screen, on the image track there is a wipe right, and her image first bifurcates, then quadruples, and so forth, arriving at a multiple of thirty-two little boxes of her in a line down the far right side of the screen. This visual splitting, squared, is a metaphor for women's fragmented consciousness and contradictory social roles, reinforced by the fragmentation of women's bodies in the mass media and all the ideological and narrative uses to which woman as a cultural icon is put. However, the major critics writing about Hershman's work have interpreted her spoken words here, accompanied by this bifurcating image, as distancing the viewer from the producer's "self." To them, Hershman's fascination with the technical and social process of "media-tion" mean that her historical self or personality becomes unknowable, especially since in a later moment she says that her consciousness depends on multiple voices or personae within her.[24] But her lines about simulation, fiction, facsimiles, and faction do not lead her to the conclusion that woman's condition is ultimately unfathomable because woman's image is so mediated and fractured culturally, but, rather, this train of thought leads her to a plea to end all distortions of *truth and value*, especially those tied to women's bodily distortions and self-abuse.

In *First Person Plural*, Hershman directly states what this process of splitting and fragmenting in the psyche entails for women, what feminine masochism is, its origins, and its ways of getting worked out—in bodily symptoms, in self-destructive behavior, in abuse of the next generation, or in directly voicing its mechanisms over and over again. Hershman tells us about her personae and enacts on screen the painful child alive within her. "You're not supposed to talk about it," says that intact child speaking directly to the camera. It is astounding to me that none of the critics of her work could comment on her courage in such a performance, especially since she comments directly on what her child's tone of voice means.

Finally, and here is where I think Hershman is most powerful, and potentially most difficult for feminist thinkers and activists around issues of incest to accept, is her understanding of, partial identification with, and even compassion for the oppressor. No one has commented on the fact that for the past thirty years it has especially been Jewish women of a certain generation who have made a commitment to theorizing pornography, sexual oppression, and women's sexual stake in sadomasochistic sexuality. These women do not say the same things, but think of the list: the feminist poet and theorist of the "lesbian continuum" among women, Adrienne Rich; the leader of the feminist antipornography movement, Andrea Dworkin; philosopher Sandra Bartky, who wrote *Femininity and Domination*; Ellen Willis, an early writer about the politics of sexuality in the *Village Voice*; Eve Kosofsky Sedgwick, author of *Epistemology of the Closet*; Judith Butler, who has analyzed the performativity of gender and sex; sadomasochist theorist, who also wrote "The Traffic in Women," Gayle Rubin; and feminist experimental filmmaker, currently working on a feature film about a woman who is an adult survivor of incest, Michelle Citron.[25] In my own background, born to a Jewish mother in 1939, I came to consciousness hearing women's voices in the domestic sphere talking about concentration camps. My personal understanding of torture came when in infantile sadism my brother and sister and I would cut worms in half to see both halves move. I consciously always understood the connection between my own consciousness and behavior and concentration camp torture. With a similar understanding, Hershman talks about her abused childhood in terms of an explicit parallel with Hitler's youth as a battered child.

In *First Person Plural,* in addition to the image of Dracula, repeated at various times, sounds of airplanes and guns, shots of Hitler and Nazi rallies, shots of war footage, and shots of a baby's face circulate a set of related connotations. Toward the end of the tape, the editing dramatically incorporates Hershman's own long pauses, biting her lip and looking down as she struggles to tell a difficult story. In the middle of the tape, over a frozen image of her mostly in shadow with her hand raised to her face as if to ward off shame and danger, she whispers the repeated phrase, "Don't talk," in the child's voice and then changes tone and says bluntly,

> I showed this tape to some friends of mine. And what I thought I said and what I thought was really obvious, it turned out they didn't hear. So I guess as hard as it is for me to find the words, I'm going to have to just say it—that when I was very young, I was physically and sexually abused.

She then draws a parallel between her own experience and that of Hitler. As the Dracula image dissolves in once again, the man's face comes up very clear this time, leaving the viewer to wonder if Hershman keyed in a photo of her father or picked an actor who looked like him. As Hershman says the following lines to the camera, the man's face fades up again, accompanied by a clanking sound on the audio track. Hershman's face, speaking the monologue, is first placed in the frame to the right of his; then the two faces are overlaid with his dominant on top. The section ends with a freeze on the man's face. During this visual evocation of male dominance and the "doubling" of the victim and oppressor, probably edited from a single day's talking to the camera, Hershman says,

> It's easier to see the demon as something other than ourselves, to project out the demon and the guilt. When you point your finger at the other, chances are that three fingers are pointing back at you.

In the tape, Hershman spoke earlier about Hitler as a battered child, noting that Hitler's brother died from a severe beating and at age eleven Hitler almost did, too. In the sequence that comes after she discusses her identification with the Dracula figure, under the image of Hershman speaking appear images of Hitler speaking at a Nazi rally and the crowd saluting the Führer. At the end of the sequence, just the images of the Nazis remain on the screen. We see Hershman's image joined with Hitler's as we saw her joined to the image of Dracula; she speaks rapidly, delivering a thesis about Hitler and her identification with the male aggressor. She articulates how creating an Other is primarily a way of expressing yet disavowing the dark side of one's own self:

> In a way, maybe he was trying to exterminate his own past in order to deal with the humiliation he suffered as a child. He once said that if Jews did not exist, he would have to invent them or invent something to take their place— as we all invent the Other. Something that projects and reflects what we are but we're afraid to see. Our own demons, the demons that we cannot see but are there in our memory, articulate and loud and amplified, speaking in their own way, speaking in a voice that can't be heard. And that's why it's so important to say things, to know, and to understand. And not be afraid of your voice, or to hear your past, or to be authentic, or to identify with what you were. They say that his grandfather was Jewish.

In a rare moment in feminist intellectual life, Hershman explains what is to be gained by understanding the mentality of the oppressor and even identifying with it in an open way. Masochism, especially in its garden variety among women, lets women claim their right to feeling and desire through indirection: it may function as the psychic impulse driving purging and bingeing, sadomasochistic fantasies, or just always falling in love with the wrong person. For Hershman to know the mentality of the oppressor is to claim the power of his lust, the right to feel and pursue desire directly, openly. It is also to see in men what their less fractured and less Other-directed egos never allow them to see. She has an insight shared by contemporary novelist Jane Smiley, who ends her novel *A Thousand Acres* with one of her character's final thoughts. This woman, without ever being able to communicate it to others, comes to understand her incestuous father's mind and to claim that knowledge as her own:

> I can't say that I forgave my father, she thinks, but now I can imagine what he probably chose never to remember—the goad of an unthinkable urge, pricking him, wrapping him in an unpenetrable fog of self that must have seemed, when he wandered around the house late at night after working and drinking like the very darkness. This is the gleaming obsidian shard I safeguard above all others.[26]

The possibility that women readers will understand and identify with Smiley's final "gleaming obsidian shard," with all its phallic implications, can be explained by what feminist film theorists Elizabeth Cowie, Mary

Ann Doane, Janet Bergstrom, and others have written about as the multiple subject positions that women occupy as media viewers. Women identify with different characters and points of view both successively and simultaneously. The psychoanalytic work commonly cited in feminist writings on women viewers' and readers' capacity for imagining all the roles is Freud's "A Child Is Being Beaten," which postulates that a boy's fantasies about parental abuse give the boy a sense of mastery by letting him watch from a distance and identify with the aggressor. Girls, Freud notes, use masochistic fantasies to gain mastery over the abusive scene as they simultaneously watch from the outside, and from the inside, with a sense of participatory identification.[27]

In contrast to the kind of control that women get from masochistic fantasies, and concurrently from watching melodramas and tales of aggression against women, male fantasies worked out in common movie and television scenes of violence rely on the female figure's being always available as a blank slate, to be projected and acted on. This most common variety of media violence against women is what Hershman calls the culture's "mediated psyche fleshed out as the female body." Hershman posits a kind of understanding and victory over masochism that comes from understanding and taking the subject position of the oppressor. And this violent imaging is very different from the ordinary film characterization of the murderer and rapist: Hershman and Smiley let the abused woman see the abuser exactly for who he is. He is not a blank slate for her to project on, but he is understood in a way he does not understand himself. What the woman now claims is the aggressor's, the man's, right to direct access to desire, indeed, to lust.

The kind of exploration of woman's psychosexual self seen in Hershman's work, or from a lesbian perspective in Margaret Stratton's *Kiss the Boys and Make Them Die* (1994), is notably absent from the most common media used in struggles for social change, the social-issues documentary. This genre (of which I am a great admirer and in which I participate as a videomaker) has more currency in feminist struggles than art media will ever have. One reason for this genre's popularity worldwide is that it usually assumes a cohesive individual subjectivity; indeed, it must do so as it tries to motivate viewers to organize for social change. The representation of the just cause assumes that a social movement's participants share a similar consciousness. In particular, it is easy for those committed to social change to adopt a traditional, battle-oriented discourse that has easy recourse to the melodramatic tropes of villains versus the oppressed, good versus evil, victory versus defeat. For example, the antipornography movement and the more generalized sentiment against violence in the media attack media products that seem to represent an expungeable Other, an easily removable source of male-generated violence. Participants in the antipornography movement and my own feminist friends who are now raising children and want to control their children's television viewing often deny the role of violent fantasy in the most ordinary childhood and adult sexual experiences. And most of the culture, right and left, massively denies the usefulness of masochism, the economy of masochism in most women's lives.

Similarly, most documentary media made about children's lives or for children, frequently for important social reasons, have the same problems, in particular denying the aggression and sadism that we know are an integral part of infantile sexuality. I frequently see the results of this kind of false consciousness here on the West Coast where pop-psychology movements teach participants how to reclaim their inner child. Even though that psychology has refined the notion of a unitary self and finds consciousness divided into the voices of child/parent/adult, it does not explain the most common genesis of a separate child persona in (mostly girls') too-early sexual awakening. It seeks to reclaim a very Wordsworthian child and not a masochistic, sadistic, or sexually savvy one. And as it denies gender differences in these inner-child figures, it tells men that they, too, need this act of reclamation—and with the same kind of urgency.

Many important social-issues documentaries have been made around the themes of incest and rape. These documentaries do not acknowledge that all women's adult sexuality, perhaps especially that of women who have suffered abuse, is always and ever an outgrowth of the old experience, something that has to be reclaimed for better as well as for worse.[28] Perhaps it is only in fiction or experimental forms that women mediamakers can depict women's sadomasochistic practice or, more common, women's sadomasochistic sexual fantasy life, for what it so often is: women's way of recuperating a rape and incest culture for pleasure at the same time that women also take up the struggle for social change.

One of the reasons, I think, that Lynn Hershman's understanding of abuse has not been used in the women's movement or acknowledged by art critics writing about her work is that she articulates a very complex and complete way of looking at how women understand men's follies and also how they participate sometimes masochistically, sometimes cunningly, and sometimes in a self-satisfying way in a modern world that is constructed according to male fantasies. In fact, many of the works constructed by experimental feminist autobiographical videomakers have this quality, although the oppressions that women experience are variously emphasized—not only heterosexuality but also the dysfunctional family and racist society. For me, the pleasure of watching the works I discuss here is the pleasure of experiencing the epistemological and emotional power of women's fragmented consciousness and of seeing how it is that the fragmented consciousness of the oppressed most accurately understands how society works. A fragmented consciousness does not preclude working for social change and, indeed, may be the prerequisite for it. As Frantz Fanon points out, those of us with the fragmented consciousness that results from living in structures of oppression are those most likely to articulate the need for revolution and encourage others to join it as the "festival of the oppressed."[29]

Regretfully, most of the liberal academics and political activists I know rarely use tapes like these in public forums or in class. It may be that these works' subject matter—their exploration of the different components, layers, discourses, and processes that constitute the self—and their fractured, disjunctive, nonteleological narrative style make their work seem not appropriate or useful to social activists. The videotapes that people regularly show in order to teach about social process usually assume the existence of coherent subjectivity rather than seeing selfhood as dynamic, containing and shaped by many kinds of discourses, and shifting over time, especially with more global historical change. However, the most effective social action results when progressive organizers and their agendas take into consideration the ways that their constituencies live within many roles, participate in contradictory discourses, and have different needs at different moments of their daily lives. At the same time that I work actively in movements for social change, both as a leftist and a feminist, I am particularly attracted to feminist art media for the way it resists the reductionism of the political discourse in which I am necessarily immersed.

♦————————————————————————

NOTES

1. Jeanne Braham, *Crucial Conversations: Interpreting Contemporary American Literary Autobiographies by Women* (New York: Teachers College Press, 1995), 4.

2. When I discuss men, women, teenagers, and girls—and their consciousness—in this essay, it is in terms of statistical probability, structures such as family dynamics, or hegemonic cultural institutions like heterosexuality that impinge on everyone's lives. Varying social contexts uniquely shape different groups of people's sexual practice, family behavior, and consciousness, and these also vary according to region, social class, and conditions of multiple oppression. The feminist scholarship I mentioned traces these cultural differences in detail.

3. Common examples include sexual dysphoria ("I am a woman inside a man's body") and post-traumatic stress disorder.

4. For a brief discussion about how theorizing race has enriched feminist theory over the past twenty years, see Rita Felski, "Modernism and Modernity: Engendering Literary History," in *Rereading Modernism: New Directions in Feminist Criticism*, ed. Lisa Rado (New York: Garland Press, 1994).

5. I am especially indebted to two distributors, Women Make Movies (462 Broadway, Suite 500C, New York NY 10013, 212-925-0606) and the Video Data Bank of the School of the Art

Institute of Chicago (112 S. Michigan, Chicago IL 60603, 312-345-3550), which between them distribute almost all of the videos discussed here. The Video Data Bank is one of the main promoters of experimental video in the United States, and Women Make Movies is one of the main outlets for women's film and video.

6. Other exemplary works of the "narration-as-primary" style include Linda Montano's early classic *Mitchell's Death*, Cheryl Dunye's *Janine*, and Margie Strosser's *Rape Stories*.

7. Sadie Benning and Susan Mogul enjoy the moment of filmmaking, although their editing styles indicate their eccentric views on the world as well. Benning traces the shape of her small social and physical world, mostly in her bedroom. Although just a teenager when she started videomaking, Benning has consistently exhibited a skilled, avant-garde videomaker's trained artistic eye and discipline over the camera (her father is well-known avant-garde filmmaker James Benning). Mogul's works *Everyday Echo Street*, about her neighborhood in Los Angeles, and *Prose Portraits, Ironies, and Other Reflections*, a travel diary of a trip to Eastern Europe, provide the pleasure of her turning the camera on the men whom she dates and also capturing the small, telling moments of her experiences in an urban environment.

8. For example, later edits of Lynn Hershman's *Confessions of a Chameleon* omit her discussion of how she supported her child through hustling after her husband left her. Partly the ellipsis comes from the fact that she regularly edits her collected *Electronic Diaries* to fit on one standard two-hour videocassette. Hershman does not discuss the omissions made in later edits of her work, since making and remaking the *Electronic Diaries*, always adding new historical material to them, seem to be part of her way of forging a self.

9. See especially Barbier's *Table of Silence* and *The Kitchen Goddess*.

10. Sidonie Smith, "Identity's Body," in *Autobiography and Postmodernism*, ed. Kathleen Ashley, Leigh Gilmore, and Gerald Peters (Amherst: University of Massachusetts Press, 1994), 271.

11. See John Berger, *Ways of Seeing* (London: Penguin Books, 1972), 45–64.

12. An important essay by Dorothy E. Smith, "Femininity as Discourse," analyzes the popular discourse around beauty in Foucauldian terms, seeing it both as disciplinary and as requiring an enormous amount of labor and libidinal energy to enact. Smith describes how this discourse produces a ruptured body consciousness: "The 'structure' of the relationship of the subject to herself is

tripartite: the distance between herself as subject and her body, which becomes the object of her work, is created by the textual image through which she becomes conscious of its defects." In *Becoming Feminine: The Politics of Popular Culture*, ed. Leslie G. Roman, Linda K. Christian-Smith, Elizabeth Ellsworth (East Sussex: Falmer Press, 1988), 50.

13. *Measures of Distance* is the title of a tape by Mona Hatoum that is the classic experimental autobiographical video about woman's personal and political boundedness.

14. Julia Kristeva, *Powers of Horror: An Essay on Abjection* (New York: Columbia University Press, 1982).

15. In his essay on the uncanny (*unheimlich*), Freud traces the roots for this German word for the terrifying back to its roots, which contain *heim*, the German word for home, and *heimlich*, the familiar or that which is related to the household. Sigmund Freud, "The Uncanny," vol. 17, *Standard Edition of the Complete Psychological Works of Sigmund Freud*, trans. James Strachey (London: Hogarth Press, 1953–74).

16. Janice Tanaka's *Whose Going to Pay for These Donuts, Anyway?* and Rea Tajiri's *History and Memory* exemplify the common use of such a mixed form for videomakers belonging to an ethnic or sexual subculture that has suffered generations of oppression. The mixed documentary-like interviews and autobiographical narration allow the maker to use the word *I* to speak for the experience of the whole group.

17. Bill Nichols, *Representing Reality: Issues and Concepts in Documentary* (Bloomington: Indiana University Press, 1991), 3.

18. Philippe Lejeune's definition of autobiography is a "retrospective prose narrative about one's own existence, focusing on the author's life, especially the story of his personality." "The Autobiographical Pact," in *On Autobiography*, ed. Paul John Eakin, trans. Katherine M. Leary (Minneapolis: University of Minnesota Press, 1989), 21. Lejeune, knowing the grammatical indeterminacy or shifting referent of the word *I*, later added that in autobiography the *I* is anchored by our knowledge of the author's proper name.

19. William James, *Principles of Psychology*, cited in John Paul Eakins, *Touching the World: Reference in Autobiography* (Princeton N.J.: Princeton University Press, 1992), 7. I am indebted to Eakins for my discussion of remembrance.

20. As Suzanne Clark, author of *Sentimental Modernism* (Bloomington: Indiana University Press, 1991) pointed out to me in conversation, traditional definitions of high modernism apply primarily to male artists and writers of the mid-twentieth century; more useful to describe the work of twentieth-

century women experimentalists is the term *modernité*, which posits the artist as forging aesthetic and developing themes within the context of her social milieu. "The French term, *modernité*, while also concerned with a distinctively modern experience of dislocation and ambiguity, locates it in the more general experience of everyday life, as exemplified in the ephemeral and transitory qualities of an urban culture shaped by the imperatives of fashion, consumerism, and constant innovation" (Felski, "Modernism and Modernity," 198).

21. Nancy Chodorow, *The Reproduction of Mothering: Psychoanalysis and the Sociology of Gender* (Berkeley: University of California Press, 1979).

22. Green told me in conversation that the title directly alludes to Anaïs Nin's *A Spy in the House of Love* (Chicago: Swallow Press, 1959).

23. By no means am I implying that all men accept the dominant valorization of a certain kind of masculinity. And certainly children's paths toward knowing the ugly side of sexuality vary. In particular, urban children learn about street problems or family violence very young, especially if they receive child care in large, publicly run institutions, where the other children often talk about these things at the age of three or four.

24. Such critics who find the referent "empty" in Hershman's *Electronic Diaries,* and who consider the tapes to be more about media process than about women's fragmented consciousness, include Michael Renov ("The Subject in History," *Afterimage* [Summer 1989]: 4–7) and David James ("Lynn Hershman: The Subject of Autobiography," in *Resolutions: Contemporary Video Practice*, ed. Michael Renov and Erika Suderburg [Minneapolis: University of Minnesota Press, 1996], 124–33).

25. For example, see Adrienne Rich, "Compulsory Heterosexuality and Lesbian Existence," reprinted in *Women — Sex and Sexuality,* ed. Catharine R. Stimpson and Ethel Spector Person (Chicago: University of Chicago Press, 1980); Andrea Dworkin, *Pornography:*

Men Possessing Women (New York: Putnam, 1981); Sandra Lee Bartky, *Femininity and Domination: Studies in the Phenomenology of Oppression* (New York: Routledge, 1990); Ellen Willis, *Beginning to See the Light: Pieces of a Decade* (New York: Random House, 1981); Judith Butler, *Gender Trouble: Feminism and the Subversion of Identity* (New York: Routledge, 1990); Eve Kosofsky Sedgwick, *Epistemology of the Closet* (Berkeley and Los Angeles: University of California Press, 1990); Gayle Rubin, "The Leather Menace," in *Coming to Power: Writings and Graphics on Lesbian S/M,* ed. Samois Collective (Boston: Alyson, 1987). Also see the essay in this volume by Michelle Citron, maker of the films *Daughter Rite* and *What You Take For Granted.* . . .

26. Jane Smiley, *A Thousand Acres* (New York: Ballantine Books, 1991), 371.

27. Sigmund Freud, "A Child Is Being Beaten," in *Standard Edition.*

28. Furthermore, with the advent of the sex debates in the women's movement, a subgenre of documentary about and for women's sexual practice has arisen, lesbian pornography. The latter includes commercial pornography, early lesbian documentary-like works from production companies like Blush, and sadomasochistic pornography that represents the preferences of various subcultural factions. The current queer, in-your-face lesbian S-M and piercing media are often made with a certain stylistic skill and have much of the taboo-breaking characteristics of the old avant-garde film and video tradition. Lesbian pornography may assume and speak directly to a woman's sexualized child but, at least in the examples we now have of it, it does not yet articulate the relation of incest to adult sadomasochistic practices, especially among women.

29. Frantz Fanon, "On Violence," in *The Wretched of the Earth,* trans. Constance Farrington (New York: Grove Press, 1968); and Julia Lesage, "Women's Rage," in *Marxism and the Interpretation of Culture,* ed. Cary Nelson and Lawrence Grossberg (Urbana: University of Illinois Press, 1988).

Selected Filmography/Videography

Editors' note: The film and video works discussed in this volume are listed below along with a representative selection of other works we find relevant to our general project. Distributors (noted here in brackets) and their addresses are listed at the end of the filmography/videography. Dates provided are derived from distributor catalogs.

The Act of Seeing through One's Own Eyes, Stan Brakhage, 1971, 32 minutes [Canyon]

Adynata, Leslie Thornton, 1983, 30 minutes [WMM]

Age 12: Love with a Little L, Jennifer Montgomery, 1990, 22 minutes [WMM]

All My Babies, George Stoney and the Georgia State Department of Public Health, 1952, 52 minutes [MOMA]

American Dream, Barbara Kopple, 1990, 90 minutes [Facets]

An American Family, Craig Gilbert, 1972, WNET, twelve one-hour episodes [Video Verité]

An Armenian Journey, Theodore Bogosian, 1988, 56 minutes [Bogosian]

Antonia: Portrait of a Woman, Judy Collins and Jill Godmilow, 1973, 58 minutes [UCEMC]

Back to Ararat, Peå Holmquist, 1988, 100 minutes [First Run]

Bicycle, Meryl Perlson, 1992, 2 minutes, available from the filmmaker at (909) 880-5820

Binge, Lynn Hershman, 1987, 28 minutes [Hershman]

The Bridge, Joris Ivens, 1928, 12 minutes [MOMA]

. . . But Then, She's Betty Carter, Michelle Parkerson, 1980, 53 minutes [WMM]

Chronicle of a Summer, Jean Rouch and Edgar Morin, 1961, 90 minutes [Corinth]

Chronicles of a Lying Spirit by Kelly Gabron, Cauleen Smith, 1992, 6 minutes [Drift]

The Cinematic Jazz of Julie Dash, Yvonne Welbon, 1992, 27 minutes [TWN, WMM]

Coal Miner's Granddaughter, Cecilia Dougherty, 1991, 90 minutes [VDB, WMM]

Complaints of a Dutiful Daughter,
Deborah Hoffmann, 1994, 44 minutes
[WMM]

Conversations with Roy DeCarava,
Carroll Parrott Blue, 1984, 28 minutes
[First Run]

The Cool World, Shirley Clarke, 1963,
104 minutes [Zipporah]

Dangerous When Wet, Diane Bonder,
1992, 5 minutes [Frameline]

Daughter Rite, Michelle Citron, 1979,
53 minutes [WMM]

Dead Birds, Robert Gardner, 1963,
83 minutes [UCEMC]

Delirium, Mindy Faber, 1993, 23 minutes [VDB, WMM]

Die Kuemmelturkin Geht (Melek
leaves), Janine Meerapfel, 1984–85,
88 minutes, Basis Film Verleih, Berlin

*Domestic Portraits, 1 & 2 (Time and
Space),* Annette Barbier, 1993, 4 minutes
[VDB]

Don't Look Back, D. A. Pennebaker,
1967, 96 minutes [Facets, October,
Pennebaker]

Excerpts, Aysha Quinn, 1983, 10 minutes, Long Beach Museum of Art Annex

The Fairies, Tom Rubnitz, 1989,
10 minutes [VDB]

Far from Poland, Jill Godmilow, 1984,
109 minutes [WMM]

Finding Christa, Camille Billops and
James Hatch, 1991, 55 minutes [TWN]

First Person Plural, Lynn Hershman,
1989, 28 minutes [Hershman]

Freebird, Suzie Silver, 1993, 11 minutes
[VDB]

Fundi: The Story of Ella Baker, Joanne
Grant, 1986, 47 minutes [First Run]

Girl Power, Sadie Benning, 1993, 15
minutes [VDB]

The Good Woman of Bangkok, Dennis
O'Rourke, 1995, 82 minutes [Direct
Cinema]

*Gotta Make This Journey: Sweet Honey
in the Rock,* Michelle Parkerson and
Joseph Camp, 1983, 58 minutes
[WMM]

Grapefruit, Cecilia Dougherty, 1989,
40 minutes [VDB]

Growing up Female, Julia Reichert and
James Klein, 1971, 50 minutes [New
Day]

Happy Mother's Day, Richard Leacock
and Joyce Chopra, 1964, 26 minutes
[Pennebaker]

Harlan County, USA, Barbara Kopple,
1976, 103 minutes [First Run]

Hayal (Shadowplays), Merlyn Solokhan,
1989–90, 70 minutes [Blank]

Hey! Baby Chickey, Nina Sobel, 1979,
6 minutes [VDB]

High School, Frederick Wiseman, 1968,
75 minutes [Zipporah]

History and Memory, Rea Tajiri, 1991,
32 minutes [VDB, WMM]

Housing Problems, Arthur Elton and
Edgar Anstey, 1935, 17 minutes
[MOMA]

I Am Somebody, Madeline Anderson,
1970, 28 minutes [First Run]

I Be Done Been Was Is, Debra Robinson,
1984, 60 minutes [WMM]

If Every Girl Had a Diary, Sadie
Benning, 1990, 6 minutes [VDB]

I'm British But . . . , Gurinder Chadha,
1989, 30 minutes [TWN]

Industrial Britain, Robert Flaherty and John Grierson, 1933, 21 minutes [MOMA]

I Never Danced the Way Girls Were Supposed To, Dawn Suggs, 1992, 7 minutes [TWN]

In Plain English, Julia Lesage, 1992, 42 minutes [Canyon, Facets]

Intervals of Silence: Being Jewish in Germany, Deborah Lefkowitz, 1990, 58 minutes [Lefkowitz]

It Happens to Us, Amalie Rothschild, 1972, 32 minutes [New Day]

It Wasn't Love, Sadie Benning, 1992, 20 minutes [VDB]

Jollies, Sadie Benning, 1990, 11 minutes [VDB]

Joyce at 34, Joyce Chopra, 1972, 28 minutes [New Day]

Kanehsatake: 270 Years of Resistance, Alanis Obomsawin, 1993, 119 minutes [Bullfrog]

Kiss the Boys and Make Them Die, Margaret Stratton, 1994, 30 minutes [VDB]

Lamento, Julia Lesage, 1986, 11 minutes, available from the filmmaker at (541) 346-3979

The Last Time I Saw Ron, Leslie Thornton, 1994, 12 minutes [VDB]

Learn Where the Meat Comes From, Suzanne Lacy, 1976, 14 minutes [VDB]

Letter to My Uncle, Deborah Lefkowitz, 1981, 15 minutes [Lefkowitz]

A Litany for Survival: The Life and Work of Audre Lorde, Ada Gay Griffin and Michelle Parkerson, 1995, 90 minutes [TWN]

Lost, Lost, Lost, Jonas Mekas, 1975, 178 minutes [FMC]

The Love Tapes, Wendy Clarke, 1978 to present, available from the filmmaker at P.O. Box 187, Topanga, CA 90290; (310) 455-0861

Measures of Distance, Mona Hatoum, 1988, 15 minutes [VDB, WMM]

Memories from the Department of Amnesia, Janice Tanaka, 1989, 13 minutes [VDB]

The Mom Tapes, Ilene Segalove, 1974–1978, 28 minutes [VDB]

Mother Right, Michelle Citron, 1983, 25 minutes, currently not available

My Wife Is Filipina, Yasunori Terada, 1993, 100 minutes [Manpukuji]

Naked Spaces Living Is Round, Trinh T. Minh-ha, 1985, 135 minutes [WMM]

Nana, Mom, and Me, Amalie Rothschild, 1974, 47 minutes [New Day]

News from Home, Chantal Akerman, 1975, 85 minutes [World Artists]

Nun and Deviant, Nancy Angelo and Candace Compton, 1976, 20 minutes [VDB]

Of Great Events and Ordinary People, Raul Ruiz, 1979, 65 minutes, currently not available in the United States

On Art and Artists: Judy Chicago, Lyn Blumenthal and Kate Horsfield, 1974, 28 minutes [VDB]

On Art and Artists: Arlene Raven, Blumenthal and Horsfield, 1979, 28 minutes [VDB]

On Art and Artists: Miriam Schapiro, Blumenthal and Horsfield, 1979, 28 minutes [VDB]

On Becoming a Woman, Cheryl Chisholm, 1987, 90 minutes [WMM]

Overstay, Ann Kaneko, 1998, 75 minutes, available from the filmmaker at (213) 465-0749

La Operación, Ana Maria Garcia, 1982, 40 minutes [Cinema Guild]

Parthenogenesis, Michelle Citron, 1975, 25 minutes, available from the filmmaker at (847) 491-7315

Peggy and Fred in Hell series, Leslie Thornton, 1987 to the present [VDB, WMM]

Pink Slip, Hildegarde Duane, 1982, 7 minutes, Long Beach Museum of Art Video Annex

Portrait of Jason, Shirley Clarke, 1967, 105 minutes [Facets]

A Prayer before Birth, Jacqui Duckworth, 1992, 20 minutes [WMM]

Pretty Fluffy. Cheezy. Bunny . . . , Alix Pearlstein, 1993, 6 minutes, Postmaster Gallery, NY

Primary, D. A. Pennebaker and Richard Leacock, with Terence Macartney-Filgate and Albert Maysles, 1960, 60 minutes [Direct Cinema]

Privilege, Yvonne Rainer, 1990, 103 minutes [Zeitgeist]

A Question of Color: Color Consciousness in Black America, Kathe Sandler, 1993, 56 minutes [California Newsreel]

Rape Stories, Margie Strosser, 1989, 25 minutes [WMM]

Reassemblage, Trinh T. Minh-ha, 1982, 40 minutes [TWN, WMM]

Remembering Thelma, Kathe Sandler, 1981, 15 minutes [WMM]

Remembering Wei Yi-fang, Remembering Myself: An Autobiography, Yvonne Welbon, 1995, 29 minutes [WMM]

Roger and Me, Michael Moore, 1989, 87 minutes [Facets, Swank]

The Scary Movie, Peggy Awesh, 1991, 9 minutes [Canyon]

Secret Sounds Screaming: The Sexual Abuse of Children, Ayoka Chenzira, 1986, 30 minutes [TWN, WMM]

Seeing Is Believing, Lynn Hershman, 1991 [Hershman]

Seeing Is Believing, Shauna Beharry, 1991, 8 minutes [GIV]

Semiotics of the Kitchen, Martha Rosler, 1975, 6 minutes [VDB]

She Don't Fade, Cheryl Dunye, 1991, 23 minutes [TWN, VDB]

Sherman's March, Ross McElwee, 1986, 155 minutes [First Run]

She's Just Growing Up, Dear, Julia Tell, 1992, 16 minutes [New Day]

Shoah, Claude Lanzmann, 1985; Part 1, 273 minutes; Part 2, 290 minutes [New Yorker]

A Shortness of Breath, Ann Kaneko, 1992, 15 minutes [TWN], or through the filmmaker at (213) 465-0749

Sink or Swim, Su Friedrich, 1990, 48 minutes [Canyon, WMM]

Spin Cycle, Aarin Burch, 1991, 5 minutes [WMM]

A Spy in The House That Ruth Built, Vanalyne Green, 1989, 30 minutes [VDB, WMM]

Storme: The Lady of the Jewel Box, Michelle Parkerson, 1987, 21 minutes [WMM]

Surname Viet Given Name Nam, Trinh T. Minh-ha, 1989, 108 minutes [WMM]

Suzanne, Suzanne, Camille Billops and James Hatch, 1982, 30 minutes [TWN]

Syvilla: They Dance to Her Drum,
Ayoka Chenzira, 1979, 15 minutes
[WMM]

Tekerleme (Tonguebreaker), Merlyn
Solakhan, 1985–86, 85 minutes
[Blank]

Territories, Sankofa Film and Video
Collective, 1984, currently not available
in the United States

Thank You and Good Night, Jan
Oxenberg, 1991, 77 minutes [Swank]

There Was an Unseen Cloud Moving,
Leslie Thornton, 1987, 60 minutes
[WMM]

The Ties That Bind, Su Friedrich, 1984,
55 minutes [Canyon, WMM]

Toechter Zweier Welten (Daughters of
two worlds), Serap Berrakkarasu,
1990, 60 minutes, available from the
filmmaker at (451) 79 74 97, Lubeck,
Germany

Tomboychik, Sandi DuBowski, 1993,
15 minutes [VDB]

Tongues Untied, Marlon Riggs, 1989,
55 minutes [Frameline]

Trick or Drink, Vanalyne Green, 1984,
20 minutes [VDB, WMM]

Unfinished Diary, Marilu Mallet, 1983,
55 minutes [WMM]

Union Maids, Julia Reichert, Jim Klein,
Miles Mogulescu, 1976, 51 minutes
[New Day]

*Vital Statistics of a Citizen Simply Ob-
tained,* Martha Rosler, 1977, 39 minutes
[VDB]

Voices of the Morning, Meena Nanji,
1991, 15 minutes [WMM]

Waiting at the Soda Fountain, Susan
Mogul, 1980, 24 minutes, Long Beach
Museum of Art Video Annex

War on Lesbians, Jane Cottis, 1992,
32 minutes [VDB, WMM]

What Happens to You?, Vanalyne
Green, 1991, 35 minutes [VDB]

What You Take For Granted . . . ,
Michelle Citron, 1983, 75 minutes
[WMM]

*Who's Going to Pay for These Donuts,
Anyway?,* Janice Tanaka, 1992, 58 minutes [VDB, WMM]

With Love from A to B, Nancy
Buchanan and Barbara Smith, 1977,
8 minutes, Long Beach Museum of Art
Video Annex

A Woman Waiting for Her Period,
Wei-Ssu Chien, 1993, 23 minutes
[WMM]

Womb with a View, Sherry Millner,
1986, 40 minutes [VDB]

The Woman's Film, Women's Caucus,
San Francisco Newsreel, 1971, 40 minutes [TWN]

Women's Movements, Annette Barbier,
1993, 28 minutes [VDB]

DISTRIBUTORS

[Blank] Blank Film
Berlin
(30) 262 5745

[Bogosian] Bogosian Productions
148 Russell Avenue
Watertown, MA 02172
(617) 924-4090

[Bullfrog] Bullfrog Films
P.O. Box 149
Oley, PA 19547
(610) 779-8226

[California Newsreel] California
Newsreel
149 Ninth Street, Suite 420
San Francisco, CA 94103
(415) 621-6196

[Canyon] Canyon Cinema
2325 Third Street, Suite 338
San Francisco, CA 94107
(415) 626-2255

[Cinema Guild] The Cinema Guild
1697 Broadway, Suite 506
New York, NY 10019-5904
(800) 723-5522

[Corinth] Corinth Films
34 Gansevoort Street
New York, NY 10014
(800) 221-4720

[Direct Cinema] Direct Cinema
P.O. Box 10003
Santa Monica, CA 90410-1003
(310) 636-8200

[Drift] Drift Production and
Distribution
709 Carroll Street, #3R
Brooklyn, NY 11215
(718) 857-4885

[Facets] Facets Multimedia, Inc.
1517 West Fullerton Avenue
Chicago, IL 60614
(800) 331-6197

[First Run] First Run/Icarus Films
153 Waverly Place, 6th Floor
New York, NY 10014
(212) 727-1711

[FMC] Film-Makers' Cooperative
175 Lexington Avenue
New York, NY 10016
(212) 889-3820

[Frameline] Frameline Distribution
346 Ninth Street
San Francisco, CA 94103
(415) 703-8654

[GIV] Groupe Intervention Vidéo
Montreal
(514) 271-5506

[Hershman] Lynn Hershman
1935 Filbert Street
San Francisco, CA 94123
(415) 567-6180

[Lefkowitz] Deborah
Lefkowitz/Lefkowitz Films
P.O. Box 94
Riverside, CA 92502-0094
(909) 682-0444

[Manpukuji] Manpukuji Cinema
1-1-25 Ohara Kamifukuoka-shi
Saitama 356
Japan
81 492 63 0713

[MOMA] Museum of Modern Art
11 West 53 Street
New York, NY 10019
(212) 708-9530

[New Day] New Day Films
22-D Hollywood Avenue, Dept. SS
Hohokus, NJ 07423
(201) 652-6590

[New Yorker] New Yorker Films
16 West 61st Street
New York, NY 10023
(212) 247-6110

[October] October Films
65 Bleecker Street, 2nd Floor
New York, NY 10012
(800) 628-6237

[Pennebaker] D. A. Pennebaker
Associates
21 West 86th Street
New York, NY 10024

[Swank] Swank Motion Pictures
201 South Jefferson Avenue
Saint Louis, MO 63103
(800) 876-5577

[TWN] Third World Newsreel
335 West 38th Street, 5th Floor
New York, NY 10018
(212) 947-9277

[UCEMC] University of California
Educational Media Center
200 Center Street, Suite 400
Berkeley, CA 94704
(510) 642-0462

[VDB] Video Data Bank
112 S. Michigan Avenue
Chicago, IL 60603
(312) 345-3550

[Video Verité] Video Verité
927 Madison Avenue
New York, NY 10021
(212) 249-7356

[WMM] Women Make Movies
462 Broadway, Suite 500E
New York, NY 10013
(212) 925-0606

[World Artists] World Artists
P.O. Box 36788
Los Angeles, CA 90036
(213) 651-0200

[Zeitgeist] Zeitgeist Films Ltd.
247 Centre Street, 2nd Floor
New York, NY 10013
(212) 274-1989

[Zipporah] Zipporah Films
One Richdale Avenue, Unit 4
Cambridge, MA 02140
(617) 576-3603

Selected Bibliography

Editors' Note: The following is a selected bibliography of works we find relevant to the general project of the volume as described in our introduction. For further and more specific bibliographic information, please see the notes for the individual essays.

Abu-Lughod, Lila. "Writing against Culture." In *Recapturing Anthropology: Working in the Present.* Richard G. Fox, ed. Santa Fe: School of American Research Press, 1991.

Agee, James, and Walker Evans. *Let Us Now Praise Famous Men.* Boston: Houghton Mifflin, 1941.

Armstrong, Dan. "Wiseman's Realm of Transgression: *Titicut Follies,* the Symbolic Father and the Spectacle of Confinement." *Cinema Journal* 29.1 (Fall 1989): 20–35.

Artel, Linda, and Susan Wengraf. "Positive Images: Screening Women's Films." Reprinted in Erens, *Issues in Feminist Film Criticism* and Steven, *Jump Cut.*

Arthur, Paul. "Jargons of Authenticity (Three American Moments)." In Renov, *Theorizing Documentary.*

Barnouw, Erik. *Documentary: A History of the Non-Fiction Film.* New York: Oxford University Press, 1974. Revised editions, 1983, 1993.

Barnouw, Erik, and Patricia R. Zimmermann, eds. "The Flaherty: Four Decades in the Cause of Independent Cinema." Special Issue. *Wide Angle* 17.1–4 (Winter 1996).

Barsam, Richard Meran. *Nonfiction Film: A Critical History.* Revised edition. Bloomington and Indianapolis: Indiana University Press, 1992.

Becker, Edith, Michelle Citron, Julia Lesage, and B. Ruby Rich. "Lesbians and Film." Reprinted in Steven, *Jump Cut.*

Beh, Siew Hwa. "The Woman's Film." *Film Quarterly* 25.1 (Fall 1971). Reprinted in Nichols, *Movies and Methods.*

Benson, Thomas, and Carolyn Anderson. *Reality Fictions: The Films of Frederick Wiseman.* Carbondale: Southern Illinois University Press, 1989.

Bobo, Jacqueline. "Black Women's Films: Genesis of a Tradition." In *Black Women Film and Video Artists.* New York: Routledge, 1998.

Brunsdon, Charlotte. *Films for Women.* London: British Film Institute, 1986, esp. 9–48.

Burton, Julianne, ed. *The Social Documentary in Latin America.* Pittsburgh: University of Pittsburgh Press, 1990.

———. "Democratizing Documentary: Modes of Address in the New Latin American Cinema, 1958–1972." In *The Social Documentary in Latin America.*

Butler, Judith. *Gender Trouble: Feminism and the Subversion of Identity.* New York: Routledge, 1990.

Carson, Diane, Linda Dittmar, and Janice R. Welsch, eds. *Multiple Voices in Feminist Film Criticism.* Minneapolis: University of Minnesota Press, 1994.

Cartwright, Lisa. *Screening the Body.* Minneapolis: University of Minnesota Press, 1995.

Clarke, Cheryl. "Lesbianism: An Act of Resistance." In Moraga and Anzaldúa, *This Bridge Called My Back: Writings of Radical Women of Color.*

Clarke, Shirley. Interviewed in Sharon Smith, *Women Who Make Movies.* New York: Hopkinson and Blake, 1975.

Cohen, Hart. "The Ax Fight: Mapping Anthropology on Film." *Ciné-Tracts* 2.2 (Spring 1979): 61–73.

Dargis, Manohla, and Amy Taubin. "Double Take." *The Village Voice* (21 January 1992): 56.

Devereaux, Leslie. "Cultures, Disciplines, Cinemas." In *Fields of Vision: Essays in Film Studies, Visual*

Anthropology, and Photography. Leslie Devereaux and Roger Hillman, eds. Berkeley and Los Angeles: University of California Press, 1995.

Devereaux, Leslie, and Roger Hillman, eds. *Fields of Vision: Essays in Film Studies, Visual Anthropology, and Photography.* Berkeley and Los Angeles: University of California Press, 1995.

Diamond, Sara. "Sex Lies with Videotape: Abbreviated Histories of Canadian Video Sex." In Renov and Suderburg, *Resolutions.*

Doane, Mary Ann. "Remembering Women." In *Femmes Fatales: Feminism, Film Theory, Psychoanalysis.* London and New York: Routledge, 1991.

——. "The Retreat of Signs and the Failure of Words: Leslie Thornton's *Adynata.*" In *Femmes Fatales.*

Dyer, Richard. *Now You See It: Studies on Lesbian and Gay Film.* London: Routledge, 1990, esp. 174–286.

Dystra, Jean. "Putting Herself in the Picture: Autobiographical Images of Illness and the Body." *Afterimage* 23 (September/October 1995): 16–20.

Eaton, Mick, ed. *Anthropology — Reality — Cinema: The Films of Jean Rouch.* London: British Film Institute, 1979.

Ellis, Jack C. *The Documentary Idea.* Englewood Cliffs, N.J.: Prentice Hall, 1989.

Erens, Patricia. "Women's Documentary Filmmaking: The Personal Is Political." In Rosenthal, *New Challenges for Documentary.*

——. "Women's Documentaries as Social History." *Film Library Quarterly* 14.1–2 (1981): 4–9.

——, ed. *Issues in Feminist Film Criticism.* Bloomington and Indianapolis: Indiana University Press, 1990.

Feuer, Jane. "'Daughter Rite': Living with Our Pain and Love." Reprinted in Brunsdon, *Films for Women.*

Frisch, Michael. "Oral History, Documentary, and the Mystification of Power: A Critique of *Vietnam: A Television History.*" In *A Shared Authority: Essays on the Craft and Meaning of Oral and Public History.* Albany: State University of New York Press, 1990.

Frota, Monica. "Taking Aim: The Video Technology of Cultural Resistance." In Renov and Suderburg, *Resolutions.*

Gaines, Jane. "Women and Representation: Can We Enjoy Alternate Pleasure?" Reprinted in Erens, *Issues in Feminist Film Criticism.*

Gibson, Gloria J. "Moving Pictures to Move People: Michelle Parkerson *Is* the Eye of the Storm." *Black Film Review* 3.3 (Summer 1987): 16–17.

Gibson-Hudson, Gloria. "Aspects of Black Feminist Cultural Ideology in Films by Black Women Independent Artists." In Carson, Dittmar, and Welsch, *Multiple Voices.*

Ginsburg, Faye. "Mediating Culture: Indigenous Media, Ethnographic Film, and the Production of Identity." In Devereaux and Hillman, *Fields of Vision.*

Gledhill, Christine. "Recent Developments in Feminist Film Criticism." Reprinted in *Re-Vision: Essays in Feminist Film Criticism.* Mary Ann Doane, Patricia Mellencamp, and Linda Williams, eds. Frederick, Md.: University Publications of America, 1984.

Gordon, Deborah. "Writing Culture, Writing Feminism: The Poetics and Politics of Experimental Ethnography." *Inscriptions* 3/4 (1988): 7–24.

Gordon, Linda. "*Union Maids*: Working Class Heroines." *Jump Cut* 14 (1977): 34–35.

——. "What's New in Women's History." In *Feminist Studies/Critical Studies.* Teresa de Lauretis, ed. Bloomington: Indiana University Press, 1986.

Grant, Barry Keith, and Jeannette Sloniowski, eds. *Documenting the Documentary: Close Readings of Documentary Film and Video.* Detroit: Wayne State University Press, 1998.

Gross, Larry, John Katz, and Jay Ruby, eds. *Image Ethics: The Moral Rights of Subjects in Photographs, Film and TV.* New York: Oxford University Press, 1988.

Guynn, William. *A Cinema of Nonfiction.* London and Toronto: Associated University Press, 1990.

Haralovich, Mary Beth. "Film History and Social History: Reproducing Social Relationships." *Wide Angle* 8.2 (1986): 4–14.

Harvey, Sylvia. "An Introduction to 'The Song of the Shirt.'" Reprinted in Brunsdon, *Films for Women.*

Hess, John. "Notes on U.S. Radical Film, 1967–80." Reprinted in Steven, *Jump Cut.*

Higson, Andrew. "Representing the National Past: Nostalgia and Pastiche in the Heritage Film." In *Fires Were Started: British Cinema and Thatcherism.* Lester Friedman, ed. Minneapolis: University of Minnesota Press, 1993.

Hine, Lewis W. *Men at Work: Photographic Studies of Modern Men and Machines.* Revised edition. New York: Dover Publications, 1977.

Holmlund, Chris, and Cynthia Fuchs, eds. *Between the Sheets, In the Streets: Queer, Lesbian, Gay Documentary.* Minneapolis: University of Minnesota Press, 1997.

hooks, bell. "Is Paris Burning?" In *Black Looks: Race and Representation.* Boston: South End Press, 1992.

——. "Madonna: Plantation Mistress or Soul Sister?" In *Black Looks.*

———. "Neo-Colonial Fantasies of Conquest: *Hoop Dreams.*" In *Reel To Real: Race, Sex, and Class at the Movies.* New York and London: Routledge, 1996.

———. "Back to the Avant-Garde: The Progressive Vision." In *Reel to Real.*

———. "Confession—Filming Family: An Interview with Camille Billops." In *Reel to Real.*

Ivens, Joris. *The Camera and I.* New York: International Publishers, 1969.

Jacobs, Lewis, ed. *The Documentary Tradition: From Nanook to Woodstock.* 2d edition. New York: W. W. Norton, 1979.

James, David. "Lynn Hershman: The Subject of Autobiography." In Renov and Suderburg, *Resolutions.*

Johnston, Claire. "Women's Cinema as Counter-Cinema." In *Notes on Women's Cinema.* Claire Johnston, ed. London: Society for Education in Film and Television, 1973.

Johnston, Claire, and Paul Willeman. "Brecht in Britain: *The Nightcleaners* and The Independent Political Film." In Waugh, *"Show Us Life."*

Juhasz, Alexandra. "Our Autobodies, Our Selves." *Afterimage* 21.7 (February 1994):10–14.

———. "They Said We Were Trying to Show Reality—All I Want to Show Is My Video: The Politics of the Realist, Feminist Documentary." *Screen* 35 (Summer 1994): 171–90.

Kaplan, E. Ann. "Interview with British Cine-Feminists." In *Women and the Cinema: A Critical Anthology.* Karyn Kay and Gerald Peary, eds. New York: E. P. Dutton, 1977.

———. "Theories and Strategies of the Feminist Documentary." *Millennium Film Journal* 12 (Fall/Winter 1982/83). Reprinted and revised in Kaplan, *Women and Film.*

———. *Women and Film: Both Sides of the Camera.* New York: Metheun, 1983, esp. 125–41.

———. "Theory and Practice of the Realist Documentary Form in *Harlan County, U.S.A.*" Waugh, *"Show Us Life."*

Kelly, Mary. "A Conversation on Recent Feminist Art Practices." *October* 71 (1995): 49–70.

King, Noel. "Recent 'Political' Documentary: Notes on *Union Maids* and *Harlan County, USA.*" *Screen* 22.2 (1981): 7–18.

Kipnis, Laura. "Female Transgression." In Renov and Suderburg, *Resolutions.*

Klein, Michael, and Jill Klein. "*Native Land*: An Interview with Leo Hurwitz." *Cineaste* 6.3 (1974): 2–7.

Kuhn, Annette. "The Camera I: Observations on Documentary." *Screen* 19.2 (1978): 71–83.

———. *Women's Pictures: Feminism and Cinema.* 2d edition. London and New York: Verso, 1994, esp. 127–90.

———. *Family Secrets: Acts of Memory and Imagination.* London: Verso, 1995.

LaCapra, Dominick. *Rethinking Intellectual History: Texts, Contexts, Language.* Ithaca, N.Y.: Cornell University Press, 1983.

———. *History and Criticism.* Ithaca, N.Y.: Cornell University Press, 1985.

Lawrence, Amy. "Women's Voices in Third World Cinema." In Carson, Dittmar, and Welsch, *Multiple Voices.*

Lesage, Julia. "For Our Urgent Use: Films on Central America." Reprinted in Steven, *Jump Cut.*

———. "The Political Aesthetics of the Feminist Documentary Film." Reprinted in Erens, *Issues in Feminist Film Criticism.*

———. "Women Make Media: Three Modes of Production." In Burton, *The Social Documentary in Latin America.*

Levin, G. Roy. *Documentary Explorations: 15 Interviews with Film-makers.* Garden City, N.Y.: Doubleday, 1971.

MacDougall, David. "Prospects of the Ethnographic Film." Reprinted in Nichols, *Movies and Methods.*

Mamber, Stephen. *Cinema Verite in America: Studies in Uncontrolled Documentary.* Cambridge: MIT Press, 1974.

Marks, Laura U. "A Deleuzian Politics of Hybrid Cinema." *Screen* 35.3 (Autumn 1994): 235–64.

———. "Sexual Hybrids: From Oriental Exotic to Postcolonial Grotesque." *Parachute* 70 (Spring 1993): 22–29.

Martineau, Barbara Halpern. "Talking about Our Lives and Experiences: Some Thoughts about Feminism, Documentary and 'Talking Heads.'" In Waugh, *"Show Us Life."*

Mascia-Lees, Frances E., Patricia Sharpe, and Colleen Ballerino Cohen. "The Postmodernist Turn in Anthropology: Cautions from a Feminist Perspective." *Signs* 15.1 (Autumn 1989): 7–33.

Mayne, Judith. "Visibility and Feminist Film Criticism." *Film Reader* 5 (1983), esp. 123–24.

McCormick, Ruth. "Women's Liberation Cinema." In Jacobs, *The Documentary Tradition.*

———. "*Union Maids.*" *Cineaste* 8.1 (Summer 1977): 50–51.

Michel, Sonya. "Feminism, Film, and Public History." Reprinted in Erens, *Issues in Feminist Film Criticism.*

Millner, Sherry. "Third World Newsreel: Interview with Christine Choy." Reprinted in Steven, *Jump Cut.*

Moraga, Cherríe, and Gloria Anzaldúa, eds. *This Bridge Called My Back: Writings of Radical Women of Color.* New York: Kitchen Table, Women of Color Press, 1981.

Mulvey, Laura. "Film, Feminism and the Avant-Garde." In *Visual and Other Pleasures.* Bloomington and Indianapolis: Indiana University Press, 1989.

————. "Visual Pleasure and Narrative Cinema." In *Visual and Other Pleasures*.

Nelson, Joyce. *The Colonized Eye: Rethinking the Grierson Legend*. Toronto: Between the Lines, 1988.

Newton, Judith. "History as Usual? Feminism and the 'New Historicism.'" *Cultural Critique* 9 (1988): 87–121.

Nichols, Bill. *Movies and Methods: An Anthology*. Berkeley and Los Angeles: University of California Press, 1976.

————. *Ideology and the Image*. Bloomington: Indiana University Press, 1981.

————. *Representing Reality: Issues and Concepts in Documentary*. Bloomington: Indiana University Press, 1991.

————. *Blurred Boundaries: Questions of Meaning in Contemporary Culture*. Bloomington: Indiana University Press, 1994.

————. "Historical Consequences of the Viewer: *Who Killed Vincent Chin?*" In Sobchack, *The Persistence of History*.

Noriega, Chon. "Talking Heads, Body Politic: The Plural Self of Chicano Experimental Video." In Renov and Suderburg, *Resolutions*.

Orvell, Miles. "Documentary Film and the Power of Interrogation: Kopple's *American Dream* and Moore's *Roger and Me*." In *After the Machine: Visual Arts and the Erasing of Cultural Boundaries*. Jackson: University Press of Mississippi, 1995.

Peckham, Linda. "Not Speaking with Language/Speaking with No Language: Leslie Thornton's *Adynata*." *Discourse* 8 (Fall/Winter 1986/1987): 103–13.

Penley, Constance. "Documentary/Documentation." *Camera Obscura* 13–14 (1985): 85.

Penley, Constance, and Andrew Ross. "Interview with Trinh T. Minh-ha." *Camera Obscura* 13–14 (1985): 87–103.

Petro, Patrice, ed. *Fugitive Images: From Photography to Video*. Bloomington: Indiana University Press, 1995.

————. "Historical *Ennui*, Feminist Boredom." In Sobchack, *The Persistence of History*.

Polan, Dana. "Brecht and the Politics of Self-Reflexive Cinema." *Jump Cut* 17 (1978): 28–32.

Pryluck, Calvin. "Ultimately We All Are Outsiders: The Ethics of Documentary Filming." In Rosenthal, *New Challenges for Documentary*.

Rabinowitz, Lauren. *Points of Resistance: Women, Power, and Politics in the New York Avant-Garde Cinema, 1943–71*. Champaign-Urbana: University of Illinois Press, 1991.

Rabinowitz, Paula. "Chapter One: Labor and Desire: A Gendered History of Literary Representation." In *Labor and Desire: Women's Revolutionary Fiction in Depression America*. Chapel Hill: University of North Carolina Press, 1991.

————. *They Must Be Represented: The Politics of Documentary*. London: Verso, 1994.

Renov, Michael. "Re-Thinking Documentary: Toward a Taxonomy of Mediation." *Wide Angle* 8.3–4 (1986): 71–77.

————. "*Lost, Lost, Lost*: Mekas as Essayist." In *To Free the Cinema: Jonas Mekas and the New York Underground*. David E. James, ed. Princeton, N.J.: Princeton University Press, 1992.

————, ed. *Theorizing Documentary*. New York: Routledge, 1993.

Renov, Michael, and Erika Suderburg, eds. *Resolutions: Contemporary Video Practices*. Minneapolis: University of Minnesota Press, 1996.

Rich, Adrienne. *On Lies, Secrets, and Silence: Selected Prose 1966–1978*. New York: W. W. Norton, 1979.

Rich, B. Ruby. "In the Name of Feminist Film Criticism." Reprinted in Steven, *Jump Cut* and Carson, Dittmar, and Welsch, *Multiple Voices*.

————. "Anti-Porn: Soft Issue, Hard World." Reprinted in Erens, *Issues in Feminist Film Criticism* and Brunsdon, *Films for Women*.

Richter, Hans. *The Struggle for the Film*. Trans. Ben Brewster. New York: St. Martin's Press, 1986.

Rodowick, D. N. *The Crisis of Political Modernism: Criticism and Ideology in Contemporary Film Theory*. Urbana and Chicago: University of Illinois Press, 1988.

Rony, Fatimah Tobing. *The Third Eye: Race, Cinema and Ethnographic Spectacle*. Durham: Duke University Press, 1996.

Rosenberg, Jan. *Women's Reflections: The Feminist Film Movement*. Ann Arbor: University of Michigan Research Press, 1983.

Rosenheim, Shawn. "Interrotroning History: Errol Morris and the Documentary of the Future." In Sobchack, *The Persistence of History*.

Rosenstone, Robert A. "The Future of the Past: Film and the Beginnings of Postmodern History." In Sobchack, *The Persistence of History*.

Rosenthal, Alan. *The New Documentary in Action: A Casebook in Film-Making*. Berkeley and Los Angeles: University of California Press, 1971.

————, ed. *New Challenges for Documentary*. Berkeley and Los Angeles: University of California Press, 1988.

Scott, Joan W. *Gender and the Politics of History*. New York: Columbia University Press, 1988.

———. "Experience." In *Feminists Theorize the Political*. Judith Butler and Joan W. Scott, eds. New York and London: Routledge, 1992.

Silverman, Kaja. *The Acoustic Mirror*. Bloomington: Indiana University Press, 1988.

———. *Threshold of the Visible World*. New York: Routledge, 1996.

Smith, Valerie. "Telling Family Secrets: Narrative and Ideology in *Suzanne, Suzanne* by Camille Billops and James V. Hatch." In Carson, Dittmar, and Welsch, *Multiple Voices*.

———. "The Documentary Impulse in Contemporary African-American Film." In *Black Popular Culture: A Project by Michele Wallace*. Gina Dent, ed. Seattle: Bay Press, 1992.

Sobchack, Vivian. "Inscribing Ethical Space: Ten Propositions on Death, Representation, and Documentary." *Quarterly Review of Film Studies* 9.4 (Fall 1984): 283–300.

———. *The Address of the Eye: A Phenomenology of Film Experience*. Princeton, N.J.: Princeton University, 1992.

———. *The Persistence of History: Cinema, Television, and the Modern Event*. New York: Routledge, 1996.

Solanas, Fernando, and Octavio Gettino. "Towards a Third Cinema." Reprinted in Nichols, *Movies and Methods*.

Solomon-Godeau, Abigail. "Reconstructing Documentary: Connie Hatch's Representational Resistance." *Camera Obscura* 13–14 (1985): 113–46.

Stacey, Judith, and Barrie Thorne. "The Missing Feminist Revolution in Sociology." *Social Problems* 32.4 (April 1985): 301–16.

Stange, Maren. "Documentary Film and Photography: Rethinking Histories." Presented at Visible Evidence II: Strategies and Practices in Documentary Film and Video. Los Angeles: University of Southern California, 19 August 1994.

Sterne, Leslie. "Feminism and Cinema—Exchanges." *Screen* 20.3–4 (1979/80): 89–105.

Steven, Peter, ed. *Jump Cut: Hollywood, Politics, and Counter Cinema*. Toronto: Between the Lines, 1985.

Strathern, Marilyn. "An Awkward Relationship: The Case of Feminism and Anthropology." *Signs* 12.2 (1987): 276–92.

Suderburg, Erika. "The Electronic Corpse: Notes for an Alternative Language of History and Amnesia." In Renov and Suderburg, *Resolutions*.

Tanner, Marcia. "Preface and Acknowledgement." In *Bad Girls Catalogue*. New York: New Museum of Contemporary Art, 1994.

Tomasulo, Frank. "'I'll See It When I Believe It.' Rodney King and the Prison-House of Video." In Sobchack, *The Persistence of History*.

Trinh, T. Minh-ha. *Woman, Native, Other: Writing Postcoloniality and Feminism*. Bloomington: Indiana University Press, 1989.

———. *When the Moon Waxes Red—Representation, Gender and Cultural Politics*. New York: Routledge, 1991.

———. *Framer Framed*. New York: Routledge, 1992.

Turim, Maureen. *Flashbacks in Film: Memory and History*. New York: Routledge, 1989.

Vertov, Dziga. *Kino-Eye: The Writings of Dziga Vertov*. Annette Michelson, ed. Berkeley and Los Angeles: University of California Press, 1984.

Waldman, Diane. "There's More to a Positive Image Than Meets the Eye." Reprinted in Erens, *Issues in Feminist Film Criticism* and Steven, *Jump Cut*.

Walker, Janet. "The Traumatic Paradox: Documentary Films, Historical Fictions, and Cataclysmic Past Events." *Signs* 22.4 (Summer 1997): 803–25.

Walker, Janet, and Diane Waldman. "John Huston's *Freud* and Textual Repression: A Psychoanalytic Feminist Reading." In *Close Viewings: An Anthology of New Film Criticism*. Peter Lehman, ed. Tallahassee: Florida State University Press, 1990.

Warren, Charles. *Beyond Document: Essays on Nonfiction Film*. Hanover, N.H.: Wesleyan University Press, 1996.

Waugh, Thomas, ed. *"Show Us Life:" Toward a History and Aesthetics of the Committed Documentary*. Metuchen, N.J.: Scarecrow Press, 1984.

Welbon, Yvonne. "Black Lesbian Film and Video Art: Feminism Studies, Performance Studies." *P Form: A Journal of Interdisciplinary and Performance Art* 35 (Spring 1995): 12–15.

Welsch, Janice R. "Bakhtin, Language, and Women's Documentary Filmmaking." In Carson, Dittmar, and Welsch, *Multiple Voices*.

White, Hayden. *The Content of the Form: Narrative Discourse and Historical Representation*. Baltimore: Johns Hopkins University Press, 1987.

———. "Historiography and Historiophoty." *American Historical Review* 93.5 (December 1988): 1193–99.

———. "Historical Emplotment and the Problem of Truth." In *Probing the Limits of Representation: Nazism and the Final Solution*. Saul Friedländer, ed. Cambridge: Harvard University Press, 1992.

———. "The Modernist Event." In Sobchack, *The Persistence of History*.

White, Mimi. "Rehearsing Feminism: Women/History in *The Life and Times of Rosie the Riveter* and *Swing Shift*." In Carson, Dittmar, and Welsch, *Multiple Voices*.

Williams, Linda. "Mirrors without Memories: Truth, History, and the New Documentary." *Film Quarterly* 46.3 (Spring 1993): 9–21.

Winston, Brian. "The Documentary Film as Scientific Inscription." In Renov, *Theorizing Documentary*.

———. *Claiming the Real: The Griersonian Documentary and Its Limitations*. London: British Film Institute, 1995.

Wolf, Margery. *A Thrice-Told Tale: Feminism, Postmodernism, and Ethnographic Responsibility*. Stanford, Calif.: Stanford University Press, 1992.

Wolfe, Charles. "Just in Time: *Let Us Now Praise Famous Men* and the Recovery of the Historical Subject." In Petro, *Fugitive Images*.

Zimmermann, Patricia R. *Reel Families: A Social History of Amateur Film*. Bloomington and Indianapolis: Indiana University Press, 1995.

———. "Fetal Tissue: Reproductive Rights and Activist Amateur Video." In Renov and Suderburg, *Resolutions*.

Contributors

MICHELLE CITRON is an award-winning independent filmmaker who has received grants from the NEA and NEH. She is professor in the Department of Radio/Television/Film at Northwestern University, where she is also director of the Center for Interdisciplinary Research in the Arts. She is the author of *Home Movies and Other Necessary Fictions* (Minnesota, 1999).

GLORIA J. GIBSON is associate professor of Afro-American studies, assistant director of the Black Film Center/Archive, and director of the Archives of Traditional Music at Indiana University. She has published numerous articles in the area of black cinema, specifically black women's cinema. Her forthcoming book *Moving Tableaux of Consciousness: The Films and Videos of Black Women* considers the work of black women throughout the African diaspora.

CHRIS HOLMLUND is associate professor at the University of Tennessee, Knoxville, where she teaches film, women's studies, critical theory, and French. With Cynthia Fuchs, she coedited *Between the Sheets, In the Streets: Queer, Lesbian, Gay Documentary* (Minnesota, 1997). Her essays on film, video, and theory have appeared in a number of anthologies and journals, among them *Screening the Male, Moving Targets, Play It Again Sam, Out of Bounds, Screen, Cinema Journal, Feminist Studies, Camera Obscura, New Formations,* and *Discourse.*

ALEXANDRA JUHASZ is associate professor of media studies at Pitzer College. She teaches and makes feminist documentary. She has recently completed the documentary *Women of Vision: Eighteen Histories in Feminist Film and Video,* with a forthcoming book on the same topic (Minnesota).

ANN KANEKO is a filmmaker and writer based in Los Angeles. Since her essay in this book was written, she has completed a feature-length documentary, *Overstay*, which has premiered in California and is currently showing in film festivals around the world. She also freelances as a cinematographer and camera operator on other independent documentaries.

ANAHID KASSABIAN is assistant professor of communication and media studies at Fordham University. She is author of *Tracking Identities: Hollywood Film Music of the 1980s and 90s,* coeditor of *Keeping Score: Music, Disciplinarity, Culture,* and editor of the *Journal of Popular Music Studies.* She is also coauthor with David Kazanjian of "Naming the Armenian Genocide" in *Space and Place: Theories of Identity and Location* and "You Have to Want to Be an Armenian Here" in *Armenian Forum,* which, along with the present essay, are parts of an ongoing collaboration on representations of the North American–Armenian diaspora.

DAVID KAZANJIAN is assistant professor of English at Queens College, CUNY. He is the author of "Race, Nation, Equality: Olaudah Equiano's *Interesting Narrative* and a Genealogy of U.S. Mercantilism," forthcoming in *Post-Nationalist American Studies,* edited by John Carlos Rowe; "Notarizing Knowledge: Paranoia and Civility in Freud and Lacan," in *Qui Parle*; and coeditor with David L. Eng of the forthcoming anthology *Loss: The Social and Psychic Work of Mourning.* He is also coauthor with Anahid Kassabian of "Naming the Armenian Genocide" in *Space and Place: Theories of Identity and Location* and "You Have to Want to Be an Armenian Here" in *Armenian Forum,* which, along with the present essay, are parts of an ongoing collaboration on representations of the North American–Armenian diaspora.

SUSAN KNOBLOCH recently received her Ph.D. in film and television from UCLA. Her dissertation is titled "More to the Picture: Rock Recording, Film Form, and Other Trouble." Her essays on rock and film, performance, and gender representation appear in several forthcoming anthologies, including *Screen Acting as Art and Profession.*

SILVIA KRATZER-JUILFS earned her Ph.D. in critical studies from the Department of Film and Television at UCLA. Her dissertation, "Exile Cinema as National Cinema: Re-Defining German National Cinema (1962–1995)," redefines the rigid and stagnant boundaries around the notion of a national German cinema and proposes a more porous and fluid idea of "national identity" and "national cinema."

DEBORAH LEFKOWITZ has been working as a documentary filmmaker since 1981. Her award-winning film *Intervals of Silence: Being Jewish in Germany* (1990) has been screened in more than fifty cities in the United States, Germany, Canada, and France. Since 1994 she has also used images from her film footage for the creation of site-specific photographic installations.

JULIA LESAGE is a videomaker, feminist critic, and cofounder and coeditor of *Jump Cut: A Review of Contemporary Media*. She teaches in the English department at the University of Oregon and is the coeditor (with Linda Kintz) of *Media, Culture, and the Religious Right* (Minnesota, 1998).

LAURA U. MARKS has written extensively on independent and experimental media and visual art for publications in the United States, Canada, and Europe and programmed experimental film and video for venues in the United States and Canada. She is assistant professor of film studies in the School for Studies in Art and Culture at Carleton University in Ottawa. Her book *The Skin of the Film: Intercultural Cinema, Embodiment, and the Senses* is forthcoming.

PAULA RABINOWITZ is professor of English at the University of Minnesota, where she teaches courses in film, American studies, feminism, and literary theory and history. During 1996 she put her years of reading proletarian fiction and watching labor documentaries to practical use as co-coordinator of the University Faculty Alliance, which organized to defend tenure at Minnesota. Her book *They Must Be Represented: The Politics of Documentary* and a long poem on cinema, "StairMaster Yeats" (in *Wide Angle*), are among her recent publications. She is currently at work on two books, *Black and White and Noir: Pulping Twentieth-Century American Culture* and *Frida, Emily, Georgia: Feminism, Painting, and the Marketing of National Icons*.

MICHAEL RENOV is professor of critical studies in the School of Cinema-Television at the University of Southern California. He is the editor of *Theorizing Documentary* and coeditor of *Resolutions: Contemporary Video Practices* (Minnesota, 1996) and *Collecting Visible Evidence* (Minnesota, 1999). With Jane Gaines and Faye Ginsburg, he is an editor of the Visible Evidence book series at the University of Minnesota Press.

DIANE WALDMAN is associate professor in the Department of Mass Communications and is affiliated with the women's studies and the cultural and critical studies programs at the University of Denver. She teaches in the areas of women and film and documentary theory, history, and production. She has published essays in various anthologies and in such journals as *Camera Obscura, Cinema Journal, Jump Cut, The Velvet Light Trap*, and *Wide Angle*.

JANET WALKER is associate professor of film studies at the University of California, Santa Barbara. She is the author of *Couching Resistance: Women, Film, and Psychoanalytic Psychiatry* (Minnesota, 1993). Teaching courses on documentary, historiography, and women and film prompted her to write "The Traumatic Paradox" (published in *Signs*, summer 1997), and her current project is a related book on history, trauma, and memory in film and video.

PATRICIA R. ZIMMERMANN is professor of cinema and photography at Ithaca College and author of *Reel Families: A Social History of Amateur Film* and *Endangered Species: Documentaries and Democracies*. With Erik Barnouw, she coedited "The Flaherty: Four Decades in the Cause of Independent Cinema," a special monograph issue of *Wide Angle*.

Index

Abu-Lughod, Lila, 16–17
Ackerman, Chantal, 75; *News from Home*, 92
Act of Seeing through One's Own Eyes, The (Brakhage), 283
Adorno, Theodor, 227
Adynata (Thornton), 289, 294, 295, 296
Age 12: Love With a Little L (Montgomery), 272
Agee, James, and Walker Evans, *Let Us Now Praise Famous Men*, 20, 60
Ahwesh, Peggy, *The Scary Movie*, 111
Alarmo, Louise, Judy Smith, and Ellen Sorrin, *The Woman's Film*, 29 n. 25, 75
Allen, Austin, 81
All My Babies (Stoney), 67–68, 73
Almy, Max, 78
American Dream (Kopple), 47, 52–60
American Family, An (Raymond and Raymond), 87–89
American Family—Revisited, An (Raymond and Raymond), 88
Amerika, 74
Anderson, Angela, and Lee Williams, *Love Boys and Food*, 97, 106
Anderson, Madeline, 75, 76, 79, 137–38; *I Am Somebody*, 74, 75, 137–38
Angelo, Nancy, and Candace Compton, *Nun and Deviant*, 112, 115
Anthropology as Cultural Critique (Marcus and Fischer), 15
Antonia: Portrait of a Woman (Collins and Godmilow), 17, 76
Antonioni, Michelango, 72
Anything You Want to Be (Brandon), 74
Apter, Emily, 302
Armenian Journey, An (Bogosian), 2–3, 203–23
Armstrong, Nancy, 45
Arnow, Harriet, *The Dollmaker*, 49
Aronowitz, Stanley, 89–90, 92
Art and Artists, On (Blumenthal and Horsfield), 105
"Ashes to Flowers" (Beharry), 231, 235–36
At Home feminist art show, 96–116
Autobiographical documentary, women's, 22–24;

and ethics of responsibility, 271–86; experimental or avant-garde, 309–37; fragmented consciousness in, 309–37; as political act, 272

Bacher, Lutz, *My Penis*, 106
Bad Girls feminist art show, 96–116
Baillie, Bruce, 74
"Bakhtin, Language, and Women's Documentaries" (Welsch), 149, 154
Bandy, Mary Lea, 79
Barbier, Annette, 313; *Domestic Portraits, I*, 322; *Women's Movements*, 322
Barnouw, Erik, 30 n. 32, 60, 70, 78; *Documentary*, 4
Barnouw, Erik, Akira Iwasaki, Paul Ronder, and Barbara Van Dyke, *Hiroshima Nagasaki August 1945*, 76
Barret, Elizabeth, 81
Barrie, James, *What Every Woman Knows*, 321
Barry, Iris, 70
Barsam, Richard, *Nonfiction Film*, 4–5
Barthes, Roland, 295
Bartky, Sandra, *Femininity and Domination*, 330
Bataille, Georges, *Erotism*, 102–3, 104–5, 108–9
Battle of Chile, The, 59
Baudry, Jean-Louis, 24
Bazin, André, 228
Beer, Elizabeth, and Agatha Kener, *God Gave Us Eyes*, 101
Beeson, Coni: *Holding*, 288; *Unfolding*, 288
Beh, Siew Hwa, 29 n. 25
Beharry, Shauna, 225, 229–31; "Ashes to Flowers," 231, 235–36; *Seeing Is Believing*, 229–36, 240
Belverio, Glenda, and Camille Paglia, *Glenda and Camille Do Downtown*, 100–101, 107
Benjamin, Walter, 7, 230–31
Benning, James, 81; *Deseret*, 81
Benning, Sadie, 77, 78, 336 n. 7; *Girl Power*, 97, 107; *If Every Girl Had a Diary*, 92; *It Wasn't Love*, 92; *Jollies*, 92
Berger, Sally, 79
Bergstrom, Janet, 332–33
Berrakkarasu, Serap, *Toechter Zweier Welten* (Daughters of two worlds), 194–96, 199–201

Betty Tells Her Story (Brandon), 74
"Beyond Chiffon" (Parkerson), 152
Bhabha, Homi, 227
Bicycle (Perlson), 101
Billops, Camille, 78, 138, 150; *Suzanne, Suzanne*, 140
Billops, Camille, and James Hatch, *Finding Christa*, 150
Binge (Hershman), 329–30
Biographical documentary, women's, 287–89; and melancholic memories, 202–23; by Parkerson, 137–57; by Thornton, 288–308; and transference, 187–201
Biology of Conception (Sanger), 98
Blackaby, Linda, 78
"Black Studies, Cultural Studies" (Diawara), 150, 152
Blackwood, Maureen, 77
Blanch, Lesley, 291–92
Blood of the Condor (Sanjine), 74
Blue, Carroll Parrott, 79, 138; *Conversations with Roy DeCarava*, 138; *Eyes on the Prize*, 138; *Nigerian Art*, 138, 156; *Varnette's World*, 138
Blumenthal, Lyn, and Kate Horsfield, *On Art and Artists*, 105
Boas, Franz, 137
Bobo, Jacqueline, 18
Bognar, Steve, *Personal Belongings*, 81
Bogosian, Theodore, *An Armenian Journey*, 2–3, 203–23
Bonder, Diane, *Dangerous When Wet*, 97, 107
Bontoc Eulogy (Fuentes), 81
Borealis (Vasulka), 82
Bossak, Jerzy, 71
Bowser, Pearl, 76, 78, 79; *Midnight Ramble*, 156
Boyle, Deirdre, 79
Boys on the Side, 108
Bradley, Ruth, 78, 79, 80–81
Braham, Jeanne, 309–10
Brains on Toast: The Inexact Science of Gender (Platt and Saunders), 105
Brakhage, Stan, 283, 322; *The Act of Seeing through One's Own Eyes*, 283
Brandon, Liane, 75; *Anything You Want to Be*, 74; *Betty Tells Her Story*, 74; *Not So Young Now as Then*, 73
Brault, Michel, 71
Brecht, Bertolt, 7, 10
Brewer, Rose M., "Theorizing Race, Class, and Gender," 139–40
Brico, Antonia, 17
Bridge, The (Ivens), 85
Bridges Go Round (S. Clarke), 72
Brown, Jeffrey, 109
Buchanan, Nancy, and Barbara Smith, *With Love from A to B*, 107
Burch, Aarin, *Spin Cycle*, 272
Burke, Edmund, 44–45, 47
Burton, Julianne, 18
Butler, Judith, 330
. . . *But Then, She's Betty Carter* (Parkerson), 139, 144–45, 152–54

Campion, Jane, 77
Carby, Hazel, 145
Carroll, Madeline, 4
Carter, Angela, 104–5; *The Sadeian Woman and the Ideology of Pornography*, 110–111
Center, The (Rothschild), 74
Chadha, Gurinder, *I'm British But . . .*, 92
Chaplin, Charlie, 51
Chenzira, Ayoka, 77; *Syvilla*, 155–56
Chicago, Judy, 105
Chien, Wei-Ssu, *A Woman Waiting for Her Period*, 272
"Child Is Being Beaten, A" (Freud), 333
Ching, Yau, 77
Chodorow, Nancy, 321
Chopra, Joyce, 71, 72, 75; *Joyce at 34*, 272
Chopra, Joyce, and Richard Leacock, *Happy Mother's Day*, 72–73
Choy, Christine, 77
Chronicle of a Summer (Rouch), 91
"Chronicle of the Human Experience, A" (Gardner), 4–5
Chronicles of a Lying Spirit by Kelly Gabron (C. Smith), 113–15
Churchill, Joan, *Sylvia, Fran and Joy*, 73
Cinema verité, 5–10, 13, 30 n. 32, 31 n. 41, 71–75, 86–87, 112–13, 133, 136 n. 27. See also Documentary realism
Cinema Verite in America (Mamber), 8
Citron, Michelle, 10, 271–86, 330–31; *Daughter Rite*, 271, 273, 275–85; *Mother Right*, 275, 278–80; *Parthenogenesis*, 18, 274–75; *What You Take For Granted . . .*, 273, 284–85
Clarke, Cheryl, 108
Clarke, Shirley, 4, 67, 71, 72, 79, 98; *Bridges Go Round*, 72; *The Cool World*, 72; *A Moment in Love*, 72; *Portrait of Jason*, 72
Clarke, Wendy, *The Love Tapes*, 90–91
Clausen, Constance, 238
Clifford, James, 17
Clifford, James, and George Marcus, eds., *Writing Culture*, 15
Clover, Carol, 109
Coal Miner's Granddaughter (Dougherty), 313
Cobbett, William, 45, 47
Cohen, Colleen Ballerino, Frances Mascia-Lees, and Patricia Sharpe, "The Postmodern Turn in Anthropology," 15–16
Cohen, Hart, 11
Collins, Judy, and Jill Godmilow, *Antonia*, 17, 76
Complaints of a Dutiful Daughter (Hoffmann), 92, 93
Compton, Candace, and Nancy Angelo, *Nun and Deviant*, 112, 115
Condit, Cecelia, 78
Confessions (Rousseau), 326
Consciousness, women's, 309–37. See also Identity; Subjectivity
Conversations with Roy DeCarava (Blue), 138
Cool World, The (S. Clarke), 72
Coolidge, Martha, *Old-Fashioned Woman*, 73
Covert, Nadine, 79
Cowie, Elizabeth, 332–33

Cox, Nell, 4
Cross-cultural documentary. *See* Intercultural and cross-cultural documentary
Custen, George, 301–2

Dangerous When Wet (Bonder), 97, 107
Daughter Rite (Citron), 271, 273, 275–85
Daughters of Two Worlds. See Toechter Zweier Welten
Davidson, Cathy, 45
Davis, Angela, 139; "Black Women and Music," 142
Davis, Peter, *The Selling of the Pentagon*, 75
Dead Birds (Gardner), 4
De Antonio, Emile, 75
De Certeau, Michel, 188
Delacour, Marie-Odile, and Jean-Rene Huleu, 290
Deleuze, Gilles, 227, 229
Delirium (Faber), 318, 322
Delson, Susan, and Jill Godmilow, *Far from Poland*, 77
De Michiel, Helen, 78
De Mott, Joel, and Jeff Kreines, *Seventeen*, 77
Deren, Maya, 67, 98
De Ruiter, Heidi, *Strut*, 105–7, 109
Deseret (J. Benning), 81
Devil Never Sleeps, The (Portillo), 81
Diawara, Manthia, "Black Studies, Cultural Studies," 150, 152
Dick, Esme, 79
Dickens, Hazel, 53
Die Kuemmeltuerkin Geht (Meerapfel), 190–94, 199–201
Doane, Mary Ann, 122–23, 134–35, 200, 302, 332–33; "Remembering Women," 188
Documentary (Barnouw), 4
Documentary Conscience, The (Rosenthal), 13
Documentary ethics, 13–17, 163–64, 271–86
Documentary realism, 6–13, 72–73, 87, 112–13, 288. *See also* Cinema verité
"Documentary, Realism, and Women's Cinema" (McGarry), 8–9
Documentary Tradition, The (Jacobs), 4–5
Dollmaker, The (Arnow), 49
Domestic Portraits, I (Barbier), 322
Don't Look Back (Pennebaker), 2–3, 9, 121–35
Double Strength (Hammer), 288
Dougherty, Cecilia, *Coal Miner's Granddaughter*, 313; *Grapefruit*, 105–7
Douglas, Mary, *Purity and Danger*, 100, 103–4
Drew, Robert, 30 n. 32, 71, 87
Duane, Hildegarde, *Pink Slip*, 105
DuBowski, Sandi, *Tomboychik*, 92, 93, 106
Duckworth, Jacqui, *A Prayer before Birth*, 272
Dunye, Cheryl, 77, 107; *She Don't Fade*, 313
Dworkin, Andrea, 330
Dyer, Richard, 288
Dykstra, Jean, "Putting Herself in the Picture," 154–55
Dylan, Bob: as filmmaker, 134; as subject of *Don't Look Back*, 121–36

Eikelman, Dale, and James Piscatori, *Muslim Travellers*, 189–90

Eisenstein, Sergei, 10, 70, 312
Elder, Sarah, 77
Electronic Diaries (Hershman), 323–35
Emshwiller, Ed, 71
Enough to Eat, 14
Epistemology of the Closet (Sedgwick), 330
Erotism (Bataille), 102–3, 104–5, 108–9
Ethics. *See* Documentary ethics
Evans, Walker and James Agee, *Let Us Now Praise Famous Men*, 20
Excerpts (Quinn), 98, 109
Eyes on the Prize (Blue), 138

Faber, Mindy, *Delirium*, 318, 322
Fairies, The (Rubnitz), 106
Family Secrets (Kuhn), 91–92
Fanon, Frantz, 335
Far from Poland (Delson and Godmilow), 77
Fatal Women (Hart), 108
Femininity and Domination (Bartky), 330
"Feminism, Film, and Public History" (Michel), 21–22
Feminist art shows: Bad Girls and At Home, 96–116
Fifty-One Per Cent, 9
"Film, Feminism, and the Avant-Garde" (Mulvey), 10–11
Filmmaker/subject relationships, 13–17, 160–76, 250–51, 273–80, 282, 286 n. 8
Finding Christa (Billops and Hatch), 150
Fink, Ida, 263
Firestone, Cinda, 75
First International Festival of Women's Films, 6–7, 74
First Person Plural (Hershman), 321, 325–27, 330
Fischer, Michael, and George Marcus, *Anthropology as Cultural Critique*, 15
Fisher, Marc, 244
Flaherty, Frances, 65, 68, 69–70, 79; as collaborator with Robert Flaherty, 76
Flaherty, Robert, 4, 64–65, 68–69; *Louisiana Story*, 46, 68; *Nanook of the North*, 4, 76. *See also* Flaherty Seminars
Flaherty Seminars, 64–82
Frampton, Hollis, 289
Freebird (Silver), 105, 107
Freud, Sigmund, 63 n. 35, 69, 114–15, 219, 336 n. 15; "A Child Is Being Beaten," 333; "Construction in Analysis," 200; "Mourning and Melancholia," 203, 207–10; *Totem and Taboo*, 103
Friedländer, Saul, 23, 263
Friedrich, Su, 77; *Sink or Swim*, 92
Frisch, Michael, 23
Fuentes, Marlon, 81; *Bontoc Eulogy*, 81
Fundi (Grant), 18
Fusco, Coco, 78
Fuses (Schneemann), 288

Gaettens, Marie-Luise, 263
Gaines, Jane, 12
Gallager, Steve, 78
Garcia, Ana Maria, 77; *La Operación*, 12

Garcia, Irma, 263
Gardner, Robert: "A Chronicle of the Human Experience," 4–5; *Dead Birds*, 4
Geertz, Clifford, *Local Knowledge*, 88–89
Gellert, Hugo, 47
Gelly, Mira, *I Am a Famous French Director*, 105
Georgakas, Dan, 19
Gerber, Racquel, 77
Giacometti, Alberto, 238–39
Gibson, Gloria J., 137–57
Gilfillan, Lauren (Helen Gilfillan Woodbridge), *I Went to Pit College*, 44, 60
Ginsburg, Faye, 16, 79
Girl Power (S. Benning), 97, 107
Glenda and Camille Do Downtown (Belverio and Paglia), 100–101, 107
Godard, Jean-Luc, 10, 29–30 n. 29
God Gave Us Eyes (Beer and Kener), 101
Godmilow, Jill, 10, 75
Godmilow, Jill, and Judy Collins, *Antonia*, 17, 76
Godmilow, Jill, and Susan Delson, *Far from Poland*, 77
Gold, Tami, 78
Golddiggers, 200
Goldenberg, Myrna, 264 n. 6
Goldhagen, Daniel, 245
Gomery, Douglas, 83 n. 7
Good Woman of Bangkok, The (O'Rourke), 170–71, 176
Gordon, Betty, 75
Gorris, Marlene, 75
Gotta Make This Journey: Sweet Honey in the Rock (Parkerson), 18, 139, 141–44, 151–52
Grant, Joanne, *Fundi*, 18
Grapefruit (Dougherty), 105, 107
Gray, Mike, *The Murder of Fred Hampton*, 75
Grayson, Helen, 4
Great Invisible, The (Thornton), 290, 301, 304
Green, Vanalyne, 78; *A Spy in the House That Ruth Built*, 272–73, 322–23; *Trick or Drink*, 313–21, 325, 329; *What Happens to You?*, 313
Grieco, D. Marie, 67, 69, 77, 78, 79
Grierson, Ruby, 4
Griffith, D. W., 53
Gross, Larry, John Stuart Katz, and Jay Ruby, *Image Ethics*, 14, 286 n. 9
Growing Up Female (Klein and Reichert), 74
Guynn, William, 24

Hae, Ygang Hang, 71
Hall, Stuart, 144
Halleck, Dee Dee, 77
Hammer, Barbara, 77; *Double Strength*, 288; *I Was/I Am*, 288; *Women I Love*, 288
Hamper, Ben, *Rivethead*, 62 n. 26
Happy Mother's Day (Chopra and Leacock), 72–73
Hard-Pressed in the Heartland (Rachleff), 55–57, 60, 63 n. 40
Harlan County, USA (Kopple), 2–3, 19–21, 52, 53–54, 55, 56, 73, 76
Hart, Lynda, *Fatal Women*, 108
Hart, Ursula Kingsmill, 290

Hatch, James, and Camille Billops, *Finding Christa*, 150
Hatoum, Mona, 78; *Measures of Distance*, 310
Hayal (Solakhan), 199–201
Hayes, Helen, 321
Hebdige, Dick, *Rambling Man*, 92
Heinemann, Marlene, 264–65 n. 6
Herbst, Josephine, *Rope of Gold*, 49
Hershman, Lynn, 321; *Binge*, 329; *Electronic Diaries*, 323–35; *First Person Plural*, 321, 325–27, 330; *Seeing Is Believing*, 313
Herskowitz, Richard, 78
Herstory (San Francisco Newsreel), 8
Hey! Baby Chickey (Sobel), 98, 110–11
Hidari, Sachiko, 75–76
High, Kathy, 78, 80–81
High School (Wiseman), 5, 28 n. 15, 89
Hine, Lewis, *Men at Work*, 46
Hiroshima Nagasaki August 1945 (Barnouw, Iwasaki, Ronder, and Van Dyke), 76
History: counterhistory, women's documentary as, 19–22; of feminism and documentary studies, 1–35; institutional history, importance of, 64–83; and memory in modernist cinema, 35 n. 107; representations of in documentary film, 187–201
History and Memory (Tajiri), 26, 92, 272, 310
Hoberman, J., 272–73
Hoffmann, Deborah, *Complaints of a Dutiful Daughter*, 92, 93
Holding (Beeson), 288
Holmlund, Chris, 10, 19, 287–308
hooks, bell, 139
Horowitz, Margaret, 128
Horsfield, Kate, and Lyn Blumenthal, *On Art and Artists*, 105
Housing Problems, 14
Huleu, Jean-Rene, and Marie-Odile Delacour, 290
Hunt, Lynn, 63 n. 33
Hurston, Zora Neale, 137, 156 n. 2
Hurtado, Margarita de la Vega, 78

I Am a Famous French Director (Gelly), 105
I Am Somebody (Anderson), 74, 75, 137–38
Idemitsu, Mako, 76, 77
Identity: construction of, 187–201; intercultural, 158–81, 187–201, 202–23, 225–27; issues in documentary film, 187–223; Jewish, in Germany, 244–66; lesbian and gay, 92–93; politics, 89–90. *See also* Consciousness; Subjectivity
If Every Girl Had a Diary (S. Benning), 92
Image ethics, 13–17
Image Ethics (Gross, Katz, and Ruby), 14, 286 n. 8
I'm British But . . . (Chadha), 92
Industrial Britain, 14
In Plain English (Lesage), 12
Intercultural and cross-cultural documentary: identity construction in, 158–81, 187–201, 202–23; issues in making, 158–81; as space for fossils and fetishes, 224–43
Intervals of Silence (Lefkowitz), 2–3, 245–65
Irigaray, Luce, 224, 233
Isabelle Eberhardt (Pringle), 292

It Wasn't Love (S. Benning), 92
I've Never Danced the Way Girls Were Supposed To (Suggs), 97, 107–8
Ivens, Joris, 68, 84–85, 88; *The Bridge*, 85
I Was/I Am (Hammer), 288
Iwasaki, Akira, and Erik Barnouw, Paul Ronder, and Barbara Van Dyke, *Hiroshima Nagasaki August 1945*, 76
I Went to Pit College (Gilfillan), 44, 60

Jacobs, Lewis, *The Documentary Tradition*, 4–5
James, William, 318
Jane (Pennebaker), 87
Jenkins, Bruce, 77
Jimenez, Mary, 77
Johnson, Claudia, 45
Johnson, Mark, and George Lakoff, 256–57
Johnston, Claire, "Women's Cinema as Counter-Cinema," 7–8
Jollies (S. Benning), 92
Jones, Jacquie, 148
Josselson, Ruthellen, 265 n. 32
Joyce at 34 (Chopra), 272
Juhasz, Alexandra, 9–11, 31 n. 45, 95–116

Kanehsatake: 270 Years of Resistance (Obomsawin), 81
Kaneko, Ann, 158–82; *Overstay*, 158–81
Kaplan, Dora, 6–7
Kaplan, E. Ann, 12
Kaplan, Nelly, 4
Kardar, Aaejay, 72
Kassabian, Anahid, 202–23
Katz, John Stuart, and Judith Milstein Katz, 271, 275
Katz, John Stuart, Larry Gross, and Jay Ruby, *Image Ethics*, 14, 286 n. 8
Katz, Judith Milstein, and John Stuart Katz, 271, 275
Kazanjian, David, 202–23
Kelly, Mary, 106
Kener, Agatha, and Elizabeth Beer, *God Gave Us Eyes*, 101
King, Noel, 19–20
Kirsa Nicholina (Nelson), 288
Kiss the Boys and Make Them Die (Stratton), 309
Klein, Jim, 74
Klein, Jim, and Julia Reichert: *Growing Up Female*, 74; *Seeing Red*, 77
Klein, Jim, Miles Mogulescu, and Julia Reichert, *Union Maids*, 19, 20–21, 76
Knobloch, Susan, 121–36
Koonz, Claudia, 264 n. 6
Kopple, Barbara, 75, 76; *American Dream*, 47, 52–60; *Harlan County, USA*, 2, 19, 20–21, 52, 53–54, 55, 56, 73, 76; and Hart Perry, 76
Koumiko Mystery (Marker), 197
Kratzer-Juilfs, Silvia, 187–201
Kreines, Jeff, and Joel DeMott, *Seventeen*, 77
Krishnan, Indu, 78
Kristeva, Julia, 10, 18–19, 99–100, 224, 243 n. 21, 316; "Psychoanalysis and the Polis," 301
Kuchar, George, 81; *Weather Diaries*, 81
Kuhn, Annette, *Family Secrets*, 91–92

Lacan, Jacques, 129–30, 134, 135 n. 3
LaCapra, Dominick, 23
Lacy, Suzanne, *Learn Where the Meat Comes From*, 98, 109–10
Lakoff, George, and Mark Johnson, 256–57
Lanzmann, Claude, *Shoah*, 26, 194
La Signora Di Tutti, 200
Last Time I Saw Ron, The (Thornton), 290, 298–300
Lawder, Standish, 74
Leacock, Richard, 30 n. 32, 39, 68, 69, 71, 87, 289
Leacock, Richard, and Joyce Chopra, *Happy Mother's Day*, 72–73
Learn Where the Meat Comes From (Lacy), 98, 109–10
Lefkowitz, Deborah, 244–66; *Intervals of Silence*, 2–3, 245–66
Leiris, Michel, 238–39
Lesage, Julia, 30–31 n. 36, 73, 287, 309–38; *In Plain English*, 12
Lesbian Herstory Archives, 146
Let Us Now Praise Famous Men (Agee and Evans), 20, 60
Let Us Now Praise Famous Men—Revisited (PBS), 20
Levi, Primo, *Survival in Auschwitz*, 263
Levinson, Julie, 78
Levitt, Helen, 4
Lin, Cheng Sim, *My American Friends*, 107
Linden, R. Ruth, 263
Lionnet, Françoise, 272, 281
A Litany for Survival (Parkerson), 146–48, 154–55
Livingston, Jennie, 77
Local Knowledge (Geertz), 88–89
Lonely Crowd, The (Reisman), 70
Long Beach Museum of Art, 97
Longbow, Zachary, 81
Lorde, Audre, 141
Lost, Lost, Lost (Mekas), 92
Louisiana Story (R. Flaherty), 46, 68
Love Boys and Food (Lee Williams and A. Anderson), 97, 106
Love Tapes, The (W. Clarke), 90–91
Lukács, Georg, 44
Lyons, Elizabeth, 73

MacDonald, Christine, 79
MacDonald, Scott, 65–66, 83 n. 16
Mackworth, Cecily, 291
Makaveyev, Dusan, 75
Makeout (New York Newsreel), 8
Making the Modern (T. Smith), 61 n. 15
Maldoror, Sara, 75
Malek Leaves. See *Die Kuemmeltuerkin Geht*
Mallet, Marilu, *Unfinished Diary*, 92
Mamber, Stephen, 30 n. 32, 87, 128, 136 n. 27; *Cinema Verite in America*, 8
Man with a Movie Camera (Vertov), 51
Marcus, George, and James Clifford, eds., *Writing Culture*, 15
Marcus, George, and Michael Fischer, *Anthropology as Cultural Critique*, 15
Mare, Aline, 78

Marker, Chris, 75; *Koumiko Mystery,* 197; *Sans Soleil,* 197
Marks, Laura U., 18–19, 224–43
Marx, Karl, 44, 46, 61 n. 15, 62 n. 26, 226–27
Mascia-Lees, Frances, Colleen Ballerino Cohen, and Patricia Sharpe, "The Postmodern Turn in Anthropology," 15–16
Massachusetts 54th Colored Infantry, The (Shearer), 156
Materre, Michelle, 79
Mayne, Judith, 9
Maysles, Albert, 30 n. 32, 71, 87
Maysles, David, 30 n. 32, 71
McCormick, Ruth, 29 n. 25
McCullough, Barbara, 138
McElwee, Ross, 39; *Sherman's March,* 166–68, 176, 272–73
McGarry, Eileen, 30 n. 36; "Documentary, Realism and Women's Cinema," 8–9
Mead, Margaret, 137
Measures of Distance (Hatoum), 310
Meerapfel, Janine, *Die Kuemmeltuerkin Geht* (Malek leaves), 190–94, 199–201
Mekas, Jonas, *Lost, Lost, Lost,* 92
Melville, Herman, *Moby Dick,* 46
Memories from the Department of Amnesia (Tanaka), 310
Men at Work (Hine), 46
Meszaros, Marta, 75
Metz, Christian, 19, 24
Michel, Sonya, 31 n. 46; "Feminism, Film, and Public History," 21–22
Midnight Ramble (Bowser), 156
Millett, Kate, *Three Lives,* 6
Millner, Sherry, 78; *Womb with a View,* 322
Minh-ha, Trinh T. See Trinh, T. Minh-ha
"Mirrors without Memories" (Linda Williams), 26, 194
Mita, Merata, 81
Mitchell, Juliet, *Psychoanalysis and Feminism,* 9
Moby Dick (Melville), 46
Modernist filmmaking, 9–10, 287–88, 310–11, 336–37 n. 20
Moffat, Tracey, 75
Mogul, Susan, *Waiting at the Soda Fountain,* 98, 105, 336 n. 7
Mogulescu, Miles, Jim Klein, and Julia Reichert, *Union Maids,* 19–21, 76
Moment in Love, A (S. Clarke), 72
Mom Tapes, The (Segalove), 99–101
Montgomery, Jennifer, *Age 12,* 272
Moore, Michael, 60, 62 nn. 20, 21; *Pets or Meat,* 49; *Roger and Me,* 47–52
Mootoo, Shani, 77
Morgan, Robin, *Sisterhood Is Powerful,* 102
Morin, Edgar, 30 n. 32, 87
Mother Right (Citron), 275, 278–80
"Mourning and Melancholia" (Freud), 203, 207–10
Mulvey, Laura, 9–10, 31 n. 41, 75, 122, 128, 129–30, 135 n. 3; "Film, Feminism, and the Avant-Garde," 10–11; "Visual Pleasure in the Narrative Cinema," 9
Murder of Fred Hampton, The (Gray), 75

Museum of Modern Art (MOMA), 74; Film Library, 70
Muslim Travellers (Eikelman and Piscatori), 189–90
Muybridge, Eadweard, 84
My American Friends (Lin), 107
My Courbet or a Beaver's Tale (Patten), 97, 107
My Name Is Oona (Nelson), 288
My Penis (Bacher), 106

Naficy, Hamid, 224 n. 30
Naipaul, V. S., 210 n. 6
Nair, Mira, 77
Nana, Mom, and Me (Rothschild), 73, 272
Nanji, Meena, *Voices of the Morning,* 92
Nanook of the North (R. Flaherty), 4, 76
National Film Board of Canada, 71
Naumburg, Nancy, 4
Neiman, Susan, 244
Nelson, Gunvor: *Kirsa Nicholina,* 288; *My Name Is Oona,* 288
Nelson, Gunvor, and Dorothy Wiley, *Schmeerguntz,* 288
Nestle, Joan, 146
New Day Films, 73–74
New ethnography, 15–17
New Latin American cinema movement, 76
New Masses, 47
New Museum (New York), 97
News from Home (Ackerman), 92
Newsweek, 97
Newton, Judith, 21–22, 23
New York Newsreel: *Makeout,* 8; *She's Beautiful When She's Angry,* 8
New York State Council of the Arts (NYSCA), 78
Nichols, Bill, 2, 24, 86–87, 94 n. 6, 271, 288, 294; *Representing Reality,* 11, 286 n. 8
Nigerian Art (Blue), 138, 156
Nin, Anaïs, 98
Nonfiction Film (Barsam), 4–5
Noriega, Chon, 18, 78
Not So Young Now As Then (Brandon), 73
Nun and Deviant (Angelo and Compton), 112, 115

Objectivity, in documentary, 84–94. *See also* Subjectivity
Obomsawin, Alanis, 81; *Kanehsatake,* 81; *Richard Cardinal,* 81
Of Great Events and Ordinary People (Ruiz), 92
Old-Fashioned Woman (Coolidge), 73
Olsen, Tillie, 43, 250
Olson, Dorothy, 79
Onwurah, Ngozi, 77, 81; *Welcome II the Terrordome,* 81
Ophuls, Marcel, 13, 75
O'Rourke, Dennis, *The Good Woman of Bangkok,* 170–71, 176
Osborne, Elodie, 79
Overstay (Kaneko), 158–81
Owings, Alison, 244, 250
Oxenberg, Jan, *Thank You and Good Night,* 92, 93
Ozu, Yasujiro, 71, 72

Paglia, Camille, and Glenda Belverio, *Glenda and Camille Do Downtown*, 100–101, 107
PapaPapa (Rivera), 81
Paper Tiger, 77
Parkerson, Michelle, 77, 137–57; "Beyond Chiffon," 152; *. . . But Then, She's Betty Carter*, 139, 144–45, 152–54; *Gotta Make This Journey*, 18, 139, 141–44, 151–52; *A Litany for Survival*, 139, 146–48, 154–55; *Storme*, 139, 145–46, 152
Parmar, Pratibha, 77
Parthenogenesis (Citron), 18, 274–75
Patten, Mary, *My Courbet or a Beaver's Tale*, 97, 107
PBS (Public Broadcasting Service), 20, 62 n. 20, 157 n. 13; *An American Family*, 87–89; *An American Family—Revisited*, 88
Pearlstein, Alix, *Pretty, Fluffy, Cheesy, Bunny*, 103
Peckham, Linda, 292, 296–97
Pecot, Marcelle, 81
Peirce, Leighton, 81
Penley, Constance, 10
Pennebaker, D. A., 71; *Don't Look Back*, 9, 39, 121–35; *Jane*, 87
People's War, 74
Perlson, Meryl, *Bicycle*, 101
Perry, Hart, and Barbara Kopple, *Harlan County, USA*, 76
Personal Belongings (Bognar), 81
Pets or Meat (Moore), 49
Philoktetes Variations, 298
Pickering, Mimi, 76
Pietz, William, 225–27, 228–29, 231, 236, 238–39
Pink Slip (Duane), 105
Piscatori, James, and Dale Eikelman, *Muslim Travellers*, 189–90
Platt, Liss, and Joyan Saunders, *Brains on Toast*, 105
Poirier, Anne Clair, 77
Portillo, Lourdes, 78; *The Devil Never Sleeps*, 81
Portrait of Jason (S. Clarke), 72
"Postmodern Turn in Anthropology, The" (Mascia-Lees, Cohen, and Sharpe), 15–16
Potter, Sally, 75
Prayer before Birth, A (Duckworth), 272
Pretty, Fluffy, Cheesy, Bunny (Pearlstein), 103
Primary, 89
Pringle, Ian, *Isabelle Eberhardt*, 292
Pryluck, Calvin, "Ultimately We Are All Outsiders," 13–14
Psychoanalysis and Feminism (Mitchell), 9
"Psychoanalysis and the Polis" (Kristeva), 301
Psychoanalytic criticism, 24–26, 121–36, 135 n. 3, 187–201, 202–23, 239–40, 316–18, 327–34. *See also* Doane; Freud; Kristeva; Lacan; Mulvey
Purity and Danger (Douglas), 100, 103–4
"Putting Herself in the Picture" (Dykstra), 154–55

Question of Color, A (K. Sandler), 155
Quinn, Aysha, *Excerpts*, 98, 109

Rabinowitz, Paula, 43–63; *They Must Be Represented*, 2, 10

Rachleff, Peter, 58, 63 n. 40; *Hard-Pressed in the Heartland*, 55–57, 60, 63 n. 40
Rainer, Yvonne, 10, 75
Rambling Man (Hebdige), 92
Ramsay, Raylene, 22–23
Randau, Robert, 290
Ranucci, Karen, 78
Rape Stories (Strosser), 272
Raven, Arlene, 105
Ray, Satyajit, 71, 72
Raymond, Alan, and Susan Raymond: *An American Family* (PBS), 87–89; *An American Family—Revisited* (PBS), 88
Raymond, Susan, and Alan Raymond: *An American Family* (PBS), 87–89; *An American Family—Revisited* (PBS), 88
Realism. *See* Documentary realism
Reassemblage (Trinh), 77
Reece, Florence, 43
Reichert, Julia, 13, 74, 75
Reichert, Julia, and Jim Klein: *Growing Up Female*, 74; *Seeing Red*, 77
Reichert, Julia, Jim Klein, and Miles Mogulescu, *Union Maids*, 19–21, 76
Reisman, David, *The Lonely Crowd*, 70
"Remembering Women" (Doane), 188
Renoir, Jean, 72
Renov, Michael, 24, 84–94; *New Subjectivities*, 40; *Theorizing Documentary*, 39
Representing Reality (Nichols), 11
Ribe, Gloria, 77
Rice, Susan, 6
Rich, Adrienne, 1, 28 n. 15, 246, 330
Rich, B. Ruby, 9, 31 n. 46, 73, 78
Richard Cardinal: Cry from a Diary of a Metis (Obomsawin), 81
Richardson, Bill, 76
Richter, Hans, 84, 88
Riefenstahl, Leni, 4
Riggs, Marlon, *Tongues Untied*, 92–93, 149
Rimbaud, Arthur, 290, 306 n. 16
Ringelheim, Joan, 264 n. 6
Rittner, Carol, and John K. Roth, 264 n. 6
Rivera, Alex, 81; *PapaPapa*, 81
Roam Sweet Home (Spiro), 81
Robert Flaherty Seminars. *See* Flaherty Seminars
Robinson, Debra, 138
Rodriguez, Marta, 76
Roger and Me (Moore), 47–52
Ronder, Paul, and Erik Barnouw, Akira Iwasaki, and Barbara Van Dyke, *Hiroshima Nagasaki August 1945*, 76
Rope of Gold (Herbst), 49
Rosenthal, Alan, *The Documentary Conscience*, 13
Rosler, Martha: *Semiotics of the Kitchen*, 110–11; *Vital Statistics of a Citizen Simply Obtained*, 98
Roth, John K., and Carol Rittner, 264 n. 6
Rothschild, Amalie, 74, 75; *The Center*, 74; *Nana, Mom, and Me*, 73, 272; *Woo Who? May Wilson*, 74
Rouch, Jean, 30 n. 32, 39, 71, 87, 90–91; *Les Maîtres fous*, 229; *Chronicle of a Summer*, 91
Rousseau, Jean-Jacques, *Confessions*, 326

Roy, Somi, 78
Rubin, Gayle, "The Traffic in Women," 320
Rubnitz, Tom, *The Fairies*, 106
Ruby, Jay, Larry Gross, and John Stuart Katz, *Image Ethics*, 14, 286 n. 8
Ruiz, Raul, *Of Great Events and Ordinary People*, 92

Sachs, Lynne, 77
Sadeian Woman and the Ideology of Pornography, The (Carter), 110–11
Safford, Kimberly, 12
Sander, Helke, 75
Sandler, Kathe, 138; *A Question of Color*, 155
San Francisco Newsreel: *Herstory*, 8; *The Woman's Film*, 8
Sanger, Margaret, *Biology of Conception*, 98
Sanjine, Jorge, *Blood of the Condor*, 74
Sankofa Film and Video Collective, *Territories*, 92
Sans Soleil (Marker), 197
Sappho Was a Right-On Woman, 107
Saunders, Joyan, and Liss Platt, *Brains on Toast*, 105
Scary Movie, The (Ahwesh), 111
Schapiro, Miriam, 105
Schiller, Greta, and Andrea Weiss, 77
Schmeerguntz (Nelson and Wiley), 288
Schneemann, Carolee, 95–96, 114, 115; *Fuses*, 98, 288
Scientific project and documentary, 84–87
Scott, Joan, 220
Screen, 19
Sedgwick, Eve Kosofsky, *Epistemology of the Closet*, 330
Seeing Is Believing (Beharry), 2, 229–36, 240
Seeing Is Believing (Hershman), 2, 313
Seeing Red (Klein and Reichert), 77
Segalove, Ilene, *The Mom Tapes*, 99–101
Selling of the Pentagon, The (P. Davis), 75
Semiotics of the Kitchen (Rosler), 110–11
Sentimentality, discourses of in documentary film, 43–63
Seventeen (De Mott and Kreines), 77
Shadowplays. See *Hayal*
Sharpe, Patricia, Colleen Ballerino Cohen, and Frances Mascia-Lees, "The Postmodern Turn in Anthropology," 15–16
Shearer, Jackie, 78, 138; *The Massachusetts 54th Colored Infantry*, 156
She Don't Fade (Dunye), 313
Sherman's March (McElwee), 165–69, 272–73
She's Beautiful When She's Angry (New York Newsreel), 8
Shoah (Lanzmann), 26, 194
"*Show Us Life*" (Waugh), 18
Shub, Esfir, 4
Silver, Suzie, *Freebird*, 105, 107
Silverman, Kaja, 9, 124, 127, 129, 131, 132, 134–35
Sink or Swim (Friedrich), 92
Sisterhood Is Powerful (Morgan),102
Sisters in the Life: First Love (Welbon), 155
Smiley, Jane, *A Thousand Acres*, 332–33
Smith, Barbara, 139

Smith, Barbara, and Nancy Buchanan, *With Love from A to B*, 107
Smith, Cauleen, 77; *Chronicles of a Lying Spirit by Kelly Gabron*, 113–15
Smith, Dorothy E., 336 n. 12
Smith, Herb E., 81
Smith, Judy, Louise Alarmo, and Ellen Sorrin, *The Woman's Film*, 29 n. 25, 75
Smith, Sidonie, 23, 315
Smith, Terry, *Making the Modern*, 61 n. 15
Smith, Valerie, 140, 149
Sobchack, Vivian, 297–98
Sobel, Nina, *Hey! Baby Chickey*, 98, 110–11
Solakhan, Merlyn: *Hayal* (Shadowplays), 199–201; *Tekerleme* (Tonguebreaker), 196–98, 200–201
Sorrin, Ellen, Louise Alarmo, and Judy Smith, *The Woman's Film*, 29 n. 25, 75
Spin Cycle (Burch), 272
Spiro, Ellen, *Roam Sweet Home*, 81
Spivak, Gayatri C., 235
Spy in the House That Ruth Built, A (Green), 272–73, 322–23
Stallybrass, Peter, and Allon White, 226
Starr, Cecile, 69, 79
Steady, Filomina Chioma, 139
Steele, Lisa, 281
Stewart, Susan, 242 n. 14
Stoddard, Kimberly, *Street Walk*, 101
Stoney, *All My Babies*, 67–68
Storme: Lady of the Jewel Box (Parkerson), 139, 145–46, 152
Stratton, Margaret, *Kiss the Boys and Make Them Die*, 309, 333
Street Walk (Stoddard), 101
Strosser, Margie, *Rape Stories*, 272
Strut (DeRuiter), 105–7, 109
Subjectivity in documentary film: as opposed to objectivity, 84–94; women's, 2, 187–201, 310, 318–20. See also Consciousness; Documentary realism; Identity
Subjects, filmmaker's relationship to. See Filmmaker/subject relationships
Suggs, Dawn, *I've Never Danced the Way Girls Were Supposed To*, 97, 107–8
Survival in Auschwitz (Levi), 263
Suzanne, Suzanne (Billops), 140
Sylvia, Fran and Joy (Churchill), 73
Syvilla: They Dance to Her Drum (Chenzira), 155–56

Tajiri, Rea, 78; *History and Memory*, 26, 92, 272, 310
Tamrong, Marlina Gonzalez, 78
Tannen, Deborah, 252
Taussig, Michael, 233
Tekerleme (Solakhan), 196–98, 200–201
Territories (Sankofa), 92
Thank You and Good Night (Oxenberg), 92, 93
Theorizing Black Feminisms, 139
Theorizing Documentary (Renov), 39
"Theorizing Race, Class, and Gender" (Brewer), 139–40

Theory of the Leisure Class (Veblen), 45
There Was an Unseen Cloud Moving (Thornton), 288–307
Thin Blue Line, The, 194
This Bridge Called My Back, 107–8
Thornton, Leslie, 19, 77; *Adynata*, 289, 294, 295, 296; *The Great Invisible*, 290, 301, 304; *The Last Time I Saw Ron*, 290, 298–300; *Peggy and Fred in Hell*, 289, 294, 295, 304; *There Was an Unseen Cloud Moving*, 288–307
Thousand Acres, A (Smiley), 332–33
Three Lives (Millett), 7
Tirado, Amilcar, 71
Todd, Loretta, 80–81
Toechter Zweier Welten (Berrakkarasu), 194–96, 199–201
Tomboychik (DuBowski), 92, 93, 106
Tompkins, Jane, 45
Tonguebreaker. See *Tekerleme*
Tongues Untied (Riggs), 92–93, 149
Totem and Taboo (Freud),103
"Tradition of the Victim in Griersonian Documentary, The" (Winston), 14
"Traffic in Women, The" (Rubin), 320
Trick or Drink (Green), 313–21, 325, 329
Trinh, T. Minh-ha, 10, 77–78, 79; *Reassemblage*, 77
Troyano, Ela, 78
Tschaka, Jackie, 78, 79
Tucker, Marcia, 99

"Ultimately We Are All Outsiders" (Pryluck), 13–14
Unfinished Diary (Mallet), 92
Unfolding (Beeson), 288
Union Maids (Reichert, Klein, and Mogulescu), 19–21, 76

Van der Veer Quick, Charlotte (Mrs. Mason), 137
Van Dongen, Helen, 68
Van Dyke, Barbara, 69, 76, 79
Van Dyke, Barbara, Erik Barnouw, Akira Iwasaki, and Paul Ronder, *Hiroshima Nagasaki August 1945*, 76
Van Dyke, Willard, 74, 77
Varda, Agnes, 4, 75
Varnette's World (Blue), 138
Vasulka, Steina, 81; *Borealis*, 82
Veblen, Thorstein, *Theory of the Leisure Class*, 45
Védrès, Nicole, 4
Vertov, Dziga,10, 71, 75, 85, 88; *Man with a Movie Camera*, 51; "We: Variant of a Manifesto," 85
Vietnam: A Television History, 20
"Visual Pleasure in the Narrative Cinema" (Mulvey), 9
Vital Statistics of a Citizen Simply Obtained (Rosler), 98
Voices of the Morning (Nanji), 92
Von Trotta, Margarethe, 75

Waiting at the Soda Fountain (Mogul), 98, 105
Waldman, Diane, 1–36
Walker, Alice, 139
Walker, James, 17
Walker, Janet, 1–36

Wallner, Martha, 78
Ward, Melinda, 77, 78
War on Lesbians, 107
Watson, Julia, 93–94
Waugh, Thomas, 14; "Show Us Life," 18
Weather Diaries (Kuchar), 81
"We: Variant of a Manifesto" (Vertov), 85
Weiss, Andrea, and Greta Schiller, 77
Welbon, Yvonne, 140; *Sisters in the Life*, 155
Welcome II the Terrordome (Onwurah), 81
Welsch, Janice, "Bakhtin, Language, and Women's Documentaries," 149, 154
Wenders, Wim, 265 n. 32
What Every Woman Knows (Barrie), 321
What Happens to You? (Green), 313
What You Take For Granted . . . (Citron), 273, 284–85
White, Allon, and Peter Stallybrass, 226
White, Hayden, 23, 256
Who's Going to Pay for These Donuts, Anyway? (Tanaka), 310
Wide Angle, 80
Wight Gallery (UCLA), 97
Wiley, Dorothy, and Gunvor Nelson, *Schmeerguntz*, 288
Willemen, Paul, 8
Williams, Lee, and Angela Anderson, *Love Boys and Food*, 97, 106
Williams, Linda, 22; "Mirrors without Memories," 26, 194
Williams, Patricia J., 139
Williams, Raymond, 45, 86
Willis, Ellen, 122, 320
Winnecott, D. W., 239
Winston, Brian, 14, 87; "The Tradition of the Victim in Griersonian Documentary," 14–15
Wiseman, Frederick, 30 n. 32, 71; *High School*, 5, 89
With Love from A to B (Buchanan and Smith), 107
Wolfe, Charles, 20–21
Woman Waiting for Her Period, A (Chien), 272
Womb with a View (Millner), 322
Women & Film, 6–8
Women I Love (Hammer), 288
Women Make Movies, 73
Women Talking, 7
"Women's Cinema as Counter-Cinema" (Johnston), 7–8
Woman's Film, The (Smith, Alarmo, and Sorrin), 29 n. 25, 75
Women's Liberation Cinema, 6
Women's Movements (Barbier), 322
Woo Who? May Wilson (Rothschild), 74
Wordsworth, William, 322, 334
Writing Culture (Clifford and Marcus, eds.), 15

Yasui, Lise, 78
Yates, Pamela, 77

Zimmermann, Patricia, 64–83
Žižek, Slavoj, 65
Zornow, Edith, 79